The European Revolutions of 1848 and the Americas

Nineteenth-Century Latin America Series

General Editor Eduardo Posada-Carbó.

The Institute's Nineteenth-Century Latin America series results from the annual workshop on nineteenth-century Latin American history held at the Institute, and is aimed at encouraging the study of various aspects of what has largely been a neglected period in the modern historiography of the region.

Publications in the Series

1 *Wars, Parties and Nationalism: Essays on the Politics and Society of Nineteenth-Century Latin America*
Eduardo Posada-Carbó (ed.) – 1995 (out of print).

2 *In Search of a New Order: Essays on the Politics and Society of Nineteenth-Century Latin America*
Eduardo Posada-Carbó (ed.) – 1998

3 *Independence and Revolution in Spanish America: Perspectives and Problems*
Anthony McFarlane and Eduardo Posada-Carbó (eds) – 1999

4 *Judicial Institutions in Nineteenth-Century Latin America*
Eduardo Zimmermann (ed.) – 1999

5 *The Politics of Religion in an Age of Revival*
Austen Ivereigh (ed.) – 2000

6 *Rumours of Wars: Civil Conflict in Nineteenth-Century Latin America*
Rebecca Earle (ed.) – 2000

Institute of Latin American Studies
School of Advanced Study
University of London

The European Revolutions of 1848 and the Americas

Edited by

Guy Thomson

Institute of Latin American Studies
LONDON

Published by
Institute of Latin American Studies
31 Tavistock Square
London WC1H 9HA
http://www.sas.ac.uk/ilas/publicat.htm

British Library Cataloguing-in-Publication Data
A catalogue record for this book is available
from the British Library

ISBN 1 900039 43 5

Contents

Notes on contributors

Guy Thomson is Reader in History at the University of Warwick. He is the author of *Puebla de los Angeles. Industry and Society in a Mexican City* (Westview, CT, 1989), and (with David LaFrance) *Politics, Patriotism and Popular Liberalism in Mexico. Juan Francisco Lucas and the Puebla Sierra* (Wilmington, DE, 1999), and has recently edited *The European Revolutions of 1848 and the Americas* (London, 2002). Since 1994 he has been working on comparative aspects of nineteenth-century Mexican and Spanish liberalism, and he is preparing a book on the Rafael Pérez del Alamo and the roots of the Spanish Democrat Party in eastern Andalusia between 1849 and 1876.

Roger Magraw is Senior Lecturer in History at the University of Warwick. He is author of *France 1815–1914: The Bourgeois Century* (London, 1983) and *A History of the French Working Class* (Oxford, 1992). He has published on a variety of aspects of French social history, including popular anticlericalism, rural radicalism, industrial management and consumerism. He is writing a social history of France.

Clara E. Lida (Argentina) is Research Professor of History at El Colegio de México. She has published extensively on social and labour movements in nineteenth-century Spain, on Spanish migration to Latin America and on Spanish–Mexican relations in the nineteenth and twentieth centuries. She is preparing a book on anarchism and clandestinity in Latin Europe after the Paris Commune.

Timothy Roberts received an MA from Brandeis University and a DPhil from the University of Oxford. He is a Visiting Assistant Professor of History at the Metropolitan State College of Denver. His publications include 'The United States and the European Revolutions of 1848', in Robert Evans (ed.), *The Revolutions in Europe 1848–1849: From Reform to Reaction* (Oxford, 2000), and 'Diplomatische Reaktionen der Vereinigten

Staaten während der Revolutionsjahre 1848/49,' [US Foreign Policy During the Euoropean Revolutions of 1848] in Wolfgang Hochbruck, Ulrich Bachteler and Henning Zimmermann (eds.), *Achtundvierziger / Forty-Eighters: Die deutschen Revolutionen von 1848/49, die Vereinigten Staaten, und der amerikanische Buergerkrieg* (Münster, 2000). He is currently studying communities of Confederate States of America expatriates in Brazil.

Nancy Naro is a lecturer at King's College, University of London. Her research interests include the process of transition from slave to free labour in the Americas, the impact of the 1848 revolutions in Brazil and South America, and gender, space and citizenship in rural Brazil. Her publications include *A Slave's Place, a Master's World. Fashioning Dependency in Rural Brazil* (New York and London, 2000), the translation from the Portuguese of *The Unedited Diaries of Carolina Maria de Jesus* (New Brunswick, 1999), and 'Safeguarding Portugal's Colonial Legacies: Pernambuco's 1848' (forthcoming). She is the editor of vol. 9 of the Nineteenth-Century Latin American Series of the Institute of Latin American Studies, *Blacks and National Identity in Latin America* (forthcoming).

David Rock is Professor of History at the University of California, Santa Barbara where he teaches the history of Latin America. Between 1974 and 1977 he served as the Assistant Secretary at the Institute of Latin American Studies at the University of London. His works include *Politics in Argentina, 1890–1930. The Rise and Fall of Radicalism* (Cambridge, 1975), *Argentina 1516–1987. From Spanish Colonization to Alfonsín* (Berkeley, 1987). He is currently working on a study of state formation and political coalitions in Argentina between 1860 and 1916.

Leonor García-Millé has an MA in History at the University of Warwick. She teaches at UNAM and at the Universidad Autónoma Metropolitana–Xochimilco. Among her fields of research are Latin American travellers in the nineteenth century and the Spanish in Mexico in the twentieth century. She has contributed a chapter, 'El retrato burocrático. Las fotografías de españoles en los documentos inmigratorios mexicanos (1939–1950)', to Clara E. Lida (ed.), *España y México en el primer franquismo: 1939–1950.* She is currently researching the resettlement of Spanish refugees in Mexico City.

Cristián Gazmuri is director of the Institute of History of the Catholic University of Chile, member of the Chilean Academy of History and member of the 'Comisión (de la Presidencia de la República) Bicentenario de la Independencia de Chile'. His publications include *Testimonios de una crisis. Chile 1900–1920* (Santiago, 1980), *Chile en el siglo XX* (co-authored)

(Santiago, 1985), *La revolución francesa y Chile* (edited and co-authored) (Santiago, 1990) and, *El '48' chileno* (Santiago, 1993), *Eduardo Frei Montalva y su época* (Santiago, 2000).

Natalia Sobrevilla Perea has a degree in History from the Pontificia Universidad Católica del Perú and an MA in Latin American Studies at the Institute of Latin American Studies, University of London, where she is currently studying for a doctorate. She is the author of 'La creación de la colonia de Pozuzo', in Giovanni Bonfiglio (ed.), *La presencia europea en el Perú* (Lima, 2001).

Eduardo Posada-Carbó is an historian, currently a Senior Teaching Fellow at the University of Warwick. He has published extensively on the history and politics of Colombia, including *The Colombian Caribbean: A Regional History, 1870–1950* (Oxford, 1996) and *¿Guerra civil? El lenguaje del conflicto en Colombia* (Bogotá, 2001). He is the general editor of this series.

Introduction

GUY THOMSON

The fall of Orleanist monarchy in February 1848, like the 'events' of May 1968 in Paris, had repercussions far beyond France, precipitating political crises not only across Europe, but also over much of the world colonised by Europeans. In Great Britain and her Empire, often assumed to be shielded from the 1848 contagion, popular movements directly attributable to the events in Europe occurred not only at home and in Ireland, but also throughout the Empire – from French Canada to Guyana, from Malta and the Ionian Islands to South Africa, from Ceylon to New Zealand. 'The upheavals in Europe,' writes Miles Taylor, 'were a crisis of Empire, as much as they were an outbreak of Revolution.'[1]

It was not only subjects living under autocracies, unreformed monarchies or under European colonial control who were affected by the revolutions of 1848. In Europe's long-independent former American colonies, the events of 1848 in Europe dramatised the failure of fledgling liberal republics to live up to their founding ideals. In New York, where the first news of Paris's February revolution arrived on 20 March, there was 'no revolutionary crisis, no June Days, no insurrection by workers or anyone else ... it was to the ballot box and not to the barricades'.[2] Yet Sean Wilentz documents how artisan radicalism and militancy peaked in the two years following the revolutions of 1848, invigorated by the influx of news and exiles from Europe. In Latin America, news of Europe's 'springtime of the peoples' also had a catalytic effect, prompting the disenfranchised – whether Mexican villagers, Colombian Blacks, Brazilian

1 Miles Taylor, 'The 1848 Revolution and the British Empire,' *Past and Present*, vol. 166, 1: Feb. 2000, pp. 146–80.

2 Timothy Roberts and Daniel W. Howe, 'The United States and the Revolutions of 1848,' in R.J.W. Evans and Hartmut Pogge von Strandmann (eds.), *The Revolutions in Europe 1848–1849: From Reform to Reaction* (Oxford, 2000), p. 157; Sean Wilentz, *Chants Democratic and the Rise of the American Working Class, 1788–1850* (Oxford, 1984), p. 387.

small farmers and shopkeepers or Chilean artisans – to take to the fields and streets, to demand representative institutions and to conceive of themselves as sovereign people.[3]

If in the Americas, as in Europe, the fraternal, egalitarian and democratic ideals of the spring of 1848 would not translate into lasting democratic gains until much later, in the short and medium term the ideas and example of European revolutions (and reactions to them) substantially changed the shape and language of politics. Riots and political crisis in Canada (Montreal and Toronto), British Guiana and Jamaica in 1848–49, resulting initially from colonial opposition to imperial economic liberalisation, soon opened up much wider political issues as the British colonial authorities grew aware of how the European example was contributing to pressure for representation among the French in Canada and Blacks in the anglophone Caribbean and Guyana.[4] Elsewhere in the Americas, as the chapters of this book show, democratic movements in Europe were reflected in the emergence of new, more radical and progressive liberal parties – the Free Soil Movement/Free Democrats in the United States, the Reform Liberals in Mexico, the 'progresista' liberal parties in Colombia and Peru, the 'Society of Equality' and the Radical party in Chile – that challenged the political groupings that had served since independence.

While in the British colonies riots and political dissent forced the authorities to instal or reform representative institutions (if only to ensure that colonial assemblies did not fall under the control of Black majorities), throughout Latin America the rejuvenation of liberalism and the political baptism (albeit fleeting) of socialism prompted the revival of a more aggressive conservatism. Colombia first acquired its 'Conservative' party in 1848, Mexico in 1849; liberalism after 1848 acquired a virulently anti-clerical character in both countries, much as in France.[5]

3 Michael P. Costeloe, 'Mariano Arizcorreta and Peasant Unrest in the State of Mexico, 1849,' *Bulletin of Latin American Research*, vol. 15, 1996, p. 67; Margarita Rosa Pacheco, 'El pueblo soberano. Sociabilidad y cultura política popular en Cali (1848–1854),' *Siglo XIX Revista de Historia* (Mexico), no. 13, Jan.–June 1993, pp. 119–57; Amaro Quintas, *O sentido social da Revolução Praierira* (Rio de Janeiro, 1967); Luis Alberto Romero, 'La sociedad de la igualdad: liberales y artesanos en la vida política de Santiago de Chile,' in *Siglo XIX. Revista de Historia*, 2:3 (1987), pp. 15–36.

4 Taylor, 'The 1848 Revolution and the British Empire'.

5 William Fowler, 'Presentación', in W. Fowler and H. Morales (eds.), *El conservadurismo mexicano en el siglo XIX* (Mexico, 1999) p. 17; Eduardo Posada-Carbó, 'New Granada and the European Revolutions of 1848,' in this volume; James F. McMillan, 'Religion and Politics in Nineteenth-Century France: Further Reflections on Why Catholics and Republicans Couldn't Stand Each Other,' in Austen Ivereigh (ed.), *The Politics of Religion in an Age of Revival* (London, 2000), pp. 43–56.

'The European Revolutions of 1848 and the Americas' is based on a workshop held at the Institute of Latin American Studies in London on 15 November 1998. This was the last of only three 150th anniversary commemorations of 1848 held in Britain in 1998.[6] The aim of the workshop was to trace the impact of European revolutions globally (by 1848 the steamship and the telegraph were rapidly making the world a smaller place). The collections of essays edited by Evans and Pogge von Strandmann, and Körner focus almost exclusively on the impact of the revolutions, and their commemoration, within Europe. Neither volume looks at the impact of 1848 in the Iberian peninsula or in Latin America. Indeed, although the impact of the 1848 revolutions in Latin America has been occasionally noted, there has been very little written on the subject. It is hoped that the essays in this volume, by exploring the impact of 1848 in the New World, will complement the Oxford and University College (London) volumes and contribute to plugging a gap in the historiography.

Although the February revolution in France was just one (and not even the first) of numerous revolutions occurring over the length and breadth of Europe in 1848, and although the revolutionary events were largely confined to Paris, with France after June 1848 becoming associated more with counter-revolution (in particular the suppression of the Roman Republic), France was the model that liberals throughout the Americas, especially in Latin America, had long sought to emulate. It is therefore appropriate that the first two chapters of this book focus on events in France.

Roger Magraw sets the scene in chapter one with an examination of the part played by radical republicans – the 'Démocrates-Socialistes' (Dem-Socs) – between February 1848 and the Montagnard uprising following Louis Napoleon's coup d'état in 1851, in the light of the vast output of French regional historiography over the past last forty years. The judgement of contemporaries, and of later historians, of the leaders of the February and July revolutions, especially the Dem-Socs, has been harsh. Unfavourable comparisons are drawn between the 'real' revolutionaries of 1789 and the 'imitation' played out by those manning the barricades in February and June 1848. Victor Hugo admitted that he preferred 'Titans wading through chaos (in 1793) to nincompoops dithering

6 Based on a conference held at University College (London) in February 1998, Axel Körner (ed.), *1848: A European Revolution? International Ideas and National Memories of 1848* (London, 2000) concentrates on how the revolutions have been commemorated and on fresh ways of studying the events 1848 (women's participation, the reflection in literature, music and songs, etc.). Resulting from a lecture series held in Oxford early in 1998, Evans and Pogge von Strandmann (eds.), *The Revolutions in Europe* explores the actual course of the revolutions, and reactions to them, within different national contexts in Europe.

(in 1848).'[7] De Tocqueville, although a participant himself in the February revolution and a deputy in July, wrote in his *Recollections* that 'The whole time I had the feeling we had staged a play about the French Revolution, rather than we were continuing it ...' Pursuing the theatrical analogy, he described the parliament elected in April 1848, in which the rustic Montagnard Dem-Socs from the south were represented for the first time, as a 'vile tragedy played by a provincial troupe'. Karl Marx's low opinion of the leaders of France's 1848 is well known: 'all facts and personages of great importance in world history occur twice, the first time as tragedy, the second as farce.'[8]

Rather than damning the revolutionaries of 1848 for their failure to carry out the legacy of 1789 by consolidating and exporting a democratic revolution, Magraw sets out to explain how regional differences in social structure and political culture, combined with France's relative economic backwardness and poor communications, obstructed effective national organisation and mobilisation by radical republicans. Far from conveying a sense of 'failure', 'farce' or 'dithering', Magraw portrays the Dem-Soc leaders as highly effective, particularly in wine-growing and forest regions in the south-east and south, in consolidating support before 1848 and in mobilising these regions on repeated occasions between April elections in 1848 and the insurrection of December 1851.

The key to the political effectiveness of the Dem-Socs was the ability of the bourgeoisie of smaller towns – lawyers, doctors, teachers, artisans and literate peasants – to tap popular support: through clubs, *chambres* and cafés; through newspapers and 'democratic catechisms' laced with Christian imagery; through popular song groups (*goguettes*) who revived the ideals and images of 1789; by responding to local economic grievances, by fostering credit and cooperative schemes, and opposing forest codes and wine taxes; and finally by organising clandestine networks in the face of mounting police and army repression. Magraw argues 'that it was precisely the existence of a neo-Jacobin, Radical republican stratum of the bourgeoisie, capable of providing both ideological and organisational leadership to popular protest, rather than the artisanal character of the urban labour force, which explains France's peculiarity as *the* home of European revolution.'

Clara Lida begins her account of the impact of 1848 in the Hispanic world with an analysis of the revolutions in France. If Magraw focuses mainly on radical republicanism in the regions, Lida is concerned above all with events in Paris in 1848, focusing especially on the part played by

7 Roger Magraw, 'The Second Republic,' in this volume, p. 17.

8 Rebecca Spang, 'First Performances – Staging Memories of the French February Revolution,' in Axel Körner (ed.), *1848: A European Revolution?*, pp. 169–74.

the 'popular urban classes', particularly artisans, and on the discourse they developed of a 'social and democratic Republic'. Although the popular revolution was defeated following the closure of the National Workshops and the 'June days', Lida argues that image of literate artisans fighting alongside 'teachers, students, journalists and artists, as well as the liberal and technical professions, that is to say people of learning and culture', exercised an enormous impact in the Hispanic world: 'when in February 1848 the Provisional Government decreed the 'right to work' as a republican right ... and authorised the right to association, it offered a new language ... which would feed the revolutionary imagination in many parts of the world.' Spain, in particular, proved particularly responsive to French radical republican imagery.

If it was the generalised collapse of the ancien regime across the length and breadth of Europe, without any army having to cross a border, that distinguished 1848 as the 'year of revolutions', it was events in France that mesmerised observers in Spain and the Americas. During the 1830s and '40s French political and social ideas – romanticism, utopian socialism, democratic socialism and republicanism – and a French model of citizenship that could be taught through manuals of sociability, urbanity and democratic rights, became particularly influential among the educated young in Spain and Latin America.[9] Long before 1848 France was a mirror in which the intelligentsia of a modernising Spain and fledgling Spanish American republics could see the future development of their own societies. In 1848 France's Democratic-Socialists in particular seemed to embody the ideal of a fusion of the intellectual, the artisan and the 'conscious' peasant, that would sweep away the corruption, *caciquismo* and *caudillismo* of restored ancien regimes, and become the harbinger of a democratic republic. French democratic socialism – or neo-Jacobinism freed of the earlier negative associations with terror, violence and warfare, and identified instead with sociability, social welfare, the right to work, education and universal suffrage – offered a formula by which the constitutional liberalism of the period of the Constitution of Cadiz (1812), that had helped shape the republics of Spanish America, could rejuvenate itself. Less relevant in the United States, which had its own traditions of popular mobilisation going back to the Revolution of 1776, France's democratic socialism/neo-Jacobinism/radical republicanism were particularly attractive in Spain and Latin America, where absolutists or elite factions had dominated politics for much of time since the Napoleonic invasion of 1808.

9 Pilar González Bernaldo, 'La nación como sociabilidad,' in François-Xavier Guerra and Mónica Quijada (eds.), *Imaginar la nación* (Münster and Hamburg, 1994), pp. 185–97.

In chapter two, Clara Lida dispels any lingering belief that the 1848 revolutions passed Spain by. The fall of Louis Philippe in February 1848 prompted a hardening of the Moderate liberal regime as first minister, General Ramón María Narváez, forced the Chamber of Deputies to grant emergency powers and to suspend constitutional guarantees. This provoked a popular uprising in Madrid on 26 March, which, after a short truce (to allow for the enjoyment of lunch at the barricades), was put down with a brutality that caused consternation in Paris and pressure for intervention.[10] Conspiracies and uprisings followed in several provincial cities, and in May Madrid experienced a second uprising. Although order everywhere was restored, Lida shows how the same 'popular classes' as in France were involved in the uprisings ('artisans and day-labourers, together with officials of the regular army, lawyers, journalists and … radical politicians'), the same ideas animated the crowds (the right to work, freedom of association and universal suffrage), and French republican symbolism and links with Italian and French republicanism (particularly Mazzini and Ledru-Rollin) were much in evidence.

Violently suppressed in the short term, the 1848 revolutions had important longer-term consequences, permanently altering Spain's political geography. Progressive Liberal internal divisions prompted the formation, in March 1849, of the Democrat Party, Spain's first party committed both to universal suffrage and social reform. Over the subsequent twenty years the Democrats dedicated themselves to legal opposition, but also to building up a clandestine national network of *carbonari* cells to challenge the prevailing Moderado constitution of 1845, which restricted suffrage to major property holders. 1848 also saw the formation in Madrid of Young Spain (*Joven España*), an internationalist association established by the utopian socialist from Cadiz, Fernando Garrido, and linked with Guissepe Mazzini. This rejuvenated movement of the Liberal left culminated in the revolution of September 1868, when a coalition of Progresistas and Democrats, led by the popular war hero General Juan Prim, succeeded in bringing down an oppressive and discredited Bourbon regime. This inaugurated a six-year period of constitutional experimentation known as the *sexenio revolucionario*, during which many of the democratic and social ideas of 1848 were attempted (albeit, as in France in 1848, largely unsuccessfully).

But what lessons could the European revolutions of 1848 teach the New World? What could European constitutional laggards teach long-established American republics (or, in the case of Brazil, a constitutional monarchy), emancipated from European monarchies and accustomed to

10 R.J.W. Evans, 'Liberalism, Nationalism and the Coming of Revolution,' Evans and Pogge von Strandmann (eds.), *The Revolutions in Europe*, p. 21.

constitutional government and charters of individual rights? One of the objectives of this collection is to explore why the events of 1848 in Europe, especially the improved (more democratic and less violent) French model of revolution, could attract so much attention in countries which already possessed quite liberal constitutions.

The impact of European revolutions of 1848 in Latin America, although minor compared with the momentous repercussions of the 'great revolution' of 1789 and the Napoleonic invasion of the Peninsula, was nevertheless palpable, magnified by the great ease and speed of transatlantic communication, and enhanced by the prior existence of elements of political modernity – such as clubs, parties and newspapers – which the European Revolutions, particularly the French, would infuse with a renewed rhetorical and symbolic content. In particular, the mid-nineteenth-century democratic image of bearded and dark-suited young men of the 'middle class' fighting for, and in intimate collaboration with, the 'people' (belonging to the same clubs and manning the same barricades) was irresistibly attractive in countries where post-Independence politics remained resolutely oligarchical.[11] The revolutions of 1848 renewed and extended Latin America's democratic vocabulary and republican symbolism. This could be seen in the 'democratic societies' of Colombia, Chile's 'Society of Equality', the use of barricades in Chile's revolution of 1851 and the popular banquets in Lima held in February 1850. The events in Europe helped groups seeking entry to politics reimagine a republican political community that had become ever more exclusive, or torn by *caudillismo*, since Independence.

If radicals and some liberals in Latin American welcomed the revival of French revolutionary idealism during the spring of 1848, moderate liberals and conservatives feared the renewal of the tendency for revolutionary events to spill over borders. But on this occasion the borders feared by Moderate Liberals and Conservatives were the internal boundaries separating the 'civilised' nation from the 'barbaric' masses.[12] Conservatives in Mexico and Brazil warned that democratisation, federalism and decentralisation would encourage Indian caste wars and slave revolts leading to emancipation, which would threaten the post-colonial social edifice. Argentine liberals such as Sarmiento, Alberdi and Echeverría, living in exile from the Rosas regime, welcomed the fall of corrupt and absolutist regimes in Europe and the revival of the French revolutionary

11 Maurice Agulhon, 'Reflexiones sobre la imagen del burgués francés en vísperas de 1848: Monsieur Prudhomme, Monsieur Homais y Monsieur Bamatabois,' *Historia Social*, 1997, no. 29, pp. 73–88.

12 Mónica Quijada, '¿Qué Nación? Dinámicas y dicotomías de la nación en el imaginario hispanoamericano del siglo XIX,' in Guerra and Quijada (eds.), *Imaginar la nación*, pp. 40–51.

tradition, but doubted whether Spanish America was ready for democracy, fearing that universal suffrage would be abused by the demagogue, as it was under Rosas and Louis Napoleon. In the United States, Tim Roberts shows how the issue of slavery (France abolished colonial slavery in April 1848) was cunningly side-stepped by all parties, each finding a way of putting progressive ideals coming from Europe to their own advantage.

Even progressive/radical liberals in Mexico, Peru and Brazil, who were in search of popular support, did not include among 'the people' at this stage either Indians or African slaves. American admirers of the revolutions in Europe, although able passionately to identify with popular struggles in Paris or with anti-dynastic national struggles of the Italian, Bohemians and Hungarians, as Leonor García shows in her account of the Chilean Benjamín Vicuña Mackenna's journey through Europe in 1850–51, were unprepared to deepen their own fragile sense of nationality by tapping hitherto unappreciated reserves of ethnic and linguistic distinctiveness. Indeed the European revolutions of 1848 seem to have encouraged a return to a more Eurocentric focus of cultural imitation, after the Creolism, nativism, proto-*indigenismo* of post-independence decades.

The United States was the first part of the New World to read about the February revolution in Paris and its continental consequences. News of the extraordinary events occurring in Europe took three weeks to arrive in New York by steamship. Edited news was then relayed by telegraph throughout a country that had been so recently and greatly expanded. The inevitable bunching of news would have made the pace of events in Europe seem even more vertiginous. Readers of *The New-York Tribune* on Monday 10 April 1848 had the following choice:

> Four days later from Europe – Arrival of the Hibernia (departed Liverpool 25 March 1848) – The Progress of France – The Financial Embarrassment – Great News from Italy – The Revolution in Lombardy – The Flight of the Viceroy – The Constitution of the Roman States – The Change in Prussia – Bloodshed in Berlin – The King doing the Honor to the Slain – Reform Concessions – A Union of German States – Liberal Men and Liberal Measures – Joy of the People – Disturbances in Bohemia – The Republic proclaimed at Cracow – Outbreaks in Hanover – Rejoicings in Sweden – Lola Montez in Switzerland – Ireland Tranquil – The Failures in Europe – The Markets, etc., etc.[13]

Roberts writes in chapter three: 'As news from Europe appeared in the US press in clusters, the 1848 Revolutions took the appearance to most US observers as a monolithic, even spiritual force, rather than as disparate movements'. Newspaper readers in Recife, Mexico City, Bogotá, Lima,

13 *New-York Tribune*, Monday morning, 10 April 1848.

Santiago and Montevideo faced the same dizzying course of events.

Tim Roberts analyses the intense US interest in the Revolutions of 1848, a fascination rooted in the reassurance that Europe was at last following the republican example set by the United States in 1776, mixed with anxiety that the events in Europe might signal 'a second revolution in US society, erupting over the issue of slavery ... more like Europe in 1848 than America in 1776; more comprehensive in its social upheaval.' US detachment from the European revolutions was combined with mimetic sensitivity to events in Europe. The United States possessed an unrivalled capacity for transforming the events and personalities of 1848 into objects of consumption: citizens in Arkansas, Wisconsin and Pennsylvania named towns after Lamartine, several plays dramatising the February Revolution in France opened in Boston and New York in spring 1848, citizens dressed in the French and the Italian tricolour, the Hungarian polka became a craze, and a cult of the Hungarian leader Kossuth preceded his visit in 1851–52. Although a generally sympathetic, often euphoric, public mood cooled notably after the June days and into 1849 as mounting violence in France recalled the revolutionary excesses of 1789, all three parties 'made the idea of revolution a natural component of the 1848 (presidential) campaign'.

The party that derived most encouragement from the events in Europe was the Free Soil Party, that favoured opening western lands for free labourers, rather than slave owners. After the February revolution in France, 'Free Soiler' leaders began to emphasise their transatlantic roots, the need to 'pluck fresh coals from the living altars of France' and to 'proclaim "Liberty, Equality, Fraternity".' The Democratic Party also capitalised on the renewed vogue in 1848 for popular sovereignty, supporting the extension of universal male suffrage to Rhode Island (where restricted suffrage still obtained), while resolving the problem of whether slavery should be allowed in the new western territories by arguing that the citizens there should decide the slave question through local municipal votes. Only the Whigs steered clear of associating themselves with the European revolutions. In the delayed presidential elections of November 1848, with events in Europe looking much less rosy, more violent and complicated, Whigs benefited from this detachment, the Mexican War hero Zachary Taylor winning with ease.

The revolutions in Germany, Bohemia and Italy and, especially, the Magyar uprising in Austria, were followed enthusiastically in the United States, although Roberts concludes that 'as revolution became anarchy, or counterrevolution, [US citizens] instead embraced their own successful revolutionary heritage to hold Europe at a distance.' With the triumph of reaction throughout most of Europe in 1851 and 1852, attention in the USA shifted to the influx of numerous republican exiles. Roberts explores the ecstatic reception, and subsequent involvement in US politics, of the Hungarian leader, Lajos Kossuth. Kossuth angered US abolitionists, by refusing to declare himself against slavery, and 'frightened Catholics ... when he lectured about a Jesuit conspiracy to take over the world'. For a brief moment, during the 1852 presidential election, the Hungarian leader's presence in the United States brought the issue of US intervention on behalf of the Magyars to the forefront of party debate. Democrats and Free Soilers (now Free Democrats), in a bid to attract German votes, at first promised US intervention to put pressure on Russia. But ultimately isolationist sentiments prevailed over Kossuth's pleas for intervention. This time the Democrats triumphed as voters deserted the Free Democrats, the third party that in 1848 had briefly promised a revolution in US politics.

Even as the USA acknowledged its distance from Europe's national struggles during the later 1850s, the democratic message of Europe's 'springtime of the peoples' became ever more audible, broadcast by exiled German '48ers' who vociferously opposed slavery and abandoned the Democratic for the Republican Party. Roberts shows how radical German Republicans contributed significantly to the ascent of Abraham Lincoln to the presidency, concluding that 'in the 1860s Americans went to war over questions that they had been prodded to debate by events in Europe a little more than a decade before'.

Mexico's initial diplomatic response to the February revolution in Paris, like that of her northern neighbour, was enthusiastic, leading in May to a renewal of diplomatic relations with France (broken off in 1845 over unpaid debt and claims). By the summer, however, comfortable feelings of republican solidarity had given way to anxiety about the influx of 'communist doctrines', a fear voiced in national newspapers of all political persuasions. Clara Lida notes how this 'red scare' was not accompanied by any careful analysis of the significance of the unfolding events in Europe, or of the meaning of these novel social doctrines: 'it was necessary to wait until the 1870s before a more comprehensive debate on the various socialist trends was experienced, leading to the emergence of organised working-class associationism.'

The aversion or blindness of Mexico's liberals to the more advanced social ideas of 1848, in contrast to the receptiveness of their counterparts in Colombia and Chile, can partly be explained by the country's dire predicament in the wake of defeat in the American War (1847–48). In the face of possible further territorial dismemberment, major peasant uprisings in the Sierra Gorda and the Isthmus of Tehuantepec, a rebellion of Apaches in the North and the Maya 'Caste War' in Yucatán, Mexican leaders were too preoccupied with national survival to be able to respond calmly to the dramatic events in Europe. Instead, the diffusion of socialist ideas and the presence European refugees in the Mexican provinces were viewed by liberals and conservatives as threats to the social order, particularly to the tranquility of the Indian population. Only after the Revolution of Ayutla in 1854 did Mexico's liberals begin to appreciate how ideals of 1848 might contribute not only to the progress of humanity, but also to their own political advance. Like the Colombian constitution of 1863, the Mexican constitution of 1857 betrays the imprint of 1848 in its radical charter of individual rights.

Brazilian elites, like their Mexican counterparts, feared the implications of the European revolutions for the social stability and territorial integrity of the monarchy. Since the eighteenth century this largely coastal, slave society had been particularly receptive to external influences stemming the European enlightenment, and the US and French revolutions. Federalist and republican ideas appealed to elites in the north-east concerned that power since the 1760s had shifted south to the new capital of Rio de Janeiro, while the free coloured and urban slave populations found it advantageous to appeal to the 'rights of man' and the sovereignty of the people in periodic urban uprisings and regional insurrections. Some response in Brazil to the events in Europe in 1848 was therefore expected.

For several decades, the '*Praieira* rebellion' in the north-eastern province of Pernambuco in 1849–51 has been offered as proof that 'the European revolutions had visible and dramatic effects', as David Rock puts it. In chapter four Nancy Naro evaluates the claim that the ideas of 1848 had a determining influence on provincial politics. The revolutions in Europe in 1848 coincided with a crisis in north-eastern Brazil associated with the emergence of a third party to challenge the Conservative and Liberal dominance of the politics of the north-eastern state of Pernambuco. The Praia party (named after the Rua da Praia, Beach Street, where its official organ the *Diario Novo* was published) was formed by dissident members of the Liberal Party in protest over the party leaders' inability to provide a share of paid positions in the provincial civil service. The new party attracted support from 'dissident traders and planters, small scale farmers, liberal professionals, newspaper publishers, artisans and the unemployed', the 'popular classes' to which Clara Lida draws attention in chapter two. There are also parallels here with the Free Soil movement in the United States; elements within Praia favoured freer access to land, monopolised in Pernambuco by the great plantations owning families. However, while the Free Soiler Party had its first convention in 1848 and borrowed in profligate style from European radicalism, the emergence of the Praia anticipated the European revolutions by six years. Indeed, the fall of July monarchy in February 1848 coincided with a concerted campaign in Brazil to remove the Praia from office and to restore Conservative and central government control over the rogue state of Pernambuco.

The Praia came to power in Pernambuco in 1845 and remained in office until September 1848. During this period, European radical ideas circulated in Recife's press as freely as anywhere in Brazil, while the example of Pernambuco under an ostensibly non-oligarchical and reformist Praia administration attracted attention among federalists, republicans and non-elite factions in other regions of Brazil, particularly in the northeast. However, Naro's analysis reveals that, once in office, Praia radicalism went little deeper than, first, replacing their Liberal and Conservative rivals on the state government payroll with their own supporters and, secondly, pandering to popular anti-Portuguese sentiment.

In their last months in office the Praia mounted a successful campaign, backed by street demonstrations, against Portuguese control of the wholesales and retail trades in Recife, eventually requiring the Portuguese navy to evacuate its citizens for resettlement in Angola. Yet Naro sees Praia's fanning of popular xenophobia as a substitute for genuine reform. The third party never became anything more than dissident faction, somewhat more popular yet still patronage based and oligarchical, of the Liberal party. The Praia's apparent receptiveness to the radical ideas and rhetoric of 1848 became more marked after its removal from office, when Praia leaders launched a rebellion against the reinstated Conservatives. Yet the rebellion between 1849 and 1851 confirmed that at the core of the Praia party were elite landowners, who for a period had been prepared to court the support of middle sectors – liberal professions, journalists, artisans, shopkeepers and small farmers – in order to challenge a monopoly of power exercised by a dominant Liberal/Conservative family network of plantation owners. The Praia studiously avoided raising the issue of slavery and, even during their rebellion, made sure that Praia forces were deployed in regions of the state where a social order still based in part upon slave labour would not be disturbed.

'Brazil's 1848' turned out to be little more than the last gasp of a third-party movement which, during its four years in power, failed to make any headway in terms of greater democratisation or popular representation. The Praia rebellion was the last of many provincial rebellions that punctuated the regency and early reign of Pedro II. During the 1850s and '60s the empire entered its heyday and not until the early 1870s did a Republican Party emerge to challenge the alternating, yet equally oligarchical, Liberal and Conservative dominance of Brazil.

If there was a part of South America in which it might have been expected that the Revolutions of 1848 would have an immediate effect, it was the Argentine Confederation under the dictator Juan Manuel de Rosas – incarnation of post-independence anti-liberal reaction. Moreover, facing Rosas's Buenos Aires across the River Plate in Montevideo were thousands of Argentine refugees, backed by a French army, planning the dictator's downfall and a return to their homeland. However, as David Rock shows in chapter five, Rosas – a committed republican – rejoiced at the news of the fall of Louis Philippe and had no reason to fear a repetition of the social disorders of Europe in a province he had successfully drilled into federalist conformity. Indeed, the internal and external situation for Rosas improved for three years after 1848.

Just as revolutionary France decided not to come to the aid of their Spanish confrères rebelling in Madrid in March 1848, Lamartine proved no more willing to support a more forward policy against Rosas than had Guizot during the July Monarchy (Rock notes how Guizot's dithering in the River Plate was a significant factor in the fall of the Orleanist regime in February 1848). Support for Rosas grew in the face of the continued French and British blockade. Yet, it was the eventual withdrawal of French forces in 1851 that precipitated the rearrangement of regional alliances under the leadership of General Justo José Urquiza, leader of the 'Independent Republic of Entre Rios', that culminated in the defeat of Rosas in the battle of Caseros in 1852.

If the ideas of 1848 could have little impact in the well-policed Buenos Aires of General Rosas, they found more fertile ground among the large community of exiled Argentines liberal in Montevideo and Santiago. Along with the Chileans, these Argentines were among the best-travelled Spanish Americans of the mid-nineteenth century, several with first hand experience of the European revolutions. Facing oppression and exile under Rosas since the 1830s, Argentina's liberal youth had looked to the French revolution of 1830 for inspiration, particularly the idea that it was the duty of the bourgeois intellectual to construct – through education and lessons in sociability, manners and urbanity – a modern, civilised republic (the role that they envisaged for themselves once the dictator was removed). Already committed francophiles, Esteban Echeverría, Domingo F. Sarmiento and Juan Bautista Alberdi welcomed the return of the Republic in 1848. Yet, Rock observes, 'compared with the events in France in either 1830 or 1870–71, the 1848 movement provoked neither a new intellectual fashion nor a body of followers or imitators'. Indeed, France's combination of popular radicalism and resurgent Bonapartist demagoguery reminded Sarmiento, Alberdi and especially the Catholic thinker Félix Frias too much of their enemy, Juan Manuel de Rosas. Only the younger Argentine Liberal, Bartolomé Mitre, working as a journalist in Chile and close to the Chilean radicals, Francisco Bilbao and Santiago Arcos, expressed enthusiasm for the democratic ideals of 1848. Behind Mitre's later reputation for the ruthless (and very successful) pursuit of the political and military aggrandisement of Buenos Aires, and his alignment with the most conservative members of the Argentine oligarchy, was a commitment, Rock reminds us, to the democratic ideas of 1848, expressed in *Professions of Faith* (a tract published in Buenos Aires shortly after Mitre's participation in the battle of Caseros which brought down the Rosas regime). The objectives of good government outlined in *Professions of Faith* included direct universal suffrage, freedom of the press, the right to hold public meetings without restriction and public education 'as a means to moralise the masses and make them fit for the enjoyment of liberty'.

Mitre's Chilean friends, Bilbao and Arcos, shared his penchant for political radicalism and military adventurism. Although Chilean radical liberals had much less short-term success than Argentina's 'Generation of 1837', or the younger Mitre (Argentina's solitary 'quarante-huitard'), who came to power after the fall of Rosas in 1852, the 1848 revolutions had a deeper impact on Chile in the longer term. This longer term legacy of the short-lived bubble of French-inspired revolutionary exaltation in Chile between 1850 and 1852 is the theme explored by Cristián Gazmuri in chapter seven.

Like their Argentine confreres, Chilean radical liberals faced autocratic and authoritarian Conservative (*pelucón*) regimes during the 1830s and '40s, although *pelucón* governments were less arbitrary, oppressive and demagogic than the Rosas regime. Like Rosas, Chilean conservatives, especially Diego Portales, were not averse to mobilising artisans. And, like the Argentine 'Generation of 1837', younger liberals in Chile turned to French social and political ideas in the aftermath of the 1830 revolution. Chileans also shared the Argentine experience of political exile, although in the Chilean case exile beyond the country (as opposed to internal exile) was usually self-imposed. Yet, while the revolutionary winds that blew over Buenos Aires in 1848 left the Rosas regime undisturbed, Chile between 1850 and 1852 witnessed the only example of a conscious attempt to apply lessons of the Paris of 1848 to the politics of an American republic.

Why did radicals in Chile believe that their remote and conservative country would provide fertile ground for political and social experimentation? The chapters by Rock, Lida, Gazmuri, Sobrevilla and García highlight the extraordinary combination of circumstances that contributed to Chile's short-lived 'springtime of the peoples': the return of Santiago Arcos and Francisco Bilbao from France, both with first hand experience of political clubs and barricades, to a more cosmopolitan Chile, flush from the onset of the California Gold Rush; the existence of a large, relatively literate and already politically initiated class of artisans in Santiago; and, the approach of presidential elections in which the *pelucones* believed they had a natural, aristocratic right to reelection. The 'Society of Equality', founded by in Santiago in February 1850 by Arcos and Bilbao, brought together liberals from the social elite and the middle class with artisans and workers. Initially conceived as a 'society of ideas', with the additional objectives of promoting mutualism and popular education, in the run up to the 1851 presidential election the society transformed itself into a nationwide network of political clubs in the service of the Liberal party (*pipiolos*). Persecution and electoral defeat pushed the *pipiolos* into two rebellions, the first in the southern province of Concepción, and then in the capital, both of which the Conservatives swiftly repressed.

Lida and Gazmuri concur that the alliance between the radical liberal intelligentsia and artisans and workers in the 'Society of Equality', however ephemeral and unsuccessful in the short term, represented both the political initiation of the Chilean working class and the start of a process which would result in a significant democratisation of Chile during the 1870s. Gazmuri shows how young *pipiolos*, brought together in the 'Society', who fought in the civil war of 1851–52 and its sequel in 1859, rose to prominent positions in Chilean government and politics during the 1860s and '70s. In particular, the founding members of the Radical party in 1858 embraced many of the ideas and forms of association first evident in the 'Society of Equality' in Santiago in 1850. More broadly, in spite of the military defeat of the *pipiolos* and the closure of the 'Society of Equality' in 1852, the impulse given to Chilean associational life by the events of 1850–51 continued. A national network of Cuerpos de Bomberos Voluntarios, masonic lodges and mutualist associations, first evident in 1850–51, served as a bedrock of later middle and working class politics.

If Chile's intellectual cosmopolitanism and strong constitutional (albeit conservative) traditions made it Latin America's most likely candidate for absorbing influences from the European revolutions of 1848, Peru, at first glance, seems to offer the least potential for receptivity to radical European ideas. Yet in chapter seven Natalia Sobrevilla demonstrates that Europe's 'springtime of the peoples' had a marked impact on Peru. After two decades of post-independence economic stagnation, wracked by conflict between regional caudillos, the onset of the guano boom during the 1840s, followed by the economic quickening associated with the California gold rush, opened up new possibilities in Peruvian politics. Moreover, expanded suffrage resulting from constitutional reforms in 1849 allowed artisans greater political participation, while economic recovery intensified debate over free trade and protectionism (marked characteristics also of Bolivian, Colombian and Mexican politics in the mid-century).

As in Chile and Argentina, more advanced liberal currents had emerged in Peru during the 1830s, associated with the founding of a liberal higher educational institution in Lima – the College of our Lady of Guadalupe – by Domingo Elías. After 1848, graduates of this school in particular were inspired by the events in Europe to raise their political profile and to pressure for reform. During the presidential electoral campaign of the winter of 1850–51 a new political grouping, the Club Progresista, was formed, presenting itself as an alternative to the prevalent *caudillismo*, demanding the abolition of Indian tribute and African slavery, and naming Domingo Elías as its candidate. Sobrevilla describes how during this election, new forms of political mobilisation imported from Europe, such as the banquet and the political club, were brought into use, both in Lima and in the provinces. After losing the election, the *progresistas* promoted Peru's first revolution to involve mass mobilisation.

Mass mobilisation was in part a consequence of internal factors, especially artisan activism over the tariff issue, and mounting competition for the support of Blacks on the eve of abolition. But Sobrevilla shows how important the European example was to the sharpening of the reform agenda. The existence in Lima of a large community of literate European artisans and liberal professionals, among whom were several refugees from the European revolutions (including Giuseppe Garibaldi between 1851–53), combined with the presence during the early 1850s of the exiled Chilean radical Francisco Bilbao, a tireless publicist of democratic ideas and founder of clubs and associations, were crucial links between Peruvian politics and ideas and events in mid-century Europe.

Peru, then, at the height of the guano boom proved to be peculiarly susceptible to the European example. The imprint of 1848 can be seen in the self-confidence and militancy of Lima's artisans, the opening of a third, 'progresista', force in Peruvian politics, with a broad national appeal, the hastening of the end to slavery, the abolition of Indian tribute and the beginning of a liberal, *indigenista*, integrationist agenda, and the promulgation in 1855 of a modern, Liberal constitution, separating Church and state and providing a charter of individual rights and guarantees.

As regards receptivity to the ideas of 1848, Peru resembled far more the other Andean republics than is usually supposed. Yet, if in Peru and Chile conservatives promptly succeeded in stemming the liberal advance, in New Granada, not only were radical liberals able to achieve power in the wake of the European revolutions (in 1849), but the Liberal Revolution endured until the late 1880s. 'Nowhere else in Latin America,' observes Malcolm Deas, 'did the events of 1848 in Europe find such eager followers and imitators as among the politicians, artisans, students and even soldiers of poor isolated New Granada.'[14] In chapter nine Eduardo Posada-Carbó assesses the impact of the events in Europe against an analysis of Colombian mid-century politics.

14 M. Deas, 'Venezuela, Colombia and Ecuador,' in L. Bethell (ed.), *Spanish America after Independence, c.1820–1870* (Cambridge, 1989), p. 533.

As in Chile and Peru, news of the 1848 revolutions arrived in Colombia on the eve of a presidential election in which Liberals were challenging a Conservative hold on power since the late 1830s. In contrast to the success of conservatives in Mexico, Pernambuco, Chile and Peru, either to resist the liberal challenge during the early 1850s, or to achieve a conservative restoration (albeit short-lived in the case of Mexico), in Colombia radical liberals won the 1849 election, successfully resisted a conservative rebellion and saw a wide range of radical reforms incorporated in the new constitution of 1853 (the civil code, universal male suffrage, abolition of slavery, the replacement of the army with a national guard and the introduction of a federal system). Although by 1854 more moderate liberals (so-called *draconianos*) had replaced the radicals (known as *golgotas*), the liberal revolution prevailed for most of the rest of the century, until the conservatives returned behind Rafael Núñez in 1886.

The question Posada-Carbó poses in chapter nine is how, and to what extent, a liberal revolution in remote Colombia was influenced by the ideas and events of revolutionary Europe. He concludes that 'the events in New Granada were neither a parody of the French revolution, nor an independent movement only slightly influenced by foreign ideas'. He shows, first, that the Liberal victory in 1849 represented no sudden opening of popular politics. Party conflicts during the early 1850s were rooted in regional rivalries and habits of popular mobilisation, going back at least as early as the 1820s. 'Democratic societies' representing artisans had existed since the early 1840s, while popular regional caudillos such as Cali's José María Obando were long accustomed to recruiting Blacks and Indians in the cause of 'popular federalism'. Colombians could therefore greet the news coming from Europe of a new kind of popular politics, with discrimination born of experience. For instance, as in Mexico, the novel European ideas of communism and socialism were generally greeted in Colombia with ridicule or contempt.

Yet, in spite of the autonomous genealogy of Colombia's Liberal Revolution, Posada-Carbó shows how Colombia was acutely sensitive to news of events in Europe and responsive to European ideas and political fashions. Using Jonathan Sperber's concept of 'varieties of revolutionary experience', he reveals a political environment characterised by a free and highly competitive press, widespread literacy, an energetic associational life, extended suffrage and popular (including female) mobilisation around elections, and widespread use of public space. None of this was new to Colombian politics. What *was* different was the sheer quantity of democratic politics, and its successful deployment. As party rivalry intensified during the early 1850s there was the same sudden and massive proliferation of democratic clubs as in Chile with the 'Society of Equality', and the same diffusion of a modern democratic vocabulary. Posada-Carbó concludes that 'the ideals of the French revolution served to increase the momentum behind a set of reforms that aimed at granting political freedom, securing individual rights, giving autonomy to the provinces, and protecting freedom of industry and trade. These reforms left an enduring legacy in the history of the republic: in the civilian outlook of its institutions, in its competitive, often violent, partisan struggles, and in the general weakness of its central government.'

1

The Second Republic and French 'Republican Socialism': 1848–51

ROGER MAGRAW

The French Radical Republicans of 1848 have not, in general, enjoyed a very high reputation. Even Republican sympathiser Victor Hugo confessed that he preferred 1793 to 1848: 'Titans wading through chaos to nincompoops dithering.' The liberal Alexis de Tocqueville – whose memoirs are suffused with distaste both for the workers' sordid, unrealisable material aspirations and demands, and for the ill-dressed and uncouth 'Montagnard' petty-bourgeois deputies who entered parliament after the April 1848 elections – insisted that, while history might have seen more wicked revolutionaries, there had been none more 'stupid'. Endlessly proclaiming their belief in popular sovereignty, they nevertheless appeared blind to the real interests and grievances of the mass – largely peasant – electorate that they had just enfranchised.[1] The neoliberal historiography, which has dominated our own era, has been equally unforgiving. François Furet's Burkean general history of nineteenth-century France insists that the revolutionaries of 1848 shared far too many of those extremist ideas (egalitarianism, direct democracy) which had caused the Revolution to veer so disastrously off course between 1789 and 1794. Only in the 1870s, once Jules Ferry's new generation of Republicans had reembraced the healthy, liberal values of 1789 – and when the massacre of thousands of Communards had allowed 'France' to reassert its control over socialist Paris – could the ship of the Revolution, battered by the storms of decades of alternating insurrection and dictatorship, finally limp home to port, and could representative constitutional government and a free-market economy be consolidated.[2]

Tim Bancroft has recently argued, with a hint of exaggeration, that '1848' has always been the 'forgotten' revolution. Official commemorations have been, at best, lukewarm. Mainstream Republicans have always favoured '1789', which gave birth to the *tricolore,* the *Marseillaise* and the

1 A. de Tocqueville, *Recollections* (London, 1948).
2 F. Furet, *Revolutionary France, 1770–1880* (Oxford, 1992).

Quatorze Juillet. For their part, the left gave priority to the martyred Communards. In 1898, at the height of the Dreyfus crisis, there were a few localised commemorations in left-wing departments, such as the Allier, and a scholarly society was established to foster study of 1848. In 1948 Léon Blum and Edouard Herriot organised an exhibition at the Bibliothèque Nationale – Lazare Carnot's project for free, secular schooling was praised – and the ashes of Victor Schoelcher, who had abolished slavery in the French colonies, were transferred to the Panthéon. But in a snowy February there were few signs of popular enthusiasm, and communist students heckled Blum for his 'betrayal' of Spain. Projects for a film on the 'springtime of freedom' and for a museum of the 1848 Revolution were both stillborn. Many suggested that the main significance of 1848 lay in providing warnings both of mistakes to be avoided – the naïve 'lyric illusions' of spring 1848, the suicidal class warfare of the June Days – and of the recurrent danger of Bonapartism against which one should be perpetually wary.[3] A recent lecture in Birmingham on the 'French and the Commemoration of their History' by F. Bédarida neglected to mention that this was a significant anniversary of 1848 – and his audience compounded the lecturer's amnesia by forgetting to ask him why he had neglected to mention the fact!

Paradoxically, Furet's bête noire, Karl Marx himself, played a major role in perpetuating this disdain for 1848. His two brilliant pamphlets – *The Class Struggles in France* (1850) and *The Eighteenth Brumaire* (1852) – contrasted the epic (bourgeois) Revolution of 1789–94 with the failed (proletarian) Revolution of 1848–51. The actors of the Second Republic sought to give themselves historical gravitas by adopting the classical/Roman rhetoric of their heroic predecessors. But the net impression of history repeating itself as tragi-comic farce was finally confirmed when the counter-revolutionary coup was delivered by a buffoon, who happened to bear the name of the great Napoleon. Some of Marx's scorn was directed against the 'moderate' Republicans of the Provisional Government of the spring of 1848, whom he accused of being mere wordsmiths, purveyors of the absurd lyric illusion that somehow their verbiage could, by itself, bridge that yawning gulf between workers and capitalists, which mass unemployment was in the process of accentuating. Unsurprisingly, given the current vogue for the 'linguistic turn', some recent studies have claimed that the rhetorical skills of Alphonse de Lamartine and other intellectuals played a pivotal political role in these months, since it was vital for Republicans to construct a discourse which could rescue the term 'Republic' from its association with warfare, blood and Jacobin Terror,

3 T. Bancroft, 'Commemorations of the Revolution of 1848 and of the Second Republic,' *Modern and Contemporary France*, vol. 6 (1998), pp. 155–68.

and to help rebuild a respectable Republican culture. Lamartine thus warned workers that, by insisting on making the red flag the banner of the new regime, 'you would strangle the Republic born of your blood in its cradle'. Many of the speeches of Republican leaders in March and April thus consisted of convoluted attempts to reconcile property rights with the 'right to work', in order to build a political constituency which might rally round ameliorative social policies, or to convince Catholic 'pères de famille' that state education reforms were not an infringement of parental rights. Honoré Daumier's portrait of the 'Family at the Barricades' sought to incorporate the insurrectionary tradition within the cosy confines of the ideology of domesticity. Organic metaphors were widely used, with the 'people' portrayed as the warm, caring 'heart' of the body politic and Republican intellectuals as its rational, thinking 'head'. The latter were, of course, committed to serving the people's interests in a selfless way. One of the more astute decisions of the conservative victors of the April elections was to retain Lamartine in the government in the hope that his rhetoric would continue for a few more weeks to soothe the workers while the right prepared to dismantle the social programmes introduced after February.[4]

However, it was the Radical-Republicans who bore the full brunt of Marx's derision. The efforts of politicians associated with the newspaper *La Réforme* – Flocon, Ledru-Rollin – to persuade the Provisional Government to support the 'Right to Work', the ten-hour day, the 'organisation of labour' and the 'craft Parliament' of the Luxembourg were scorned as attempts to buy off workers' anger with meaningless sops. They were accused of betraying the workers by failing to offer full support to the June Days insurrection, a rising portrayed by Marx *not* as a desperate, defensive reaction to the abolition of the National Workshops, but as socialist-led and as reflecting workers' awareness that nothing more could be expected from a bourgeois Republic. The support of (a tiny minority of) workers for Raspail rather than for Ledru-Rollin in the December 1848 election was taken as evidence of a definitive breach between the workers' conscious vanguard and the Radicals, whose indecisiveness during the June 13 1849 abortive *journée*, called to protest at Louis Napoleon's attack on the Roman Republic, was cited as evidence of their petty-bourgeois 'Parliamentary cretinism' and their unwillingness to support strategies proposed by workers' secret societies. Above all, Marx was highly critical of the Démocrates-Socialistes who from 1849 to 1851 sought to assemble and hold together a 'broad left' political and electoral coalition. Led by 'progressive' bourgeois – lawyers, doctors and journalists – this

4 J. Livesey, 'Speaking the Nation: Radical Republicans and the Failure of Political Communication in 1848,' *French Historical Studies* (1997), pp. 459–80.

attracted some workers who, Marx lamented, remained very much junior partners. For the naïve, illusory, 'utopian' dream of the Dem-Socs was to defend the world of small-shopkeepers, craftsmen and peasant farmers against the juggernaut of large-scale capitalism via promises of government support for cheap credit and for cooperatives and mutualist associations.

In 1850 – when *The Class Struggles in France* was written – Marx was allying with Stefan Born in Germany, who was seeking to disentangle workers from alliances with bourgeois democrats. Marx insisted that French workers, stripped of all previous illusions, were following a similar strategy, establishing their own autonomous movement and preparing to seize the initiative by a ('Blanquist') coup. Such bold 'voluntarist' tactics by the workers' vanguard would serve to galvanise the intermediate classes into confrontation with the forces of finance and commercial capitalism that oppressed them. Revolutions *could be* the 'locomotives of History'. The momentum generated by the revolutionary process itself could overcome the 'structural' obstacles posed by the 'immaturity' of the class system ... ('Different classes in France had to count their epochs of development in weeks where previously they counted them in half-centuries').

By the time of the *Eighteenth Brumaire*, however, such revolutionary optimism and voluntarism had long faded. Not only did Marx view the upturn in the European economy in 1850 as marking the end of the prolonged depression which had fuelled the revolutionary movements, but he now insisted that earlier hopes of a successful worker revolution had always been illusory since French and European industrial capitalism was still underdeveloped and, thus, the 'islands' of proletarian militancy too small and easily isolated. The tone was now ironic and fatalistic/deterministic. Revolutions were viewed as natural phenomena subject to physical laws; hence any attempt to short-circuit these processes was seen as futile.[5]

However, as Bernard Moss has emphasised, Marx's views in the 1848–51 period were in constant flux, as changing circumstances altered his revolutionary tactics. During 1848–49 Marx's opinions on the best strategies for the French to pursue were very different from those which he later came to espouse, and his assessment of the Radical-Republicans, much more generous. Marx's ambivalence stemmed from his failure to develop any one coherent interpretation of the role and significance of Jacobinism in the Great Revolution. Were Jacobins simply the most tactically flexible of the bourgeois factions, willing to make opportunistic

5 B. Moss, 'Marx and Permanent Revolution in France: the Background to the *Communist Manifesto*,' *Socialist Register* (London, 1998), pp. 47–68, and, 'Marx and Engels on French Social Democracy: Historians or Revolutionaries?,' *Journal of the History of Ideas*, vol. 46, (1985).

concessions to the popular classes in the Year II in order to defeat internal counter-revolution and its foreign allies? Or did Jacobinism contain within itself the seeds of a form of embryonic social-democracy, exemplified by its willingness to question unlimited property rights, in its aspirations towards state welfare and secular education, and its Rousseauist distaste for wide disparities of wealth? Marx himself derived many of his concepts of the 'bourgeois' French Revolution from liberal historians like Guizot, and was never *entirely* convinced of Jacobinism's subversive potential. However, one might argue that it was precisely the existence of a neo-Jacobin, radical republican stratum of the bourgeoisie, capable of providing both ideological and organisational leadership to popular protest, rather than the artisanal character of the urban labour force, which explains France's 'peculiarity' as *the* home of European revolution. After 1830, the Société des Droits de l'Homme, which sought to harness Republican and popular resentment at the 'confiscation' of that revolution by the Orleanist grande bourgeoisie, was led by lawyers and students. But it recruited heavily among Parisian artisans with a programme that included support for trade union rights and producer cooperatives, as well as for male suffrage and progressive taxation. Equally, much of the rhetoric of the emerging workers' movement was a creative adaptation of bourgeois anti-aristocratic discourses that distinguished between 'parasitic' and 'productive' classes. When political repression and censorship after 1834 smashed Republican organisations, many activists, both bourgeois and working class, entered the clandestine world of secret societies.[6]

It was direct experience of this world of French radicalism in the early 1840s that informed Marx's ideas in the *Communist Manifesto*. In 1846 he insisted that 'all (workers) have at least the obscure feeling that social equality of rights is implicit in democracy. Except for those who do not count all European democrats are more or less, communists at heart.' Hence he urged that the embryonic workers' movement should ally with bourgeois democrats and with the range of subordinate non-proletarian petty bourgeois, artisanal and peasant strata. Thus, throughout 1848–49 Marx discouraged in France and in Germany any maximalist, ultra-left tactics which might disrupt this alliance. He gave general support to the policies of the Radical-Republicans. Inevitably this support was not uncritical. For one thing he felt that the French left was too heavily imbued with the myth of France's historic role as the bastion of Revolution to grasp fully the need to internationalise the Revolution. Despite Lamartine's attempt to reassure the European powers that under the

6 B. Moss, 'Republican Socialism and the Making of the Working Class in Britain, France and the U.S.A.,' *Comparative Studies in Society and History*, (1993), pp. 390–413.

Republic French ideas, not revolutionary troops, would 'charge with bayonets', France did offer sanctuary to foreign radicals and there were attempts to mobilise support for the Poles in May 1848 and for the Roman Republic in June 1849 (Lyon workers had a tradition of supporting Italian nationalists). However, Marx believed too few appreciated that 'revolution in one country', even one as important as France, would be doomed and that success would only come when the left mobilised a crusade against *both* British capitalist hegemony *and* tsarism.[7]

Reevaluating French 'social democracy': towards a historiographical reassessment

The historiography of the Second Republic was revitalised in the 1960s and 1970s, initially by a number of major French studies of the provinces, and then by a wave of monographs on aspects of urban and rural mobilisation by younger US historians influenced by the (then) 'new social history'.[8] Once the Second Republic had been dismissed as a largely Parisian phenomenon that had rapidly and gratuitously alienated the peasantry, by imposing an additional land-tax, and the bulk of 'moderate' provincial opinion by funding the National Workshops to maintain Parisian workers in idleness. Hence the election of Louis Napoleon as president in December 1848, with a massive 74 per cent of the vote, was interpreted as the death-knell of a republic with little support beyond a few major cities, even if its death throes were prolonged over a period of three years. Now, however, Agulhon – a sometime Marxist who has subsequently 'matured' into the doyen of left-Republican/lay orthodoxy – insists that the Second Republic should be accorded an important status as *the* moment of the democratic 'apprenticeship' during which progressive *notables* tutored the newly-enfranchised masses in Republican ideas.[9] Similarly historical sociologist Charles Tilly claimed to discern a significant watershed between 'archaic' forms of localised protest (grain-riots; tax-revolts; forest-invasions) still prevalent during the depression of 1846–47 and 'modern' forms of political and industrial mobilisation (although Agulhon and others suggested that intensified political and police repression in 1850–51 pushed some of the left's popular supporters back to more 'archaic' forms of expressionist or violent protest).[10]

7 L. C. Jennings, *France and Europe in 1848* (Oxford, 1973).

8 P. Vigier, *La Seconde République dans la région alpine*, 2 vols. (Paris, 1963); M. Agulhon, *La République au village* (Paris, 1970); A. Corbin, *Archaïsme et modernité en Limousin: 1845–80*, 2 vols. (Paris, 1975).

9 M. Agulhon, *The Republican Experiment: 1848–52* (Cambridge, 1983).

10 C. Tilly, 'How Protest Modernised France 1845–55,' in W. Aydelotte (ed.), *The Dimensions of Quantitative Research in History* (Princeton, 1972).

Although one may not agree with the 'modernisation theory' implicit in some of this literature, by the end of the 1970s a strong case had been made, supported by extensive empirical research in diverse regions, for viewing the Second Republic, despite its rapid demise, as marking a crucial stage in the development of French popular politics. In April 1848, in the first elections held under mass suffrage, much of the peasantry voted for crypto-royalist *notables* and radicals won under 80 of the 900 seats. Thirteen months later the 'Party of Order' won some 54 per cent of the votes. However, its immediate reaction was to voice alarm at the gains made by the Dem-Soc left, which secured 36 per cent of the vote, over 200 seats and a majority in one third of departments. The electoral map of 1849, it has been remarked, bears a striking resemblance to that of 1936, when the Popular Front secured the first socialist-led government. Hence much of the historiography of the 1960–70s, even that of Marxist or 'new-left' historians, adopted a much more sympathetic tone towards the radicals of the Second Republic than had Marx after 1850–51. These radicals were, after all, operating in a society where the power of landed *notables*, large 'paternalist' employers and a largely reactionary clergy remained intact in many areas, and where, except very briefly in the spring of 1848, the forces of the state were ruthlessly used against them. They were attempting to mobilise a popular base among a newly enfranchised and extremely heterogeneous electorate within which the 'working class' formed only one element. It would have made little political sense to have informed millions of petty bourgeois, craftsmen and peasants that, however much one sympathised with their conjunctural and structural problems, long-term capitalist development would consign them inexorably to the rubbish heap of history! Hence the emphasis came to be on the imaginative ways in which, under very difficult circumstances, the Dem-Socs sought to assemble and to hold together the first ever 'social-democratic' mass movement in Europe.

Left-wing mobilisation in the Second Republic: the achievements of the 'démocrates-socialistes'

Obviously it is difficult to present the history of the Dem-Socs as a 'success story'. They lost the 1849 election and, after prolonged state harassment, the remnants of their organisation were shattered by the 1851 coup. In the intervening period they were undoubtedly weakened by tactical indecision and by ideological and social tensions among both activists and supporters. However, recent historiography has emphasised the tenacious comeback that they staged after the multiple disasters of 1848 (the alienation of peasant voters by the 45 centimes land-tax, the crushing of Parisian workers in the June Days, the inability to mount any effective challenge to the seductive populism of Louis Napoleon in the presidential elections). The Dem-Socs exhibited real organisational skills and their imaginative attempts to win support from a wide range of social groups suggests a more nuanced understanding of the complexities of the French social structure and the grievances of its 'intermediary' but subaltern classes than that of Marx. Throughout they were operating under great difficulties. The political clubs which, as P. Amann showed, acted as the focus for political debate and electoral organisation in the spring of 1848, had been banned after the June Days.[11] Solidarité Républicaine, that emerged in early 1849 as the national focus of the left's regrouping, was in turn outlawed. Much of the movement's activity thus came to be based around its extensive network of local newspapers, whose editors, many of them deputies, used their offices as political headquarters and whose distribution networks, often employing sacked worker militants or itinerant journeymen, acted as the main channel for the diffusion of propaganda. Increasingly draconian laws against *colportage* made such activities increasingly hazardous and dozens of editors were prosecuted and jailed for offending against tough press laws.

As Ed Berenson has argued, radical propagandists showed great skill in adapting to both the forms and content of popular culture.[12] Journalists like Pierre Joigneaux, himself the son of a Burgundian wine-carter, adapted the *Almanach*, the staple reading matter of the peasant *veillée,* by augmenting its usual blend of agricultural and medical tips and adventure stories with 'conversations' with old peasants recalling the horrors of seigneurialism, to which, it was suggested, the neo-royalists of the Party of Order wished to return France.[13] Although many Dem-Socs themselves were Voltairean sceptics, they were aware that many of their potential popular supporters, though often anticlerical, retained respect for Christianity. Hence their 'catechisms' argued for a 'social gospel' of fraternity and mutual solidarity, a religion which was portrayed as that of Christ the Carpenter, who had thrown the usurers from the temple. This Christ's image adorned the walls of artisan cooperatives. Such a religion was a far cry from that of the Catholic clergy which had sold out to the rich. And in a culture where much popular sociability centred around 'free-and-easy' song groups (*goguettes*), the left had the services of song-writers like Pierre Dupont whose '*Chants des Vignerons*' promised a 'social

11 P. Amann, *Revolution and Mass Democracy: The Parisian Club Movement in 1848* (Princeton, 1975).

12 E. Berenson, *Populist Religion and Left-Wing Politics in France 1830–52* (Princeton, 1984).

13 R. Magraw, 'Pierre Joigneaux and Socialist Propaganda in the French Countryside, 1848–51,' *French Historical Studies* (1978), pp. 599–640.

Republic' (*'La Belle'*) in which, at last, peasants would be freed from the clutches of usurers and tax-collectors.[14]

Dem-Soc ideology blended Republicanism with a loosely defined 'socialism' which made extensive use of the rhetoric of 'associationism', mutual aid and 'fraternal' solidarity. Its programme promised progressive taxes and free secular education, cheap state credit for artisan and peasant producer and consumer cooperatives, trade-union rights, repeal of the Forest-Codes and wine-taxes, and nationalisation of mines and railways. Its 'targets' included royalist landowners, usurers and 'financial feudalism', but not necessarily 'productive' industrialists. Indeed Prothero has suggested that the movement's middle-class leadership may have tried to direct its artisanal supporters towards cooperatives in order to discourage thought of strikes (or insurrections) which would have alarmed prospective bourgeois supporters.

Inevitably there were strategic conflicts within the movement. The majority of its deputies, who viewed the failed insurrections of 1848–49 as disasters, insisted that one should refuse to be provoked by incessant state harassment and put one's faith in the elections of 1852, since the by-election gains in 1849–50 and the constitutional ban on Louis Napoleon standing for a second term, suggested that prospects were bright. However, a dissident group, the 'New Mountain', insisted that growing evidence of an impending coup meant that this electoral option was no longer viable and that organisation of paramilitary secret societies was essential. By May 1850 this latter faction urged that the new law disenfranchising migrant workers and anyone with a criminal record (around 30 per cent of voters) necessitated a show of force in response. But the leadership simply organised a protest petition. There was talk of the disenfranchised marching to the polling booths in 1852, hunting guns in hand, to demand the right to vote.

Undoubtedly, too, there were social tensions within the movement. In 1850–51 some bourgeois moderates quit, alarmed either by state persecution or by the 'extremism' of the popular rank-and-file. Some of the latter, as Huard has shown for the Gard, *were* prone to use a rhetoric which suggested the need to return to the Terror of the Year II and to play *boules* with the skulls of the royalist 'whites' (a language familiar to readers of Richard Cobb).[15]

14 I. Prothero, *Radical Artisans in England and France, 1830–70* (Cambridge, 1997). For a recent analysis of the transmission of memories of 1848 to the later labour movement via popular songs see A. Körner, 'Ideas and Memories of 1848 in France: Nationalism and Internationalism in the *Goguette* between 1848 and 1890,' in A. Körner (ed.), *1848: A European Revolution?*, pp. 85–105.

15 R. Huard, *Le mouvement républicain en Bas-Languedoc, 1848–81* (Paris, 1982).

However, it is misleading to suggest an unbridgeable gulf between 'petty-bourgeois' and 'proletarian' wings of the movement. Nor was the left moribund or in disarray in 1850–51. The premises of *Eighteenth Brumaire* are simply too deterministic. The results of this bitter political conflict were not predestined nor a foregone conclusion. The 'threat' of a left-wing victory in 1852 was not 'invented' by Bonapartist bureaucrats seeking a justification for a coup. Rather, they viewed this as a genuine possibility, even if, as Forstenzer has suggested, their vivid, medicalised rhetoric, portraying a France infected by 'gangrene' and 'cancer', by a 'plague' spread by the carriers of the 'disease' of socialism, may sound slightly paranoid.[16]

Left-wing mobilisation in the Second Republic: the 'Republic of the Peasants'

The historiographical breakthrough of the 1960–70s was the (re)discovery of the 'red' Republican peasant, 'a character', one historian claimed, 'until then not recognised, even unthinkable'. Hitherto, it had been assumed that urban-based Republicans had simply squandered the opportunity to exploit the widespread discontent smouldering in the countryside since the harvest failures of 1846–47. Unwilling to offend bankers, the Provisional Government had sought to reduce the spiralling deficit by imposing an additional land tax, thereby driving peasant voters straight into the arms of crypto-royalist *notables* and provoking a prolonged tax revolt which served as the prelude to the massive populist rural endorsement for Louis Napoleon, perceived as the anti-Republican and anti-tax candidate.

Most writing about the Second Republic thus assumed that this was virtually all that needed to be said about its rural politics. As property-owners, peasants 'naturally' feared socialism; hence the peasant volunteers who warmed de Tocqueville's heart by going from Normandy to Paris to help massacre the workers in the June days. 'Essentially religious' they rallied behind village *curés* against 'godless' urban ideologies. Unable to conceive of 'politics' in anything but personalised terms, they could rally to a Bonapartist messiah but not to the 'abstract' concept of a Republic. And some of these stereotypes clearly inform many – not all – of the observations of Marx and Engels. Peasants represented barbarism within society. Engels talked of the 'native stupidity of the French peasant'. Isolation and illiteracy meant that peasant class-consciousness was

16 T. Forstenzer, *The French Provincial Police and the Fall of the Second Republic* (Princeton, 1981); J. Merriman, *The Agony of the Republic: The Repression of the Left in Revolutionary France* (Princeton, 1978).

rudimentary. It was their passivity which helped to ensure that in December 1851 France would be 'delivered unresisting into captivity'. Ironically, of course, in the long run their fascination with Bonaparte would prove fatal, Marx argues, for by accelerating the development of capitalism, a Bonapartist regime would doom inefficient peasant petty production to more rapid extinction.

And yet Marx's pamphlets contain ample evidence for an alternative reading of the rural politics. He noted how Louis Napoleon was too tied to his conservative backers to carry out the populist promises on cheap credit that had won him votes, how resentment at wine-taxes and the Forest Code, and sympathy with persecuted teachers, were pushing peasants into the arms of the 'reds', that there were peasant 'Cévennes' as well as peasant 'Vendées'.[17]

Much of the historiography of the 1960–70s sought to explain why certain rural regions proved responsive to the appeal of the left. These did not include most of northern and western France. In May 1849 the right won 202 of 214 seats in Normandy, Brittany and the Vendée. The conservatism of such regions was explained, in part, by the social control exercised over dependent agricultural labourers by big tenant farmers who, leasing from bourgeois owners, dominated the capitalist, market-orientated estates of Flanders, Picardy and the Ile-de France. In the west, aristocratic landowners, aided by the clergy, maintained firm 'paternalistic' control over their devoutly Catholic sharecroppers and farm-servants in Brittany and the Vendée. More generally, Brustein argues, villages or regions dominated by sharecropping or tenant farming have tended (into the present century) to be dominated by the right. Tenants (*fermiers*) were often relatively prosperous, forming a locally dominant '*fermocratie*' in Artois in the north. Sharecropping tended to survive in less market-orientated regions, and sharecroppers were often isolated from wider social or market contacts and fearful of eviction if they challenged the landowner. Since they paid their rents in kind, they were also less badly hit than cash-crop farmers by the low agricultural prices that persisted throughout the Second Republic.[18] Moreover, except in the wine-growing Midi, agricultural labourers formed few collective solidarities. Farm-servants who lodged with the farmer felt superior to day-labourers or seasonal harvesters. Many labourers were younger sons of peasant farmers who might one day inherit the family farm. Though there were grain-riots in 1846–47, agricultural strikes were rare and brief. Instead, labourers' resentments found an outlet in physical violence, arson, or in migration to the towns.

17 D. Fernbach (ed.), *Surveys from Exile: K. Marx and the Revolutions of 1848* (London, 1973).
18 W. Brustein, *The Social Origins of Political Regionalism: France 1848–1981* (Berkeley, 1988).

Finally there are fairly strong correlations between the map of rural conservatism and that of religious practice. Many of the 'clerical' regions whose clergy rejected the 1790 oath of allegiance to the Revolution went on to support the Counterrevolution. Memories of persecution by Republican armies then sustained a martyrology that nurtured reactionary politics for generations. In short, 'cultural' factors and local historic memories, not just social structures or landholding patterns, could play a decisive role in determining political behaviour.

Explanations for the geography of rural radicalism similarly invoked a combination of socio-economic, cultural and political factors. Studies of twentieth-century peasant mobilisation suggest that the 'middle peasant' is often the crucial figure. Too small to be economically secure, he is dependent on the sale of cash crops and thus vulnerable to market fluctuations. At the same time, ownership of a small farm provides a degree of potential 'independence' denied to dependent sharecroppers or labourers, while market contacts provide links to the towns and potential access to 'cultural brokers' and to ideologies which may offer explanations for and solutions to multiple grievances. The extent of peasant cash-crop farming in France before the completion of the rail network during the Second Empire has too often been underestimated. Hundreds of thousands of small *vignerons* were dependent on sale of their wine in order to purchase food, pay taxes, because for all its life-giving properties few can live by wine alone! *Vignerons*, who already had along history of violent protest to wine-taxes (*droits réunis*), which as flat-rate taxes discriminated against producers of cheap table wines, found themselves hit by collapsing prices in 1848–50. Wine-growing regions, with the exception of areas of 'quality' wines or those dominated, like the Beaujolais, by a form of share-cropping, were thus bastions of the left. Around Dijon, in Burgundy, the left won 50 per cent of the vote, and 70 per cent in the Mâconnais. In Lower Languedoc, where a wine mono-culture was beginning to develop, a 'Manifesto of the Extreme Left' opened, not with calls for workers of the world to unite, but with a demand for the salvation of threatened winegrowers because 'wine is the purest product of the love affair between sun and soil, the consoler of the afflicted ...'[19] Moreover, wine was a labour-intensive crop, and one which supported a variety of complementary trades (cork-, barrel- and bottle-makers; carters, etc). *Vignerons* thus tended to live in large villages with a vigorous café-culture and strong communal sociabilities.[20] Here was an audience, receptive to Dem-Soc promises to abolish the wine taxes and to support the 'practical socialism'

19 L. Loubère, 'The Emergence of the Extreme Left in Lower Languedoc, 1848–51,' *American History Review*, (1968), pp. 1019–51.

20 M. Agulhon, *La République au village*.

of cooperative projects, such as those in the Jura which would facilitate wine storage to avoid sale at low prices just after harvest and establish barter schemes allowing *vignerons* – and cheese producers – to purchase goods from local stores with vouchers for which the stored goods acted as collateral. Similarly, Vigier's study of the Alpine region showed how small peasants engaged in production of raw silk and other 'industrial' crops had borrowed in order to purchase extra land in the good years before 1845, only to find themselves in debt to 'usurers' and facing possible expropriation in the depression. Bonapartist officials were in no doubt that it was the left's promises of cheap credit that explained their electoral gains in the central belt of the Drôme.[21] Even more spectacular were the six seats won by the Dem-Socs in the neighbouring Ardèche where populist hostility to 'usurers' had hitherto usually been expressed in the atavistic sectarian hatreds of Catholic peasants for Protestant financiers. And although there did remain traces in Alsace of traditional rural anti-semitism against 'Jewish' moneylenders, many indebted peasants appeared responsive to Dem-Soc propaganda which insisted that most 'usurers' were Catholic and French, that peasants could expect no relief from a government which was allied with the forces of 'financial feudalism'.

Another set of disputes which had the potential to provide rural support for the left were those generated by resistance to the erosion of communal and usage rights vital to the economic viability of countless peasant households. The Forest Code of 1827 restricted the access of villages, which traditionally had been permitted to graze livestock, gather wood, collect mushrooms, etc. During the subsequent decades there were tens of thousands of prosecutions annually for forest offences, and many more for poaching, after the 1844 Act introduced a 25-franc hunting permit. From the late 1820s onwards peasants in the Ariège (Pyrenees) conducted a prolonged *'révolte carnavalesque'* during which, following the calendar of the festive year, they adopted female dress (as during carnival) and conducted *charivaris* to harass the forest guards and the forge owners.[22]

There is no historical consensus on the question of just how deeply such disputes politicised rural communities. Some have interpreted these as 'archaic', 'pre-political' outbursts, emphasising the low literacy levels and cultural isolation of many forest villages.[23] Yet many such areas did vote heavily for the left in 1849. In the months following the election prefects expressed alarm at the frequency of gun battles between forest

21 P. Vigier, *La Seconde République dans la région alpine.*

22 P. Sahlins, *Forest Rites: The War of the Demoiselles in Nineteenth-Century France* (Cambridge, MA, 1994).

23 T. Margadant, *French Peasants in Revolt: the Insurrection of 1851* (Princeton, 1979).

guards and poaching gangs and at incidents in which large groups of villagers marched with drums and red flags into the forests to 'reclaim' them. Such widespread disorders were cited as proof of the deplorable and insidious spread of subversive doctrines into remote areas. The radical press featured provocative stories in which Robin Hood or village poachers featured as culture heroes. Although on balance the evidence does appear to suggest that such conflicts could engender enhanced political awareness which the left might hope to channel, some qualifications should be noted. Firstly, as Margadant has emphasised, forest areas did not, in general, harbour many of the secret societies which mushroomed in 1850–51 and which played such a key role in organising resistance to the Bonapartist coup. Hilly Morvan provides an interesting example in northern Burgundy of the limitations of 'radicalisation' of a forest region. The area had some contacts with Paris since *flotteurs* floated logs downriver to the capital. In the local small-towns (e.g. Château-Chinon) there were radical lawyers, petty bourgeois and artisans (one of the Dem-Soc deputies elected by a sizeable 'red' vote in 1849 was a Christian-socialist primary teacher). The targets of popular anger in the countryside were landowners. Their systematic exclusion of villagers from the forests generated not merely mass invasions of their estates in 1848–51, and attacks on chateaux, but also a resurgence of the rhetoric of 1789–94; denunciation of 'seigneurs' as parasites and traitors in league with France's foreign enemies, mixed with cries of '*Vive Robespierre!*' and calls for the guillotine. Yet the ideological content of this populism was always rather fluid. In 1848 forest areas had voted overwhelmingly for Louis Napoleon – and (see below) Bonapartism continued to retain its image, both during the Second Republic and beyond, as a guarantee against a return to the seigneurial past, despite the *modus vivendi* which Louis Napoleon had established with the Legitimist elites of the 'Party of Order'. The Morvan thus remained largely calm in December 1851. Principled opposition to the coup in the area came mainly from the petty bourgeois and artisan radicals of the small towns.[24]

Eugen Weber's classic *Peasants into Frenchmen* (1976) argued that the bulk of the peasantry was eventually integrated into 'the nation' only in the final decades of the nineteenth century as the rail network drew rural petty-producers into wider markets and conscription and compulsory primary schooling in French eroded regional linguistic and cultural particularisms. The rural world of the 1840s was, Weber claimed, still 'archaic', characterised by localism, economic autarchy, deep suspicion of all 'outsiders', illiteracy, patois-speaking, superstition and fear. Hence it would be absurd to attribute to the peasantry of the Second Republic any real

24 M. Vigreux, *Paysans et notables du Morvan* (Paris, 1986).

understanding of or commitment to national 'politics'. Peasants faced acute problems, had deep-seated grievances and hatreds. But these were largely expressed through 'traditional' forms of localised violence against taxmen, 'usurers' and local towns. What some historians have perceived as evidence of 'politicisation' was little more than the localised support of peasant 'clients' for local *notables*, whether Republican lawyers or Catholic-royalist landowners.[25] A variant of Weber's approach has recently become fashionable among historians who portray the French countryside, in terms strikingly similar to those used by Orlando Figes about the pre-Revolution Russian peasantry, as a world of endemic violence and brutality, of inter-village conflicts and intra-village feuds.[26]

In pardonable, but perhaps exaggerated, reaction against this 'archaism' model, Margadant's analysis of the peasant support for the 1851 insurrection emphasised the strong forces of cultural 'modernisation' at work in the countryside. Market agriculture – and cultural contacts with market towns – was already widespread among peasant petty-producers and those involved in rural proto-industry. 'Anti-urban' sentiments were stronger in northern France, where conservative peasants feared the 'socialism' of the cities, than in much of the Midi. Literacy and school attendance were rising steadily, particularly since the 1833 Guizot Education Act. Anticlericalism was widespread in many regions and rejection of the clergy's teachings on birth control was evidenced by the rapid decline in the birth rate in, for example, wine-growing areas of Burgundy.[27] Yet, although Margadant's emphasis on a culturally 'modernising' peasantry open to political mobilisation is, on balance, more plausible than Weber's model, his claims that Dem-Soc rural successes owed little to 'archaic' grievances against tax officials, forest owners and 'usurers' are surely exaggerated. Moreover, it remains difficult to accept any simple 'modernisation' explanation of the left's rural implantation. The most literate parts of France were north and east of the 'St Malo-Geneva' line, whereas many of the departments of high Dem-Soc voting in central and southern France had low literacy levels (Allier; Creuse; Arièg, etc.).

Hence, the most persuasive 'culturalist' reading of rural politics remains that of Agulhon who analysed the 'filtering down' of radical-Republican politics to the peasantry and rural artisans of Provence.[28] Agulhon argued for a complex and fruitful dialectic between cultural change and aspects of 'traditional' folk culture. Literacy had nearly doubled

25 E. Weber, *Peasants into Frenchmen* (Stanford, 1976).

26 A. Corbin, *Le village des cannibales* (Paris, 1990); F. Chauvaud, *De Pierre Rivière à Landru: la violence apprivoisée au 19e siècle* (Brépols, 1991).

27 T. Margadant, *French Peasants.*

28 M. Agulhon, *La République au village.*

(to 60 per cent) in the Var since 1830. The cultural control of the clergy was being eroded, in part because of resentment at their puritanical attempts to curb the boisterous hedonism associated with religious *fêtes.* In the wine-growing areas of Bas-Provence much of the population lived in large villages and 'agro-towns'; peasants had regular contact with artisans, professionals and petit bourgeois who were challenging the hegemony of royalist landowners and their clerical allies. Popular cafés and *chambrées* came to copy the politicised sociability of petty-bourgeois *cercles*, subscribing to newspapers and holding political discussions. Thus a popular/plebeian 'public sphere' was developed. At the same time, these *chambrées* often doubled as mutual aid and benefit societies and reflected the strength of community solidarities. Vigorous defence of communal forest rights had led to prosecutions for forest offences and court cases in which villagers claimed historic usage rights, cases in which villages were represented by Republican lawyers. Moreover, there was a still-vital popular culture of *fêtes,* carnival, collective dances (*farandoles*), folk songs which, as Bonapartist authorities clamped down on formal political organisations, could serve as a perfect medium for protest. The *mannequin* burned at the end of the carnival procession wore royalist white or looked remarkably similar to the local Bishop or Prefect. *Farandole* dancers wore red ribbons, Provençal folk songs predicted that 'the Mountain will flower ...' P. McPhee has observed a similar mobilisation of Catalan folk-culture in the coastal plain near Perpignan, another radical stronghold.[29] What is striking – perhaps surprising – is the apparent lack of tension between the Dem-Socs' neo-Jacobin ideology and the role of *occitan*, Provençal and Catalan folk-culture in its mobilisation in the Midi. For in the 1790s Jacobin patriotism had appeared ferociously hostile to regionalist cultures and to *patois*, which it equated with Catholic-royalist counter-revolution.

More generally one might conclude that the left did best in areas where it could rely on some degree of 'cultural brokerage', such as that supplied by seasonal migrants in the Limousin, who spent summers working in the Parisian construction industry and who alarmed local *notables* by importing ideas and practices from the capital.[30] Finally the left's rural propaganda contained a strong 'proto-narodnik' strand, designed to appeal to sentiments of communal solidarity. Pierre Joigneaux, for example, tried to persuade his readers that peasant culture was not, as the right claimed, one of individualistic private property owners, but one which valued solidarities, mutual aid, communal usage rights,

29 P. McPhee, 'Popular Culture, Symbolism and Rural Radicalism in Nineteenth-Century France,' *Journal of Peasant Studies*, (1978), pp. 238–53.

30 A. Corbin, *Archaïsme*.

and where communal dances were held to help flatten the soil in preparation for building the homes of newly-married couples. In short, there was an age-old, doctrineless, village 'communalism' (which meant that peasants were 'socialists' without knowing it).

Between 1849 and 1851 the provincial left was exposed to incessant police and bureaucratic harassment. A 'state of siege' was declared around Lyon from 1849 and extended to some other departments (e.g. Cher) in the months before the coup. Journalists were prosecuted and laws against the *colportage* of propaganda tightened. Radical village mayors were dismissed and their municipal councils dissolved. Thousands of suspect teachers, accused by Thiers of being socialist rhetoricians responsible for the corruption of the villages, were sacked and the influence of the clergy on schools increased following the 1850 Falloux Law. Cafés were placed under police surveillance, *fêtes* and village *bals* banned and cooperatives, accused of being a front for seditious political activities, hounded out of existence. What was the net impact of this persecution? Marx argued that 'the regime of the gendarme, consecrated by the priest' inevitably 'demoralised the immature masses'. And certainly, as Merriman argued, there do appear to be examples (e.g. Saône-et-Loire; Morvan; Narbonnais, etc.) of radicalised areas where the arrest of local leaders, and the severing of the links between the Dem-Socs' regional leadership and local activists, made any coherent response to the coup very difficult.[31]

However, there does also appear to be strong evidence that heavy-handed but patchy repression actually served to strengthen villagers' political commitment. The rural police force was simply too small for effective surveillance of thousands of villages. And, as some public prosecutors warned, sending troops or paramilitary gendarmes to shut cafes, ban village dances or arrest wedding guests carrying red bouquets was likely to be entirely counterproductive and create more opposition from hitherto 'apolitical' villagers outraged at such disruption of their social life. Police became, as McPhee observed, 'lost in a chase through popular culture'.[32] Moreover the trials of local journalists often became stages for radical oratory; local juries were often inclined to acquit. 'Martyred' mayors often returned from jail to a hero's welcome. There appears to be a strong correlation between communes whose municipal leaders had suffered from 'persecution' and those involved in subsequent resistance to the coup. Repression also served to drive Dem-Soc organisation underground, into a network of hundreds of secret societies, many of which

31 J. Merriman, *The Agony of the Republic*; C. Guthrie, 'Reactions to the Coup d'Etat of 1851 in the Narbonnais,' *French Historical Studies* (1983), pp. 18–46.

32 P. McPhee, *The Politics of Rural Life: Mobilisation in the French Countryside 1846–52* (Oxford, 1992).

had elaborate initiation rituals and oaths of secrecy and of commitment to fight for the 'social and democratic Republic'. And as bourgeois leaders were either arrested or scared away by the potential dangers, or by fears of the 'extremism' of the movement, leadership increasingly fell into the hands of 'popular' elements. Forty-eight per cent of secret society leaders in four Midi departments by 1851 were peasants or artisans, and it was these men who played a key role in organising local resistance to the coup.[33] Marx, who by 1851 had come to view the left as already demoralised and defeated, saw the conservatives' 'justification' for the coup as a necessary action to avert a potential Dem-Soc victory in 1852 as an implausible excuse. However, as Forstenzer's analysis of the bureaucracy makes clear, prefects and public prosecutors were convinced that this threat remained serious. And even if one might discount the lurid terms in which this was described (the countryside 'infected' with a 'plague' carried by 'diseased' socialists), the extent of the resistance to the coup does suggest that their fears were not entirely the result of paranoia.

There have been three interpretative models offered for the insurrection of December 1851. Contemporary Bonapartist and conservative commentators justified the coup by portraying the 'brutality' of the insurgents as evidence of the threat from which France had been rescued. They were accused of being bent on pillage and rape, and the (rare) examples of the killing of gendarmes, as at Bédarieux or Clamécy, were cited as proof of their murderous intent.[34] The Republican journalist Ténot, writing in the late 1860s, outlined the interpretation which was to become the official version of the Third Republic (which issued medals to the 'heroic' surviving insurgents in the 1880s). Rejecting the stereotype of savage rustic brutes, Ténot portrayed the insurgents as convinced, legalistic Republicans forced into taking up arms against a threat to the constitution. The pitchforks and sickles carried as they marched on local towns were cited not, as by the right, as evidence of their rustic savagery, but rather of their heroic determination to confront armed troops. Indeed, the left argued that, although the insurgents were motivated by genuine political conviction, their goal was not a mere 'formal' Republic but one which would carry out the promises made by the Dem-Socs. During the brief period during which rebel columns controlled local towns they often attacked tax offices, burned the records of 'usurers' and made clear their hostility to the rich.

Historians who favour *longue durée* structural analysis of rural societies might well question the significance of the apparently ephemeral radical

33 T. Margadant, *French Peasants*.

34 J. Martinet, *Clamécy et ses flotteurs* (La Charité-sur-Yonne, 1975); C. Johnson, *The Life and Death of Industrial Languedoc, 1700–1920* (Oxford, 1996), pp. 145–6.

mobilisation of the Second Republic. Although thousands of peasants, village artisans and agricultural labourers were among those arrested during and after the coup, one might argue that after 1851 the 'threat' of rural radicalism receded. Two decades of relative rural prosperity under the 'authoritarian populism' of the Bonapartist regime calmed the mood in some regions, while the demographic pressures which had exacerbated the problems in some forest and upland areas were eased by out-migration of the potentially volatile young. And yet such conclusions need to be qualified. A radical countryside did reemerge in the prolonged agricultural depression of the late nineteenth century. In 1914 eight of the 12 departments with the largest socialist vote were rural departments in central and southern France, and, as noted above, the electoral map of 1936, the year of the Popular Front, bears striking resemblance to that of 1849. Oral history has often suggested that the events of 1848–51 were etched in local memory. G. Cholvy, researching popular religious practice in Lower Languedoc in the 1960s, encountered an old woman who claimed that her family had not entered the village church since one of its members, an 1851 insurgent, was betrayed to the police by the local curé.[35] Researchers in the Allier in the same period came across elderly peasants who still associated '1852' with the promise of *'la Belle'*; the social Republic. In the Drôme, not only did oral tradition in peasant families preserve the memory of 'the tower of Crest', in which the 1851 insurgents had been incarcerated, but the commander of the local *maquis* in 1943–44 equated Vichy and the Nazis with the 'whites', and urged his resistance fighters to remember that they were the proud heirs of the heroic rebels of 1851.[36] In short just as memories and myths of the 'genocide' of the 1790s nurtured a counter-revolutionary, Catholic-Royalist tradition in the Vendée for two centuries, so the legacy of 1848–51 served to ensure that in some rural regions populist grievances were likely to be channelled by the left rather than, as elsewhere in Europe, by the radical-right.

Left-wing mobilisation in the Second Republic: the 'Artisan Republic'

Since the role of the working class in the Second Republic is both less 'surprising' than that of the peasantry and rather better-known, comments will be restricted to a few, rather schematic, general observations. First, it was clearly the impressive and precocious militancy of French workers that provided Marx with his model for the 'revolutionary proletariat' in the *Communist Manifesto*. Because the 'bourgeois revolution'

35 G. Cholvy, *Religion et société au XIXe siècle: le diocèse de Montpellier* (Lille, 1973).

36 R. Pierre, *Ah! Quand viendra la Belle?: Résistants et insurgés de la Drôme, 1848–51* (Valence, 1981).

of 1789–1830 had felt obliged to utilise the discourse of the 'Rights of Man', and of 'Liberty, Equality, Fraternity' in order to give its cause universal resonance, and because its ideological spokesmen (Sièyes; St Simon, etc.) had sought to justify the struggle against the aristocracy as that of 'productive' against 'parasitic' classes, French workers had been provided with a whole ideological arsenal which might easily be appropriated for use against the capitalist bourgeoisie, as well as with invaluable experience of participation in revolutionary struggles.[37] Furthermore, because of the relative backwardness of French capitalism, the French bourgeoisie were never in a position to make the type of concessions to labour through which mid-Victorian Britain achieved a degree of stability.

Marx's analysis of French working-class politics in 1848–51 is clearly misleading in a number of respects. He appears to divide urban workers into three categories. The 'lumpenproletariat' of the big cities were portrayed as semi-criminal, unemployed or underemployed. Lacking any firm class-consciousness, they might easily be recruited by the elites to fight for 'order'. The second category was made up of 'artisans', whose intermediate status made them politically volatile. Threatened by the growth of industrial capitalism, and by their growing subordination to merchants, they tended to dream of 'illusory' and 'utopian' schemes that might somehow rescue doomed petty-production. Finally, the 'proletariat' were seen as the participants in the heroic struggle of the June Days, which suggested that they were on the verge of mature class-consciousness. However, France's gradual and uneven industrial development meant that, as yet, the bastions of proletarian strength were too scattered and isolated to push through a successful revolution (or so Marx came to believe by 1850).

However, the consensus among historians is that the 'authentic' industrial proletariat was much less militant and mobilised in these years than either artisans or, indeed, sections of the peasantry. There were instances of strikes, political demonstrations and radical voting in factory textile towns such as Lille or Rouen, in mining centres like Anzin or St Etienne and in metallurgical centres such as Le Creusot. However, in general, mobilisation in such towns was fragile and ephemeral. Much of the textile proletariat was unskilled, female or very young.[38] Many miners and heavy metallurgy workers lived in company towns and were dependent on a single 'paternalist' employer. Because of the prevalence of child labour, literacy rates in textile towns like Lille were lower than in the

37 T. Judt, *Marxism and the French Left* (Oxford, 1986).

38 W. Reddy, *The Rise of Market Culture: The Textile Trade and French Society, 1750–1900* (Cambridge, 1984).

surrounding countryside. There were, of, course, some exceptions to these generalisations. As C. Johnson has shown, the southern factory town of Lodève became a leading Dem-Soc bastion in Lower Languedoc. But, unlike mill-towns in the north, many of its workforce were third generation factory workers who had had the chance to develop solidarities and patterns of resistance, and many retained cultural contacts with the increasingly radicalised peasantry of the region, while sharing their passion for poaching![39]

Conversely, local studies agree that most of the militancy which Marx ascribed to the 'proletariat' was, in fact, that of 'artisanal' workers, albeit often of those facing a variety of threats to their trades. The most radical city in France was Lyon whose economy was dominated by France's largest export sector, the silk industry, which was still reliant for its 'quality' products on skilled weavers (*canuts*). However, ongoing efforts by merchant-capitalists to reduce costs, by moving the weaving of cheaper cloths outside the city to peasant-weavers, and by reducing the rates (*tarif*) paid to the *canuts*, had provoked insurrections in 1831 and 1834, and made the city the bastion of a variety of cooperative socialist projects and radical groups.[40] Similarly Limoges, another radical bastion, had a labour force dominated by skilled workers in the porcelain industry.[41] Aminzade's comparative study of radicalism in three French cities shows that Toulouse, still dominated by craft industries, had the strongest Radical-Republican movement. In St Etienne, the left had strong support among ribbon-weavers but found it more difficult to secure a foothold among miners and heavy-metallurgical workers. 'Proletarian' Rouen, by contrast, failed to develop any firm ties between radical political leaders and the factory labour force of its large textile mills.[42]

Similarly, Paris remained largely an artisanal centre, indeed Europe's largest and most diverse. The 'proletariat' of the June Days were, thus, largely skilled workers, in particular from the construction and small-metal trades.[43] The wide range of mutualist and cooperative projects attempted during the Second Republic clearly had their greatest appeal

39 C. Johnson, *Life and Death of Industrial Languedoc.*

40 R. Bezucha, *The Lyon Uprising of 1834* (Cambridge, MA, 1974); M.L. Stewart-McDougall, *The Artisan Republic: Lyon 1848–51* (Kingston/Montreal, 1984); R. Liebmann, 'Repressive Strategies and Working-Class Protest: Lyon 1848–51,' *Social Science History* (1980).

41 J. Merriman, *The Red City: Limoges and the French Nineteenth Century* (Oxford, 1985).

42 R. Aminzade, *Ballots and Barricades: Class Formation and Republican Politics in France 1830–71* (Princeton, 1993).

43 C. Tilly and L. Lees, 'The People of Paris in June 1848,' in R Price (ed.), *Revolution and Reaction* (London, 1975).

among craft workers, in particular tailors and shoemakers, who established producer cooperatives.[44]

The apogee of historiographical enthusiasm about 'radical artisans' came during the heyday of the E.P. Thompson's 'new social history' in the 1970s. Artisans were perceived as facing threats not merely from factories and machines but from female 'dilution', the erosion of apprenticeship training, the subdivision of labour processes, 'sweating', the advent of ready-made clothing and from growing subordination to merchant control. However, it was argued, artisans were in a position to wage a protracted fight against these threats because they could mobilise important 'resources': skills and craft-pride, the solidarities of established *quartiers* (Lyon's Croix-Rousse; Faubourg St Antoine, etc.), where they lived, worked and socialised in a vibrant café culture. Traditions of organisation going back to the *compagnonnages* of the ancien regime might, as Sewell argued, be adapted to the needs of the post-Revolution age.[45] In the process of struggling to protect their trades, it was suggested, these artisans transcended the confines of 'craft-consciousness' and of narrow 'sectionalism', and began to value themselves as the 'working class'. It is difficult in the 1990s to accept an unreconstructed version of this progressive meta-narrative, and, indeed, in the past two decades a motley collection of bourgeois sociologists, post-modernists, feminists and even the occasional structural Marxist, has sought to question the heroic 'myth' of the 'radical artisan'. Among the key points raised by this recent historiography are that, first, by no means all artisans were radical. In some cities of the Midi (such as Nîmes) atavistic Protestant/Catholic sectarian rivalries meant that many Catholic artisans remained royalist, although there is evidence that the political momentum of 1848 helped to win Catholic-royalist stevedores in Marseille over to the left.[46] Secondly, and contrary to Marx's assertion, the notorious *Garde Mobile* which

44 B. Moss, *The Origins of the French Labor Movement: The Socialism of Skilled Workers* (Los Angeles, 1976) However, there remains some dispute among labour historians about the significance of producer cooperatives in the Second Republic. Should they be viewed as evidence of a widespread desire among artisans to establish worker-controlled industries which could compete with and eventually replace capitalist industry? Or were they essentially pragmatic, short-term projects established by unemployed craftsmen? I. Prothero tends to support the latter interpretation, as does M. Sibalis, 'The Parisian Tailors in 1848: The "*Association Fraternelle des Ouvriers Tailleu*",' in R. Aldrich and M. Lyons (eds.), *The Sphinx in the Tuileries* (Sydney, 1999).

45 William H. Sewell, Jr, *Work and Revolution: The Language of Labor from the Ancien Regime to 1848* (Cambridge, 1980).

46 W. Sewell, 'Uneven Development and the Autonomy of Politics: The Dockworkers of Marseille in 1848,' *American Historical Review* (1988), pp. 604–37.

helped to defeat the June Days was not made up of 'lumpenproletarians', but rather, of young, unmarried workers from the same trades which contributed the bulk of the insurgents. Traugott uses this evidence to suggest that loyalties and identities may be generated by institutional/organisational participation, not (just) by class. One might also suggest that younger artisans might not have spent sufficient time in the workshops to develop any firm solidarities, or that the habitual treatment of young workers by established artisans was often so brutal that the *Gardes Mobiles* may have enjoyed their chance to take revenge.[47] Thirdly, although the Lyon silk industry provides an example of apparent unity between master silk weavers and their journeymen against a common enemy, the merchants, even here there were tensions between sober, cautious autodidact masters and the more boisterous culture and sociability (and greater propensity for political violence) of the young journeymen who established the *Voraces*, a paramilitary group which sought to take over sections of the city in 1848–49. Elsewhere the workshop may well have been the site of conflicts rather than of solidarities. Journeymen tailors might strike when masters were forced to cut wages in order to remain competitive. In the building trades, one of the most hated figures was the subcontractor (*tâcheron*). In the spring of 1848, workers petitioned the Luxembourg 'trades parliament' to abolish the subcontracting system. And yet Martin Nadaud, a radical activist and a Dem-Soc deputy in 1849, had attempted at one stage to establish himself as a *tâcheron*.[48] Fourthly, in some cases craft solidarities were more an obstacle than a contribution to worker unity. The *compagnonnages* were notorious for perpetuating rivalries and violent, ritualised confrontations both between and within trades. The decision of individual trades to each put up their own candidates for the April 1848 elections split the left's vote and lost it several seats. Fifthly, and above all, as Jacques Rancière has warned, one must interrogate closely the entire rhetoric about the craft-proud 'radical artisan'. Clearly some militants were from trades such as tailoring and shoemaking, already largely degraded by 'sweating'. Rather than wishing to spend the rest of their lives sewing *petit point* they often wished, above all, to escape from their trade. Their aspirations were as citizens not as craftsmen. Discourses about pride in craft skills often were the preserve of romantic intellectuals, or of autodidact former artisans who had left the workshop behind them and who were attempting to refute bourgeois

47 M. Traugott, *Armies of the Poor: Determinants of Working-Class Participation in the Insurrection of June 1848* (Princeton, 1985).

48 C. Harrison, 'Laissez-Faire and *Marchandage* in the Paris building trades in 1848,' *French Historical Studies* (1997), pp. 357–80.

denigration of the 'labouring and dangerous classes'.[49] And finally, the 'skilled artisan' was, of course, male. Recent feminist historiography has justifiably argued that in the 'Artisan Republic' there was no very obvious place for women workers. Many male craftsmen blamed women workers for undercutting their wage rates and 'diluting' their skills. Tailors explicitly attempted to exclude seamstresses from their organisations.[50] Proudhon, trained as a printer, was a confirmed misogynist who insisted that women had no place in the workshop. Undoubtedly, therefore, gender issues proved to be one crucial weakness of the left in the Second Republic. One might, indeed, argue that the advent of male suffrage served to exclude women to a degree which was not the case when direct action (e.g. food riots) was the main vehicle of popular politics. This is not to say that the left was uniformly misogynist, nor that women played little role in its mobilisation during the Second Republic. Although the Dem-Socs were the heirs of a Jacobin tradition which had regarded women as too 'irrational' and 'priest-ridden' to be 'citizens', and although its 'fraternalist' rhetoric still had problems recognising the existence of 'sisters', some Dem-Soc deputies did express support for working-class feminist Jeanne Déroin's campaign for women's political rights. Women supported the barricade fighters of the June Days and, in some cases, were among the insurgents. They were active in coordinating propaganda in 1849–51; female cork-workers in the Var were involved in resistance to the coup.[51]

The Legacy of 1848: Some 'Lessons' of the Second Republic.

Republicans and Dem-Socs had abundant time in exile, or in Bonapartist prisons, to ponder the lessons of their defeat. Moderate Republicans concluded from the experiences of 1848–51 that the only way to establish a durable Republican regime would be to distance themselves from the neo-Jacobin and socialist overtones of the Second Republic and to reassure the mass of small and medium property owners in regions such as

49 J. Rancière, 'The Myth of the Artisan: Reflections on a Category of Social History,' in S. Kaplan (ed.), *Work in France* (Cornell, 1986). For a recent discussion of the debate on the 'radical artisan' see R. Magraw, 'El "artisano radical": nuevas reflexiones sobre esta categoria de la historia social,' in J. Paniagua, J Piqueras and V. Sanz (eds.), *Cultura social y política en el mundo del trabajo* (Valencia, 1999).

50 J. Scott, 'Men and Women in the Paris Garment Trades,' in P. Thane and G. Crossick (eds.), *The Power of the Past* (Cambridge, 1984).

51 D. Berry, *Women and Political Insurgency in France* (London, 1996). For an attempt to synthesise recent approaches in feminist, gender and cultural history with changes in the world of work in mid-nineteenth-century France, see P. McPhee, 'The Changing Contours of 1848,' in R. Aldrich and M. Lyons (eds.), *The Sphinx in the Tuileries.*

Normandy that the Republic could stand for a combination of progress, stability and order, and active collaboration with provincial industrialists. As Elwitt and others have shown, this was the successful strategy adopted in the late-1860s.

The hostility of the majority of the clergy to the Republic (exemplified by the joy with which they greeted the coup), together with the electoral influence which they wielded, particularly in much of western and northern France and in the southern Massif, led to further intensification of republican anticlericalism. In the 1830–48 period, the clergy had not appeared to be too closely identified with the 'Voltairean' Orleanist bourgeoisie. Indeed some on the left, inspired by Lamennais and the vogue for romanticism, had dreamed of a society in which a 'social gospel', preached by a less hierarchical and more democratic clergy, would provide the moral basis for a 'socialism' built upon fraternity, associationism and mutual aid. The disciplining by the hierarchy of the minority of 'democratic' priests who supported the Revolution shattered such illusions. The tone both of republicanism and of the labour left became more uniformly secularist after 1851.

The right's paranoid vilification of village schoolteachers at the time of the Falloux Law showed clearly that it viewed control of mass education as one key to the maintenance of its hegemony. Among the first initiatives taken by the reviving republican movement in the 1860s was to establish the Ligue de L'Enseignement to revive Carnot's 1848 campaign for compulsory secular education. This was not just a strategy of bourgeois Republican moderates hoping to use education to assert their own hegemony. The Ligue's members included artisans and even Burgundian peasants, for this was an issue with wide popular appeal.

The chastening experiences of the Second Republic also taught republicans to be deeply suspicious of a directly elected executive president, for Bonapartism had proved to be the nemesis of the republican left. Marx's analysis of Louis Napoleon's apparent ability to appear all things to all men ('because he was nothing he could be everything') was both perceptive and yet not entirely adequate. Hugo's scorn for 'Napoleon the Little' left unexplained how an incompetent buffoon had succeeded in coming to power in Europe's most politically mobilised society. Marx offered a 'significant' explanation. There was a stalemate in the class war. The squabbling elites, split between rival royalist factions and conservative republicans (that is between different class fractions of the bourgeoisie), were too divided to rule directly. The subordinate classes were both too mobilised and militant to allow the unpopular elites to rule, and yet too heterogeneous and immature to seize power themselves. However, it is important to appreciate just why Bonapartism proved so difficult for the left to combat. Much of the tone of radicalism in the Second

Republic was that of neo-Jacobin populism. Yet, as Menager has emphasised, this was precisely what 'popular Bonapartism' had come to signify in France since 1815. During his 'Hundred Days' in 1815, and during his St Helena exile, Napoleon 'reinvented' himself as the 'People's Emperor', whose aim had been to secure the gains of the Revolution, to protect the people against the return of seigneurialism, clericalism and the tithes, and whose wider goals were to set the peoples of Europe free from the tyranny of their reactionary dynastic rulers. In a post-1815 world dominated by restored Bourbons, the Holy Alliance and British plutocracy, many 'little' Frenchmen espoused this myth, and 'seditious cries' denouncing the Bourbons in the 1820s were often couched in Bonapartist terms. Some of the workers on the barricades of 1830 hoped that Napoleon's son – 'the little King of Rome' – might be installed. Important figures on the Dem-Soc left, such as Joigneaux and Nadaud, were sons of neo-Jacobin fathers, one a wine carter, the other a migrant building worker, who admired Napoleon. Louis Napoleon played his populist cards with great skill. Before 1848, he developed a reputation as a critic of Orleanist economic liberalism; someone concerned with the 'social question' and with France's humiliating subordination to Metternich. During his triumphant entry into French electoral politics in 1848, his appeal to peasants and workers was as an opponent of the moderate Republicans, who had imposed the 45 centimes land-tax and provoked and crushed the June Days. Many peasants who voted for him in December 1848 thought they were voting against the Forest Codes, the wine-tax, usurers, the danger of a return to seigneurialism and the tithes. In 1849–51 his failure to 'deliver' on his 'social' promises, his appointment of conservative *notables* to cabinet posts and his 'betrayal' of the Roman Republic, threatened to undermine his radical credentials. And yet he remained an astute populist politician. He proved capable of playing the role of opponent of the more unpopular policies of his own ministers, by hinting, for example, that the May 1850 electoral Law, which disenfranchised some 30 per cent of the electorate, had been pushed through against his wishes. In areas of rural France where peasant radicalism was still fuelled by bitter anti-seigneurial memories – Burgundy, the Dordogne, the Limousin, the Dauphiné – there appeared to be little contradiction in peasant minds between their Bonapartist vote of December 1848 and their 'red' vote of May 1849. Indeed some peasants, Vigier claims, took up arms against the 1851 coup believing that this was a royalist attempt to overthrow the president of the Republic. Moreover, in the following two decades, the rural electoral successes of the Bonapartist regime were to be founded, in part, on shrewd populist gestures (such as an easing of the Forest Codes) not just on intimidation, repression or economic prosperity. In 1870, as A. Corbin has shown, anti-seigneurial Bonapartist peasants in the Dordogne tortured to death a local aristocrat on market day on the pretext that they thought him to be (because of the 'treason' of the aristocracy in 1792) a Prussian spy! Similarly, the regime's willingness to confront the Habsburgs in northern Italy in 1859 won it support among artisans in 'red' Lyon. A century later, of course, Gaullism was to exhibit a similar capacity to steal sections of the left's natural constituency. Phillippe Seguin, a key figure in Chirac's neo-Gaullist party, has written a book on Louis Napoleon and presided over the recent renaming of the square near to the Gare du Nord as the 'Place Napoleon III'. After 1848, radical activists in general sought to jettison their earlier admiration for Bonapartism. It was, however, not always easy for them to persuade their popular supporters to do likewise.[52]

The experiences of the Second Republic also help to explain some of the subsequent ideological and organisational divisions in the labour movement. The long period of political repression after 1851 clearly made it difficult to achieve the type of incorporation of labour, or at least of the labour aristocracy, achieved by liberal Britain at the height of its mid-Victorian hegemony. And the massacre of the Communards appeared to drive home the lesson that the state was the repressive tool of the capitalist elites. Trade unions were not to be legalised until 1884. However, various alternative strategies might follow on from such experiences and insights. One might attempt, as in 1869 in cities like Toulouse, to rebuild a Radical Republican/Republican Socialist political coalition. Conversely, suspicion of any such alliance with the progressive wing of the bourgeoisie might result in attempts to build an autonomous workers' party. Alternatively, Proudhonist suspicion of all politics might produce an emphasis on the need to concentrate on building a mutualist society via cooperatives, mutual aid and mutual credit schemes, or result in a pragmatic combination of localised, largely unorganised, direct action, viewed by Alain Cottereau as one of the distinctive peculiarities of the French.

52 B. Menager, *Les Napoléon du peuple* (Paris, 1988); R. Magraw, 'The People's Emperor?: Louis Napoleon and Popular Bonapartism,' *Modern History Review*, vol. 8, no. 7 (1997), pp. 28–30.

2

The Democrating and Social Republic of 1848 and its Repercussions in the Hispanic World*

CLARA E. LIDA

In the historiography of the 1848 Revolutions it has become commonplace to highlight the fact that, while several western and central European countries underwent social and political upheaval, the Hispanic world, both in Europe and America, felt little more than gentle and fleeting gusts from the revolutionary storm. Research has only just begun on the impact of French democratic ideas and forms of sociability in Spain during in the 1850s. For Brazil and Spanish America there has been some interest in the echoes of the events in France in Pernambuco, Chile and Colombia between 1848 and 1854. Argentina and Mexico have received little attention in this regard. In Argentina, as David Rock shows in chapter five, liberals likely to be sympathetic to the ideas of 1848 were living in exile in neighbouring countries, or were absorbed in the struggle against the Rosas dictatorship. Hence, the revolutionary events in Europe were hardly felt in that Platine Republic, with the exception of the blockade of Buenos Aires ordered by Louis Philippe. With the fall of Rosas in 1852 the country opened its doors to liberalising influences, and the bases for a liberal republic were laid with the promulgation of the Constitution in 1853. Ideas and polemics, characteristic of France in 1848, then became widespread, as Rock shows. As for Mexico, the general opinion is that the disastrous war against the United States, and the onerous peace treaties that followed, overshadowed any possible interest in the Revolution in Europe. Mexico was too immersed in its own national distress to be concerned with events in Europe. The French example of a democratic republic would only have served as unwelcome reminder of

* This chapter owes much to the comments of my colleagues Josefina Z. Vázquez, Erika Pani, Marco Palacios and Carlos Illades, as well as to the collaboration of Mónica Bucio and Susana Sosenski. Denah Lida offered her fine sense of language in revising this text.

the North American democracy that had just inflicted such a humiliating defeat on the country.[1]

The overriding view, then, is that Spain and Spanish America are the notable absentees in the revolutionary wave of 1848, and remained on or beyond the fringe of any possible influence. The aim of this chapter is to qualify this view by exploring how the events of 1848 were felt in Spain, Colombia, Mexico and Chile. The timing of the effects of the 1848 revolutions differed in each country. In Spain social unrest and revolutionary movements coincided with the extraordinary events in Paris in February 1848. By contrast, in Chile and Colombia, although the events in Europe were reported throughout 1848, the political consequences came later: in 1851 in Chile and between 1849 and 1854 in Colombia. Mexico was even later in echoing the events of 1848. Here, a comparable democratic openingwas not experienced until the Revolution of Ayutla in 1855 that inaugurated the Liberal 'Reforma', culminating in the radical constitution of 1857.

If the timing of revolutionary upheaval differed, so too did the course each country followed in incorporating the legacy of 1848. This chapter does not propose to document the considerable scope of this legacy. The aim is rather to highlight two themes that will serve as guiding, analytical threads. The first is the appearance, as the first barricades went up in Paris as early as February, of the popular demand for a 'social and democratic Republic'. This not only transformed the symbolic and imaginative boundaries of politics but also revolutionised social discourse beyond France's frontiers, in spite of the crushing of the popular movement in June.

The second theme is to define the social composition of the 'popular urban classes' who, between February and June, defended the idea of a 'social and democratic republic'. The chapter will later describe how these social formations in Paris resembled, *mutatis mutandis*, their counterparts that were beginning to emerge in Spain and Spanish America.

France

What was meant by a 'democratic and social Republic' in the spring of 1848 in France? And what was the social composition of the urban

1 It is not possible here to discuss the Lusitanian uprisings in Portugal in 1848, nor those of Pernambuco in Brazil in 1848–1849, whose links with 1848 in France are evident and were viewed with interest by contemporaries in other Iberian countries. I am grateful to Marco Palacios for having called my attention to the importance of this episode. The Pernambuco uprising is examined by Nancy Naro in chapter four of this volume. Also significant is the Bolivian movement known as 'the republic of artisans', during the presidency of Manuel I. Belzú (1848–1855), though as yet little has been written about it.

revolutionaries? In reply to the first question, we must examine three elements which make the concept of a 'democratic and social republic'. First, for those taking part in the Revolution, it was clear that the state had been usurped by an abusive monarchy, backed by a traditionally privileged and corrupt elite. There was no doubt in their minds that, in its place, a non-patrimonial republic should be established and that the legitimate basis and support for this republic should be 'the sovereign people'. Even those who had given their backing to the Revolution, but for whom the monarchy was not necessarily a form of government to be repudiated, provided it was upright, constitutional and parliamentary, embraced the concept of the republic, in the original political sense of the *res publica* (common weal). They defended the notion that a republic should be supported by all citizens without distinction, and that it should also provide all citizens with free and fair institutions established by a virtuous and upright government. Thus, two differing ideas about the most appropriate form of government shared common ground about what constituted good government.

Secondly, for equality to be effective in relation to the republic, citizens' rights would have to extend to all. In other words, the Republic had to be, by definition, democratic, for only in a representative system can (male) citizens fully exercise their rights, which included: direct universal suffrage for all men over 21, with the consequent right to vote and be voted for; the right of citizens to take arms, defend themselves and organise themselves into civil militia such as the National Guard, and the right of all to enjoy the fundamental freedoms of expression, press and assembly and, therefore, association. These enfranchising principles of civil equality, which eliminated a property-oriented electoral aristocracy, allowed the provisional government to proclaim naïvely: 'with the promulgation of this law there are no more proletarians in France'.[2] Thus, the diverse and plural political players who had opposed Louis Philippe, from the liberal monarchists and Moderate republicans, to the more radical and socialist sectors, seemed to agree that the democratic Republic (or, at least the democratic *res publica*) was a common denominator acceptable to all.

Thirdly, in 1848, a new political factor emerged: the social dimension. Not that 'social' was new to the political vocabulary. For several decades prior to 1848, early socialists had considered social policy as central to a society split by ever deeper inequalities. What was new in 1848 was the combination of the social dimension with republicanism and democracy.

2 Françoise Mélonio, '1848: la république intempestive,' in François Furet and Mona Ozouf (eds.), *Le siècle de l'avènement républicain* (Paris, 1993), p. 409. See also Pierre Rosanvallon, 'La république du suffrage universel,' in *ibid.*, pp. 371–89.

To include society as a whole in matters relating to government, the Republic would not only have to be democratic politically, but also embrace a new social order to include all citizens on the basis of equal material rights. For democracy to be social, it had to be rooted in a common and innate right for every citizen. In 1848, this right was defined as 'the right to work' ('le droit au travail'). If the democratic Republic was also social, then the right to work became the central articulating axis of all sectors of society. As Françoise Mélonio has pointed out, this right would be to the social order what universal suffrage is to the political one: an instrument of reconciliation and rapprochement between classes. This was one of the great promises of the February Revolution, and the confirmation that, at last, the Republic was 'one and indivisible'.[3] In other words, the new republican state should be built on the idea of work as the universal guarantee of citizen rights, unlike the patrimonial monarchical state which, until then, had defined individual rights in terms of ownership. For the revolutionaries, this had implied the usurpation of other people's work and the alienation of its proceeds among the few.[4]

Because of this redefinition of work and its fruits as the inalienable property and right of the producer, the French revolutionaries claimed that those historical players who lacked the property necessary to guarantee their rights, and thus had been deprived of any form of social participation and political guarantees, could now not only enjoy these rights but become agents themselves in the collective transformation of society. In including within its ranks workers as citizens with equal rights, the Republic was seen not only as democratic but also as social. It amalgamated the aspiration of perfecting the political system with the common will to change society and the economy in order to unite all the citizens who comprised an all encompassing, inclusive new republic.

Thus, when in February of 1848 the Provisional Government decreed the 'right to work' as a republican right, and, at the request of Louis Blanc, set up the National Workshops to provide work and trade for all those in need, established the Luxembourg Commission to solve workers' demands, and authorised the right to association (hence, to the organisation of labour), it offered a new language, as well as laws, institutions and policies, which would feed the revolutionary imagination in many parts of the world. Likewise, the decree of 5 March 1848 that introduced direct universal male suffrage meant the culmination of a process begun in 1789 with the consolidation of the principle of political equality. In this way, the 'democratic and social Republic' radically redefined the state which,

3 Mélonio, '1848: la république intempestive,' pp. 409–10.

4 On this topic see the important analysis in William H. Sewell, Jr, *Work and Revolution in France* (Cambridge, 1980).

instead of basing itself on the wealth of the few, considered the work by all as the foundations of an harmonious society, and equal rights as the essence of republican democracy.[5]

This 'Republic of Labour' was, of course, short-lived. The mounting differences between, on the one hand, workers, radical republicans and diverse socialist groups, considered 'Communists' (evoking the phantom of Jacobin terror and threat to property), and on the other, Moderates and conservatives, resulted in the bloody 'June days'.[6] In the popular mobilisations of the spring of 1848, organised by workers' associations, radical republican and socialist clubs and societies of Paris, tens of thousands took part (in March, for example, some authors have calculated demonstrations of between 150,000 and 200,000 people), hoisting the red flag, symbol of what some explicitly called the 'Republic of artisans', as a challenge to the tricolour favoured by the Moderates.[7] In this context, the term 'artisan' acquired a revolutionary meaning that went beyond the mere connotation of work and productivity.[8]

Finally, a key moment was the Assembly's decree of 21 June, which ordered the dismantling of the National Workshops which, as far as the workers were concerned, shattered the social contract established since February regarding the right to work. This paved the way for the last significant social mobilisation of the Revolution, which took place between 22 and 26 June and was organised on such a scale that for four days the popular classes succeeded in occupying half of eastern Paris. Victims of repression amounted to 1,500 dead and more than 11,000 imprisoned.

5 Roger V. Gould, *Insurgent Identities. Class, Community, and Protest in Paris from 1848 to the Commune* (Chicago, 1995); Rosanvallon, 'La république du suffrage universel'.

6 When, in January–February 1848, Karl Marx began the *Manifesto of the Communist Party* by asserting that the spectre of Communism was haunting Europe, it is undoubtedly because he was very familiar with the impact of Pius IX's encyclical *Qui pluribus* (1847) condemning communism as an 'execrable' and destructive doctrine, and with the European bourgeois fears of the different revolutionary socialist doctrines which proposed the collective appropriation of property (Owen, Cabet and Weitling), the insurrectional seizure of power (Blanqui and Weitling), the class struggle and doing away with private property (*Bund der Kommunisten*). Furthermore, Marx spoke of the abuse of the term communist with which the ruling powers stigmatised the opposition movements. Later we shall show how these tensions were also in evidence in the Hispanic countries.

7 On radical clubs and societies see Peter Amann, *Revolution and Mass Democracy. The Paris Club Movement in 1848* (Princeton, 1975); Maurice Agulhon, *Les Quarante-huitards* (Paris, 1975), pp. 117–28, explains the use by Alphonse de Lamartine and Louis Blanc of opposing symbolism in demonstrations.

8 Malcolm Deas, 'La presencia de la política nacional en la vida provinciana, pueblerina y rural de Colombia en el primer siglo de la República,' in Marco Palacios (ed.), *La unidad nacional en América Latina. Del regionalismo a la nacionalidad* (Mexico, 1983), p. 162.

From that moment it became clear the republic would no longer be democratic and social, nor would it be red. Even less would it be of an inclusive nature. Rather, it would be tricolour, liberal and Moderate, if not openly conservative and exclusive, terminating eventually in the Second Empire. Or, to use the words of Alexis de Tocqueville, 'a republic without republicans, a democracy without the people'.[9]

In this context it is important to ask ourselves about the social composition of the radical and socialist republican crowds which, in the spring of 1848, played such a combative role in Paris. From the studies that exist on the June rebels we know that a high percentage were artisans and qualified workers, largely carpenters, tailors, shoemakers, hatters, typesetters, weavers, construction workers, mechanics, transport workers (above all railway workers), who made up more than 70 per cent of those arrested. A second group was made up of wage earners in household service and public employment, who represented some seven per cent. Finally, small proprietors made up close to four per cent, artists and individuals connected with the liberal professions a little less than three per cent, and a little more than three per cent were members of the armed forces and the police. It should be pointed out, on the other hand, that those from the deprived and marginal sectors of society, that is, men and women without a trade or without a regular job, accounted for hardly more than three per cent of the total.[10] In synthesis, the popular classes of Paris were, above all, working men and women with a recognised trade, employment or profession who, in spite of their varying occupations, all had similar income,[11] and whose existence depended upon their work as their essential patrimony.

I have analysed these popular classes in greater depth in another study.[12] Here I wish only to underline the fact that, during the second third of the nineteenth century, in many non-industrialised societies, or in those societies in the process of industrialisation, these popular classes embraced men and women from a wide social spectrum. In the urban areas they included craftsmen and workers from workshops and factories, as well as those employed in domestic service, together with owners of small establishments, whose earnings were hardly enough to keep themselves

9 Speech of 5 Oct. 1848, quoted by Mélonio, '1848: la république intempestive', p. 402.

10 Roger Price, *The French Second Republic. A Social History* (New York, 1972); Charles Tilly and Lynn Lees, 'Le peuple de juin 1848,' *Annales. Économies. Sociétés. Civilisations*, vol. 29, (1974), pp. 1061–91; Gould, *Insurgent Identities*. On the social composition of the different political sectors in 1848, see Agulhon, *Les Quarante-huitards*, pp. 23–36.

11 Price, *The French Second Republic*, p. 166, based on the estimates by E. Labrousse.

12 Clara E. Lida, 'Clases populares en España y Europa,' *Historia Social* (Valencia) vol. 27, (1997), pp. 3–21.

and, perhaps, one hired hand. The popular classes also included those with a certain education, such as teachers, students, journalists and artists, as well as the liberal and technical professions, that is to say, people of learning and culture. As we shall observe when looking at the Hispanic world, these different occupational groups shared the same democratic aspiration of enjoying free access to the political sphere, and of asserting the right of work. Their social preoccupations frequently brought them together in a common struggle that radically redefined existing assumptions about citizenship and property.

In looking at the Revolution of 1848 in Paris my first aim has been to explore the idea of a democratic and social Republic as a guiding thread which will assist us in our analysis of the impact of the Revolution in the Spanish speaking world. Secondly, I have described the social profile of the popular urban actors participating in this conflict. After 1848 these ideas and actors played key political and social roles, albeit with significant variations in the different countries to which I now turn.

Spain

There is a widespread view that in the Iberian Peninsula 1848 came and went without any significant repercussions.[13] This ignores the attempts at revolution that occurred throughout the year, as well as the longer-term effects of 1848 upon the development of the Spanish republican and democratic movement, culminating in 1868 in the overthrow of Queen Isabel II. Moreover, this interpretation ignores the impact that social issues raised by 1848 had on socialist and workers' associationism, leading up to the introduction to Spain of the International Working Men's Association in 1868, and the subsequent emergence of anarchism and Marxism.

From 1846, Spain had been troubled by a rash of Carlist rebellions, mainly in Catalonia ('els matiners'), but also in the Basque country, Aragon and Valencia, in support of the pretender to the Spanish throne, Charles VI, Count of Montemolín. In February of 1848, Carlists had actually succeeded in taking certain cities in Catalonia, defeating forces of the Moderate liberal government headed by General Ramón María Narváez.[14] These attacks had mobilised the government and the army to such an extent that, when the Paris Revolution broke out, Narváez was already on the alert for any kind of social movement that might threaten

13 Robert Gildea, *Barricades and Borders. Europe, 1800–1914* (Oxford, 1987), p. 171.

14 A detailed history is in Antonio Pirala, *Historia Contemporánea. Anales de la Guerra Civil* (Madrid, 1893), vol. II. More recently, for 'els matiners', Joan Camps i Giró, *La guerra dels matiners i el catalanisme polític, 1846–1849* (Barcelona, 1978).

the stability of the monarchy, be it Carlist or any other opposing group. In addition, Narváez was personally informed that there were radical groups – democratic, socialist and republican – in Spain conspiring against the government.[15]

In this context, four days after the fall of Louis Philippe, on 27 February 1848, the president of the Spanish government presented to the Cortes (the Spanish Parliament) an emergency powers bill which included the suspension of individual guarantees. The bill was approved by the Moderate majority and ratified by Queen Isabel on 13 March. The first effect, then, of the French Revolution of 1848 in Spain, was the introduction of a legal dictatorship that enabled Narváez to prevent a revolutionary movement taking place in Spain, similar to events occurring beyond the Pyrenees. Such repression also allowed him to continue the struggle against the Carlists and to prevent any possible rapprochement between Montemolín and his followers, other disenchanted monarchists and even some republicans.

In fact, during the debates in the Cortes, the Moderates took the alarming view that the republican model was not only inflammatory and anarchical but also the epitome of destruction and chaos: 'Republic means anarchy in France, war in Europe',[16] to which the progressive liberal opposition replied, in the words of a radical, Nicolás María Rivero, that 'Revolutions are not a whim of the people; they are always a necessity, never a whim'. Taking the argument a step further, Rivero concluded by questioning the legitimacy of a monarchy when this monarchy 'has been unable to fulfil its mission'.[17] Another representative of the opposition pointed to the dangers of dictatorship exacerbating republican sentiments 'where there were previously none'. To avoid revolution, instead of repressive laws, parliament should promulgate democratic measures such as the introduction of universal suffrage, the establishment of a National Militia, the reform of local government and the reduction of taxes (the latter inspired by the severe economic crisis affecting the Peninsula since 1846, but which had intensified in the autumn of 1847).[18]

Thus, while the Moderates defended extreme measures to prevent anarchy and revolutionary conflagration from spreading throughout Spain, the more critical sectors of Congress uttered veiled threats against the monarchy and put forward measures which implied that Spain could

15 Sonsoles Cabeza Sánchez-Albornoz, *Los sucesos de 1848 en España* (Madrid, 1981).

16 Speech by Francisco Martínez de la Rosa in *Legislatura, 1847–1848*, 1 March 1848, p. 1515. This and other quotes from the same source taken from Cabeza Sánchez-Albornoz, *Los sucesos de 1848 en España*.

17 Speech by Nicolás María Rivero, in *Legislatura, 1847–1848*, 4 March 1848, p. 1637.

18 Speech by José María Orense, in *Legislatura, 1847–1848*, 2 March 1848, pp. 1529–30.

safeguard its stability only if Congress were prepared to democratise the *res publica*.[19] From the centre of Spanish politics, then, demands arose for political reform inspired the principles of the democratic Republic in France.

The opposition was not mistaken when warning against the harm that repression would have on political order. Two weeks after emergency powers had been granted, the Progressives, as well as those more explicitly identified with republicanism, and even with socialism, who had increased in numbers in a clandestine manner for at least a decade, decided to move from conspiracy to direct action.[20] In spite of some disagreement among the conspirators, on the evening of 26 March 1848 barricades went up in different parts of Madrid and the first uprising against the Moderate government began.

It is likely that Narváez had been tipped off regarding the uprising, judging by the scale and ferocity of forces deployed against the rebels. The fighting ended early the following morning, leaving a number of dead and wounded on both sides, as well as numerous prisoners. The republican and socialist activist, Fernando Garrido, estimated that 'perhaps more than a hundred family men died [...] or were wounded' and that 'in the army there were also regrettable losses'.[21] As a consequence of the events of 26 and 27 March, a war tribunal was created to judge those involved in the insurrection. Some death penalties were passed which, at the request of the queen, were commuted to imprisonment. Remaining constitutional guarantees were also suppressed, including freedom of the press. For five weeks (until 4 May) Madrid was declared to be in a state of siege; the law dealt severely with the idle and suspicious and many were sentenced and deported to prisons overseas.[22]

In spite of the defeat of the uprising of 27 March in Madrid, another took place in Barcelona on the following day, and a third broke out two

19 Perhaps one of the most extreme attitudes, adopted by the more conservative sectors in Spain and Europe, was that of Juan Donoso Cortés in his famous speech in the Cortes on 4 Jan. 1849 (also known as the 'Speech on Dictatorship'), in which he envisaged two political options: 'it is a question of choosing [...] between the dictatorship of the dagger and the dictatorship of the sword,' and he concludes: 'I choose the dictatorship of the sword because it is more noble,' Juan Donoso Cortés, *Discursos parlamentarios* (Madrid, 1915).

20 Iris M. Zavala, *Masones, comuneros y carbonarios* (Madrid, 1971), and *Románticos y socialistas. Prensa española del XIX* (Madrid, 1972); Clara E. Lida, *Anarquismo y revolución en la España del XIX* (Madrid, 1972); Jordi Maluquer de Motes Bernet, *El socialismo en España, 1833–1868* (Barcelona, 1977).

21 Fernando Garrido, *Historia del reinado del último Borbón de España* (Barcelona, 1868), vol. III, p. 39.

22 Francisco Pi y Margall and F. Pi y Arsuaga, *Historia de España en el siglo XIX*, 7 vols. (Barcelona, 1902–1903), vol. III.

days later in Valencia. Both movements suffered a fate similar to the Madrid insurrection. Nevertheless, after an apparent period of calm which lasted a month, during which republicans, democrats and socialists continued to conspire and reorganise, in the early hours of 7 May (three days after the state of siege was lifted), yet another uprising took place in Madrid. On this occasion, armed civilians received reinforcements from several regular companies belonging to the regiments of Spain and Chiclana as well as from various commissioned officers, but, as with the previous uprising of 26 March, the government responded with equal force, although the consequences were a lot more serious, with a considerable number of casualties on both sides. Repression was immediate: eight military men and five local rebels were shot and more than 700 persons were exiled to Africa, the Philippines, the Mariana Islands, the Balearic Islands, the Canary Islands and the West Indies. Moreover, the state of siege was introduced once more in Madrid and many members of the opposition fled government persecution by leaving the country or going underground.[23]

Undaunted by the failure of insurrections in Madrid, conspiracies and uprisings also took place in the provinces, in Seville on 13 May, for example, with mainly army representation, but some civilian support too. Similar uprisings and conspiracies took place in Murcia, Cartagena, Zaragoza, Galicia, Algeciras, Ceuta and other cities, but all were severely put down. In other words, in less than six weeks, between March and May 1848, civil and military revolts and conspiracies occurred in different parts of Spain, some of which, in spite of their weakness, emulated the insurrections taking place in the rest of Europe.

In 1848, the aims and objectives of Spanish rebels and their supporters manifested, in some sense, the French revolutionary spirit of a democratic and social Republic. Above all, the concept of democracy, which implied greater political rights and a much broader concept of citizenship, was shared by the rebels, irrespective of party affiliation. As in Paris, the notion of republic as a form of government was expressed among the members of radical clubs and associations in Spain. But unlike France, Spain had a very limited number of these. On the other hand, the meaning of republic as *res publica*, or 'common weal', if not as an alternative to monarchy, spread. The idea of a government prepared to defend the *res publica* by means of the Constitution and the Law, while at the same time safeguarding the integrity of the nation and the state, infiltrated the ranks of progressive monarchists who, in turn, insisted that 'it is impossible to govern unless it is solely and exclusively within the law, which is the

23 Pi y Margall and Pi y Arsuaga, *Historia de España en el siglo XIX*, vol. III.

practical justice of the world'.[24] The social factor was also present among Spanish revolutionaries. The Spanish artisans and workers, and the socialist leaders who took part in the Peninsular uprisings, also fought so that the 'right to work', and of the fruits of labour, were recognised as the true rights to citizenship, in strong opposition to the propertied and privilege oriented system that prevailed at the time.

One further demand was the right of freedom of association, or more specifically, the right to 'the organisation of work' – also the name of a newspaper edited by the socialist republican, Fernando Garrido, in Madrid, in 1848.[25] For Garrido the organisation of work meant the right already advocated by Louis Blanc in his famous tract on the creation of 'social workshops', associations of producers to protect workers from competition and exploitation of capital. Moreover, Garrido demanded the abolition of property as an exclusive right, as only 'a small number of privileged persons' enjoyed such a right which 'prejudiced the majority who own nothing'.[26]

It is possible to conclude, then, that in 1848 in Spain a movement took place whose revolutionary goals were not very different from the rest of Europe, although it is clear that the strength and scope of the democratic movement in Spain was on a more reduced scale. As in France, the events in Spain owed much to the support received from republican, democratic and socialist clubs, associations and newspapers in which the urban popular classes took part. By the same token, just as in France, in addition to the radical and revolutionary elements, there were more moderate groups whose objectives were restricted to the democratic transformation of parliamentary institutions within a constitutional monarchy. In Spain, from the outset of the uprisings, the latter carried more weight than the former. The small republican and socialist minority, who sought support from the popular classes in demanding their rights, were outnumbered by property-owning, progressive and democratic monarchists. Both groups represented but a very small segment of society which had to contend with powerful anti-democratic interests in a country overwhelmingly populated by rural and marginal classes.

Although isolated and defeated, Spanish rebels did receive some support from abroad. In a practically unknown French pamphlet, published

24 Speech by Manuel Cortina, in 'Revista Europea', *Legislatura, 1847–1848*, pp. 315–16.

25 *La Organización del Trabajo* adopted the title of the series of articles written by Louis Blanc in 1839, later collected in pamphlet form [1st ed. 1840; 5th ed. 1848]. This Spanish newspaper, although it was closed in May 1848, after the defeat of the insurrection in which Garrido himself was involved, spread among its readers the socialist ideas of the time, which were frequently referred to as 'communist' and 'anarchist'.

26 F. Garrido, 'Communism,' *La Organización del Trabajo*, 28 April 1848, p. 130.

in Paris in 1848 by a certain Monsieur Perreymond, we learn that in the French capital a 'Spanish Democratic Committee' had been created. This group defended the idea of a Republic and called for 'Iberian Union', as Giuseppe Mazzini had done years before with respect to Italy and Europe as a whole.[27] These republican refugees in Paris organised a demonstration to support and second the Madrid revolt on the same day of the revolt itself, 26 March, confirming that the uprising had been planned in advance. The Spanish demonstrators waved the tricolour flag, not the tricolour flag of the French moderates, but a variant of the flag that had been hoisted by Colonel Riego against the absolutist monarchy of Fernando VII in 1820. Its red, yellow and blue symbolised the unity of the Iberian Republic.[28] Two weeks later, on 11 April, these same republicans organised a burial service to commemorate the Spanish rebels who had died 'in the name of freedom'.

Strictly speaking, there was no revolution in Spain in 1848 because the rebel forces were never strong enough to overthrow the Moderate government and gain control, much less topple a monarchy, secure the transformation of the state and install a democratic and republican regime. On the other hand, it is evident that Spain was deeply affected by events in Europe in 1848, even if the attempts to join other continental revolutions were carried out by small groups and ended in failure. And even though the urban uprisings in Spain were ephemeral in nature they did reflect events taking place in Paris and involved, as in France, male and female members of the popular classes. Broadly speaking, these popular classes were similar in social composition to the rebels barricading the streets of Paris: artisans and day-labourers, together with officers and soldiers of the regular army, lawyers, journalists and, of course, radical politicians.[29]

27 Clara E. Lida, 'Conspiradores e internacionalistas en vísperas de la Revolución,' Clara E. Lida and Iris Zavala (eds.), *La Revolución de 1868. Historia, pensamiento y literatura* (New York, 1970), p. 50, and notes 4 and 5. Although the question of the contacts between French and Spanish republicans before February 1848 has received little attention, we do know that there existed several links. For example, Amann refers to the republican, Napoléon Lebon, an executive member of the radical *Club des clubs*, who was exiled in Spain before the Paris Revolution; see Peter Amann, *Revolution and Mass Democracy*.

28 The author explains that the colours of Riego were green, yellow and red, but that in 1830, while the red and yellow remained, the green, which was the colour of Freemasonry, had been changed for the blue of the then flag of Portugal to express the idea of an Iberian Union, Perreymond, *L'Espagne démocratique. Compte-rendu des manifestations du 26 mars et du 11 avril 1848* (Paris, 1848), p. 41, pamphlet in Bibliothèque Nationale, París. On the 'war of symbols', see footnote 8 above.

29 The mobilisation of such heterogeneous social sectors was characteristic of all the movements, the same in Milan as in Hungary, in Berlin and, as we shall see later, in Spanish America too, Alan Sked, *The Survival of the Habsburg Empire: Radetzky, the*

Likewise, on many of the barricades the cry 'Long Live the Republic' could clearly be heard.[30]

In spite of these defeats and the intense repression by Narváez, 1848 in Spain produced new and potentially democratic and revolutionary consequences. In politics, the radical wing of the Progressive Liberal party split off to become the new Partido Demócrata (the Democratic Party), founded in 1849.[31] What was different about this new party was its ability to bring together diverse opposition groups, including republicans and socialists, who became stronger and more determined to fight not just the Moderates in office, but the Spanish monarchy, and to set up a democracy based upon popular sovereignty. Also evident was a marked increase in associationist and socialist propaganda among Spanish day-labourers, not to mention the persistent appeal to the popular classes to fight for the right to work as a primordial right of all citizens. Hence, in Spain after 1848, the republic, as well as the social question, found shelter and developed at the very heart of politics, especially in the Democratic Party.

All these elements help explain the growth of democratic, republican and socialist movements in subsequent years. During the 'Bienio progresista', between 1854–1856, Democrats and radical Progressive Liberals succeeded, with the help of massive mobilisation of workers (and the display of red flags), in displacing the Moderate government, although, in the end, the Moderates staged a successful comeback behind General Leopoldo O'Donnell. Moreover, the influence of the ideas of 1848 can be seen in the various uprisings between 1857 and 1863, each increasingly anti-monarchist, and more republican and socialist. And the final echo of 1848 was the successful Revolution of 1868, when an alliance of the different

---

Imperial Army and the Class War, 1848 (London, 1979), and Roger Price, *The Revolutions of 1848* (London, 1989). It is also interesting to note that in the abundant iconography of the period, the scenes depicting the barricades in the different cities show workers wearing loose shirts and caps shoulder to shoulder with those dressed in frock coats and top hats; although the majority of those taking part were men, women also appear. Of the latter, the Mexican newspaper *El Siglo XIX* (12 July 1848) would later report that in Paris, during the events of July, of all 'those barbarian people' taking part the 'cruellest by far' were 'certain women'. Quoted by Erika Gabriela Pani Bano, 'Para nacionalizar el Segundo Imperio. El imaginario político de los imperialistas,' México, Centro de Estudios Históricos de El Colegio de México (unpublished doctoral thesis), 1998, pp. 169–70.

30 F. Garrido, *Historia del reinado del último Borbón*; Pi y Margall and Pi y Arsuaga, *Historia de España en el siglo XIX*, vol. III. For a view that considers these events as mere 'disturbances' and perceives Spain as escaping the upheavals of 1848, see Daniel Headrick, 'Spain and the Revolutions of 1848,' in *European Studies Review*, vol. 6, (1976), pp. 197–223.

31 Initially called Progressive Democratic Party, Antonio Eiras Roel, *El partido demócrata español (1849–1868)* (Madrid, 1961).

democratic groups succeeded, once and for all, in ousting Isabel from the throne and establishing the Republican party. This was followed by the appearance in Spain of the First International and the decisive arrival of the ideas of Karl Marx and Mikhail Bakunin.

1848 in Spanish America

While it is true that in Spanish America in 1848 there were no revolutionary movements worthy of the adjective, the impact of events in Europe, particularly in Paris, on several countries in the area cannot be ignored. This influence was of varying intensity, timing and duration. The effect of 1848 can be observed in Chile in the short term, between 1850–1851; in Colombia during the five-year period from 1849 to 1854; in Argentina following the overthrow of the Rosas dictatorship in 1852 with the triumph of democracy and the promulgation of the federal republican Constitution in 1853; and, in the case of Mexico, in the longer term, particularly with the Revolution of Ayutla in 1854–1855 and the constitutional debates of 1856–1857.

The fact that Spanish American nations had become independent republics at a very early stage, and were no longer encumbered by monarchy, might suggest that 1848 had little relevance in a largely republican Hispanic America. Nevertheless, while few questioned the republican form of government, the republics themselves faced democratic and social pressures not unlike those besetting Europe. It was not long before echoes of these conflicts in Europe began to be heard in Spanish America, stimulating ideological debate but also political action. Colombia between 1849 and 1854 is where the influence of the Paris Revolution of 1848 was most clearly evident, although Chile's Society of Equality ('Sociedad de la Igualdad'), formed between 1850 and 1851, drew many of its democratic and socialist ideas from France.

Colombia

It is uncertain whether the shift to radical liberal rule that occurred in Colombia with the election, in March 1849, of General José Hilario López, with the backing of artisans' associations and democratic clubs, was directly influenced by the Revolution in France.[32] It is more likely to have been the result of Colombia's political and social reality. In any case, it is evident that ideological currents in Colombia coincided with the

32 In 1838 the 'Co-republican Democratic Society of Progressive Artisans and Farmworkers' was created and in 1847 the 'Society of Artisans' which changed in the following year to 'Democratic Society'.

democratic ideology of the French revolutionaries. The press provided considerable coverage of the interest engendered in Colombia by events in France, and newspapers debated for or against French social thought and the transforming ideas of European social romanticism.[33]

Enthusiasm was such that conservative sectors finally felt obliged to print a newspaper entitled *El Socialismo a las Claras* (1850), specifically to refute the doctrines of the different socialist thinkers (Owen, Fourier, Saint-Simon, Proudhon and others); and, just as in other countries, to label them and their followers 'communists', 'anarchists' and social 'disrupters' ('disolventes'). Other newspapers, however, came out in support of socialism and widely disseminated the new ideas. Thus, between January and February 1849, *El Alacrán* ran a series of articles entitled 'Communism'; *La Revolución*, in May 1849, comprehensively covered the socialist ideas being debated in Europe; and the newspaper *El Comunismo Social*, towards the end of 1850, defended socialism, mutualism and associationism against capitalism and free enterprise, because these destroyed the working classes. For its part, in 1850, the newspaper *El Orden* appeared, not to attack socialism but, on the contrary, as a means of defending a 'new order' and a state that would protect the working people from hunger and destitution. In addition, such was the interest aroused by Louis Blanc's National Workshops, that in 1850 they were reinterpreted to suit Colombian reality, and called instead 'Industrial Workshops', designed not to provide work for the unemployed, but to train in a trade those without one.[34] What is remarkable in the case of Colombia is the wide extent of press discussion of socialist theories, and the impact this had on political discourse and action of a radical nature.

During the liberal government of López a series of radical laws was passed, just as in France. These laws defined, among other reforms,

33 Jaime Eduardo Jaramillo Uribe, 'Las sociedades democráticas de artesanos y la coyuntura política y social colombiana de 1848,' in *Anuario Colombiano de Historia Social y de la Cultura*, vol. 8, (1976), pp. 5–18; 'La influencia de los románticos franceses y de la revolución de 1848 en el pensamiento político colombiano del siglo XIX,' in *Eco*, vol. 31, 188 (1977), pp. 127–47; and, 'Etapas y sentido de la historia de Colombia,' in Mario Arrubla (ed.), *Colombia hoy* (Bogotá, 1989), pp. 38–45. The impact of social romanticism linked to 1848 derserves closer attention. Still lacking for the Hispanic world is an approximation similar to that of Paul Bénichou, *Le temps des prophètes. Doctrines de l'âge romantique* (Paris, 1977). As far as Spain is concerned Zavala, *Románticos y socialistas* offers a pioneering glimpse. For Spanish America, see Germán Carrera Damas's stimulating reflections in *De la dificultad de ser criollo* (Caracas, 1993).

34 Jaramillo Uribe, 'Las sociedades democráticas de artesanos', and 'La influencia de los románticos franceses'; Anatolii Fedorovich Shulgovski, 'La "Comuna de Bogotá" y el socialismo utópico,' *América Latina* (USSR) vol. 8, (1985), pp. 45–56, and vol. 9, (1985), pp. 47–56.

citizens' freedoms and rights, including women's rights, the abolition of the death penalty for political crimes, freedom of the press, the elimination of ecclesiastical and military privileges, the introduction of civil marriage and the abolition of slavery. However, even though these political changes were democratic, the essentially liberal nature of the government was revealed above all in its economic policy, with the abolition of monopolies, the liberalisation of foreign trade and the disentailment of communal lands, among other measures.[35]

This clear liberal emphasis was expressed in the Constitution of 1853, although it fell far short of the radical and socialist discourse mentioned above.[36] This explains why artisans, socialists and radicals from Bogotá and other Colombian cities began to feel disillusioned with measures which, while perhaps bestowing upon the Republic a more democratic character, actually offered greater protection to elite interests (landowners, financiers, traders and exporters).[37] In this context, the 1853 elections saw a split in the Liberal Party and the radicalisation of the army. Amid these conflicts, on 17 April 1854, the military insurrection of General José María Melo took place.

Focused upon Bogotá, although spreading to other urban centres, this movement lasted almost eight months, ending on 4 December 1854.[38] As far as we know, Melo's support, as in the other countries already referred to, was made up of the popular classes; a conglomeration of urban artisans and workers, professionals, students and radical politicians, grouped in Democratic Societies, as well as members of the army and the civil militias. For its part, the National Guard, like the mobile National Guard in France, comprised artisans and workers, employees and small property

35 Jaime Eduardo Jaramillo Uribe, 'La influencia de los románticos franceses', and 'Etapas y sentido de la historia de Colombia'. On the different faces of liberalism in Colombia and the efforts towards modernity by the mid-nineteenth century, see Marco Palacios, *Parábola del liberalismo* (Bogotá, 1999), pp. 143–236.

36 These same years saw the proclamation of the Argentine Constitution of 1853 and that of Mexico, in 1857, both democratic and liberal.

37 Palacios, *Parábola del liberalismo*, pp. 222–3, calls this a clash between 'the learned revolution' and the 'plebeian revolution'.

38 On the popular discontent of what the author calls 'the plebeian movement', see Francisco Gutiérrez Sanín, *Curso y discurso del movimiento plebeyo 1849–1854* (Bogotá, 1995). Malcolm Deas highlights political events in areas other than capital cities, Deas, 'La presencia de la política nacional'. Stoller points out how, in these years, in San Gil, local patricians interpreted the violence of artisans as a direct result of governmental centralism and appealed to the sentiments of local autonomy to protect the social order. Richard Stoller, 'Ironías del federalismo en la provincia del Socorro, 1810–1879,' in *Fronteras* (Instituto Colombiano de Cultura Hispánica), vol. 2, (1998), pp. 11–32.

owners.[39] The rebels, as in Paris and Madrid, identified themselves by wearing red ribbons and hailing the 'Republic of Artisans'. They also cheered the army, since Melo had adopted the Bolivarian idea that 'the army is the people in arms'.[40]

The popular nature of Melo's uprising is revealed by information on the repression suffered at the hands of his opponents, the 'Constitutionalists' (who drew together liberals and conservatives).[41] Melo was sentenced, together with the military chiefs and rebels, to long periods of imprisonment or exile. Melo himself was banished to Mexico where he later served in the army of Juárez, eventually dying there. Civilian rebels holding public posts were dismissed and teachers and students accused of sedition were expelled from the universities. But, in the end, those who received the severest sentences were the democrats, radicals and socialists, who belonged, mostly, to the Democratic Societies and were sent to military prison camps. Extremely severe, too, was the corporal punishment inflicted upon rebels in certain regions such as Cali. Those who undoubtedly took the brunt of the reprisals were the artisans whose associations were closed down, their members imprisoned and more than 300 sentenced to hard labour in the region of Panama where many died.[42]

To summarise, in Colombia between 1849 and 1854 political changes bestowed a democratic complexion upon republican ideology. Moreover, in Melo's revolution in 1854, the social factor emerged decisively to threaten privileged propertied groups, both liberal and conservative. Nevertheless, these events in Colombia, which in April 1854 called to mind a 'democratic and social Republic' similar to that of Paris in 1848, by December had ended in utter defeat. From then on, not only did the revolutionary threat of the popular classes cease to be a danger, but republican participation was henceforth reserved for the group which had emerged in triumph from the revolution: the liberal and conservative oligarchies. While capable of differing in political and economic matters,

39 Under Louis Philippe the Parisian National Guard had been a clearly bourgeois institution whose members were chosen from the voters of every *arrondissement* with the economic power to buy their uniforms and arms. Instead, the Revolution made it mandatory for all men between the ages of 25 and 50 to serve in this civil militia; the state had to supply all the military equipment, and the officers were selected by the troops, Amann, *Revolution and Mass Democracy*; Mark Traugott, *Armies of the Poor* (Princeton, 1985).

40 *Gaceta Oficial*, Bogotá, 24 April 1854, cited in Shulgovski, 1985, II, p. 47.

41 Marco Antonio Palacios Rozo refers to the rebels as 'levellers' ('niveladores') in 'El estado liberal colombiano y la crisis de la civilización del siglo XIX,' in *La delgada corteza de nuestra civilización* (Bogotá, 1986), pp. 46–51.

42 Margarita Pacheco, *La fiesta Liberal en Cali* (Colombia, 1992), and Gutiérrez Sanín, *Curso y discurso del movimiento plebeyo*.

even to the extent of waging devastating civil wars, these liberal and conservative oligarchs, once 'the patrician republic' had triumphed 'over the republic of artisans', henceforth shared a common anti-democratic and socially exclusionist bias.[43]

Chile

It is unnecessary to go into great detail with the Chilean case, since the studies of Luis Alberto Romero, Cristián Gazmuri and Sergio Grez Tosso have revealed, in great depth, how the new ideas and social forces that appeared in France in 1848 culminated in Santiago in 1850 in the creation of the Society of Equality (Sociedad de la Igualdad), and in armed insurrection in April 1851. These historians have revealed Chile's peculiarities, the clashes between moderate and progressive liberals, property owners and the popular classes – particularly artisans – and between radical intellectuals and politicians and the conservatives.

The revolution in Paris had a direct influence on radicals such as Santiago Arcos and Francisco Bilbao, the so-called 'Chilean Girondins', and contributed to opening up discussion of democratic and social ideas (which had first surfaced in the literary societies, political clubs and societies of artisans in the 1830s).[44] All this had a notable influence on the analysis and debate on Chile's social problems, on the organisation of associations of artisans, and on the widening and deepening of a radical democratic ideology among intellectuals who directly opposed the restrictive and oligarchic nature of the conservative governments. These radical intellectuals and artisans were determined to make the Chilean Republic democratic, and to inject it with a social dimension.

The Society of Equality emerged out of this context, its objective being to promote secularisation and democratic rights, which earned its members epithets such as 'blasphemers', 'heretics' and 'Jacobins'. At the same time, the Society also propagated European socialist ideas: the protection of labour, the right to association, the creation of schools for artisans and the establishment of banks for workers. Through its newspaper, *El Amigo del Pueblo*, a comprehensive analysis was made of the social rights of the working classes, synthesised in defence of the right to

43 Palacios, *Parábola del liberalismo*, p. 224.

44 Title of the book of one of the supporters of the group, Benjamín Vicuña MacKenna, *Los girondinos chilenos* (Santiago, 1902). On the influence of France on the founders of the Society of Equality, see, above all, Luis Alberto Romero, *¿Qué hacer con los pobres?* (Buenos Aires, 1997); and Cristián Gazmuri, *El '48' chileno. Igualitarios, reformistas radicales, masones y bomberos* (Santiago, 1992).

work.[45] Chilean historians have explained that this proposal lacked the radical character that such rights had acquired in France. Still, the doctrines expounded initially in *El Amigo del Pueblo* and, from June 1850. by its successor, *La Barra*, represented a significant step to defining and popularising republican principles, symbols, ideas and images. These were, above all, democratic, but also social, as suggested by the use of terms 'anarchist', 'saintsimonian' (as synonymous of 'men without God and laws') and 'communist'.[46]

Between August 1850 and April 1851, during the presidential elections, so-called 'Egalitarians' ('Igualitarios') mobilised against the conservative candidate, Manuel Montt. Conservatives became convinced that radicals and artisans threatened the political and social order. In November 1850, after opposition demonstrations in the provinces, the government decreed a state of siege and intensified repression against the Society of Equality and its members, both in the capital and beyond. On 20 April 1851, in opposition to the June elections which, it was predicted, would be dominated by the conservatives, surviving 'Egalitarians', together with radical liberals backed by members of the army and the militia, attempted an uprising but were once again defeated. Despite these blows, in the second half of 1851 uprisings took place in several Chilean provinces. These insurrections approached the scale of a civil war but were finally crushed by the conservative government in early 1852. The extent of repression was considerable: from November 1850 until January 1852, several of the leaders, like Arcos, were taken prisoner and even deported; others, like Bilbao, went underground or fled. The most unfortunate, however, were those workers sent to the penal colonies in the south. In the words of one eye witness, 'the imprisonment of artisans continues diligently'.[47]

We can venture the opinion that in spite of ups and downs the revolutionary winds which had reached Chile in 1848 continued to blow, creating in time new circumstances propitious for the setting up of a democratic republic, in spite of conservative power. Nevertheless, many

45 We should remember that the title of this publication is not only an echo of Marat's newspaper during the Great Revolution, but of a more recent one, whose Parisian editor was Dr François V. Raspail, a revolutionary defender of the democratic and social republic of 1848.

46 Sergio Grez Toso, *De la 'regeneración del pueblo' a la huelga general. Génesis y evolución histórica del movimiento popular en Chile (1810–1890)* (Santiago de Chile, 1997), p. 317. Information on *El Amigo del Pueblo*, in Gazmuri, *El '48' chileno*, pp. 76–9, and also in Jack Ray Thomas, 'The Role of the Press in the Chilean Rebellion of 1851,' in *The Americas*, vol. 36, (1979), pp. 59–78, who also cites the attacks on this newspaper and its supporters by *El Verdadero Chileno*.

47 Benjamín Vicuña Mackenna, *Diario*, quoted in Romero, *¿Qué hacer con los pobres?*, p. 73.

decades were to elapse before there was any decisive progress in the implementation of the principles of the social republic. However, it is clear that with the Society of Equality and similar societies formed in several other towns, Chile's popular classes enjoyed their first associationist and democratic experience. Grez Tosso is right when he says that these years produced 'a significant leap, an irruption unknown in the country until then' of the popular classes, particularly the artisans.[48] Nevertheless, in the future, each of the sectors involved in this process, the radical liberals, on the one hand, and the artisans and wage-earners, on the other, would choose and develop their own paths, paths that would seldom cross.

Mexico

In Mexico the repercussions of 1848 in France were not felt in any systematic manner until much later. When the revolution in Paris took place Mexico was recoiling in defeat at the hands of the United States. Moreover, since 1847 the country had been shaken by Indian uprisings in the Sierra Gorda and in Yucatán, as well as by Apache invasions on the northern border. In addition, diplomatic relations between Mexico and France, which had been suspended since 1845 during the monarchy of Louis Philippe, were not renewed until May 1848. Although French affairs were of interest to the Mexican government, most of the official documents which have been consulted for the period are concerned mainly with 'the Mexican debt' with France and the intentions on the part of the French government to pressure the United States into withholding from the indemnities agreed on in the Treaty of Guadalupe the amount owed to France by Mexico. There do exist, however, certain communiqués dispatched by the official in charge at the Mexican Foreign Ministry, Luis de la Rosa, who, on 11 March, had sent cordial congratulations to the French republican government and had instructed Mexico's chargé d'affaires in Paris, Fernando Mangino, to convey to the minister of foreign affairs, Alphonse de Lamartine, 'the good and friendly wishes which inspire Mexico with hope for the full development of democratic principles in France'.[49] Almost a month later, Mexico's chargé d'affaires in Spain was asked to assess the general reaction to events among members of the court of Isabel II, making it clear to them 'that in Mexico that movement which has converted France into a sister Republic

48 Grez Toso, *De la 'regeneración del pueblo' a la huelga general*, p. 372. This study of the development of the working classes in Chile is the most complete to date.

49 Archivo Histórico de la Secretaría de Relaciones Exteriores, México (AHSRE), Leg. 25, exp. 302. doc. 9269, 11.III.1848.

has been well received'.[50] At about the same time, the chargé d'affaires in Paris received a communiqué underlining the fact that the President of Mexico, Manuel de la Peña, 'would like to receive details [...] about these momentous events', and the February *journées* were referred to as 'the astonishing revolution'.[51]

However, by mid-way through the year the Mexican attitude had changed. On 1 June, the new Mexican minister, the moderate liberal Mariano Otero, in reply to a note of 22 April from the chargé d'affaires in France expressing concern 'about the danger of French communist doctrines spreading throughout the [Mexican] Republic', stated that he would bear in mind the measures proposed 'to avoid the emigration of communists' to Mexico.[52] Thus, as in other countries, the fear of 'communism', a concept undoubtedly unfamiliar to most, qualifies the enthusiasm with which Mexicans initially had greeted the events in Paris.

Beyond the diplomatic sources, there is very little mention of the events of 1848 in correspondence and personal writings of the politicians of the period. The moderate liberal, José María Luis Mora, was minister plenipotentiary in England in 1848 and may have been the first to inform the Mexican government, on 29 February, of the 'astonishing revolution'. But he warned against 'the disastrous future it heralds' and 'the universal disruption of order and peace'.[53] Two commentaries made in subsequent months were just as negative concerning the future of the French Republic whose internal security is 'continually at risk on account of the communist conspiracy'.[54] Mid-way through the year, after the Parisian June days, and as a result of the war waged in Yucatán by the Mayas (the so-called 'Caste War'), Mora proposed that the Mexican government favour white emigration to Mexico and take advantage of the failure of the 'workers' uprising' due to 'communist instigations', and the subsequent repression, in order to facilitate the arrival in the country of those persecuted, since 'the majority of these men are not depraved people but robust and hard working' men, of whom the French government wishes to rid itself, and of whom Mexico could well avail itself, achieving 'the fusion of every race and colour [...] in one'.[55] Three days earlier, he had

50 AHSRE, Leg. 16-03-46, exp. h/513(44)8482/1, 10.IV.1848.

51 AHSRE, Leg. 25, exp. 302, doc. 9268, 11.IV.1848.

52 AHSRE, Leg. 25, exp. 302, doc. 9270, 1.VI.1848.

53 José María Luis Mora, *Obras completas. Obra diplomática* (México, 1988), Vol. VII, p. 164. Mora's expression of 'astonishing revolution' is surprising, since it is almost identical to the one used by de la Rosa on 11 April. This could mean that Mora was the first to give the Mexican government news of the events in France.

54 Mora, *Obras completas. Obra diplomática*, VII, p. 203, 30 June 1848.

55 Mora, *Obras completas. Obra diplomática*, VII, p. 276, 31 June 1848.

already indicated, with insight, that 'French workers, like Irish workers, do not rise up because they lack morals but out of extreme misery'.[56]

For his part, Valentín Gómez Farías, whose radical liberal opinions earned him labels such 'sansculotte', 'anarchist' and 'demagogue', in his personal correspondence with his sons, particularly Benito, then living in London, ebulliently hailed the Republic and expressed the hope that 'the revolutionary movement [would] spread to Spain and other [monarchical] nations'.[57] His enthusiasm for the French revolutionary initiative moved him to reflect on the contrast with Mexico: 'Everywhere one feels things are changing, only among us [Mexicans] is there fear of action, only among us does one sleep soundly amid social collapse. What degradation!'[58] At the end of April he reflected further: 'The time has come for the People to recover their rights, for the good and by force [since] they have been deceived long enough, they have been made to wait long enough.'[59] After these comments made in the spring of 1848, the topic no longer appears in his letters, although his son Benito continued to send him news from Europe in subsequent years, at least until the proclamation of the Second Empire.

Very opposing views were expressed by the ageing Conservative, Carlos María de Bustamente, who had little sympathy for the revolutionary Republic. In his 'Historical Journal' he copied and commented upon certain news items about France appearing in the Mexican newspapers, above all *El Monitor Republicano*.[60] He praised Louis Philippe: 'He was a good king to all and sundry [although] wicked towards Mexicans', and he condemned 'the unjust manner in which the French have behaved' towards him. Moreover, he was against a revolution which changes the monarchical system 'for the old Republican one [based] upon the disastrous principles of the last revolution in 1792'. And a few pages later he referred to the French as 'a people experienced in massacres and slaughters'.

These few examples are enough to convey the meagre and contradictory manner in which the Mexican government and politicians reacted to the changes taking place in France, a reaction not always based on adequate information. In part, this was due to the slowness with which news on European events reached Mexico, often two months late and by differing means. In some cases, news arrived via packet boats docking in Veracruz; in others, by telegramme, the information frequently truncated,

56 Mora, *Obras completas. Obra diplomática*, VII, p. 205, 28 July 1848.

57 Archivo de Don Valentín Gómez Farías, University of Texas, Austin, in microfilm at the Instituto José María Luis Mora, México, (AVGF) 10 May 1848, doc. 2955.

58 AVGF, 14.IV.1848, doc. 2960.

59 AVGF, 28.IV.1848, doc. 2963.

60 My gratitude to Josefina Z. Vázquez for this information.

incomplete, even false. Most other news was extracted directly from newspapers printed in the United States, England and Spain, or even via Cuba, since Mexico did not have its own correspondents abroad. A review of the Mexican press reveals the poor quality of information available; at best news is descriptive of European events, but it is also void of significant commentary or analysis. In 1848 the newspapers most concerned with the revolutionary theme were *El Monitor Republicano*, with radical liberal tendencies, *El Siglo XIX*, moderate liberal in approach, and *El Universal*, conservative and Catholic.

The first news of the overthrow of Louis Philippe began to reach Mexico, in the last two weeks of April. *El Monitor* was enthusiastic in expressing the opinion that 'Paris has often made heroic efforts, great revolutions. Today, it is called upon to give yet another example to the people', foreseeing that 'the whole of America will receive with pleasure the news of the reestablishment of the republic in France'. *El Monitor*'s editors expressed the hope that the Republic would favour 'the weak nations'.[61] The events in Europe also served as a pretext for the newspaper to deal with domestic problems and to reject conservative and monarchical efforts in Mexico. On 12 May, *El Monitor* praised the liberalism of the French Revolution against the 'servile objectives' of the uprising of General Paredes. On 7 June it stated that it would be impossible to make Mexico accept a monarchy 'which is rejected by the most civilised nations of the old continent'.

However, by May, we can observe how the influential *El Eco de Comercio* rang the alarm bells vis-à-vis 'the principles of a most impassioned republicanism' which took into account 'the uneducated working classes'. The paper also warned against 'the people', which in France means 'the pleb, the rabble'.[62] The most notable change in press coverage took place in mid-June with information of the events of May. *El Comercio* changed its tone, referring now to the demonstrators as 'disorderly men, ultra-revolutionaries, communists', and a few paragraphs later it spoke of the anti-social system which the 'anarchists' were sponsoring.[63] In August,

61 *Monitor Republicano* (MR), 11 April, 14 April and 17 April 1848, respectively. A week later, the influential *El Eco del Comercio*, referred to the revolution of February as the 'great event which has completely changed the face of Europe, perhaps the whole world, in one week' (25 April 1848), quoted by Pani Bano, 'Para nacionalizar el Segundo Imperio,' p. 167. In Chapter III, Pani carries out an interesting review of the Mexican press in order to examine the vision held by Mexico of France and Spain before the Empire of Maximilian, and offers other news complementary to those quoted here.

62 *El Eco del Comercio*, 2 May and 6 May 1848, respectively, quoted in Pani Bano, 'Para nacionalizar el Segundo Imperio,' p. 169.

63 *MR*, 16 June 1848.

the first news and comments on the Parisian June days appeared and *El Monitor* began to elaborate further on the dangers of socialism and communism, claiming that the former wants 'equality for all' while the supporters of the latter 'seek the levelling of all fortunes'.[64] The disinformation on social ideas was evident, yet the opposition to these was emphatic when the newspaper, in September, explained in categorical terms that 'the right to work is communism itself'.[65]

If in the spring of 1848 *El Monitor Republicano* and other liberal newspapers applauded the first news of the Revolution as a true breakthrough in republican consolidation, with the events of May and the June days the attitude of all Mexican newspapers, regardless of tendency, was clearly against the social theories and the popular classes, to which they referred in very simplistic if not Manichaean terms. An excellent example of this was provided by *El Monitor* itself on 6 January 1849, when it labelled Louis Napoleon 'a communist prince'. In fact, from the autumn of 1848 the Mexico City press referred to the revolution and its supporters in an increasingly negative manner. For its part, on 13 January 1849, the conservative newspaper *El Universal* ran a long article in which it compared the revolutions of 1789 and 1848, expressing the view that the former was a blood bath brought about by 'depraved' and 'lunatic' beings, while the latter was less 'unjust', although it too violated every social and moral principle by attacking property and the 'Supreme Being'. The writer concluded by pointing his finger at those really to blame for these events: 'The socialist and terrorist clubs created by the Republic of 48 [which] shared the same disruptive and bloody tendencies as the famous club of the Jacobins'.[66]

An exception to this hostile climate of opinion was *El Socialista*, published in Guadalajara in 1849, whose goal seemed to be was to restore the reputation of Socialism.[67] Both *El Universal* and *El Monitor* referred

64 *MR*, 7 Aug. 1848.

65 *MR*, 26 Sept. 1848.

66 *El Universal* (*Univ.*), 13 Jan. 1849. The Catholic newspaper, *La Voz de la Religión*, echoed the fear of heresy and the threats by the 'socialist sect' (*La Voz de la Religión*, Vol. II, (9 June 1849), pp. 721–2) in a manner similar to that of the Bishop of Guadalajara, Diego Aranda, in 1847, when he published a pastoral letter on Pius IX's encyclical (see note 7 above). I wish to thank Guillermo Nájera for sharing this information with me.

67 There exist only indirect references to this newspaper as it has not been possible to locate surviving issues. However, thanks to Juan B. Iguíniz, *El periodismo en Guadalajara, 1809–1915* (Guadalajara, 1955), pp. 69–70, we know that its founder was an Italian doctor, José Indelicato, who settled in Guadalajara after visiting Brazil, Argentina, Peru and Ecuador. *El Socialista* appeared between 2 Jan. and 28 Feb. 1849, and ran a total of nine issues. Carlos Illades ventures the opinion that perhaps Sotero Prieto (a Mexican socialist who was in Cadiz around 1837 and was linked to the

to this new newspaper. *El Universal* saw the appearance of *El Socialista* as a threat: 'the first foundations of socialist doctrine are being laid ... (as) ... aberrations ... (against) ... the holy books.'[68] *El Monitor*, for its part, reproduced, without any commentary, a leading article in which the theories of Fourier and socialism were explained.[69]

The following year, in 1850, the moderate liberal newspaper *El Siglo XIX* announced, without further explanation, that 'the democratic-socialist party' had appeared in Mexico.[70] Two days later it stated that a 'liberal-progressive party' had been created in Toluca, with ideas 'even more barbarian than those of socialism and communism', inasmuch as it has asked the Indians for their vote, promising them lands and water and support against the oppression in which they find themselves.[71] Throughout 1850, references to socialism, communism and republican democracy appeared at regular intervals in the Mexican press, the first two as anathema, and the third as in need of defining its boundaries. The terms socialism and communism acquired such negative connotations that the newspapers even used these labels in attacking each other. Thus, *El Universal* was openly critical of *El Monitor Republicano* branding it 'socialist' and, with such an ideology, accusing it of covering up for certain politicians and their 'gangs', who were nothing other than supporters of 'mad, stupid and evil individuals'. *El Universal* also railed against 'the socialists' of *El Siglo XIX* whom it labelled 'outlaws' and 'advocates of theft'.[72] For its part, *El Monitor* defended itself by pointing out that the accusation 'of being socialist means either a complete ignorance of the term itself or a treacherous calumny aimed at casting us an unmerited affront'. *El Monitor* then attacked, without naming them, certain politicians who were sponsoring 'the setting up of clubs openly professing such destructive dogmas as those of Proudhon'.[73] For its part, *El Siglo XIX* denied being socialist and called upon its readers 'to wage war against socialism'.[74]

Fourierist group of Joaquín Abreu) took part in founding the newspaper towards mid-century, inasmuch as he was actively involved in promoting the associationism of workers in the Jalisco capital at about that time; Carlos Illades, 'De los gremios a las sociedades de socorros mutuos,' in *Estudios sobre el artesanado urbano en el siglo XIX.* (Mexico City, 1997), pp. 101–17 (1st ed.: *Historia Social*, vol. 8, (1990), pp. 73–87). Dr Indelicato was viewed with hostility by local society who pressed him to leave, but not before he had launched in February 1854 another publication, *La Revista*, which lasted until the beginning of June.

68 *Univ.*, 19 Jan. 1849.

69 *MR*, 20 Jan. 1849.

70 *Siglo XIX* (*S. XIX*), 18 April 1850.

71 *S. XIX*, 20 April 1850.

72 *Univ.*, 31 Oct. and 27 Dec. 1850, respectively.

73 *MR*, 21 Oct. and 30 Nov. 1850, respectively.

74 *S. XIX*, 24 July 1850.

In brief, what is striking in the Mexican case, is the sudden change from initial support for the February Revolution to widespread caution, and the rapid loss of enthusiasm throughout the spring. This change of attitude was common to all the different sources consulted, with the exception of certain manifestations of hostility present from the beginning when it was realised that the French liberal Republic could well become democratic and social.[75] As the months went by sympathy for the revolution was replaced by a discourse of fear and condemnation which repudiated popular mobilisation with constant references to 'anarchy' and 'communism'. This discourse spread to the towns where peasant communities were fighting for land. Hence, when in March 1849 the 'Political and Eminently Social Plan' ('Plan político y eminentemente social') was promulgated by the 'Regenerating Army of Sierra Gorda' ('Ejército Regenerador de Sierra Gorda') in Río Verde, San Luis Potosí, *El Monitor* described its followers as 'rabble, newly coined socialists' and 'anarchists' whose ideas 'beguile and will always beguile (...) the country dwellers'.[76] However, unlike other Hispanic countries, what strikes one most about Mexico is the dearth of public and informed discussion on democratic and social ideas.[77] In fact, it was not until mid-way through the 1850s that an open debate was begun on democratic ideas, which culminated directly in the Reform laws and the Constitution of 1857. Yet,

75 Mora, for example, as early as 1830 categorically opposed more widespread access to the right to citizenship, closely linking it to ownership, and sought to secure 'exclusion from it of all those unable to inspire any kind of confidence whatsoever, that is to say, those non-property owners', those to whom he refers on another occasion as 'the tail end classes of society'. José María Luis Mora, *Obras completas. Obra política* (Mexico City, 1986), vol. I, p. 370: 'Discurso sobre la necesidad de fijar el derecho de ciudadanía en la República y hacerlo esencialmente afecto a la propiedad.'

76 Quoted by J. González Martínez who studied this movement in his M. A. thesis. My thanks to the author for providing me with a copy of this as yet unpublished research. Joaquín González Martínez, 'Una sublevación campesina: El movimiento regenerador de Sierra Gorda'. México, Universidad Autónoma Metropolitana-Iztapalapa (unpublished MA thesis) 1983, pp. 90–102.

77 The spread of socialist ideas in Mexico was slow and sporadic, Gastón García Cantú, *El socialismo en México (siglo XIX)* (Mexico City, 1974) [1st ed., 1969]; Illades, 'De los gremios a las sociedades de socorros mutuos'. On the other hand, references tended to be biased, as in the case of José María Tornel, the War Minister at the time, who in December 1843 published in *El Museo Mexicano*, a very personal translation of 'Walks in London' by Flora Tristán, not so as to present the ideas of the French socialist on the rights of women and workers, but to criticise England and question Owen and the socialists, whom he considered materialists, atheists, and 'true conspirators against human happiness [who] deserve to be stoned in the public square', María del Carmen Vázquez Mantecón, *La palabra del poder. Vida pública de José María Tornel, 1795–1853* (Mexico, 1997), pp. 139–40.

as far as social ideas were concerned, it was necessary to wait until the 1860s and, more resolutely, until the 1870's, before a more comprehensive debate on the various socialist trends was experienced, leading to the emergence of organised working-class associationism.[78] In synthesis, it can be said that sympathy for the Liberal Republic, but not for the Democratic Republic, existed in Mexico as soon as the February events in Paris were known. But the only acceptable republic would seem to have been a republic without revolution, without a popular dimension, a moderate republic restrictive in the rights it conferred upon citizens, and without any social dimension, similar to that observed by Tocqueville ('a republic without republicans, a democracy without the people').[79]

To conclude, in the case of Mexico, in the period from the Paris revolution of 1848 to the coup d'état of Louis Napoléon in 1851, the social problems occupying the centre of public affairs were, above all, those linked to indigenous mobilisation and their struggle for land.[80] In the field of politics, attention was focused exclusively upon the struggle between different regional and national factions. Moreover, there was no mobilisation of Mexico's urban popular classes during this period, comparable to what has been observed occurring in other countries included in this study.[81]

In the longer term, the echoes of 1848 in Europe, hardly audible in Mexico initially, began to be heard loud and clear after the victory of the Ayutla Revolution in 1855, during the political debates leading up to and following the promulgation of the Reforma laws and the Constitution of 1857.[82] This constitution, which included the freedom of work and the

78 Carlos Illades, *Hacia la república del trabajo. La organización artesanal en la ciudad de México, 1853–1876* (Mexico City, 1995); Mario Trujillo Bolio, *Operarios fabriles en el Valle de México (1864–1884)* (Mexico City, 1997); Clara E. Lida and Carlos Illades, 'El anarquismo europeo y sus primeras influencias en México,' in Ward Albro (ed.), *Flores Magón and Mexican Anarchism* (Forthcoming).

79 See note 10 above.

80 Leticia Reyna, *Las rebeliones campesinas en México (1819–1906)* (Mexico City, 1988); Guy P.C. Thomson, 'Popular Aspects of Liberalism in Mexico, 1848–1888,' in *Bulletin of Latin American Research*, vol. 10, (1991), p. 265.

81 Sonia Pérez Toledo, *Los hijos del trabajo. Los artesanos en la ciudad de México: 1780–1853* (Mexico City, 1996); Carlos Illades, *Hacia la república del trabajo*; and for a study the first associative practices and demands concerning the right to work in the mid-nineteenth century, Carlos Illades, 'De los gremios a las sociedades de socorros mutuos'.

82 For the wide range of topics debated in the period of the Reforma, see the indispensable works of Jacqueline Covo, 'Los clubes políticos en la revolución de Ayutla,' *Historia Mexicana*, vol. 26, (1977), pp. 438–55, *Las ideas de la reforma en México, 1855–1861* (Mexico, 1983), and, '*Le Trait d'Union,* periódico francés de la ciudad de México, entre la reforma y la intervención,' *Historia Mexicana*, vol. 35, (1986), pp. 461–76. Also Thomson, 'Popular Aspects of Liberalism'; Pani Bano, 'Para nacionalizar el Segundo Imperio'.

right to association, as individual freedoms and rights constituting the rights of man, was more influenced by the French Constitution of November 1848 than has been acknowledged.[83] The Constitution of 1857 constituted a legal platform for the implementation of a Democratic Republic.[84] Nevertheless, in spite of the expansion of the male vote, for decades this was accomplished more in theory than in practice.[85] On the other hand, the Social Republic did not appear, although in the Workers Congress of 1876 invocation to the 'Republic of Work' enjoyed a fleeting moment on stage.[86] The Social Republic would await a further half a century, until the Mexican Revolution, when the right to work was established in the Constitution of 1917.

Conclusions

At the end of this wide-ranging review of the Hispanic world, we can conclude that 1848 marked the emergence of a plural and, often, contradictory *imaginaire* which converted the revolution of 1848 into a moment of democratic and egalitarian optimism for the more radical social sectors, or an example of disorder and social threat for the more moderate and conservative factions. This would explain why the Bonapartist model, imposed upon France at mid-century, would be vindicated by the antirevolutionary sectors as a large-scale dam built by an authoritarian yet constitutional state to hold back the advance of radical democratic doctrines, together with those of a social nature broadly labelled socialist and communist.

This was very much in evidence in Mexico after the proclamation of the liberal Constitution of 1857, when moderate and conservative sectors of Mexican society reacted against the democratic and progressive, but not as yet social, republic of Benito Juárez and the so-called 'pure' liberals, not only by means of armed insurrection but also by approaching Napoleon III himself with a view to setting up in Mexico a Bonapartist-

83 Mélonio, '1848: la république intempestive'. That Mexicans kept abreast of discussions of the French constituents can be seen, for example, in Guillermo Prieto's reference to the discussion between republican monocameralists, represented by Lamartine, and the bicameralists such as the monarchist, Odillon Barrot, Francisco Zarco, *Historia del Congreso Extraordinario Constituyente [1856–1857]* (Mexico, 1956), pp. 1069 and 1052.

84 Francisco Zarco, *Historia del Congreso*, and *Congreso Extraordinario Constituyente, 1856–1857* (Mexico City, 1957).

85 See a compilation of federal election regulations between 1857 and 1901, in Antonio García Orozco, *Legislación electoral mexicana. 1812–1977* (Mexico City, 1978).

86 Illades, *Hacia la república del trabajo*.

type monarchy in the figure of Maximilian.[87] In Colombia too, after the five-year period of artisan radicalism and constitutional experimentation from 1849 to 1854, popular mobilisation diminished, although on the Constitution of 1863 was Latin America's most radical, until it was repealed in 1886 by Rafael Núñez in the conservative Restoration. In Chile, the mobilisation of artisans and radical liberal political assertiveness was much more shortlived than in Colombia, although, through their participation in the Society of Equality, Chilean wage earners enjoyed a foretaste of the political influence would acquire in the early twentieth century. Meanwhile, as Gazmuri's demonstrates in chapter seven, many radical liberals who had entered politics during the crisis of 1850–51 would contribute importantly to the reshaping of Chilean political life during the 1850s and 1860s.

In Spain, we have already mentioned that the brief *bienio progresista*, from 1854 to 1856, was crushed by moderate and progressive monarchists who saw in the political stability and material accomplishments of the Second Napoleonic Empire a model to emulate. The struggle for a democratic and social Republic thus continued there in a clandestine fashion until its first victory in 1868, with the fall of the monarchy of Isabel II. It culminated in the proclamation of the First Spanish Republic in 1873. This Republic, however, was to be very different from the social and democratic Republic of 1848, in that the federalism of the Paris Commune of 1871, as well as the new forms of organisation arising from the First International, were to have a significant influence upon it.

In fact, the First Republic was unwittingly split in two from birth: on the one hand, there was the Democratic Republic, made up of the reformist and radical parliamentarians; on the other, the Social Republic, longed for by the revolutionary working classes. This division continued after its defeat in 1874, when the Bourbon restoration took place. The two tendencies fused into one for only fleeting and intermittent periods in the Second Republic and the Civil War, between 1931 and 1939.

In the differing trajectories evident in the Hispanic world, we can observe the vigorous emergence in public life of social sectors which, until that point, had remained on the fringe of debate and political participation and for whom 1848 aroused awareness of their rights as citizens, and the redefining of the premises upon which these rights were based. However, for the working class majorities which made up the popular classes, the problem was not only political but above all social. For the *res publica*, or Republic, to be effectively democratic, citizens' rights had to be inclusive; no longer based upon the exclusive criterion of individual

87 On the influence of the Napoleonic model in Mexico, see Pani Bano, 'Para nacionalizar el Segundo Imperio'.

property, but rather taking as their basis the only value which these classes considered universal: the value of work. And so, a shift occurred from a redefinition that was essentially political to another of a social character. Thus, in converting the citizen into a synonym for worker, the Democratic Republic in turn would become Social.

Nevertheless, in this process which, as we have seen, varied in duration according to the country in question, the plural nature that initially characterised the popular classes, with time, would undergo a gradual redefinition and display a dual specificity. There would be those who, from the standpoint of democratic liberalism, called upon the social sectors enjoying greater social mobility to take part in political competition, and those who understood social goals as part and parcel of the demands and struggles of the working classes.

In conclusion, recalling Maurice Agulhon's view of the Second Republic as a huge 'apprenticeship in republicanism', for the Spanish and Hispanic American republicans the Revolution of 1848 also signified the beginning of a long apprenticeship in the construction of new forms of democratic participation and social rights.[88] In the republics of Spanish America 1848 defined the frontier between popular sovereignty and authoritarianism. In Spain, even more, 1848 meant a boost to republican principles and an alternative to a discredited monarchy. In all these countries, the key lesson to be learned was the ability to trace a dividing line between republicanism and patrimonialism, between the Republic for all and Republic for the few. But 1848 also meant an apprenticeship in collective social rights as opposed to individual privileges; that is, the Republic of the few vis-à-vis the Republic of many. In other words, although the process was very slow, after the revolutionary events of the spring of 1848 many began to learn that for the Republic to be truly Democratic it also had to be Social.

88 Maurice Agulhon, *1848, ou l'apprentissage de la république, 1848–1852* (Paris, 1973).

3

The United States and the European Revolutions of 1848*

TIM ROBERTS

The United States did not itself undergo a revolution in 1848, nor did it intervene in Europe during the mid-century European revolutions. Such omissions, taken alone, suggest that the United States took little heed of European turbulence. Yet the reactions of ordinary US citizens and statesmen to the European revolutions reveal much about the USA's political culture and prejudices.

Some elements of US society in 1848 suggest its differences from Europe. In the United States all adult white males could vote, native-born and immigrant alike. This was a right for which European revolutionaries struggled and died in 1848. The US Constitution guaranteed republican government, a commitment that European monarchs, unless or even if they were physically threatened, vigorously resisted. In 1848 victorious US armies occupied lands conquered from Mexico stretching from Texas to California, after a war surprising for the ease of US victories following one after the other. Speaking in 1848, President James Polk crowed that 'while the people of other countries struggle to establish free institutions under which man may govern himself, we [US citizens] are in actual enjoyment of them – a rich inheritance from our fathers.'[1] To be sure, revolutionary upheaval was not something that linked the United States to Europe in 1848.

Yet the USA took notice of Europe in 1848, often, like their chief executive, by comparing the news of the European revolutions with what they remembered of the USA's own revolutionary origins. By 1848 the United States was some seventy-five years old: an ancient regime compared to the fledgling democratic regimes established in Europe at mid-century. 1848 surprised US observers because events that year offered the prospect that a democratising Europe would follow the example of an

* Material for this chapter is based on Timothy M. Roberts, 'The American Response to the European Revolutions of 1848,' DPhil Thesis, University of Oxford, 1998.

1 Polk, 'Fourth Annual Message,' 5 Dec. 1848, in James Daniel Richardson (ed.), *Compilation of the Messages and Papers of the Presidents* (New York, 1927), vol. VI, p. 2479.

established USA. France declared a republic. The German states convened a national parliament, based on popular representation. Italians established popular regimes in Venice, Sicily and Rome. Hungary rose against its historical master Austria. In 1848 Europe showed a new aspect: a yearning to change dramatically, to declare, if not secure, popular sovereignty. This was a shock to people in the USA: was it possible Europe was imitating, or even surpassing, the USA in developing liberal democracy? The USA assessed revolutionary Europe and, egocentrically, took stock of itself.

This kind of collective self-assessment was woven through the ways the USA expressed interest in revolutionary Europe, in political speeches, legislative resolutions, street parades and meeting hall celebrations. In the process they reflected on the components of their own revolutionary identity. That identity, as variously conceived in the USA, shaped responses to the question raised by Europe, of what kinds of people should claim the right of self-government, as President Polk had indicated.

The pressures exerted by their own revolutionary history, the mounting problems of slavery in the USA, and the uniform failures by 1850 of the European revolutions themselves, ultimately led people in the USA to react to the European revolutions in two ways. They used Europe to salute US revolutionary origins. They also examined Europe to consider the prospect of a second revolution in US society, erupting over the issue of slavery. Such a second revolution, the USA feared, would be more like Europe in 1848 than the British American colony in 1776, more comprehensive in its social upheaval. This was a time when disputes over slavery grew ever more rancorous. Yet via the fate of revolutionary Europe most US citizens at mid-century could conclude that the unique condition of liberty in their own country was still better than it was in Europe. This was the reaction to the European revolutions.

Revolutionary Repercussions in the USA, 1848–1849

The news from Europe arrived in the USA in the mid-nineteenth century in a unique way. Transatlantic steamers could deliver as much as six weeks' worth of news, all of which was often condensed and published in the next day's newspapers. News from Europe was spread widely by new telegraph lines. Many citizens across the republic thus learned of foreign events at roughly the same time and had roughly the same information. Even US soldiers, encamped in Mexico in the spring of 1848, could read and rejoice, as one put it, that the 'refulgence of [our] glorious stars' had penetrated the 'noxious fogs of European despotism'.[2]

2 Menahem Blondheim, *News over the Wires* (Cambridge, MA, 1994), pp. 49–62. US soldier quoted in Robert Johannsen, *To the Halls of the Montezumas* (New York, 1985), p. 303.

Moreover, as news from Europe appeared in the US press in clusters, the 1848 Revolutions took the appearance to most US observers as a monolithic, even spiritual force, rather than as disparate movements. Early on, such a force was ascribed to US influence, augmented by God's providence. The US Minister to France, Richard Rush, acting on his own authority, hastily extended recognition to the Provisional Government in Paris; no other nation had yet done so. But Rush's action was readily confirmed by the Polk administration when news arrived in Washington in late March.[3] The *Richmond Enquirer* reported the 1848 upheavals by exclaiming, 'The victory is won! American principles are triumphant! What a sublime spectacle does Europe present to the American patriot!' The *New York Tribune* noted the coincidence of the outbreak of the French Revolution with George Washington's birthday, a public holiday. Perhaps most lustily, the *Baptist Banner* of Louisville, Kentucky, rejoiced at the significance of news that Pope Pius had been struck with apoplexy on the anniversary of US independence. Such reports portrayed the European upheavals as a uniform event, animated by both a US national and a divine will. Foreign news in the US press was simplified and highly interpretative. This made it easy for those in the USA to be inspired by what was happening across the Atlantic.[4]

To be sure, not every US newspaper wrote about overseas events with such exuberance, even at the outset of the revolutions. The Washington *National Intelligencer,* an old Federalist and then Whig organ, attacked the French revolutionaries. 'That Gallic people,' as the *Intelligencer* wrote caustically, 'want the braver instincts that [support] law, right, and freedom. We do not deny the right of revolution ... but we regard it as a right not to be lightly resorted to by *any* people.'[5] Likewise, the Catholic press reacted negatively even to the first signs of European upheaval. The *Catholic Herald* of Philadelphia spoke of the 'threat' in Europe of 'an eruption of democracy and republicanism from the caverns and bowels of the earth'.[6] For critics of radical events in Europe, it was one thing to salute the idea of struggling violently for greater liberty. It was another thing for suspicious or unproven peoples to actually undertake that struggle.

But such opinions, at least in the first part of 1848, were in the minority. In contrast to the *Catholic Herald,* the *Baptist Banner* showed an eschatological view typical of the Protestant press, rejoicing 'that the

3 Henry Blumenthal, *A Reappraisal of Franco–American Relations, 1830–1871* (Chapel Hill, NC, 1959), pp. 13–14.

4 *Richmond Enquirer,* 14 April 1848; *New York Tribune,* 5 April 1848; [Louisville, KY] *Baptist Banner,* 23 Aug. 1848.

5 *Daily National Intelligencer,* 27 March 1848. Emphasis in original.

6 [Philadelphia] *Catholic Herald,* 4 May 1848.

people of Europe are becoming acquainted with ... ethics ... When the millennial reign of Christ shall bless the earth ... we shall have pure Government.'[7] *The National Intelligencer* had many critics because of its scepticism. According to the *Richmond Enquirer*, to 'follow the *National Intelligencer* we must first blot out the bright page of our country's history, when our fathers of '76 raised the flag of liberty.' President James Polk wrote Minister Andrew Donelson in Germany that the '*National Intelligencer* and a few Federal leaders, true to their instinctive hatred of free principles', were the exception to most of the USA's enthusiasm. Accordingly, Polk was simply doing the people's work when he appointed Donelson 'Minister Plenipotentiary to the Federal Government of Germany', even though such a thing as the 'Federal Government of Germany' did not yet exist.[8] Early in 1848, published and official opinion in the United States rejoiced at the 'springtime of the people', owing largely to the apparent US spirit obliterating the practical difficulties of staging a revolution.[9]

In addition to written expressions, US citizens showed their interest in Europe in other ways as well. During the revolutionary period in Europe from 1848 to 1852 they interpreted the exciting foreign news in name-taking, consumer purchases, forms of dress and entertainment, academic exercises and street demonstrations. Continuities and changes in US sentiments about the European revolutions may be traced in such cultural expressions. In 1848, more than later, US enthusiasm reflected a sense that Europe and the USA were indeed growing closer together, based on the prospect for democratic change in Europe and the flattering impression that that prospect had on most US observers.

The French Second Republic drew US attention in the spring of 1848. The fate of the whole of Europe west of Russia seemed to rest in French hands. The USA heartily celebrated the leadership of the French poet and national historian Alphonse de Lamartine, especially his resistance to the adoption of the red flag of revolution over the Hotel de Ville, and his diplomatic circular pledging France's commitment not to attack other countries. The Massachusetts senator, Charles Sumner, wrote of Lamartine that his 'position is one of incalculable influence, not only over the destinies of France, but the progress of civilization'. Citizens in Arkansas, Wisconsin and Pennsylvania named towns after the French romantic

7 *Baptist Banner*, 5 April 1848.
8 Buchanan to Donelson, 15 Aug. 1848, in John Bassett Moore (ed.), *Works of James Buchanan* (New York, 1960), VIII, pp. 147–9.
9 *Richmond Enquirer*, 21 March 1848; James Polk to Andrew Donelson, 2 April 1848, in St George L. Sioussat (ed.), 'Letters of James K. Polk to Andrew Jackson Donelson, 1843–1848,' *Tennessee Historical Magazine* 3 (1917), pp. 72–3.

leader. Lamartine's eloquence and rejection of more radical elements of the French uprising made him a dashing but palatable figure across US social circles. And the people of the USA endowed the French people and their uprising with the qualities Lamartine himself possessed.[10]

US renditions of events in Europe showed in cultural ways as well. In the spring of 1848 stage plays like *The Last of the Kings and The Insurrection of Paris, or, The People's Triumph* opened in Boston and New York, respectively.[11] Citizens wore the red, white and blue French tricolour and the red, green and white cockade of Italian unification from New York City to the frontier village of Madison, Wisconsin.[12] The Hungarian polka became widely popular in the USA for the first time, propelled by its political connotations. A Philadelphia ballroom instructor wrote that radical European dances like the polka, 'modified by ... deviations ... to which ardent republican sentiments ... naturally give birth,' could liberate the USA from its 'serfdom to the fashionable whims' of the Old World. In early 1848 their adoption and adaptation of the trappings of revolution helped the USA to feel a kinship with the actual struggles going on across the Atlantic.[13]

Enthusiasm evinced in the northern and western areas of the country was shared in the south. No theatre productions illustrating revolution debuted in southern cities, but this was not surprising. Southern theatre patrons had long-standing aversion to works with political themes, and temperance reform, strong in the south in the 1840s, weakened interest in the theatre generally late in the decade.[14] But southerners responded in other ways. Torchlight processions took place in Richmond, Virginia. The city of Atlanta, as did many cities along the Atlantic seaboard, anticipated the rumoured arrival of the deposed King Louis Philippe by voting him 'several hundred acres of excellent land'. New Orleans, with a sizeable immigrant population, hosted numerous 'reform banquets', modelled, albeit remotely, on the protests that launched the Paris uprising. At one such bacchanal 'three dark-eyed Creole girls impersonated Liberty,

10 Sumner quoted in Larry J. Reynolds, *European Revolutions and the American Literary Renaissance* (New Haven, CN, 1988), p. 22; *Alphabetical List of Towns and Counties* [from the 1880 US Census] (Alamo, CA, 1975); Henry Gannett, *American Names* (Washington, 1947).

11 *Charleston Courier*, 3 April, 1848; Reynolds, *European Revolutions*, p. 18; George C.D. Odell, *Annals of the New York Stage* (New York, 1931), V, p. 350.

12 *New York Tribune*, 1 April 1848; [Madison] *Wisconsin Argus*, 30 May 1848.

13 Norman E. Saul, *Distant Friends* (Lawrence, KS, 1990), p. 174; Charles Durang, *Durang's Terpsichore; or, Ball Room Guide* (Philadelphia, 1848), pp. 150, 161.

14 James H. Dormon, Jr., *Theatre in the Antebellum South, 1815–1861* (Chapel Hill, NC, 1967), pp. 131, 153; Charles S. Watson, *Antebellum Charleston Dramatists* (Tuscaloosa, 1976), pp. 129 ff.

Charity, and Pity. With ... fascinating smiles [they] collected a handsome contribution for those wounded in Paris.'[15]

With the reversal of events in Europe, however, US reaction changed accordingly. The large event changing minds in the USA was the 'Bloody June Days' of Paris, when labourers put up barricades to protest the dissolution of the labour relief workshops established by the Provisional Government. Government troops under General Eugene Cavaignac attacked the barricades with artillery, and hunted down and slew insurgents through the streets of the city.

A few members of the US press, partly reflecting their domestic sympathies, condemned the events of the June Days only reluctantly. The *Richmond Enquirer* and the *New York Tribune* both saluted the valour of the Paris working men against the 'selfish bourgeoisie and the savage soldiery' of Paris. The two papers, however, differed on how to solve the French labour conflict. The *Tribune*, edited by the labour reformer Horace Greeley, stuck to its earlier endorsement of the new French government's efforts to provide welfare to destitute French labourers. The *Enquirer*, on the other hand, called for ever greater extension of the suffrage, because elections would 'show the horror felt' over the government's crackdown on labour radicals. Both papers, however, saluted the 'Andrew Jackson-like' Eugene Cavaignac for his enforcement of law and order.[16]

Most reviewers were less sympathetic with French labour radicalism. The widely read *New York Herald* condemned the whole concept of workers' expectations of government assistance, and saluted the 'suppression of the mob'. The *Herald* warned that 'if government can interfere either to promote or retard the interest of any class of society, it can do so with all ... If it can interfere with the labourer, it can interfere with the mechanic, and with the professional.' A New York diarist registered US shock at the news of class violence: 'The workmen of Paris ... [dregs of the city] ... [were] arrayed against the existing order ... Blood ... spattering the public buildings, flowing, gurgling along the gutters ... Some [Americans] are [now] inclined to revoke hasty conclusions ... [about] the moral advance of everything.'[17]

US exercises saluting Europe fell off significantly after early 1849. Tri-coloured revolutionary headwear grew less visible, as the more subversive, less fashionable colour red came to symbolise overseas events. The *New York Herald* attributed the June conflict to the 'incendiary doctrines of

15 *Richmond Enquirer*, 28, 25 April 1848; Gunnar J. Malmin (ed.), *America in the Forties: The Letters of Ole Munch Raeder* (Minneapolis, MN, 1929), p. 170.

16 *Richmond Enquirer*, 21, 25 July 1848; *New York Tribune*, 14 July 1848.

17 Cyprian Porter Willcox, unpublished diary, entry for 15 July 1848, University of Georgia Special Collections.

Communists and Fourierists', whose presence was confirmed by 'the banner red'. The *Illustrated London News*, widely read in the United States, affirmed that the '"Red Republicans" have justified their name. The middle classes wanted no red flag.'

US theatre productions reflected this theme of fear. In the autumn of 1848 the Bowery Theatre in New York presented *The Destruction of the Bastille, or Terror's Reign*. The Park Theatre contributed *The Barricades*, in which the celebrated soprano Anna Bishop rendered the Marseillaise while costumed as an officer of the French National Guard. Previously, stage plays had celebrated the heroism of overseas events. Now, they portrayed the excesses of revolution, evoking images of the worse elements of the French Revolution of the 1790s. Or, as in *The Barricades*, US productions championed the maintenance of law and order.[18] The Red Scare of late 1848 and 1849 made the people in the USA recoil at, rather than embrace, the idea that the European revolutions might have an impact on the United States.

The Campaign of 1848 and Revolutionary Europe

Besides being the year of European revolution, 1848 was an election year in the United States. Democrats, Whigs and the Free Soil Party, a minority party, contested the presidency. In the context of US land acquisitions from Mexico, the important issues of the campaign were the fate, slave or free, of the western territories, as well as the boldness of Free Soilers to break with the traditional two-party system.

None of the three presidential candidates – the Democrat Lewis Cass, the Whig Zachary Taylor, the Free Soiler Martin Van Buren – made demonstrative statements in support of the European revolutions. It was a campaign, however, in which candidates tended not to make demonstrative statements about much of anything, so sensitive were the issues of territorial slavery and party loyalty. Still, amid many people's excitement over Europe, all three parties, although each in its own way, put the concept of revolution and events in Europe to use. Coupled with references to the Founding of the USA typical of antebellum campaign seasons, circumstances made the idea of revolution a natural component of the 1848 campaign.[19]

The Free Soil Party came perhaps as close as any group in the USA to emerging as a contemporary corollary of the 1848 European revolutionaries.

18 Odell, *Annals of the New York Stage*, vol. V, pp. 321–2, 414.

19 Jean H. Baker, 'Ceremonies of Politics: Nineteenth-Century Rituals of National Affirmation,' in William J. Cooper, Jr., Michael F. Holt and John McCardell (eds.), *A Master's Due* (Baton Rouge, 1985), p. 166.

The party name derived from its supporters' commitment to preserve, through pending federal legislation known as the Wilmot Proviso, the new US lands opening in the west for settlement by free labourers, rather than by supporters of slave labour. Free-labour ideology was not new in the USA in 1848, but the Free Soil Party convened officially in that year, holding its first convention and nominating a national ticket. Free Soilers drew inspiration from radicalism in Europe, not so much to create free government, as in Europe, but to cure a US regime of dangerous shortcomings.

Free Soil party leaders and other party communications often invoked the European revolutions. The vice presidential candidate of the party, Charles Francis Adams, son of the former president John Quincy Adams, at first disparaged European turbulence. But as he was drawn into the Free Soil camp Adams's sense of a relationship between the USA and Europe became more apparent. In the summer of 1848 Adams ruminated that 'in republics men become machines moved at the will of an idea carried into organization', and in campaign speeches compared the situation of the stand-pat Whig Party to that of the ousted French monarch Louis Philippe.[20] Adams's colleague in Massachusetts, Senator Charles Sumner, vigorously affirmed the historical and transatlantic roots of the Free Soil movement. Sumner declared Free Soilism 'a continuance of the American Revolution', and for its strength it should 'pluck fresh coals from the living altars of France'. 'Let us, too,' Sumner pleaded, 'proclaim "Liberty, Equality, Fraternity".'[21]

Besides antislavery men like Adams and Sumner, a second element of the Free Soil Party in 1848 was the New York 'Barnburners', former Democrats who now clustered around the Free Soil nominee, Martin Van Buren. Barnburners, motivated out of hatred of the Polk administration for its stingy awards of patronage after the election of 1844, sought a third party movement to an extent as revenge on the Democratic party.

Yet Barnburners also spoke of Europe. The New York Free Soiler Samuel Tilden addressed the New York state legislature in the spring of 1848 to hail France's establishment of national labour workshops and workday hour limits.[22] In reply the legislature declared that the 'French Republic was a monument to those who established our own govern-

20 Charles Francis Adams' Diary, entries for 18 March, 16 June 1848, Massachusetts Historical Society; David Donald, *Charles Sumner and the Coming of the Civil War* (New York, 1960), p. 142.

21 Frank Otto Gatell, '"Conscience and judgment": The Bolt of the Massachusetts Conscience Whigs,' *Historian*, 21 (Nov. 1958), p. 41; Charles Edward Lester, *Life and Public Services of Charles Sumner* (New York, 1874), p. 166.

22 On the labour movement of 1848 see William H. Sewell, Jr, *Work and Revolution in France* (Cambridge, 1980), pp. 243–76.

ment, that what was deemed an experiment has become a model for imitation by nations.'[23] On election day 1848, the *New York Evening Post* editor William Cullen Bryant asked, 'Shall the republic ... to which millions struggling for emancipation in Europe turn for their encouragement ... no longer be an asylum of the oppressed? Above all others the labouring man has a deep interest in this question.'[24] New York Free Soilers conflated news of labour gains in Europe with the pregnant labour situation in the United States, to appeal to the patriotism and indignation of the US labour vote. Shamefully, they argued, Europeans were enacting a US revolutionary promise of the rights of free working men.

Friends of Free Soil had no monopoly on revolutionary rhetoric in the late 1840s, however. It was the national platform of the Democratic Party that overtly attached the European revolutionary initiative to a domestic agenda: 'In view of the people ... erecting republics on the ruins of despotism in the Old World ... an increased duty is devolved upon the Democratic party to advance "liberty, equality, and fraternity", by continuing to resist all monopolies and exclusive legislation.' This hearkened to the destruction by the party's founder, Andrew Jackson, of the Bank of the United States. The Democratic platform hailed the new French revolution for establishing 'principles for which their Lafayette and our Washington fought: the inherent and inalienable right of the people to make and amend their forms of government in such manner as the welfare of the community may require.'[25]

Senator Lewis Cass from Michigan, the Democratic candidate, hoped to translate enthusiasm for the idea of the people 'making and amending their forms of government' into electoral success. The hawkish Cass had gained favour in the west and the south for leading the Polk administration's Mexican War agenda in Congress. 'We want almost unlimited power of expansion,' he declared in describing US aims against Mexico. US soldiers' sacrifices and military victories, according to Cass, had 'redeemed' the country's reputation in the eyes of the world, offsetting criticism of US military belligerence. Land acquisition and national redemption were rewards for people capable of self-government, which was, Cases wrote, 'the very first article of the democratic creed'.[26] Democratic party congratulations to French revolutionaries reminded the US electorate that a creed of self-governing peoples was not simply rhetoric.

23 'Address of the Democratic members of the Legislature of the State of New York,' in *Papers of Martin Van Buren*, microfilm reel 30 (Washington, 1960).

24 Quoted in Allan Nevins, *The Evening Post* (New York, 1922), pp. 243–4.

25 Donald Bruce Johnson and Kirk H. Porter, *National Party Platforms 1840–1960* (Urbana, IL, 1961), p. 12.

26 Quoted in Willard Carl Klunder, *Lewis Cass and the Politics of Moderation* (Kent, OH, 1996), pp. 164–5, 199.

Cass gained the Democratic nomination via his policy of popular sovereignty, which he offered as an alternative to the policy of the pending Wilmot Proviso – having first endorsed the Proviso and then retracting his support – for federal regulation of slave labour in the western territories. Under popular sovereignty, Cass held that citizens in the territories should decide the slave question locally, and that Congress should accept the local will. The doctrine was nostalgic, for it appealed to the days of the early republic when new states had sent the Continental Congress manifestos declaring the right to govern themselves at the local level.

Cass sought to capitalise, however, on the contemporary appeal of the idea of popular sovereignty in 1848, mixing international events with domestic issues. Excitement over the Dorr Rebellion was still brimming in 1848. The Dorr Rebellion had erupted in Rhode Island in 1842 over that state's failure to eliminate property requirements for voting and holding state office, as was done in most states in the early republic. But in Rhode Island, the antiquated colonial charter of 1663 had been left in place. Before being arrested by federal troops, Thomas Dorr led a movement that lay siege to the Rhode Island state assembly, attempted to break into a US Federal arsenal, and declared a 'people's' democratic state government and constitution. Martial law was imposed, and Dorr and his supporters were arrested. Dorr was sentenced to life imprisonment; he was released after serving twenty months. In its violence over the issue of voting rights, the Dorr Rebellion was perhaps the closest counterpart in the United States to the European revolutions of 1848.

The issue of popular sovereignty raised by the Dorr Rebellion was the substance of *Luther v. Borden,* heard by the US Supreme Court in 1848. Benjamin F. Hallett, a Democratic party leader and author of the Democratic national platform in 1848, was the attorney for the Dorr party, with Nathan Clifford, the US Attorney General under the Polk administration, serving as co-counsel.[27] Hallett declared to the US Supreme Court that the issues raised by the Rhode Island conflict amounted to a referendum on US belief about self-government: 'whether the basis of popular sovereignty is a living principle or a theory.' Hallett recurred to both US history and the European upheavals to frame his argument – such rhetoric issued again and again in US discourse in 1848. '[Our] glorious experiment ... would fail if we now decide that the people [cannot] hold a convention without' governmental consent. 'Such a construction ... would [sanction] despotism [and] repudiate the doctrines of the fathers.' Moreover, declared Hallett, it would 'discourage ... the oppressed millions

27 *Luther v. Borden*, 7 Howard 1 (1849); Marvin E. Gettleman, *The Dorr Rebellion* (New York, 1973), pp. 184–5.

of the old world.'[28] Both the US past and the European present seemed hard at stake in the popular sovereignty debate.

The Supreme Court ruled against the Dorr party in *Luther v. Borden* on grounds that the issue of popular sovereignty should be decided via state legislation, not the courts. Yet the plea to sanction popular sovereignty did not die within the walls of the Court; Benjamin Hallett's argument was quickly distributed as a street pamphlet. Publishers of the pamphlet emphasised the international currency of popular rule. 'Shall [the United States] recede until … regenerated Europe shall [be] so far in advance of her[?] … The French republic has … repudiated the despotic doctrine that reforms can emanate only from the will of the sovereign. Surely young America will not now take up this cast-off garment of deposed kings!'[29] Democrats, like Free Soilers, invoked radicalism in Europe to appeal to the patriotism of (potential) voters in the upcoming national election, tying domestic policy to transatlantic events.

The Whig campaign, in contrast to the Free Soil and Democrat efforts, contained little reference to Europe, nor for that matter any other issue, so divided over the slavery issue were Whigs at their convention in 1848. The Mexican War hero Zachary Taylor was nominated for his war record and his complete lack of political experience; he had never voted before 1848. Whig party managers thus spent time portraying Taylor as the second coming of the USA's first citizen soldier, George Washington, and muzzling their candidate's public campaign appearances.[30]

In a negative campaign technique, Whigs questioned the republican allegiance of Lewis Cass, their main rival for the White House, using his long public record against him. Cass had served as US minister to France a decade before the 1848 Revolutions, ensconcing himself comfortably in the court of King Louis Philippe. He was, in fact, scolded by the US State Department in 1840 for conducting official communications in French, the subtleties of which Washington did not trust.[31] Moreover, Cass published a laudatory study of the French government, praising Louis Philippe as the epitome of 'all magistrates, monarchical or republican', and hailing the 'great personal freedom' prevailing in France.[32] In 1848 Cass no longer

28 *Right Of the People to Establish Forms of Government. Mr. Hallett's Argument in the Rhode Island Causes, before the Supreme Court of the United States, January 1848* (Boston, 1848), pp. 7, 47, 62.

29 *Ibid.*, 'Note'.

30 See Joseph Gales, *Sketch of the Personal Character and Qualities of General Zachary Taylor* (Washington, 1848).

31 [Secretary of State] John Forsyth to Lewis Cass, 21 July 1840, John Y. Mason Papers, Virginia Historical Society.

32 Lewis Cass, *France, its King, Court, and Government,* quoted in the *National Intelligencer*, 27 March 1848.

defended the French monarchy but instead helped organise the US Senate's resolution to congratulate the French people for ousting Louis Philippe from the throne. Such a reversal made sense, given the enthusiasm of the US public and especially Cass's northwest constituency over the first news of the French upheaval. But in the summer and autumn of 1848, Cass's change regarding France was a foil for Whigs to impugn his reliability on the crucial question of slavery in the western territories.

Illustrating the Whigs' coupling of international news with domestic issues, the *Richmond Whig* detected in Cass's earlier praise for the French monarch, his enthusiasm now for the French republic, and his uneven course on territorial slavery a disturbing pattern of vacillation. The *Whig* noted that in the past Cass had been 'most at home among crowns and coronets ... [T]he sovereign's smile to him [was] like the rising sun to the vegetable world.' Now, the *Whig* noted, Cass 'is the most radical of radicals ... making senate speeches about the new French Republic upon all occasions. Likewise, the *Whig* continued, Cass had initially supported the Wilmot Proviso, the manifesto of the Free Soil Party. But then 'a revolution took place [in Cass's position] ... produced, no doubt, by the prospect of obtaining southern votes to sustain Presidential pretensions.'[33] For the Whig and its party namesake, even the hint of a 'revolution' in policy-making had dangerous implications; Lewis Cass's propensity for 'revolutionary' change was a strike against him. In contrast the Whig candidate Zachary Taylor posed little threat to agitate the republic in 1848.

If the presidential election had been held in the spring or even summer of 1848, when people in the USA shared an excitement about revolutionary events in Europe, its results might have been different. As it was, for the first time, on 7 November 1848, all voters went to the polls on the same day. Such an arrangement eliminated the influences of earlier states' voting results in later states' polls. But it also meant that voters together could assess a political climate charged by the theme of revolution in light of the demise of the revolutionary movements in Europe rather than their ascendancy. The 'Bloody June Days' in Paris were reported in US newspapers beginning in mid-July, as was the Austrian crackdown on the student-led insurgency of Prague. Such events separated the Free Soil Convention of August 1848 from the fall of the monarchy of Louis Philippe the previous spring, allowing anti-Free soil sentiment to speak to the times. A New York lawyer, George Templeton Strong, lamenting his financial difficulties in the autumn of 1848, remarked with heavy irony, 'I shall turn Socialist, Fourierite, Free Soiler, and Red

33 'General Cass,' *Richmond Whig and Public Advertiser*, 2 June 1848.

Republican.'[34] A Pennsylvania pamphleteer warned that 'if God permit the Free Soil party to control the extension of slavery ... anarchy or military despotism' must ensue.[35] A New York essayist wrote that the 'ferocious and desperate attempts' of the 'outcasts' of Europe to effect change 'present striking proof ... of the necessity for slave labour'.[36] The US political corollary of revolutionary Europe erupted after the time when the reception of the idea of transatlantic revolutionary change was at its highpoint. Free Soilers became tainted with the worst prospects, to US eyes, that the European revolutions could offer.

If avant-garde Free Soilers were disappointed by the momentum swing of transatlantic events, then Democrats, whose chances of actual electoral success, after all, were much more real, were injured indeed. Lewis Cass hoped to ride the enthusiasm of military victory to presidential success, especially in the northwest. Certainly, he received the European immigrant vote; until the mid-1850s German- and Irish-Americans voted for the Democratic party in large numbers. But, as the election drew near, Cass's assertions of the destined spread of US hegemony became suspect, especially if they implied US commitments across the Atlantic. Fears arose that Cass, if elected, might embroil the United States in a now chaotic and uncertain Europe. Whig Senator Daniel Webster declared publicly that Cass was 'the most dangerous man in whom the powers of the executive could be placed'.[37] Even his own party questioned what Cass might do. His 'western Radicalism concerning foreign relations' worried one Democratic organiser in Virginia. 'Amid the whirl of revolutions abroad ... I distrust him.'[38] Such suspicions, coupled with questions about Cass's perceived equivocation on the question of territorial slavery, drove voters especially in the south into the Whig camp.[39] The election year 1848 belonged to the Whigs and Zachary Taylor, whose strategy called for a reduction of US revolutionary zeal rather than its cultivation.

34 George Templeton Strong, *Diary*, edited by Allan Nevins and Milton Halsey Thomas (New York, 1952), entry for 21 Oct. 1848, I, p. 332.

35 [Jacob Leisler], *Letters to the People of Pennsylvania on the Political Principles of the Free Soil Party* (Philadelphia, 1850), pp. 2, 14, 20, 21.

36 William Murdock, *Address on the Free Soil Question* (Washington, 1848), pp. 12, 19, 40.

37 Quoted in Klunder, *Lewis Cass*, pp. 217–18.

38 James A. Seddon to Robert M. T. Hunter, 16 June 1848, in 'Correspondence of Robert M. T. Hunter, 1826–1876,' edited by Charles Henry Ambler, *American Historical Association Report*, 1916, II:91.

39 Holman Hamilton, 'Election of 1848,' in Arthur Schlesinger, Jr. (ed.), *History of American Presidential Elections 1789–1968* (New York, 1971), II, p. 892.

US Interest in Central Europe

As the USA lost enthusiasm for events in France, people turned their attention to events in central and southern Europe. Popular disturbances in Italy, Germany and Hungary erupted concurrently with those in France, but with the establishment of martial law in France, events elsewhere took precedence in the US press. Concerning Germany, people in the USA focused mainly on the Frankfurt Parliament, especially news of the parliament's deliberations to produce a constitution for all of the German people. Southerners in particular perceived and were impressed by German deliberateness. The South Carolina statesman John C. Calhoun, who had led opposition to the US Senate's resolution to congratulate the French Second Republic, wrote, 'I have ... hope for Germany ... Her old institutions ... furnish an excellent foundation on which to erect a federal constitutional Government.'[40] Stating a racial perspective common for the period, the *Southern Quarterly Review* opined that 'free institutions ... succeed [only] with certain classes of men. We question the success of democratical [sic] government among any present European nation, save the Anglo-Saxon and the German.'[41] The less European peoples were perceived to have to struggle for liberal democracy, the more likely, it was believed in the USA, they were to attain it.

Events in Italy perhaps most caught people in the USA by surprise. Italian patriots overthrew Habsburg rule in Venice and Milan and Spanish rule in Sicily, and declared a republic in each city. Most astonishingly, early in 1849 it was learned in the USA that Roman citizens had forced Pius IX to flee the Vatican and proclaimed a republic. Margaret Fuller, in Rome writing for the *New York Tribune* – she was the first US reporter ever to cover a foreign war at first-hand – sent word that 'the people is [sic] ignorant, [but] the Roman Eagle recommences her flight.'[42] Of any European people, Italians had seemed least likely to achieve a new secular order. US Catholics took a keen interest in the fate of the European Catholic Church, and of the papacy in particular. The USA's leading Catholic spokesmen, the journalist Orestes Brownson and the Irish-American Archbishop of New York, John Hughes, contrasted the European upheavals sharply with the American Revolution. The failure of the European revolutions, they explained, showed their fundamental irresponsibility and rabid secularism. By contrast the American Revolution

40 John Calhoun to Thomas G. Clemson, 13 April 1848, J. Franklin Jameson (ed.), *Annual Report of the American Historical Association for the Year 1899*, vol. II: 'Correspondence of John C. Calhoun,' (Washington, 1900), pp. 748–50.

41 'The National Anniversary,' *Southern Quarterly Review* 2 (1850), p. 175.

42 *New York Tribune*, 4 April 1849, in Margaret Fuller, *These Sad but Glorious Days*, edited by Larry J. Reynolds and Susan Belasco Smith (New Haven, 1991), p. 255.

was grounded in precedent, and enacted by a 'fair majority of the reasoning part of the community'.[43]

For their part, evangelicals in the USA, who for generations had prophesied the destruction of the Pope as a millennial harbinger, were particularly enthralled with events in Rome. Secular and religious groups organised not only relief efforts for Roman citizens but the distribution of Bibles into the Italian peninsula. These acts of proselytisation were flavoured with ethnocentrism, however. Theodore Dwight, an advocate in the USA of Italian independence, explained the Roman people's sudden revolutionary vigour as a religious conversion experience. 'The Italians have suddenly, without world suspicion,' he wrote, 'become devoted Protestants.'[44] When French troops overran the Roman Republic to prepare for Pius's return early in 1850, the *Christian Magazine of the South* attributed the sad turn of events to US evangelicals' laxity. 'If Protestant Christians had believed in republican freedom as the fruit of Biblical circulation … this calamitous restoration would never have occurred. Had France been attended to in 1848, no France in 1849 would have attempted this infamous interference.'[45] The revolution in Rome was lamented not for its own demise but for betraying the negligence of evangelicals in the USA in disciplining new European Protestant converts.

More than anywhere else, it was the revolution in Hungary that most stirred US emotions after 1848. Comparatively little was known of the Hungarians, and so people in the USA could imagine more freely the Magyars' struggles with Austrian and then Russian forces. It has been said of one prominent US citizen that he liked revolutions best when they were long ago and far away.[46] The Hungarian revolution presented both qualities to US observers. It was in eastern Europe, far away from the United States. And it evoked for people in the USA their own struggle of 1776 against British tyranny; in its images it seemed to be happening long ago.

Hungarians, like the North American colonials, were an historically settled people, defined by a common ethnicity, language and Protestant faith, and a faithful satellite of an imperial parent. Like the US patriots, Hungarians had been wronged by the parent's crackdown on customary

43 Orestes Brownson, 'Legitimacy and Revolutionism,' *Essays and Reviews Chiefly on Theology, Politics, and Socialism* (New York, 1852), pp. 389–415; John Hughes, *The Church and the World* (New York, 1850), p. 25.

44 Joseph Rossi, *The Image of America in Mazzini's Writings* (Madison, WI, 1954), pp. 31–6; Theodore Dwight, *The Roman Republic of 1849* (New York, 1851), p. 237.

45 'Bibles in Rome,' [Columbia, South Carolina] *Christian Magazine of the South* 7 (Aug. 1849), 240.

46 Thomas J. Pressley, 'Bullets and Ballots: Lincoln and the "Right of Revolution",' *American Historical Review* 67 (April 1962), pp. 647–62.

freedoms. There were rallies cheering the 'Struggle of 1776' throughout the west of the USA in 1849, including Springfield, Illinois, where congressman Abraham Lincoln pledged support for the Magyar cause.[47] Likewise at a rally in Philadelphia speakers compared the Hungarian commander Arthur Gorgey to the North American revolutionary hero Francis Marion, and the hero Lajos Kossuth to George Washington and Patrick Henry.[48] The Hungarian uprising was an occasion for revisiting and saluting the Founding of the USA.

Some in the USA were critical of Hungary, especially Catholics and individuals who examined the details of Hungary's claims for sovereignty. Catholic spokesmen blasted Lajos Kossuth as a godless anarchist, especially for his friendly communication in Europe with Giuseppe Mazzini, the vanquisher of Catholic authority in Rome. As people in the USA had earlier read the positive attributes of Lamartine into the character of the French people, so did US Catholics condemn the Hungarian cause on account of their perception of Kossuth himself.[49] The eminent New England scholar Francis Bowen revealed that the Hungarians' independence movement preyed on the repression of Slavic minorities. But such protests were muffled, and even penalised, in the enthusiasm over the Hungarian reprisal of US Independence. In Bowen's case, his criticisms were the occasion for his dismissal from a Harvard professorship.[50]

Perhaps responding to public opinion, secretary of State John Clayton ordered a US attaché in Germany, A. Dudley Mann, to observe secretly if circumstances might warrant US recognition of an independent Hungary. Mann did not reach Hungary before the Hungarians surrendered, foiling the Taylor administration's desire 'to be the very first to congratulate [Hungary], to hail her entrance into the family of nations.'[51]

The US government's actions regarding Hungary did not remain confidential. When Mann's instructions were published by Congress in

47 'Resolutions of Sympathy with the Cause of Hungarian Freedom,' [*Illinois Journal*, 7 Sept., 1849], in Abraham Lincoln, *Collected Works*, edited by Roy P. Basler (Brunswick, NJ, 1953), I, p. 62.

48 *Philadelphia Public Ledger*, 21 Aug. 1849.

49 See excerpts from the Catholic *Boston Pilot*, quoted in John H. Komlos, *Louis Kossuth in America 1851–1852* (Buffalo, NY, 1973), pp. 148–9; Daniel R. Miller, 'American Christians and the Visit of Louis Kossuth,' *Fides Et Historia*, 20 (June 1988), pp. 5–17.

50 [Francis Bowen], 'War of the Races in Hungary,' *North American Review* 70 (Jan. 1850), pp. 78–136; Samuel E. Morison, 'Francis Bowen, An Early Test of Academic Freedom in Massachusetts,' *Massachusetts Historical Society Proceedings* 5 (Feb. 1936), pp. 507–11.

51 John Clayton to A. Dudley Mann, 18 June 1849, United States Congress, Senate, Senate Documents, 31st Congress, 1st session, docs. no. 40–48, in US Serial Set (Washington, 1979), serial no. 558.

1850, the Austrian chargé d'affaires in Washington, the Chevalier J.G. Hulsemann, protested to Secretary of State Daniel Webster against US interference in Austria's domestic affairs. Webster's response to the Chevalier Hulsemann reflected ambivalent sentiments in the USA about European revolutions, notwithstanding shows of public support.[52]

Webster at first rebuked Hulsemann sharply. To the Austrian's warning that US involvement in Europe would be met with commercial retaliation, Webster snorted 'as to such hypothetical retaliation ... the United States are willing to take their chances and abide their destiny.' Webster thus met Hulsemann's warning with, it seemed, a threat of his own as to possible US belligerence.

Elsewhere in his letter, however, Webster was less combative. He explained that the Mann mission reflected only an urge to display US sentiment about Europe, not to interfere. The United States claimed no right to participate in foreign revolutions. Yet 'circumstances have made [the USA] ... representatives of purely popular government'; thus they 'could not ... conceal from mankind the causes' for their current global position. 'The successful [US] example of free government ... contemplated in other countries,' was the 'necessary consequence of the American Revolution'. Webster's defiance of the House of Habsburg turned out to be more a shielding action than an attack: indeed, wrote Webster, 'It is only in defence of his own government that the undersigned has expressed himself.'[53] In fact, Webster revealed that the underlying motive for his flamboyance was to inflame patriotic passions within the United States to shame any talk of the break-up of the Union over slavery; he released his Hulsemann letter to the US public.[54] At mid-century the fleeting successes of the European revolutions were cheered in the USA. But as revolution became anarchy, or counterrevolution, they instead embraced their own successful revolutionary heritage to hold Europe at a distance. Such a manoeuvre distinguished the United States from a flawed and conflicted Europe, and provided a respite from troubling domestic conditions.

The Phenomenon of Revolutionary Refugees

The last large events in the United States over the 1848 Revolutions were the displays produced when notable European revolutionary refugees

52 Donald S. Spencer, *Louis Kossuth and Young America* (Columbia, MO, 1977), pp. 30–42; Merle Curti, 'Austria and the US 1848–1852,' *Smith College Studies in History*, 11 (April 1926), pp. 152–79.

53 'Correspondence with the Chevalier Hulsemann,' in Daniel Webster, *Works*, ed., Edward Everett (Boston, 1853), VI, pp. 488–504.

54 Webster confided his motives in a letter to George Ticknor, 16 Jan. 1851. *Writings and Speeches*, XVI, p. 586.

came to the republic in late 1851 and 1852 asking for relief. By this time European reaction was fully entrenched. In 1849 Frederick William IV trumped the Frankfurt Assembly by offering the German people a constitution, something which the 'Professors' Parliament' had never produced.[55] In Italy Pius IX returned to the Vatican in 1850, assisted by French military occupation of a defeated city of Rome. Louis Napoleon, calling himself Napoleon III, executed a coup in 1851 that gave him dictatorial authority, wiping out the civil rights programme the French republic had initiated. Now fallen European revolutionaries hoped to stir the USA to rekindle from a distance what European patriots had been unable to sustain in the face of resurgent old authority. One European celebrity, the Hungarian Lajos Kossuth, in particular provoked sympathisers in the USA into public exercises and inspired statements about US and European conditions in the past and present. These US exercises to celebrate the presence of this revolutionary refugee revealed important differences between the outlook and aspirations of actual European revolutionaries and their potential US benefactors.

Cannon and rifle salutes greeted the Hungarian hero when he arrived in Manhattan in December 1851, following the decision of the United States Congress to transport him from Europe to the USA. Kossuth was welcomed by the New York mayor, accompanied by the Richmond Guards, the same corps that received and attended the Marquis de Lafayette on his US tour in 1824. Kossuth began a speech, but was cut off by crowds who rushed the podium. The Guards, who had been invited only to add colour to the event, instead had to repel well-wishers mobbing Kossuth and his small group of Magyar followers. Finally the Hungarians escaped the throng, and embarked in carriages for a military procession up Broadway Avenue.

The Broadway welcome of Kossuth was 'a scene such as the world seldom beholds', as the *New York Times* described it.[56] Repeated across the northern and western parts of the country, the event signalled a return to the extraordinary displays of revolutionary sentiment in the spring of 1848. On sidewalks and in stores vendors hawked a litany of 'Kossuth articles': 'the "Kossuth khaban," "Kossuth boots," "Kossuth gloves," "Kossuth cigars," "Kossuth punch," "Kossuth" everything, from the most delicate lace to the grossest human food,' according to a report.[57] A rostrum in front of the New York City Hall, where Kossuth spoke briefly,

55 The constitution imposed by the Prussian monarch restricted suffrage and imposed a tiered voting system, disenfranchising lower-income groups. It was less liberal than what the Frankfurt Parliament had in mind. See Elmar M. Hucko (ed.), *The Democratic Tradition: Four German Constitutions* (New York, 1987), pp. 3–23.

56 *New York Times*, 6 Dec. 1851.

57 *New York Tribune*, 8, 29 Dec. 1851, 6 Jan. 1852.

was covered by bunting shaped in the forms of the Hungarian tricolour and the French and US liberty cap. Hotels, stores and saloons hoisted portraits of Lajos Kossuth, George Washington, the Turkish Sultan and the British Lion. (The latter two images commemorated the temporary asylums provided Kossuth by Turkey and Britain.)

The organisation of the Hungarian's parade procession showed a sense of past revolutionary valour acted out by diverse contemporary bearers of that sentiment. Military regiments marched in the parade's first division, comprised conspicuously of immigrant as well as native volunteers. The Irish Volunteers, the La Fayette Fusileers, German Hussars and the Washington Guard, 'in old style with blue and buff coats, high boots, and powdered wigs and tails,' as an observer described them, gave the division a martial flavour. The second division included Kossuth, the mayor, other officials – ranging from the US district attorney to the county coroner – and Revolutionary War veterans. The third division included firemen's companies, German turners, exiled from Germany for their revolutionary associations, and representatives of New York unions: omnibus proprietors, journeymen tailors and butchers. These labour groups all marched behind a banner, 'The Sons of Liberty'. Different constituencies aligned in the Kossuth cause. They included bourgeois and working-class groups, natives and immigrants, in a celebration of the defeated, and the defeat of, the romantic European revolutionary.[58]

It has never been necessary for someone to live in the United States very long, or very well, to be able to recall the country's origins in a revolution. The experience of embracing fallen European revolutionary refugees unified different groups in the USA by prodding them to evoke a distinct US revolutionary heritage.

Yet even while Kossuth was the recipient of US generosity, he began to alienate some observers and began the ignominious finale of his experience in the USA. He refused to declare himself against slavery, enraging abolitionists who saw a double standard in his requests for assistance to liberate Hungary.[59] He frightened Catholics, especially when he toured the west and lectured about a Jesuit conspiracy to take over the world.[60] His appeal to southerners waned once he actually arrived in the southern states. Despite his neutrality on slavery, his ideas for US action in Europe were received coldly, in the words of one southern state legislature, as

58 Spencer, *Louis Kossuth and Young America*, pp. 5–9; Francis and Theresa Pulszky, *White, Red, Black* (New York, 1853), I, pp. 51–75; *New York Times*, 6 Dec. 1851; Marcus Cunliffe, *Soldiers and Civilians* (Boston, 1968), pp. 223–6, 402–3.

59 Spencer, *Louis Kossuth and Young America*, p. 69.

60 Miller, 'American Christians and the Visit of Louis Kossuth,' 5–17; Henry F. Brownson (ed.), *Orestes A. Brownson's Middle Life* (Detroit, MI, 1899), pp. 418–24.

'anti-American'.[61] Kossuth, the visiting European radical, was celebrated in the USA as a martyr. But his audience then asserted a different US revolutionary experience, and could not bring themselves to truly embrace his cause.

The Campaign of 1852 and Revolutionary Europe

Especially as regards the parties' reaction to the visit of Kossuth, the presidential campaign of 1852, like its predecessor of 1848, invoked transatlantic revolutionary themes, although in a different way. Parties were recovering from their extreme labours to pass the Compromise of 1850, which temporarily solved the slavery dispute by granting both pro-slavery and antislavery forces pieces of favourable legislation. The Compromise in large part undermined the drive for a third party, as Democrats and Whigs persuaded voters that it represented a final solution of the slavery question. The Free Democratic Party, which is what Free Soilers of 1848 now called themselves, received only half of its 1848 total vote.[62]

The visible element of the European revolutions in the 1852 election was the presence of Kossuth. He urged the formation of a German-American voting bloc 'without party respect' for the political candidate who would support European intervention. Many Democrats responded favourably to Kossuth's pleas. At an elaborate banquet in Washington, Kossuth heard one Democrat after another endorse the principle of intervention, either as a reflection of new US power, or as a reciprocation of the foreign intervention from which the Americans had benefited in the War for Independence.

Yet the two most prominent luminaries at the banquet, Lewis Cass and Stephen Douglas, remained aloof. Cass's reputation for equivocation had doomed him in 1848. In 1852 he did nothing to change that image. He first called for US aid to Hungary, then changed his mind. At the Kossuth banquet he declared that the United States should 'insist' that Russia not interfere with Hungary, a statement that in its weakness was worse than either silence or a more firm declaration. Douglas, likewise, did not toast Kossuth, but condemned the Whig administration of Millard Fillmore for interfering with the recent filibustering expedition of Narciso López against Cuba. Douglas calculated his criticism to gain support in the south, since many southerners supported US intervention in Cuba for its potential as a slave colony. But southerners had interpreted Kossuth's cordial reception in the north as a misdirected gesture

61 Louisiana legislature resolution reported in the *New Orleans Daily Picayune*, 21 March 1852.

62 Frederick J. Blue, *Free Soilers* (Urbana, IL, 1973), pp. 232–3.

organised by Europhile Democrats and Negro-loving Free Soilers. Douglas won southern sympathy, but his presidential campaign faltered amid publicity he received from the zealous *Democratic Review* editor, George Sanders, whose exhortations for an active European policy frightened voters as the Democratic national convention approached.[63] Revealing the emerging emphasis among all parties *on not losing* the liberty that did exist within the United States, the Democratic platform of 1852 resolved 'that in view of the condition of popular institutions in the Old World, a high and sacred duty is devolved … upon the democratic party of this country … to uphold the rights of every State … and to sustain *among us* constitutional liberty.'[64] Democrats nominated Franklin Pierce, a New Hampshire governor, whose appeal lay in his independence from Washington, his support for the 1850 compromise and his lack of interest in Europe. Such events repudiated both Democratic fervour about the potential for change in Europe apparent in 1848 and Kossuth's plea for a bold US presence in Europe in 1852.

Whigs were even less circumspect than Democrats, categorically rejecting the idea of a liberation of Europe by the USA. The Whig platform pledged the party's sympathy for 'struggling freedom everywhere', but invoked the teachings of 'the Father of the Country' against 'propagating our opinions, or imposing upon other countries our forms of government … [except for] teaching by example … the blessings of self-government.' Whigs nominated the war hero (in 1812 and 1846) Winfield Scott, who, somewhat like Pierce, was attractive for his lack of opinion on slavery and foreign intervention, the sensitive issues of 1852.[65]

It was the Free Soil supporters, now the Free Democratic Party, who gave the most demonstrative signs of hearkening to Kossuth's plea for a national policy of activism in Europe. The Barnburner Democrats, responsible for much of the Free Soil support in 1848, in 1852 returned to the main Democratic Party. Thus the Free Democratic Party consisted principally of Massachusetts and Ohio antislavery Whigs. The party platform condemned the Compromise of 1850 and especially the Fugitive Slave Act. Perhaps to attract supporters still eager to intervene in Europe, or, in tacit acknowledgement of the idealism of their cause, the Free Democrats resolved that 'every nation has a right to alter its government … Foreign interference with that right is a violation of the law of nations … [E]specially is it the duty of the American government, the chief republic

63 Spencer, *Louis Kossuth and Young America*, pp. 113–16, 160–1; Arthur James May, *Contemporary American Opinion of the Mid-Century Revolutions in Central Europe* (Philadelphia, 1927), pp. 117–18.

64 *National Party Platforms 1840–1860*, p. 18. Emphasis added.

65 *Ibid.*, p. 20; Mark W. Summers, *The Plundering Generation* (New York, 1987), pp. 187–94.

of the world, to protest against ... the intervention of kings and emperors against nations seeking to establish for themselves republican or constitutional governments.'[66] This was precisely the kind of endorsement that Kossuth had asked for. In a speech to New York Germans in June 1852, he called for 'German citizens [to] unite with a third independent party' espousing interventionism.[67] But in the national election German-Americans remained Democrats anyway, vindicating the Democrat Franklin Pierce's idea that their vote still could be taken for granted. Charles Sumner, a supporter of the Free Democrats, privately voiced the sharp isolationist sentiment that connected all of the parties in 1852, which Kossuth's interventionist pleas, although received with public enthusiasm, had served to uncover. 'Individuals may do as they please,' wrote Sumner, '[but] Kossuth errs – all err who ask any intervention by GOVERNMENT ... I am [an] enthusiast for Freedom, but that is not practical.'[68]

The Legacy of the 1848 Revolutions in the USA

Europe from 1848 to 1852 went from the dreams of liberal democracy to the familiarity of imperial rule and the reality of martial order. Similar events in different forms began at the same time in the United States. The Mexican War and excitement in Europe fostered a US third-party movement, seeking, in a way, a revolution in US politics. But, as in Europe, the results of that search were anticlimactic: voters returned in droves to the two major parties in 1852, in numbers decisive for the Democrats.[69] In the wake of Franklin Pierce's 1852 election, Horace Greeley wrote 'we have been wickedly beaten by a coalition of the Go-Slowly factions against us. I mean now to lie quiet a while and see how the world goes on.'[70] The *New York Tribune* editor had earlier evinced perhaps the most support of any journalist for transatlantic social change during the years of European revolution. But he plodded back to the old Whig party in 1852 rather than seek political overhaul. Based on these contemporaneous, conservative episodes, the USA and Europe both seemed to be returning to the *status quo ante bellum.*

66 *National Party Platforms 1840–1860*, p. 19.

67 *New York Tribune*, 26, 28 June 1852; George Templeton Strong, *Diary*, II, p. 98, entry for 27 June 1852.

68 Charles Sumner to John Bigelow, 13 Dec. 1851, in John Bigelow, *Retrospections of an Active Life* (New York, 1909), I, p. 123.

69 William E. Gienapp, *Origins of the Republican Party 1852–1856* (New York, 1987), pp. 28, 31; William O. Lynch, 'Antislavery Tendencies of the Democratic Party in the Northwest, 1848–1850,' *Mississippi Valley Historical Review* 11 (Dec. 1929), pp. 330–1.

70 Horace Greeley to Mrs Bruce Kirby, 6 Dec. 1852, Horace Greeley Papers, New York Public Library.

Yet by 1854 indications of change in the USA were afoot. By the 1850s the federal government had wrestled with the jurisdictional problems of slavery for decades. Shortly after mid-century, US policy-makers acted, they hoped, to solve slaveholders' demands for national protection. The Kansas–Nebraska Act of 1854 allowed slavery to be carried farther into the western territories than ever before, subject to local settlers deciding for or against the institution.[71] However, that idea provoked more conflict than it resolved. It increased antislavery support across the north via the perception of the revolutionary intentions of the 'slave power' to spread slavery beyond timeworn boundaries.[72] The Kansas–Nebraska Act, wrote a New Yorker, 'is ... to change the common law of the United States from freedom as the fathers of the Republic understood it to slavery as the modern slave propagandist proclaims it.'[73] Antislavery support grew not as revolutionary movement but as a defensive manoeuvre against a perceived pro-slavery revolutionary threat, this time with clearly indigenous rather than international origins.

Helped as it was by growing sectional resentment, antislavery support also mounted gradually from the increased presence of liberal German refugees in US politics, refugees from the failed European revolutions. German 48ers, as they were called, brought a resentment of aristocracy they gradually levelled at protectors of slavery. In the early 1850s, i.e., largely before their loyalties moved from the Democratic Party to the Republican Party, 48ers affirmed that their interests were the same as those of the US Revolution. But in the second half of the decade radical German Republicans under the leadership of Karl Schurz played a significant role in the ascendancy of Abraham Lincoln, first as a US senator, then in 1860 as president. In this transition from Democratic to Republican support, many German revolutionary refugees changed their point of reference, expressing their resistance to slavery in the USA as the calling of true partisans of *European* democracy.[74] As it did in 1848, US political culture in the late 1850s would struggle between hanging on to the national revolutionary beginning, the spirit of '76, and embracing different, more modern revolutionary messages from Europe, the spirit of '48.

In 1856 William Stiles, the former US minister to Austria, spoke at the Georgia Democratic State Convention. Stiles spoke not to exhort party

71 The Kansas–Nebraska Act revoked the Missouri compromise of 1820, which had divided slave from free territories along a line running west from the state of Missouri. The Kansas–Nebraska Act thus opened all lands not already settled to slavery, on the basis of local decision, or 'popular sovereignty.

72 Gienapp, *Origins of the Republican Party*, pp. 76–7, 364–5.

73 Preston King to Samuel Tilden, 13 Oct. 1854, Samuel Tilden Papers, New York Public Library.

74 Bruce L. Levine, *Spirit of 1848* (Urbana, IL, 1992).

operatives but, ironically, to analyse the causes of the US Revolution. He explained that 'our revolution is ordinarily regarded [like] the struggles that occurred but a few years since in Austria, Hungary, Italy, and France; the only distinction [being] the difference between success and failure.' However, Stiles maintained, there was a difference in revolutionary objective as well as one of success versus failure. 'It was not for human rights the [US] colonists contended ... It was the right of local self-government.'[75] Presumably Stiles drew such a distinction in order to be able to claim that the US Revolution had nothing to do with the ending of slavery. But he also revealed the ambiguity about their own revolutionary heritage that came from US experience of the European revolutions. The USA's revolution had worked, thereby setting the republic apart from the revolutionary futility of Europe and doing much to create the image of an exceptional US experience and identity. Yet the USA's revolutionary accomplishment in the eighteenth century was something less than that for which the European struggles of the mid-nineteenth century aspired. The great effect of the 1848 Revolutions on the USA was not what the 1848 Revolutions achieved – but what they aspired to and failed to accomplish.

The mid-nineteenth-century struggle for the causes of local government and human rights spanned the Atlantic. In Europe, those causes generally were united. In the USA, advocates for local government and advocates for human rights were often in opposition. Most people in the USA were not prompted by the 1848 Revolutions to try to extend their Revolution's accomplishments to overhaul US society at the mid-nineteenth century. But a decade later the USA would undergo a conflict whose upheavals and attendant suffering dwarfed the preceding conflicts in Europe. In the 1860s the US states went to war over questions that they had been prodded to debate by events in Europe a little more than a decade before: whether the accomplishment of local government of the US Revolution was worth the struggle to defend, and whether an unbroken protection of human rights the US Revolution had not achieved was worth the struggle to attain. In their failed quests for greater liberty the 1848 Revolutions did not so much follow the US example of a republican revolution as they provided a glimpse of coming, more comprehensive conflicts of democracy and nation-building on both sides of the Atlantic.

75 William H. Stiles, *Address delivered before the Georgia Democratic State Convention held at Milledgeville 4 July 1856* (Atlanta, 1856).

4

Brazil's 1848: The Praieira *Revolt in Pernambuco, Brazil*

NANCY PRISCILLA NARO

The focus of this chapter is the Brazilian monarchy's last major regional rebellion, the *Praieira* Revolt (1848–1851), and its impact on the northeastern province of Pernambuco. In particular, the chapter explores the relationships among economic, social and political events that culminated in the Praia Revolt in this slave society, considering also the response of Praia leaders to the events that were unfolding in France. Traditionally described as Brazil's 1848, the Praia revolt is presented here as a provincial political movement that highlighted the uneasy relationships between local and provincial power, and the central government in the imperial court of Rio de Janeiro. Popular mobilisation over inequalities of land, class and access to jobs that marginalised poor farmers and artisans add a social dimension that, in combination with the movement's liberal and socialist overtones, lend to the Praia Revolt similarities with the 1848 'Springtime of the People' in France. Economic aspects of the movement suggest, in addition, that turbulence in international markets had an impact on sugar prices and affected planters and their creditors. Soaring food prices and interest on loans jeopardised producers who, together with poor people in the urban port of Recife, were swayed by street orators and sensationalist newspapers that highlighted social inequalities. The chapter argues that material crises, in combination with social tensions and provincial political rivalries accompanied, but were not outweighed by social visions of Praia leaders that were inspired by the revolutionary events in Europe. The article concludes that the Praia Revolt reflected class and regional tensions over centralising measures imposed by the central government during Brazil's steady, if not painless, process of nineteenth-century state building.

Global Dimensions of 1848: Latin America

Eric Hobsbawm identified 1848 as the first global revolution, with a delayed impact on Colombia, but an immediate impact upon Brazil's northeast.[1] In Colombia, the support of artisans, tradesmen and students behind the *progresista* candidate influenced the successful outcome of the election of a Liberal to power in March 1849. The reforms undertaken during the Liberal presidency included the abolition of slavery, but also echoed several social and political aims of 1848 European protests. Eduardo Posada-Carbó has described the period as one of 'rapid economic, social and political reforms that approved the introduction of direct elections and male universal suffrage, the adoption of absolute freedom of the press, and a series of drastic measures against the Catholic Church.'[2] However, he questions whether popular mobilisation and radical politics in Colombia were directly linked to events in Europe, and concludes that internal politics had a greater impact on events there than did direct influences from Europe.

Elsewhere in Latin America intellectuals debated the democratic and liberal ideals upheld by French revolutionaries. Clara Lida highlights the literary societies, political clubs and artisan groups in Chile and Mexico, where discussion of social ideas, proclamations of liberty and citizens' rights echoed what was issuing from liberal presses in Colombia.[3] In Brazil, earlier revolutionary events in the thirteen US colonies and in France had fuelled radical liberalism in the pre-independence *Inconfidência Mineira* in 1789 and the 'Tailors' Conspiracy' a decade later in 1798. The radical strand reemerged in the liberal-secessionist stands of priests in Pernambuco in the pre-Independence movement of 1817.[4] The idea of reorganising Brazil around a Republic fired political elites in these pre-Independence conflicts that abated briefly in 1822 when Brazil ruptured the colonial pact with Portugal but remained a monarchy under the crown of the Bragança

1 Eric Hobsbawm, *The Age of Revolutions, Europe 1789–1848* (London, 1962), and *The Age of Capital 1848–1875* (London, 1975), p. 78.

2 Eduardo Posada-Carbó, 'New Granada and the European Revolutions of 1848,' in this volume.

3 Clara E. Lida, 'The Democratic and Social Republic of 1848, and its Repercussions in the Hispanic World,' in this volume. See also, Hans-Joachim Konig, 'El movimiento revolucionario del 7 de abril de 1854. Artesanos y soldados contra el proyecto modernisador de los liberales en Nueva Granada,' Congreso de AHILA, Porto, 23 Sept. 1999.

4 In the short-lived, aborted pre-Independence *Inconfidência Mineira* movement in the Captaincy of Minas Gerais in 1789, discontented merchants, shopkeepers, miners and other taxpayers shared with a small number of intellectuals and low ranking militia officers' enthusiasm for an independent republic. Republicanism was at the forefront of the agenda of mulatto artisans and their supporters who, adversely affected by the urban costs of living in Salvador, Bahia, launched the Tailors' Rebellion in 1798. Leslie Bethell (ed.), *Colonial Brazil* (Cambridge, 1985); Emilia Viotti da Costa, *The Brazilian Empire: Myths and Histories* (Chicago, 1985), p. 34; Carlos Guilherme Mota, *1817* (São Paulo, n.d.).

dynasty.[5] Two years into Independence, however, secessionist and republican sentiments flared in the province of Pernambuco during the Confederation of the Equator, a short-lived regional protest that rejected the centralising features of the 1824 Constitution and proclaimed a united, secessionist Northeast. Advocates of republicanism stirred the country from time to time during the following decades, although only in the aftermath of the War of the Triple Alliance (Paraguayan War) in 1870 did a Republican Party become an official third contender in the political arena that was disputed between Liberals and Conservatives.

The economic bearing of Europe upon Latin America was directly discernible. Post-independence governments, including the Brazilian monarchy, received technological assistance from Great Britain, France and other emerging European powers as they embarked on the process of state-building. Exports of coffee from Colombia and Brazil, and sugar-cane from the Campeche areas of the Yucatán Peninsula, Venezuela, the Tucumán area of Argentina and northeast Brazil were vital components of fledgling post-independence economies. European economic quavers had an unsettling effect on producers of export commodities in Latin America in the 1840s when falling sugar prices in international markets arrested production for the export market. Domestic agrarian crises were also major factors in local and regional social movements. Popular protests against restrictions on land use for crop production, forced recruitment, and brutal exploitation by powerful local landowners mobilised *ladinos* on sugar estates in Campeche, mestizos in coastal Venezuela and poor free farmers in Colombia and Brazil. The nature of the protests, mainly quelled by national armies, recalled popular movements among the poor and disenfranchised of Europe.[6]

Pernambuco: A Regional Power on the Brink of Hard Times

The economic clout that the northeast enjoyed during the colonial period declined as coffee shifted the economic axis to the southeast during the 1830s, rapidly overtaking sugar-cane as the principle economic mainstay

5 Viotti da Costa, *The Brazilian Empire*, chapter one and p. 34.

6 In Hungary the revolution's roots were in the countryside. On European social movements see Eric Hobsbawm, *A era do capital* (Rio de Janeiro, 1977), p. 85. Louis Bergeron, François Furet, and Reinhart Koselleck (eds.), *La época de las revoluciones europeas 1780–1848* (Madrid, 1980). For Latin America in the 1840s, Tulio Halperín Donghi, *Historia de América Latina* (Rio de Janeiro, 1975), pp. 115–51; Nelson Reed, *The Caste War of Yucatan* (Stanford, 1976), chapter 8; Conselheiro Lisbôa, *Relação de uma viagem a Venezuela, Nova Granada e Equador* (Brussels, 1866), pp. 4, 42, 78, 89; John Lombardi, 'The Abolition of Slavery in Venezuela, 1820–1854,' in Robert Brent Toplin (ed.), *The Abolition of Slavery in Brazil* (Kingsport, 1972), pp. 237–42.

of post-Independence Brazil. Whereas sugar exports represented 23 per cent of Brazil's total exports to coffee's 17 per cent between 1821 and 1825, international demand reversed those figures and coffee exports reached 40 per cent of the total value of exports in the early 1830s in contrast to almost unchanging figures for sugar (23 per cent).[7] Exports of sugar, cotton and hides were vital to the economic wellbeing of the northeast and, as Brazil's second most important port, Recife was the entrepot for imported goods destined to markets between Alagoas in the northeast and Maranhão in the north. Sugar-cane and other agricultural products were transported from the neighbouring provinces of Paraíba and Alagoas to Recife, where, together with Pernambucan products, they were shipped to sugar markets in Liverpool, London, Trieste and Genoa, cotton markets in Liverpool, and markets for hides in Genoa and Le Havre.[8]

The 1840s were not propitious times for Pernambuco's producers. International sugar prices were falling and passage of the Aberdeen Bill in Britain further restricted imports of slave-produced sugar. The percentage of sugar to total exports was 26 per cent for the decade; the figures for cotton in the same period declined to 7.5 per cent.[9] Falling international sugar prices, coupled with falling exchange rates of the British pound to the Brazilian real, led to pressures by foreign merchants on local creditors, who in turn threatened to foreclose on the estates of indebted planters. Cattle herds were decimated by drought that ravaged the backlands in the first half of the decade, cotton harvests were affected by blight from 1840 to 1845, while manioc, which was the basic dietary staple of the poor, was in short supply.[10]

The economic crises that afflicted the province in the 1840s aggravated already glaring social disparities between wealthy planters, who owned vast coastal estates (*engenhos*), numerous slaves and townhouses in the capital port city of Recife, and the majority of the provincial population. Eighty-six per cent of Pernambuco's inhabitants lived inland. It is also noteworthy, given Brazil's dependence upon slave labour, that the majority of the Pernambucan population was free, representing 77 per cent of the provincial total in 1842 and 79 per cent in 1855.

Wealthy planter-elite families who were able to diversify production

7 Peter Eisenberg, *Modernisação sem mudança* (São Paulo, 1977), Table 2, p. 34.

8 Great Britain, Foreign Office, FO 13 & 128, Brazil Correspondence, Consular Dispatches from Pernambuco, Cowper to Palmerston, 1849, and 'Table Showing the Foreign Ports to which the Produce of the Province of Pernambuco was Exported during the Year ending 31 December 1847.'

9 Peter L. Eisenberg, *The Sugar Industry in Pernambuco: Modernization without Change, 1840–1910* (Berkeley, 1974), Tables 1 and 2, pp. 5, 9–10.

10 Nancy Priscilla Naro, 'Brazil's 1848: The Praieira Revolt' (unpublished PhD dissertation, University of Chicago, 1981, p. 115).

to minimise losses incurred from falling international sugar prices and exchange rates were able to ride out the uncertainties of the 1840s. Most producers were not so fortunate. Single-owners of small and medium-sized cotton-producing estates in the less fertile clay strip of the north and southern interior of Pernambuco's *zona da mata* (sugar-producing area) were hard-pressed to recover losses from blight in the 1840s. Attracted by the price disparities between sugar and cotton, many became indebted to Portuguese merchants, moneylenders and large coastal landowners as they hastened to undertake or expand sugar-cane production.[11] Planters in Goiânia, Pau-d'Alho, Nazaré da Mata, Limoeiro and the southern areas of Bonito and Agua Preta were at a disadvantage to coastal producers who benefited from rich *massapê* soils, proximity to the port of Recife and the intricate river system that irrigated southern, fertile, coastal soils. In addition, they faced export tariffs mounting to 10 per cent and uncertain foreign markets for cotton. High prices for slaves, who were mainly concentrated in the coastal sugar-producing areas, intensified with British surveillance of the African trade, while alternatives to slave labour among unskilled and semi-skilled migrant labourers from the drought-afflicted backlands were swept up by the large coastal sugar estates. On the peripheries of the sugar belt, economic tensions played into the deteriorating political climate of the 1840s.

Mounting Opposition to the Conservative Rego Barros Provincial Presidency

During Brazil's Regency in the 1830s two national Liberal and Conservative parties emerged, although local and regional considerations frequently outweighed national programmes. In general, conservatives were recruited from the regional export oligarchies and advocated free trade, the moderating power of the emperor and a centralised government.[12] In Pernambuco, conservative provincial president Francisco Rego Barros, who was appointed under the cabinet of 19 September 1837, was granted an extended mandate by the Conservative 1842 cabinet to rule until 1844. Rego Barros also derived immediate benefit from the 1840–1841 Laws of the Regression (Institutional Acts) that placed commanding provincial

11 The Portuguese merchants who handled retail and wholesale trade were the principal moneylenders to planters whose future crops served as collateral for purchases of imported materials, such as machinery, farming tools, as well as the Africans who would use them, Antônio de Figueiredo, *O Progresso*, cited in Amaro Quintas, *O sentido social da Revolução Praieira* (Rio de Janeiro, 1967), p. 24.

12 José Murilo de Carvalho, *Teatro de sombras: a política imperial* (Rio de Janeiro, 1988), p. 154; a fuller version is found in his *A Construção da ordem* (Rio de Janeiro, 1996) ch. 8.

political appointments (local and provincial police, National Guard, and judiciary) under the authority of imperial ministries in Rio de Janeiro, where he and his family enjoyed imperial favour.[13] Extensive kinship ties that linked the Rego Barros family with other important ruling coastal planter elites and sugar exporters favoured these families with control over coveted and lucrative tax farming contracts, protection of key slave trading routes, slave markets, and the importation, commerce and distribution of goods that were destined for neighbouring provinces. The Rego Barros government, in tandem with Portuguese slave traders and retail merchants, administered a small but powerful vertical hierarchy of political power and economic influence that members of the political opposition found impossible to challenge.[14]

The Brazilian Liberal Party favoured limitations on the moderating power of the emperor, supported provincial and local autonomy, protection of local manufactures, election rather than appointment of police and judicial officials, and separation of police and judicial functions. The leader of the provincial Pernambucan Liberal Party, Rego Barros's kinsman Antonio Francisco Holanda Cavalcanti de Albuquerque (hereafter referred to as Holanda) was the most senior Liberal provincial spokesman and held, in addition, a lifetime appointment to the imperial senate. Despite his official opposition to Conservatives in Pernambuco, his family loyalties to Conservative political elites outweighed his liberal political positions. In 1842, in protest over Holanda's inability to negotiate a share of the paid positions in Rego Barros's tightly controlled provincial civil service, public works or in commerce, dissident traders, planters, small-scale farmers, liberal professionals, newspaper publishers, artisans and the unemployed defected from the Liberal party. With the collaboration of future Praia congressmen, Joaquim Nunes Machado, Urbano Sabino Pessoa de Mello, and Jerônimo Vilella de Castro Tavares, and with the editors of leaflets and provincial newspapers, they formed the National Party of Pernambuco (Partido Nacional de Pernambuco).[15] The *Diario Novo* newspaper, mouthpiece of their opposition faction, was owned by Luiz Inácio Ribeiro Roma and his two brothers, sons of the Catholic priest Padre Roma, an advocate in the 1817 movement for a constitutional assembly to establish a republic.[16] The location of *Diario Novo* on the Rua

13 Under the 1840 Procedural Code and the December 3 1841 Institutional Act spelling out a single party system.

14 A detailed evaluation of the political nature of the Rego Barros government is to be found in Naro, *Brazil's 1848*, chapter two.

15 Francisco Augusto Pereira da Costa, *Diccionário biographico de pernambucanos celebres* (Recife, 1882). Isabel Marson, *A rebelião praieira* (São Paulo, c.1975), p. 49.

16 Naro, 'Brazil's 1848', p. 98.

da Praia (Beach Street), in the heart of Recife, equated the street in the popular mind with the National Party; hence, the popular name '*Praieira*'.

The Onset of Liberal Rule and the Transition to Praia Government in Pernambuco

The Praia successfully launched six candidates to occupy Liberal seats in the imperial Congress, and in the January 1844 elections the Liberal Party achieved significant countrywide gains. The benefit of Liberal rule was not immediately felt in Pernambuco, despite the new National Party's intensified opposition to Rego Barros and its campaign to be acclaimed the sole voice of the provincial Liberal Party. But the Praia lacked the support in other provinces to enable it to compete effectively with the Conservative/Liberal sugar-planting elite that enjoyed such longstanding favour with the emperor. Hence, Liberal party stalwarts loyal to Holanda defected to the Conservative Party, leaving the Praia as a mere faction with a limited regional power base.

The Praia Party, then, was a dissident wing of the Pernambucan Liberal Party whose principal objective was to govern the province. To that end the Praia sought the support of judges, provincial and imperial congressmen, journalists and planters in a campaign to denigrate the Rego Barros-Cavalcanti planter oligarchy, which it labelled *baronistas* (titled nobility), *trapixeiros* (owners of warehouses on the quays and of sugar mills) and *guabirus* (rats), in reference to their alleged misuse of public revenues for private purposes and their joint control over the Conservative and Liberal Parties. In May 1844 the Liberals came to power nationally. The Liberal ministry dissolved the Congress, and Pernambucan Conservative congressmen returned to Pernambuco leaving Holanda as the principal provincial negotiator over provincial matters, in particular the appointment of Rego Barros's successor to the provincial presidency. The first two Liberal successors to Rego Barros were native Pernambucans who changed little. The third appointee, however, was an outsider who, within a month of taking office, dismissed 300 Rego Barros political appointees in the provincial police, the National Guard and the army, replacing them with Praia partisans.[17]

Meanwhile, The *Diario Novo* became the official government daily and on 10 August 1844 announced the launch of the Praia as a political party:

17 The three presidents of Pernambuco were Marcelino de Brito, Thomaz Xavier and Manoel de Souza, Joaquim Nabuco, *Um estadista do Imperio: Nabuco de Araújo, sua vida, suas opiniões, sua época*, vol. I (São Paulo, 1936), pp. 56–7.

> The Praia is a powerful party which has almost unanimous provincial support, a party which embraces open and national causes. Throughout the province it has won the backing of landowners and *engenho* owners who repudiate personalistic politics. Our party is intelligent, powerful, wealthy, and deserving of trust.[18]

The Chichorro de Gama da Gama Government

From 11 July 1845 to 26 April 1848 Antônio Pinto Chichorro de Gama da Gama, a Bahian supporter of the Praia, served as president of Pernambuco. Under his presidency the Praia came into its own. The party launched a two-fold offensive against Conservative rivals and foreigners, fully implementing the 1840–1841 reforms by replacing civil servants in the lowest echelons of public service, such as porters and bailiffs, with Praia supporters.[19]

The Praia under Chichorro de Gama also launched a campaign to denounce inequalities in land distribution that they held to be a principal cause of the province's social ills. One Pernambucan political observer, Antônio Pedro de Figueiredo, described by Pernambucan historians as an influential Socialist and Republican writer who eventually fell out with the Praia, a *Cousin Fusco* (dark-skinned version of the French philosopher Victor Cousin) of the times, observed in his journal, *O Progresso*, that:

> Today more than three-quarters of the population of our province is concentrated in a 10 to 15 league stretch from the coast. With few exceptions, almost all of the land belongs to a small number of large landowners who cultivate but a tiny portion of their holdings but refuse to sell the rest. Some 200 to 300,000 of our compatriots live on lands from which they can be evicted within a matter of hours; humble vassals of the landowner whose hatreds, political party, and company they are bound to support.[20]

Figueiredo linked the monopoly over land to dependent social relationships that subjected poor freedmen to the powerful clique of local political bosses, termed *coroneis,* in recognition of their commands in the National Guard. Large landowners were held accountable for the instability of leasing arrangements, as well as for refusing to sell uncultivated tracts of land, and were accused of obliging poor farmers to become dependent on them for transportation, marketing and personal favours. Under the conditions that Richard Graham has called the 'unspoken bargain', benevolence

18 *Diario Novo,* 10 Aug. 1844.

19 Nabuco, *Um estadista do Imperio,* p. 57.

20 Antônio Pedro de Figueiredo, *O Progresso,* vol. 2, pp. 158–9. See Vamireh Chacon, *História das idéias socialistas do Brasil,* 2nd ed. (Rio de Janeiro, 1981), p. 25, and Amaro Quintas, *O sentido social,* pp. 131–4.

and force were the two components of this unequal system of control.[21] It was not uncommon for a poor freeman to seek co-parenthood with a patron for personal protection, to secure work or avoid recruitment into the army. Association with the powerful was a route into service in the private forces of a landowner, the local police or the National Guard. Desertion from one patron to a rival planter was an invitation to revenge, with the offender facing eviction, arrest and even death.

Praia pamphleteers and speechwriters drew upon Figueiredo's arguments regarding land, labour and social inequalities in order to mobilise the free population against landed elites. In addition, the Praia launched a campaign against restrictions in the job market, beginning with a manifesto to artisans that promised trade schools, improvements in health care and the founding of orphanages. The Praia campaign protested against recent trade arrangements with France and Great Britain that allowed the importation of foreign manufactured goods and undercut local artisan production. Most significantly, however, Portuguese immigrants were singled out in the Praia press, and in the speeches of street orators, for monopolising the market for free skilled labour by favouring their countrymen for positions as clerks and artisans, for demanding high rates of interest for loans and for profiting from the importation of cheap and abundant African slave labour that displaced the free working population of the province.

The Praia Provincial Administration and Conservative Reprisals

In addition to social reforms Chichorro de Gama endorsed legislation to weaken the Conservative Party. Taking advantage of an electoral law of 19 August 1846 that charged provincial presidents with the organisation of electoral colleges, Chichorro de Gama gerrymandered important Conservative parishes and municipal strongholds. His government also annulled a provincial law whereby police and civil service appointees from the previous Rego Barros government had been granted lifetime positions.[22] The administration replaced Rego Barros appointees on the police payroll with Praia supporters, and, through additional recruitment, increased local forces from 600 in 1846 to 800 in 1847.

Conservative opponents labelled the Praia a band of ambitious, starving, turbulent, discontented agitators, lacking judgement to govern:

21 Richard Graham, *Patronage and Politics in Nineteenth-Century Brazil* (Stanford, 1990), p. 33.

22 Naro, 'Brazil's 1848', p. 124, and Table 12 'Population Changes in the Ten most Populated Pernambucan Districts,' p. 125.

> With few exceptions, ambition, self-promotion, or illusion drew the inferior and ignorant classes of the population, who, judging themselves disinherited from social benefits, or oppressed by tyrannical laws offensive to their imagined rights, harvested in their hearts feelings of hatred, envy, and vengeance against the superior classes.[23]

They accused the Praia of encouraging violence and disorder by strengthening public authority to counteract the sizeable private forces of prominent Conservatives. The Conservative *Lidador* broadsheet, under the title 'Proletarians will soon occupy all the Judgeships', charged the Praia with invading the engenhos of political enemies and appointing illiterate and unqualified commanders to the police and National Guard.[24]

Was violence replacing discourse, as the people claimed a stake in the political system? According to Conservative Joaquim Nabuco, by exploiting social inequalities and ethnic divisions, the Praia rallied massive popular support that gave it an unassailable majority in the province.[25] Conservative provincial police chief, Jerônimo Martiniano Figueira de Melo described the political mood in the province:

> As a necessary and infallible consequence of these manipulations the Province divided into two parties. To the first, fostered by mutual attraction, were attracted all the landowners, businessmen, and capitalists; all of the enlightened classes; all of the highest echelons. To the other party, with a few exceptions (almost always the effect of ambition, self-interest, or illusion), were attracted the inferior and ignorant classes of the population who, judging themselves disinherited from social welfare, or oppressed by tyrannical laws that offended their supposed rights, nourished in their hearts feelings of hatred, envy and revenge of the most serious nature against the superior classes. Those who heard their language, knew their aspirations, and foresaw the deplorable consequences that would result if they were realised, were forced to take precautions.[26]

23 Rio de Janeiro. Arquivo Nacional. Correspondência do Presidente de Pernambuco para o Ministro de Império, IJ8, 1846–1847.

24 *Lidador*, 18 May 1847.

25 '[o] partido Praieiro, que tinha incontestavelmente a grande maioria da provincia, podia julgar-se de antemão victorioso', Nabuco, *Um estadista do Imperio*, p. 62.

26 'Como consequência necessária e infalível destes manejos resultou que a Província se dividisse em dois Partidos: que a um deles destivessem ligados, por mútua atração, todos os proprietários, negociantes e capitalistas; todas as classes ilustradas; todos os primeiros empregados da Província; e que ao outro, guardadas algumas exceções (quase sempre efeita da ambição, do interesse ou da ilusão), aderissem as classes inferiores e ignorantes da poulação que, julgando-se deserdadas dos bens sociais ou oprimidas por leis tirânicas e ofensivas dos seus supostos direitos, nutriam no coração os sentimentos de ódio, de inveja e de vingança contra as classes superiores no mais elevado ponto de exaltação, e inspiravam assim os mais sérios cuidados a quantos ouviam a sua linguagem, observavam suas aspirações e perscrutavam no futuro as

Conservatives in the province and in Rio further accused Chichorro de Gama of endorsing fraud and of overriding the provincial legislative assembly in the 1846 elections for the imperial Senate, from which he emerged as victor. Amassing support among the Conservative majority in the Senate, the defeated Conservative slate of Pernambuco succeeded in having the election annulled. Rescheduled for 1847, the election was again annulled after repetition of the 1846 results.

Fearing reprisals in the aftermath of these annulments, Conservative planters on the southern sugar frontier areas of Una, Escada and Vitoria de Santo Antão began to mobilise private armies to defend their estates against expected incursions by the Praia police. In Iguaraçu and Rio Formoso campaigns were launched from estates of Praia sympathisers, which served as political bases, as did several others located near to the border with the province of Paraíba.[27]

1848

In January 1848, the Conservative *Diario de Pernambuco* heralded the New Year on a sombre note:

> May you bring us happier days than these which just passed! ... No-one of good faith will disagree that our situation is very critical; commerce is stagnating, agriculture has changed little from the days of our fathers; bankruptcy looms over our finances; public education clamours for reforms that will align it with the civilised European countries; the right to hold land is deplorably regulated; labour awaits measures to rescue the sizeable and miserable working class from the assaults of sordid avarice; pauperism threatens us with all of its unspeakable consequences.[28]

The greeting was addressed to all Pernambucans at a moment when ebbing demand in foreign markets coincided with domestic agrarian crisis. The message highlights the repercussions in Pernambuco of Brazil's confrontation with Britain over the continuing transatlantic slave trade, the imperial court's distraction from domestic issues by the war in the Rio de la Plata, and the revolt raging in the interior of the province. The references to Europe's educational reforms reveals the widespread concern among provincial Conservatives that the social reforms currently being demanded in Europe would also be embraced by the Praia administration.

tristes consequências que resultariam se elas se realizassem.' Jerônimo Martiniano Figueira de Melo, *Crônica da Rebelião Praieira em 1848 e 1849* (Rio de Janeiro, 1850), pp. 4–5.

27 Naro, 'Brazil's 1848', p. 131.

28 *Diario de Pernambuco*, 3 Jan. 1848.

Figueiredo, the radical mulatto editor of *O Progresso*, welcomed the dethronement of Louis Philippe on February 24 and supported the Paris workers at their barricades in June 1848, extolling the 'supremacy of general over private good, the right to life, and the intervention of the state in commerce and industry'.[29] Yet his editorial in an April edition of *O Progresso* warned that the importation of the principles of Liberty and Fraternity to Brazil would be mistaken:

> What is Fraternity in a society that has deified egoism in all its forms and imprinted on its banner this immoral slogan: *chacun pour soi, chacun chez soi?* What can the term Liberty mean in a society in which the masses depend on a small number of men who, in fact, exercise over them the rights of life and death at the mercy of capital?[30]

Nevertheless, 'Liberty, Equality and Fraternity' served as convenient slogans for the Praia's successful campaign to exclude the Portuguese from trade. Portuguese control over overseas and retail trade was pervasive in Brazil and Praia proposals to exclude them attracted support nationally, in spite of being rejected by the national congress. Demands to deport the Portuguese were popular mainly in Recife, where violence towards Portuguese citizens peaked in December 1847, June 1848 and January 1849, eventually prompting a rescue mission by the Portuguese government.[31]

Yet the slogans of 'Liberty, Equality and Fraternity' that were used to justify the Praia campaign against the Portuguese were not invoked when it came to came to much greater inequality of slavery. As Afonso d'Albuquerque Melo, a Praia supporter, declared in August, 1848:

> We cannot do without slaves, and through the gradual introduction of European immigrants a little at a time [slavery] can end without any surprise at its demise. This said, the Equality proclaimed by the Republic cannot favour the slaves among us and whoever desires a republican government in

29 *O Progresso*, n.d., cited in Quintas, *O sentido social*, p. 163.

30 'Que é a Fraternidade, num grêmio social que deificou o egoísmo sob todas as formas, e escreveu na sua bandeira esta imoral divisa: *chacun pour soi, chacun chez soi?* Que é que pode significar o vocábulo Liberdade numa sociedade em que as massas dependem de um pequeno número de homens, que, de fato exercem sobre elas um direito de vida e de mortes por mercê do capital?' *O Progresso*, 20 April 1848.

31 In the aftermath of the stoning of a dancehall and assaults on Portuguese as they left the hall in January 1849, many sought refuge aboard British naval ships anchored in Recife harbour. Provisions on British ships were insufficient and, as a result of the lack of safeguards to protect Portuguese citizens, the resident Portuguese Consul requested urgent assistance from his government. On 25 May 1849, three shiploads of Portuguese clerks, merchants, overseers, and retail traders and their families embarked on Portuguese vessels and were taken to settle the southern frontier of Angola, in Mossamedes.

> Brazil cannot wish to end slavery, since this would mean the annihilation of the Republic.[32]

As 1848 unfolded, there was little promise of relief from the economic crisis besetting much of the Brazilian northeast. Foreign businessmen abandoned trade in the ports of the northeast; those who remained suspended credit in light of worsening conditions.[33] Local authorities bemoaned the shortage of funds and alerted the central government to the increasing violence and crime.[34] Government concern over political and social unrest in Pernambuco, and its potential effect on neighbouring provinces, compromised support in Rio for the Praia government. In addition to the annulment of the results of the two senatorial elections, Praia nominations to National Guard commands were rejected in June 1848 due to 'excessive partisan spirit among the candidates'.[35]

The Conservative opposition intensified in pamphlets, broadsheets, speeches and private letters to friends and political allies in the Court. Private forces were placed on alert in Rio Formoso, Nazaré-da-Mata, Limoeiro and the Escada borders with Agua Preta. In an abrupt gesture, Holanda resigned his senate seat and returned to Pernambuco to reclaim his leadership of the Liberal Party in the province. The return of this revered native son rekindled traditional party loyalties and generated a dissident group within the Praia, the 'Praia Novo', who regenerated the traditional Cavalcanti-Rego Barros Conservative/Liberal coalition of ruling families.

The Praieira *Revolt*

In September 1848 the Conservatives were returned to national office under a Conservative cabinet at the head of which was Pernambuco's

32 'Nos não podemos deixar de ter escravos, e só com o tempo, e com a introdução de colonos europeus, se os pode ir acabando pouco a pouco, e sem que se sinta de repente a sua falta; por isto, a Igualdade que proclama a república não pode ser entre nós para os escravos, e quem deseja o governo republicano no Brasil não pode querer acabar com a escravatura, porque será isto o mesmo que aniquilar a República.' Afonso d'Albuquerque Melo, *A Verdade*, 21 Aug. 1848, cited in Figueira de Melo, *Autos do inquérito da Revolução Praieira* (Brasília, 1978), introduction by de Vamireh Chacon, p. xxvii.

33 Lisbon, Arquivo do Torre de Tombo, Ministério de Relações Exteriores, Consul e Pernambuco, Batista Moreira to Ministério, 12 July 1848.

34 Rio de Janeiro, Arquivo Nacional, *Relatório que o Exmo Presidente de Província de Pernambuco apresentou a Assembléia Legislativa da Província* (Recife, 1845–1850), *Relatório da Repartição dos Negocios da Justiça apresentado a Assembléia geral Legislativa* (Rio de Janeiro, 1840–1850).

35 Edison Carneiro, *A insurreição Praieira* (Rio de Janeiro, 1960), p. 181. Naro, 'Brazil's 1848', p. 135.

elder statesman and former regent of Brazil, Pedro de Araújo Lima. Five Conservatives in a row succeeded Chichorro de Gama to the presidency of Pernambuco, beginning with Herculano Ferreira Pena, who took office on 17 October 1848. Under his administration Conservatives assumed the important provincial positions of Commander at Arms and Chief of Police, placing their followers in the civil service, National Guard commands and police. Praia incumbents were passed over or denied reinstatement. On 7 November 1848, in desperation, they issued a call to arms, launching the first stage of the Praia Revolt. An armed group of Praia planters, poor freemen, artisans, migrant workers and dismissed civil servants, armed with weapons and ammunition they were said to have amassed during the Chichorro de Gama administration, headed north from Olinda.

Resembling a 'primitive' social movement, the first stage of the revolt involved skirmishes, assaults, the burning of cane fields and liberation of prisoners from local jails. Most of the confrontations took place on the inland peripheries of the sugar zone in and around 20 *engenhos* that served as hideouts, headquarters and munitions deposits for both sides. Some towns, such as Nazaré da Mata, were also taken. Actual numbers of participants were small – estimates hover around 0.4 per cent of the free Pernambucan population. The Pena administration dispatched troops to confront and halt the advance of this small Praia army. The first major encounter took place at the Engenho Mussupinho in Iguaraçú on 14 November 1848 where Praia forces were attacked by troops of the regular army, private forces, and battalions of recruits from a neighbouring *engenho*.[36]

Rival planter groups led and equipped migrants, unemployed, and resident free farmers who were rapidly enlisted into police and National Guard forces.[37] Others were mobilised by private armies to patrol the sugar zone and dispatch information on enemy movements. In the southern *zona da mata*, prominent Conservative landowners, Francisco Rego Barros and José Velloso de Silveira, reported to government troops, police, army and National Guard commanders on the movements and whereabouts of Praia forces. Agua Preta was the southern stronghold of José Velloso da Silveira, an important leader of the *Cabanos* movement of the 1830s, and a controlling figure in the contraband slave trade between Pernambuco and the neighouring province of Alagoas. A long-standing associate of Rego Barros and bandit leaders in Alagoas, Velloso was able

36 Carneiro, *Insurreição*, p. 18; Naro, 'Brazil's 1848'. The issue of personal animosity behind the attack was reported in the *Diario Novo*, 27 Nov. 1848, p. 3.

37 Naro, 'Brazil's 1848', ch. 6, for details of skirmishes in forested areas and *engenhos* in the northern, southern, and western frontiers of the sugar zone.

to call upon the assistance of local potentates. On one occasion, when the acting police chief of Agua Preta claimed that his forces were unable to stop the advances of the Praia, a Conservative judge requested arms and ammunition from Velloso 'to quell the proponents of anarchy, causers of so many evils'.[38]

The provincial capital, Recife, was also placed on alert. In early November 1848 President Pena postponed local elections for councils and JPs for one month, after which he postponed them indefinitely. Under his presidency, the *Diario de Pernambuco* was restored to its former official standing, replacing the Praia's *Diario Novo*. Imperial measures also contributed to the erosion of Praia support: two Praia vice-presidents were dismissed from provincial office and 25 judges removed from their county posts. Meanwhile, a prominent Conservative judge, statesman and senator, José Thomaz Nabuco de Araujo, was appointed to the first criminal ward of Recife, from where he would preside over the trial of Praia defendants in August, 1849.

Police raids on his home and newspaper, and rumours of his imminent arrest, precipitated the flight from Recife of João Ignacio Ribeiro Roma, publisher of the *Diario Novo* and a leading Praia intellectual. Ribeiro headed for the interior to coordinate Praia forces under the command of *engenho* owner Manuel Pereira de Moraes. Meanwhile, Antonio Borges de Fonseca, a Paraiban journalist and lawyer who had fought in the 1817 and 1824 rebellions, organised Praia reinforcements in the forests of the sugar zone northwest of Recife. The departure of these two leading figures for the battlegrounds of the interior coincided with the arrival in Recife of Praia congressman, Joaquim Nunes Machado, whose leadership marked a turning point in the Praia movement. As fighting escalated in the interior Nunes Machado launched an appeal for support from liberals in neighbouring provinces and prepared for the eventual mobilisation of interior forces to advance on Recife, an event that took place on 2 February 1849.

The Second Stage of the Praia Movement

The second stage of the Praia Revolt was ushered in by a political manifesto issued by eight Praia congressmen on 25 November 1848. The manifesto held President Pena accountable for the persecution of the locals, the conversion of ships of war into prison ships, the sacking of *engenhos* and raids on the *Diario Novo* involving the physical mistreatment

38 Recife. *Arquivo Público do Estado de Pernambuco*, Promotor Público, Francisco Gonçalves de Rocha, para Herculano Ferreira Pena, Presidente da Província, Rio Formoso, 19 Nov. 1848.

of its owner.[39] Lamenting that the heavens over Pernambuco had collapsed since the departure of President Chichorro de Gama and his successor from the province, the manifesto, entitled 'What are We to Do?' stated:

> (We will) Accompany our compatriots in their glorious defense, protest in the name of the constitution and the emperor against these atrocities which have been committed by an imperial appointee, and hope that the name of Senhor Herculano Ferreira Pena may be detested by honourable Pernambucans and by all Brazilians.[40]

Another non-Pernambucan, Manoel Tosta, replaced President Pena on Christmas Day 1848. The *Diario Novo* alerted its readers:

> It is well to note that the government of Rio de Janeiro could not find one single Pernambucan worthy of serving in this province. The president, the secretary, the Commander of Arms, the police chief, the commander of all front line troops and even the Relação (Appellate Judge) were not born here ... does this present situation differ significantly from that of the former colonial regime?[41]

In the week after President Tosta's inauguration, in the midst of a raging civil war, the Praia eight congressmen issued a further proclamation calling all free men to arms to restore their rights, and vowing to fight for the convocation of a constituent assembly. Deprived of their constitutional guarantees, including that of habeas corpus, the Praia congressmen claimed to be 'forced by daggers and guns to defend themselves from the hired assassins hired from Pena's public treasury'.[42] Appealing to Pernambucans to save the province from the ignominy of another Portuguese conquest, the manifesto called for reform of an inept central government and promised that Brazilians, not foreigners, would reap the fruits of their labour. It ended:

> ... to arms, a thousand times to arms and may we race to avenge our abused nationality, our battered rights, and the independence of Brazil which is threatened by the Portuguese.[43]

39 *Manifesto dos Deputados justificando os movimentos armados e mostrando-os independentes de sua vontade e intencões*, 'O que nos cumpre fazer? Acompanhar os nossos concidadãos na sua gloriosa defesa, protestar em nome da Constituição e do Imperador contra tantas atrocidades cometidas pelo seu Delegado, e votar à execração dos pernambucanos honrados, e de todos os brasileiros o nome do Senhor Herculano Ferreira Pena.' Urbano Sabino Pessoa de Mello, *Apreciação da Revolta Praieira em Pernambuco* (Rio de Janeiro, [1849], repr. Braslia, 1978), p. 73.

40 *Diario Novo*, 25 Nov. 1848. Figueira de Melo, *Autos do inquérito da Revolução Praieira*, pp. xxx–xxxi.

41 *Diario Novo*,

42 Pessoa de Mello, *Apreciação*, p. 203.

43 Pessoa de Mello, *Apreciação*, pp. 203–4.

Praia leaders and congressmen attempted to enlist regional support against central government appointment of outsiders to provincial presidencies. Praia congressman, Joaquim Nunes Machado, appealed for recognition of the Praia cause from his native state of Alagoas. In addition, the southern Praia command enlisted the aid of Pedro Ivo Velloso de Silveira, rival of José Pedro Velloso de Silveira, for control of the contraband trade on the southern provincial border. On the outskirts of Recife, João Inácio Roma and Antonio Borges de Fonseca established command posts on private estates at strategic junctures in order to maintain communications with Praia informants in Recife. In Recife, Praia broadsheets and street orators appealed to crowds for support for demands to reinstate dismissed civil servants in police and National Guard posts and to institute social reforms.

A second manifesto, signed by seven commanders of the 'Northern Liberal Army' (and probably authored by Antonio Borges da Fonseca, a longstanding proponent of a Republic), appeared on 1 January 1849. Although it was swiftly disowned by the Praia as a Conservative plot, the manifesto entitled 'To the World' echoed the 1824 Confederation of the Equator's call for unity in the North. It credited 'Divine Will' with success in unseating the monarchy and demanded a constituent assembly to undertake a judicial reform to guarantee basic rights to Brazilians of universal suffrage and freedom of the press. It called for preference for Brazilians in government employment, Brazilian ownership and control of retail and wholesale trade, separation of government powers, extinction of the moderating power of the emperor, federalism, individual freedoms, abolition of forced recruitment and annulment of legislation dealing with standard interest rates.[44]

Scholars of the *Praieira* Revolt, who link the social demands and the language of Praia leaders to the utopian socialism of Fourier, Lacordaire and Louis Blanc, argue that the influence of events in France upon the timing, rhetoric and social content of the movement in Pernambuco is unmistakable.[45] Yet even Antonio Borges da Fonseca, the main advocate of a Republic, grounded his appeals on local grievances against the excesses of the Rego-Barros-Cavalcanti coalition and the Emperor's appointments of non-native sons to govern the province. In 1844, in addition to his criticism of monarchy in general, and the interference of the central government in provincial matters, he targeted foreigners – Portuguese, English and French – whom he urged Pernambucans to expel.[46] His most

44 Rio de Janeiro. Biblioteca Nacional, Manuscripts Section, *Autos de Inquêrito da Revolução Praieira*, Document 3, 'Ao Mundo,' 1 Jan. 1849, pp. 107–9.

45 Quintas, *O sentido social*; Chacon, *História das idéias*, pp. 17–167.

46 *O Verdadeiro Regenerador*, 7 Sept. 1844. Cited in Luiz de Nascimento, *História da imprensa em Pernambuco* (Recife, 1966–1969), p. 208.

scathing commentaries moved beyond partisan disputes and, although credited with an affinity to Robespierre and Fourier, he sought inspiration in the Apostle's Creed when he appealed to the common people in his '*Credo Político*' in *O Foguete* on 29 June 1844:

> I believe in the People, the only power almighty, creator of associations and of governments. I believe in the Constituent Congress, [the People's] only son, our organiser, that was conceived by American civilisation, born of the national vote, and suffered dissolution under Pedro I, being crucified, dead and buried, descending from prominence, and emerging in its primitive state, in this province in the Confederation of the Equator. It was seated on the side of the people, all powerful, from where one day it will come to judge the Aulicos and traitors. I believe in the sovereignty of the people, in the Brazilian nation, in exclusive Brazilian national power. I believe in the resurrection of the Constituent Assembly, and in the life eternal of liberty. Amen.[47]

Popular Pressures: Urban Mobs

Crowd action was significant during the second stage of the movement. Disruption focused on the port of Recife as artisans, unemployed workers, farmers, vagrants and beggars protested social injustices, such as the wealthy planters' monopoly of land and the Portuguese merchants' monopoly over the retail trade. Inflammatory diatribes against the Portuguese in Praia dailies, such as that of Inácio Bento de Loyola in *Voz do Brasil*, were reminiscent of the 1817, 1834 and 1832 movements and linked to the events of December 1847 when numbers of Portuguese were assaulted and beaten, and their homes and shops sacked. In late June 1848 an incident involving a schoolboy, who was struck when a Portuguese cashier, whom he had been taunting, threw a weight at him, set off looting in the commercial districts of central Recife and resulted in five deaths and the wounding of forty Portuguese to demands of '*Mata Marinheiro!*' ('Kill the Portuguese!'), a blood-curdling cry that was to be heard frequently during 1848 and 1849.[48] A petition supported by 2,000

47 'Creio no povo, único poderoso, criador das associações e dos governos; creio no congresso constituinte, único filho seu, nosso organizador, que foi concebido por obra da civilização americana, o qual nasceu do voto nacional, e padeceu dissolução sob o Poder de Pedro Primeiro, sendo crucificado, morto e sepultado, descendo de categoria; e subindo depois ao seu primitivo estado, nesta província pela confederação do Equador, ficou sentado ao lado do povo, único poderoso, onde um dia há de vir julgar aos áulicos e traidores; creio na soberania do povo, na brasileira nação, que deve ser somente dos brasileiros, creio na ressureição da constituinte, e na vida eterna da liberdade. Amém.' Chacon, *História das idéias*, p. 138.

48 The schoolboy, a brother of a prominent Praia partisan, took his morning recess in front of a meat-packing house on the *Rua da Praia* where he made threatening

signatures presented to the Pernambucan provincial assembly on 27 June 1848 demanded all single Portuguese be expelled and replaced by Brazilians.[49]

The Arrest and Trial of the Praia

On 2 February 1849, the movement entered its third and final stage as Praia armies from the north and south of the province coordinated an attack on Recife. Aiming to seize control of the province after deposing the provincial president and chief of police, the siege of Recife not only took the government by surprise, but found a city divested of its strongest military contingents, that had embarked on a campaign to capture Praia forces in the South of the province. Pro-government volunteers, navy recruits and regular troops held the Praia at bay until the main government forces mounted a two-pronged attack resulting in the rebels' defeat. A manhunt for Praia supporters in Recife resulted in numerous arrests and imprisonments. Two hundred fighters in Praia regiments were eventually offered amnesty for deserting the Praia movement. This gesture virtually dismantled the Praia army.

With the defeat of the rebels, crowds shifted their loyalties back to the Conservatives with resounding cries of 'Long Live the King, Death to the *Cabanos*', echoing popular response to the rebellion that took place in the interior of Pernambuco in 1835. The 3,000 milréis bounty on the heads of Praia leaders would surely have influenced crowd sentiments.[50]

Provincial President Manoel Tosta mounted a personal campaign to capture Pedro Ivo de Silveira in the south of the province, where he authorised troops to burn crops and confiscate slaves and machinery of suspected Praia supporters. The gesture backfired. Tosta's actions threatened

---

gestures with a cane at a Portuguese clerk. The clerk retorted and the boy struck him with the cane at which point the clerk hurled a weight at the head of the lad who fell unconscious to the ground. Rio de Janeiro, Arquivo Nacional, IJ1 324, *Oficios da Presidência da Província dirigidos ao Ministro dos Negócios de Justiça*, Rio de Janeiro; Biblioteca Nacional, *Annaes do Parlamento Brasileiro. Câmara dos Senhores Deputados*, 'Speech of Deputy Urbano Sabino Pessoa de Mello, July 13, 1848' (Rio de Janeiro, 1889), pp. 69–71. *O Lidador* (Recife), 4 July 1848. Lisbon, Arquivo do Torre do Tombo, Ministério de Relações Exteriores, Consul Joaquim Batista Moreira to Ministro de Relações Exteriores, 28 June, 1848. Further details in Naro, *Brazil's 1848*, ch. 3.

49 Lisbon, Arquivo do Torre do Tombo, Diversos 3048, Correspondence from Batista Moreira to Ministério, 1848. Recife, Instituto Arqueológico Histórico Geográfico Pernambucano, *Justa Apreciação do Predomínio do Partido na Província* (Praia version).

50 The term *cabanos* (cabin dwellers) refers to rebels in general, but is taken from the 1835 movement, *Diario de Pernambuco*, 5 Feb. 1849, and Pessoa de Mello, *Apreciação* (1978), p. 95.

to destabilise the boundaries between public and private authority with harmful consequences for the authority of all landowners over land and labour. Sugar planters rallied against the president and their demand for his removal from the province was answered in July 1849. Tosta had also lost favour with foreign dignitaries who protested his disdainful treatment of, and withdrawal of diplomatic immunity from, British and French consular officials during his searches of Recife consulates for Praia supporters.[51]

Trial and Judgement

Forty-four of an estimated 1,000 survivors of the Praia movement, which at its peak totalled some 2500 participants, were brought to trial on August 17, 1849. The Conservative senator, Jozé Thomaz Nabuco de Araujo, presided as judge over the court proceedings. The trial records reveal that all of the defendants held occupations, although many were unemployed artisans, cadets, traders or civil servants. Testimonies from landless farmers, small landowners, ex-National Guardsmen and policemen revealed that they were motivated to join the Praia for a number of reasons. Some were promised good pay and working conditions for their families; others claimed to be threatened with imprisonment or eviction if they refused to join up. A few obeyed the orders of their *senhores* but none claimed to have joined for political conviction. Informed that the Praia aimed to convoke a constituent assembly to reform the constitution, some favoured these aims, but, when pressed to elaborate on them, were not able to do so. All nine leaders who stood trial were given life sentences.[52] Additionally, the court levelled charges against approximately 20,000 inhabitants, belonging to eleven villages, who were accused of 'criminally undermining the Empire and the Constitution'.[53]

The central government made conciliatory gestures in the aftermath of the Praia trial. The presidents who had effectively wiped out the movement were not chosen to restore order to the province. The last of the Conservative provincial presidents to be involved with the Praia movement was Honorio Hermeto Carneiro Leão, Brazil's most prestigious

51 Great Britain. Foreign Office. Brazil. Correspondence. Consular Despatches. Cowper to Palmerston, 13 April 1849 and undated Despatch 23.

52 They were Dr Felipe Lopes Neto, Dr Jerônimo Vilela de Castro Tavares, Antonio Borges da Fonseca, Feliciano Joaquim dos Santos, Antonio Feitosa de Melo, Leandro Cesar Paes Barreto, Henrique Pereira de Lucena, Antonio Correia Pessoa de Melo, and General José Ignacio Abreu e Lima, Rio de Janeiro. Biblioteca Nacional – Seção de Manuscritos. Autos do Inquérito (1978), p. 432.

53 The villages were Iguaraçu, Itamaracá, Pasmado, Maricota, Cruanji Caruaru, Goiana, Nazaré da Mata, Bezerros, Tracunhaém and Agua Preta.

senator, who arrived in Pernambuco on 2 July 1849.[54] His government restored freedom of the press, restored constitutional privileges to Praia congressmen, and freed political prisoners who were awaiting sentence. His conciliatory gestures backfired when Praia leader, Pedro Ivo Velloso de Silveira, mobilised 800 to 2500 armed men and sought reprisals for the manhunt carried out under President Tosta. Events in the province threatened a return to armed confrontation and a concerned emperor apprised the assembled legislators on the events of 1850 in Pernambuco:

> The province of Pernambuco is not entirely pacified. Desperate men who, deaf to the voice of my imperial clemency, retreat to the forests in order to persist in their criminal pursuits, seek once again to disrupt the public peace. My government continues to use forceful means to extinguish this revolutionary germ.[55]

The Conservative government dispatched troops to the backlands in search of bandit hideaways. The forests around Recife were searched for Praia rebels. And the southern areas of Agua Preta and Bonito were targeted to capture Praia leader, Pedro Ivo. Once again rival political camps reacted to the outside intervention of a non-native president. The government underestimated the intra-provincial personal and family networks that, despite political antagonisms, were resilient. The Conservative ex-president, Francisco Rego Barros, who had arranged a private meeting with Pedro Ivo at his estate, assured him of an imperial pardon if he agreed to leave Pernambuco. Yet, on his departure from the Rego Barros engenho, Pedro Ivo barely escaped government troops whom the provincial president had ordered to surround and capture him. This affront to the authority of the Rego-Barros-Cavalcanti families prompted their withdrawal of support from the provincial president, a stand which they reversed when Praia forces regrouped to threaten Recife and proclaim the secession of the province from the Empire.

Consolidation of the Centralised State

In the aftermath of the Praia movement the imperial government celebrated the Empire's return to peace and public order. Yet in Recife these claims were premature. Backlands raids continued on cattle ranches along the frontier of the sugar zone. In Pau d'Alho, Nazaré da Mata and Limoeiro, ten thousand people besieged the town centres in 1852, 'commit-

54 Nabuco, *Um estadista do Imperio*, p. 103.

55 Rio de Janeiro, Biblioteca Nacional, *Annaes do Parlamento Brasileiro. Camara dos Senhores Deputados*, Primeiro Ano da Oitava Legislatura, Sessão de 1849, vol. 1 (Rio de Janeiro, 1879), p. 85.

ting the greatest excesses, to the point of disarming police detachments'.[56] This popular protest, known as the Ronca da Abelha movement, stemmed from authorisation of a national registry of births and deaths in mid-1851. The timing of the measure not only coincided with the abolition of the trans-Atlantic slave trade and the passage of the Land Law in 1850, but with mid-century legislation that aimed to curb vagrancy. Fearful of becoming the targets of private and public measures to replace slaves, poor freemen rallied in protest against the encroachment of the authority of the state over their lives. Although short-lived, the 1852 rebellion, and later protests in 1868 that united angry villagers in successful movement against the introduction of the metric system – known as the revolt of the *Quebra Quilos* ('Break the Kilos') – reminded authorities of the potential of people of the backlands to reject new laws and to otherwise impose limitations on state power.[57]

Conclusions

The *Praieira* Revolt lasted from 1848 to its final demise in 1851 at the cost to the central government of two million milréis ($1,160,000), the loss of 850 lives, and some 1,700 wounded in the conflicts, not to mention extensive damage in Recife and the hinterland of the sugar-producing *zona de mata.*[58] Yet, unlike the violent *Cabanagem* and *Balaiada* movements of northern Brazil in which 30,000 slaves, freemen and planters lost their lives in the former alone, the Praia movement did not engulf the entire province or result in a violent slave rebellion.[59] Praia forces were made up of freemen and most combat took place near the borders of the province and on the inland peripheries of the sugar-cane-producing coastal areas, away from where the slave population was concentrated.

56 Arquivo Nacional, *Relatório do Ministro de Justiça, Euzebio de Queirós Mattoso da Câmara, apresentado para a Assembleia Geral Legislativa* (Rio de Janeiro, 1852); Relatório do Presidente da Província de Pernambuco para o Ministro de Justiça, 1851.

57 Hobsbawm, *Primitive Rebels.* Since the 1852 protest emerged in towns that were active in the Praia movement, I cannot accept the dissociation of that movement from the Praia Revolt. See Hamilton de Mattos Monteiro, *Crise agrária e luta de classes. O nordeste brasileiro entre 1850 e 1889* (Brasilia, 1980). In 1868 widespread popular protest over the introduction of the metric system resulted in destruction of scales in retail shops throughout settlements in the Northeast. The measure was withdrawn. See Roderick Barman, 'The Brazilian Peasantry Reexamined: The Implications of the Quebra-Quilo Revolt,' *Hispanic American Historical Review*, vol. 57 (1977), pp. 401–24.

58 General Mello Rego, cited in Horacio de Almeida, *Brejo de Areia. Memórias de um Município* (Rio de Janeiro, 1957), p. 187.

59 Murilo de Carvalho, *Teatro de sombras*, p. 15.

The organisation of the major Praia campaigns and their suppression suggests that there was consensus among all parties as to the need to avoid widespread disorder that might damage the economy, destabilise the plantation complex or bring about uncontrollable social disorder.

Praia orators generated support by appealing to those who were already discontented over forced recruitment of local producers into the armed forces, the Portuguese monopoly of credit and of the retail commerce, and the lack of agrarian reform. Matters that affected daily life and survival outweighed partisan or philosophical issues of Republicanism and Socialism. Praia orators and press also gained support from planters on the peripheries of the coastal sugar belt who wanted access to land, civil service positions, availability of low interest loans and credit, unrestricted intra-provincial trade and a free and competitive labour market.

Notwithstanding the appeal of European ideas, and the interest in European events among free labourers and farmers during the 1840s, their popular protests were channelled by Praia leaders who directed collective anger towards the Portuguese, immediate political foes, monopoly over landholdings and, finally, against the intervention of the central government in provincial affairs. In contrast to Europe, where universal suffrage and freedom of employment were inextricably linked to rights demanded by individual citizens, most Pernambucans were enmeshed in unequal relations characterised by hierarchies of dependency, from which there were no available public route of escape. The free poor population of Pernambuco depended on political favour either from social superiors, who exerted arbitrary and often quite violent control over the slave and free populations, or from those who controlled political appointments and employment in the rural milieu. In addition, indebtedness to wealthy planters and Portuguese moneylenders was further aggravated by the Portuguese monopolies over commerce and craft occupations.

Praia demands gained some support in other parts of Brazil and echoed popular protests in Europe, yet the Praia was not aiming to engage the country in civil disorder. Incidents of street violence and demands for the Brazilianisation of commerce apart, it must be remembered that, unlike events in France, the Praia did not have widespread endorsement for the convocation of a constituent assembly which might have proclaimed a Republic. Praia Congressman, Joaquim Nunes Machado, consistently supported the monarchy even as he appealed for help from the neighbouring provinces of Alagoas and Paraíba to counter the interference of the central government in what was perceived to be an internal provincial dispute.

The direction of events in the province, and especially the street violence and anti-Portuguese gestures that accelerated in mid-1848 and 1849, has led students of the *Praieira* to present the movement as Brazil's

'Springtime of the People'. The Portuguese were not only targeted for favouring the restoration of colonial rule in the 1820s and 1830s, but were still blamed in the 1840s for crises over the slave trade and for any ills affecting overseas and local commerce. The departure of Portuguese merchants and their families in 1849 represented a significant, if minor, Praia victory. In fact, one encounters few parallels in the Americas of the random targeting of the Portuguese, whose fate was finally determined by the Portuguese government's authorisation of a rescue mission that transported the refugees to settle the southern frontier of Angola.

The tensions between the central government and Pernambuco suggest that in the pre-1850 period the Brazilian state had not assembled a bureaucratic or political apparatus that could effectively placate or fully accommodate powerful local family interests. Rival and often interrelated planter elites, such as the Rego Barros and Holanda Cavalcanti clans and their supporters, disputed police, judicial and electoral positions, motivated more by personal considerations than partisan interests. For Conservative provincial leaders, cordial relations with the central government were sorely tested by the imperial appointment of outsiders to the provincial presidency (Chichorro de Gama for the Praia and three Conservative presidents after the onset of Conservative rule in 1848) that upset fragile inter-elite planter alliances. Kinship proved stronger than principle in the conflicts, as was demonstrated when the central government, unable and unwilling to continue to fortify the province with imperial troops, acceded to the demands of Conservative planter families for political leadership in the province as a condition for their continued support for the monarchy.

Order and unity under a monarchy became the pivotal points of conflict and negotiation in this political movement. In Pernambuco the maintenance of order was directly related to the ability of the provincial government to control political and civil service appointments. Although the centralising laws of the early 1840s applied to Brazil as a whole, the Praia movement highlights the pervasive recourse to clientelism (*mandonismo*), and the exchange of political and personal favours at local, provincial, and national levels that maintained the unequal social relations of the commercial plantation complex. In contrast to Mexico and other Latin American countries, where the military and armed confrontations were paramount in the state-building process, the Praia movement is one more confirmation that the bureaucracy was the mainstay of order in imperial Brazil.[60]

60 On this topic see Murilo de Carvalho, *A Construção da ordem* and *Teatro de sombras*; Fernando López-Alves, *State Formation and Democracy in Latin America, 1810–1900* (Durham, NC, 2000).

The importance to the government in power of its control over political appointments was stated by the Praia in the broadsheet, *A Estrela*, at the onset of the Chichorro de Gama presidency:

> Order is so identified with the government in office that one cannot defend its restrictions on future private claims to public land.[61]

Yet, fifteen years after the *Praieira* movement, the Pernambucan president's official report claimed that institutionalised violence still prevailed. Private and public law were still inter-related, and the upper echelons of society did not engage in social reform. He stated:

> As long as leaders in society offer an incentive to crime through their practices of seduction and violence; as long as the law is nothing in relation to the caprice of the powerful and bearers of authority; as long as the law is simply the lever for favours or persecutions instead of being rigid and equal for all; the punishment for some that constitutes a reward for others, then crimes will abound and their perpetrators will be the agents of authority, the police, and the political ward healers.[62]

61 *A Estrela*, in Luiz de Nascimento, *História da imprensa*, p. 196.
62 Relatório que o Exmo. Presidente de Pernambuco apresentou a Assembléia Legislativa Provincial (25 July 1865), cited in Hamilton de Mattos Monteiro, *Crise agrária e luta de classes* (1980), pp. 109–10.

5

The European Revolutions of 1848 in the Rio de la Plata

DAVID ROCK

In some parts of Latin America, the European revolutions of 1848 had visible and dramatic effects. An historian of the *Praieira* rebellion in the Brazilian province of Pernambuco devoted a whole chapter to what he called its '*Quarante Huitard* Spirit'.[1] The Pernambuco movement erupted in November 1848 in a radical intellectual milieu in which influences from France were exceptionally strong. The manifesto of the revolutionaries issued on New Year's Day 1849 reiterated many of the same demands as those in France on the inception of the Second Republic. Among them were freedom of the press, free education and universal suffrage. In an issue reminiscent of the renunciation of the death penalty in France in 1848, the revolutionaries demanded a ban on corporal punishment in the National Guard. The demand of the Pernambuco revolutionaries for 'the guarantee of work for every Brazilian citizen' sought to translate into the local context the issues that in France led to the creation of the National Workshops. As a salute to the legendary leader of the nationalist struggle in Hungary, one of the newspapers in Pernambuco supporting the revolution named itself *Kossuth*. In an attempt to discredit them by identifying them with the radical movement in Europe, local conservatives referred to the newspapers supporting the rebellion as the 'Red Fraternity'.

The *Praieira* revolution displayed the same confused and sometimes unrealistic objectives as many of the movements in Europe. Its leader, Antônio Borges da Fonseca, was a true radical republican but his ambition to extend the movement beyond Pernambuco into a full-fledged uprising against the Brazilian Empire remained unfulfilled. Although the rebellion occurred in a region of *ingenios* and attracted substantial support among

1 Amaro Quintas, *O sentido social da Revolução Praieira* (Rio de Janeiro, 1967). This movement acquired its name because the *Diário Nôvo*, the leading liberal newspaper supporting the insurrection, had its premises on the Rua do Praia (Beach Street) in Recife.

the rural population, the revolutionaries made no commitments to land redistribution or the destruction of slavery. Despite the French-style rhetoric of the local intelligentsia and the attempts to establish parallels with Europe, the rebellion remained at root a xenophobic outburst against Portuguese retailers, usurers and merchants. As a Brazilian politician declared, 'Europe clamours for the organisation of labour and preaches Communism. Here the same clamour translates into the cry of "War on the Portuguese!" It stems from the issue of retail commerce.'[2]

Chile provided a second illustration of the impact of the 1848 revolutions in Latin America. In that country French influences found one of their chief expressions in the Society for Equality founded in 1850 by Francisco Bilbao and Santiago Arcos. A radical exponent of liberal Catholicism, Bilbao was banished from his native land in 1845. His notorious work *La sociabilidad chilena* was condemned as blasphemous and burned by the public executioner in Santiago. For several years afterwards Bilbao lived in France where he became friendly with several prestigious French intellectuals including Edgar Quinet and Jean Marie de Lamennais. He spent the early part of 1848 observing the gestation of the revolutionary movements in northern Italy. He witnessed the battles on the barricades during the 'June Days' in Paris. In late 1848 and early 1849 he wrote numerous articles including many supporting the freedom of Poland and attacking the French military intervention in Rome to restore Pope Pius IX. Disillusioned by the failures of the revolutionary movements in Europe, Bilbao returned to Chile in early 1850 to rekindle them in his native land. Arcos, the cofounder of the Society of Equality and Chilean by birth, received his upbringing and education in France. Despite his father's high standing as a wealthy financier, as a young man he became an enthusiast for the writings of the utopian socialists and determined to pursue their programmes. Returning to Chile in early 1848 he plunged into radical politics. Close contact with French culture and writings became a distinguishing feature of all the leading young Chilean radicals in this era. Nineteen year-old Benjamín Vicuña Mackenna, another of Bilbao's associates, spent the night before the outbreak of the revolt of September 1851 reading *L'Histoire des Girondins*, the famed, if mostly apocryphal, study of the French Revolution by Alphonse de Lamartine. Leading members of the Society of Equality assumed the *noms de plume* of prominent Girondins. Bilbao adopted the pseudonym Louis Antoine de Saint-Just and Arcos styled himself Jean-Paul Marat. Vicuña Mackenna's work, *Los girondinos chilenos* opened with the sentence, referring to Chile, 'the

2 A description of the rebellion appears in Fernando Segismundo, *História popular da Revolução Praieira* (Rio de Janeiro, 1949).

French revolution of 1848 had a powerful echo'.[3]

The Society of Equality established in February 1850 imitated the 1848 revolutions by attempting to unite upper class liberals and intellectuals with the artisans of Santiago, an alliance reminiscent of those that briefly flourished in Paris, Vienna and Berlin. Echoing the orotund rhetoric of revolutionary France, the Society acknowledged the supremacy of Reason, the sovereignty of the People, and pledged to uphold 'Universal Fraternity'. The movement spread beyond Santiago briefly, attracting substantial popular support, but fell foul of the government when liberals opposed to the election of conservative Manuel Montt as the president of Chile in 1851 took it over for propaganda purposes. In November 1850 the government closed the Society and imposed a state of siege. In 1851 two rebellions erupted in Chile, but neither managed to ignite the popular movement to which Bilbao and Arcos aspired, and both were swiftly defeated. The rebellion of April 1851 in the streets of Santiago found support only among small segments of the army and a few artisans recruited by Bilbao. In that guise the movement became more reminiscent of the military *pronunciamientos* of Spain than the popular *journées* of France. The second rebellion in Chile in September 1851 became a regional uprising led by liberals in northern and southern Chile respectively. In that form it resembled the regionally based movements common throughout Latin America in the nineteenth century.

Argentina and Uruguay were two other Latin American countries apparently primed to receive a strong impact from the events of 1848 in Western Europe. Buenos Aires and Montevideo, the leading cities of the Rio de la Plata region, betrayed the same strong European cultural influences as Pernambuco and Chile. Before 1848 two of Argentina's leading liberal *pensadores*, Esteban Echeverría and Domingo F. Sarmiento, lived in or travelled through France and other parts of Europe. After 1848 a third major figure, Juan Bautista Alberdi, spent a good part of the rest of

3 Benjamín Vicuña Mackenna, *Los girondinos chilenos*, prologue by Cristián Gazmuri (Santiago, 1989); Vicuña Mackenna, *Historia de la jornada del 20 de abril de 1851. Una batalla en las calles de Santiago* (Santiago, 1878). The extensive secondary literature on this issue includes Luis Alberto Romero, 'La sociedad de la igualdad: liberales y artesanos en la vida política de Santiago de Chile,' in *Siglo XIX. Revista de Historia*, vol. 2, issue 3 (1987); Elías Ugarte Figueroa, *Francisco Bilbao, agitator y blasfemo* (Santiago, 1967); Julio César Jobet, *Santiago Arcos Arlegui y la 'Sociedad de la Igualdad'* (Santiago, 1942); Jack Ray Thomas, 'The role of the Press in the Chilean Rebellion of 1851,' *The Americas*, vol. xxxvi, July 1979, pp. 59–78; Alberto J. Varona, *Francisco Bilbao. Revolucionario de América. Vida y pensamiento. Estudio de sus ensayos y trabajos periodísticos* (Buenos Aires 1973); Gabriel Sanhueza, *Santiago Arcos. Comunista, millonario y calavera* (Santiago, 1956); Sergio Guzmán Ortega, *Vida y obra de Francisco Bilbao*, unpubl. PhD diss. University of California, Riverside, 1970.

his life in France. Campaigning from exile for a national congress and a constitution, and combating the dictatorship of Juan Manuel Rosas, the Argentine liberals saw themselves as fighting many of the same battles for political emancipation as their European counterparts. In a typical manifestation of European influence in Argentina, Giuseppe Mazzini's 'Young Italy' movement provided a model for the 'Young Argentina' movement founded by Echeverría later known as the Generation of 1837.[4] Between the late 1830s and the early 1860s Argentina pursued a broadly similar path to Italy during the Risorgimento. In both countries a liberal cultural movement became the spearhead for an assault against conservative forces and a vehicle to establish a united liberal state. In this period communications between the Rio de la Plata and western Europe grew more extensive than elsewhere in Latin America thanks to a rising inflow of European goods and population. French and British merchants regarded the Plata and the lengthy river system to its north as the commercial gateway into South America. Small communities of Europeans comprising at least half a dozen nationalities lived in Buenos Aires and Montevideo. For most of the 1840s, and up until 1852, informal political links existed between the Rio de la Plata and France. The French virtually ruled the city of Montevideo, since that city depended on their military and naval support for protection against the besieging army of Rosas's ally in Uruguay, General Manuel Oribe.

The web of ties with Europe suggested that the revolutions of 1848 would have an equal, or even greater, effect in the Rio de la Plata than in Pernambuco or Chile; in fact their impact remained relatively slight.[5] The most obvious reason was the presence of the despotic regime led by Rosas, which in 1848 stood at the height of its power. The followers of Rosas proclaimed him the Restorer of the Laws. His opponents commonly depicted him as a South American version of the reactionary European absolutists upheld by the Church and the landed classes. Echeverría, for example, claimed that *rosismo* marked the reincarnation of the colonial

4 The organisation later became known as the May Association and then as the Generation of 1837. Good analyses of the Generation of 1837 include Natalio R. Botana, *La tradición republicana* (Buenos Aires, 1984); William H. Katra, *The Argentine Generation of 1837* (Madison, 1996); Fabio Wasserman, 'La Generación de 1837 y el proceso de construcción de la identidad nacional argentina,' *Boletín del Instituto de Historia Argentina y Americana 'Dr Emilio Ravignani'*, 3rd Series, no. 15, 1997, pp. 7–34.

5 See Tulio Halperín Donghi, 'Liberalismo argentino y liberalismo mexicano: dos destinos divergentes,' in *El espejo de la historia* (Buenos Aires, 1987), p. 156. 'The 1848 revolution that in the rest of Hispanic America marks the beginning of what is seen in retrospect as an awakening from a long lethargy, only affects for an instant the costly acquired political realism of the Argentines.'

authority of the Bourbons.[6] Yet, as Echeverría and the other leading liberals knew, Rosas was a political figure of much greater complexity than a mere imitator of Europeans. A staunch republican and a declared enemy of monarchy in the Americas, he ruled as the elected governor of the province of Buenos Aires. His influence over the other provinces of Argentina stemmed not from any formal authority over them (except in the sphere of foreign affairs) but from treaties, alliances and informal agreements. Rosas wielded unrestricted dictatorial power in Buenos Aires by legislative vote; periodic plebiscites endorsed his leadership with overwhelming majorities; some contemporaries even described him as a socialist because he embodied and personified state power.[7] He made no pretence of being liberal, but he commonly depicted himself as the democratic leader of a naturally democratic society that sprang from the open pampas, the habitat of the free-roaming gauchos. Rosas became a barrier against the influence of the 1848 revolutions in two senses. He not only repressed dissent but he also ruled with popular support, including that of many of the artisans, the critical group in many of the European revolutionary movements of the time. Under his rule movements in Buenos Aires like the *Praieira* rebellion and organisations like the Society for Equality became inconceivable. Never a friend of any monarch, Rosas had a particularly strong aversion for the House of Orléans because of its armed interventions in the Rio de la Plata. 'More than anyone else perhaps [Rosas] applauded the February Revolution,' a contemporary noted. 'Not that he favoured revolution in general, but he disliked Louis Philippe and [François] Guizot.'[8] He rejoiced in the fall of these enemies, but had no sympathy for the popular insurrections in Paris that achieved their downfall, and he immediately clamped down on the slightest show of support for the revolutions in Buenos Aires. When the Sardinian consul in the city refused to quell a celebration among his countrymen in support of the liberal movements in Italy, Rosas expelled him.

Despite the presence of Rosas, the revolutions of 1848 had some influence in the Rio de la Plata, although for the most part in a subtle and indirect fashion. Firstly, to a slight degree, the effects of 1848 ran in the opposite direction, from South America to Europe, in the sense that French involvement in the Rio de la Plata played a part in the February revolution in France. Secondly, the fall of the Orléans monarchy disrupted

6 Esteban Echeverría, *El dogma socialista de la asociación de mayo* (Buenos Aires, 1958), p. 64. This edition includes the *Ojeada retrospectiva* of 1846 in which this particular charge against Rosas appears.

7 Roberto Etchepareborda, *Rosas. Controvertida historia* (Buenos Aires, 1972), p. 63. Quoting Alfred de Brossard.

8 Alfred de Brossard, *Considérations historiques et politiques sur les Républiques de la Plata dans leurs rapports avec la France et l'Angleterre* (Paris, 1850), p. 377.

French foreign policy and delayed the withdrawal of French forces from the Rio de la Plata. The delay in the withdrawal enabled the maturing of the coalition led by General Justo J. Urquiza, which in early 1852 overthrew Rosas. Thirdly, the 1848 revolutions left a mark on the liberal intellectuals of the Generation of 1837 who shaped the formation of a national state in Argentina in the 1850s and early 1860s. For the most part the revolutions validated and fortified the conservative leanings of the intellectuals, as opposed to pushing them in radical directions. The intellectuals remained liberal, but they became more strongly anti-democratic and opposed to socialism; government, they held, existed not to protect popular rights but to promote wealth. 'Economic policy ought to be the only policy in these countries,' wrote Alberdi. He wanted governments that would 'fill [them] up with wealth, population, business, and good living'.[9] Such materialist and positivist goals had little in common with the 'Spirit of '48'.

The revolutions of 1848 and the fall of Rosas

In early 1848 Buenos Aires remained under a partial blockade by French and British naval forces. Shippers first landed and paid taxes on their goods in Montevideo. Coastal vessels then took them to Buenos Aires. The tariff duties on imported goods in Montevideo financed its government and its military forces, which chiefly comprised French and Italian legionnaires including Giuseppe Garibaldi. In the 1840s Montevideo was heavily European. Most of its inhabitants, observed Sarmiento when he passed through the city in 1846, 'are neither Argentines nor Uruguayans but Europeans who have taken possession of a piece of territory in America.'[10] The French presence in the Rio de la Plata began in the late 1830s when the Orléans regime intervened to protect French citizens in Buenos Aires from alleged persecution by Rosas. In 1845 France and Britain intervened jointly against Rosas, imposing a blockade in order to protect the independence of Uruguay. The British also wanted to break Rosas's ban on the internal trade in Argentina and to open up markets along the rivers north of the Rio de la Plata to direct contact with British merchants.

The blockade failed to weaken either Rosas or Oribe, his Uruguayan ally, or to force Rosas to open the rivers to European merchants. The British soon wanted to abandon the intervention because it did more

9 Jorge Mayer, *Las bases de Alberdi. Edición crítica, con una nota preliminar, la reconstrucción de los textos originales y sus variantes, las fuentes y notas ilustrativas* (Buenos Aires, 1969), p. 46. Quoting *El Comercio*, 28 Aug. 1847.

10 Domingo Faustino Sarmiento, *Viajes. Edición Crítica*, edited by Javier Fernández (Madrid, 1993), p. 27.

damage than good to British trade. They became suspicious that the French were planning to use Montevideo as a base to establish a formal colony in the region that would further injure British interests. Meanwhile, in France powerful, although not dominant, political forces pulled in the opposite direction from the British, towards intensifying the intervention. As the leading opponent of the Orleanist ministry headed by Guizot, in 1846 Adolphe Thiers demanded military and naval action against Oribe and Rosas. He referred to Montevideo as 'that French colony', and complained repeatedly that the British government exercised too much influence over French policy.[11] As if to vindicate this criticism, in late 1847 Lord Palmerston, the British foreign secretary, persuaded Guizot to join him in sending a negotiator to the Rio de la Plata. Under the instructions of their respective governments, the two negotiators were to seek peace with Oribe and even allow him to conquer Montevideo if he disavowed Rosas and committed himself to the independence of Uruguay. Once Uruguay had escaped the influence of Rosas, the British and the French would lift the blockade against Buenos Aires. The proposed plan met British needs for the resumption of unrestricted trade, but failed to satisfy the supporters of French colonialism in the Rio de la Plata. The agreement between Palmerston and Guizot provoked renewed accusations in the French Chamber of Deputies that the latter was subservient to Britain and neglected French national interests.[12] Such attacks merged into the broader onslaught against Guizot that reached a climax in late February 1848 when the ministry and then the regime itself collapsed. In this way French intervention in the Rio de la Plata helped provoke the fall of the House of Orléans. In one historian's judgement, it contributed 'a considerable share to the lamentable failure of the foreign policy of Guizot, which was one of the principal reasons for his downfall'.[13]

The planned policy of abandonment pursued by Guizot in concert with Palmerston created a sense of hopelessness among the defenders of Montevideo. Some of the legionnaires deserted and set up home across the Rio de la Plata in Buenos Aires; others, such as Garibaldi, returned to Europe (in his case in time to lead his famous military campaigns in Italy). When news of the French revolution finally reached Montevideo in May 1848 it raised hopes of a more militant French stance against Oribe and Rosas. The celebrated circular issued by Lamartine, foreign minister in the new republican government, asserted that France reserved

11 John F. Cady, *Foreign Intervention in the Rio de la Plata, 1838–1850* (Philadelphia, 1929), p. 203.

12 Speeches attacking Guizot appear in Benjamin Poucel, *Les otages de Durazno. Souvenirs du Rio de la Plata pendant l'Intervention Anglo-Française de 1845 à 1851* (Paris, 1864), pp. 307–9.

13 Cady, *Foreign Intervention*, p. 236.

the right to support democratic principles and oppressed minorities. A pro-French Uruguayan resident in Montevideo, José Luis Bustamante, echoed the expectations created by Lamartine in many parts of Europe. 'The people of Montevideo,' he wrote, placed all their hopes 'on the new policy the French Republic was assuming in Europe, offering protection to all the peoples of the earth whose independence was being threatened. The eloquent words of Lamartine echoed in La Plata like the celestial voice of an angel of hope and consolation.'[14]

Expectations that a French army would land in Montevideo to defeat Oribe and confront Rosas remained unfulfilled. Before the revolution in Paris Lamartine had registered his opposition to the French intervention in the Rio de la Plata, and after the revolution he showed no sign of changing his mind. As foreign minister in May 1848 he signalled his abandonment of the policy proclaimed in the circular by rejecting a petition to support the independence of Ireland. In June 1848 Baron Jean Louis Gros, the diplomat sent by Guizot to negotiate with Oribe, shored up the government and the now dwindling defending army in Montevideo by granting the city a month by month subsidy. The administration in Montevideo pledged to repay the subsidy later through proceeds from foreign trade. The succession of governments in France in 1848 then virtually ignored the Rio de la Plata – except briefly as a possible destination for the prisoners from the June Days – until April 1849 when the National Assembly ratified the subsidy. In a response typical of the Uruguayans living in Montevideo, Bustamante exclaimed his relief. '¡Libertad a Montevideo! ¡Protección a la población francesa en la Plata! ¡Salud a la República Francesa!'[15] Debates on the subsidy in the National Assembly illustrated the conflicting directions of French policy continuing from the Orléans period. The majority now favoured the policy of defending Montevideo against Oribe and preventing its domination by Rosas. A minority led by Thiers urged still more positive action to promote French interests in the region, even as far as making war on Rosas. Alfred de Brossard, a soldier prominent in the defence of Montevideo, expressed views typical of the faction that supported asserting French interests in the region. The policy of the Second Republic (which reaffirmed France's determination to defend rather than abandon Montevideo), he declared,

14 José Luis Bustamante, *Los cinco errores capitales de la intervención anglo-francesa en el Plata* (Buenos Aires, 1942), p. 362 (Reprint of 1st ed. of 1849). Rosas too received a report of the Lamartine circular from Tomás Guido, his diplomatic representative in Rio de Janiero. See Julio Irazusta, *Vida política de Juan Manuel de Rosas a través de su correspondencia* (Buenos Aires, 1970), vol. 6, *La intervención anglo-francesa 1847–1848*, p. 183.

15 Bustamante, *Los cinco errores capitales*, p. 363.

represented little improvement on the 'feebleness and hesitation' that had characterised the Orléans monarchy.[16]

The 1848 revolution had a less visible impact on the direct relations between the French government and Rosas. Following the revolution French policy continued to follow the lead of the British, who remained anxious to end their political and military involvement in the area. In March 1849, while negotiating with the British, Rosas agreed to acknowledge the independence of Uruguay, but again refused to open the rivers to foreign shipping.[17] The French envoy sent to Buenos Aires, Joseph Le Prédour, secured a similar agreement from Rosas, but it failed to gain political support in Paris because it offered no safeguards for French interests in Montevideo. In early 1850, a small force of French marines arrived in the Rio de la Plata and was used by Le Prédour to pressure Rosas to withdraw the Argentine troops supporting Oribe in the siege of Montevideo. Le Prédour and Rosas concluded a definitive agreement in August 1850, when Rosas withdrew his troops from Uruguay and the French disbanded the foreign legion in Montevideo.

The withdrawal of the Europeans seemed a major victory for Rosas. French policy-makers began repudiating their previous policy. Writing in the *Revue de Deux Mondes* in mid-1851, Thomas Page, a French functionary with long experience in the affairs of the Rio de la Plata, argued that the Anglo-French intervention had served only to strengthen Rosas. The subsidy paid by the French government to defend Montevideo during recent years proved an expensive waste, achieving little more than maintaining a refuge in Montevideo for the Unitarios, the Argentine exiles from Rosas. The Unitarios succeeded, Page claimed, in misleading French governments into believing that the city was crucial to French interests. The current diplomatic settlement was the best solution, because if France were to attempt an invasion of the region, he warned, the whole continent would echo to the cry of '¡Mueran los extranjeros!'[18] Under the Second Republic, the French government followed the path indicated by Page when it withdrew its forces from the Rio de la Plata. A decade later the Second Republic's successor, the Second Empire, decided to ignore all the dangers of intervention when Napoleon III authorised the ill-starred invasion of Mexico. Events in Mexico largely fulfilled Page's prophecy.

One aspect of the assessment by Page proved quite wrong. Rather than strengthening Rosas, French policy helped to unite and assist his

16 Brossard, *Considérations*, p. 287.

17 David McLean, *War, Diplomacy and Informal Empire. Britain and the Republics of La Plata, 1836–1853* (London, 1995), p. 165.

18 Thomas Page, 'Le Paraguay et les Républiques de la Plata,' *Revue de Deux Mondes*, April–June 1851, p. 456.

enemies, and to bring about his downfall. The ultimately decisive conflict between Rosas and Urquiza, the governor of Entre Rios, began in 1846 when Rosas sought to restrict the access of the landowners of Entre Rios to foreign markets. He forced them to accept payments for their goods in the depreciated paper currency issued by the province of Buenos Aires. In an effort to escape Rosas's control, the ranchers of Entre Rios started to export their goods through Montevideo, thereby becoming increasingly dependent on that city retaining its independence. When the French commenced their withdrawal from Montevideo, Urquiza and his followers feared losing their markets or having to pay taxes to Rosas. Under these conditions Urquiza began to plot the overthrow of Rosas. In the late 1840s Rosas found himself engaged in a second conflict with Imperial Brazil, which chiefly concerned rivalries for influence in the Brazilian borderlands and Paraguay. The Brazilian government strongly opposed Rosas gaining control over Montevideo. It feared that on doing so he would then extend his influence into the rebellious Brazilian province of Rio Grande do Sul and reclaim the political dominance over Paraguay that Buenos Aires had exercised before the wars of independence. By protracting the French presence in Montevideo (even if by accident rather than design) the French revolution of 1848 created an opportunity to cement the alliance between Urquiza and the Brazilians. In 1847 Urquiza rejected an alliance with Brazil; three years later, in 1850, when faced with the prospect of losing access to the port of Montevideo, he enthusiastically accepted it. The alliance between Urquiza and the government of Brazil set in motion the well-known sequence of events that ended in the downfall of Rosas. In September 1850 the Brazilian government broke diplomatic relations with Rosas. In May 1851 Urquiza repudiated Rosas's authority and, in order to conclude a formal alliance with Brazil, declared Entre Rios a sovereign state. In October 1851 the allies defeated Oribe and raised the siege of Montevideo. Finally, in February 1852, Urquiza defeated Rosas in the battle of Caseros.[19]

Responses of the Intellectuals

In an autobiography, Vicente Fidel López, the eminent nineteenth-century Argentine historian, recalled the impact of the French revolution of 1830 in Buenos Aires. 'No one today,' he wrote, 'can possibly understand the enormous moral impact of that event on the university youth of

19 Among the numerous descriptions of these events see John Lynch, *Argentine Dictator. Juan Manuel de Rosas* (Oxford, 1981); José María Rosa, *La caída de Rosas* (Buenos Aires, 1968); Beatriz Bosch, *Urquiza y su tiempo*. 2nd. ed. (Buenos Aires, 1980), pp. 151–220.

20 Vicente Fidel López, *Evocaciones históricas* (Buenos Aires, 1929), p. 39.

Argentina.'[20] More than forty years later the influence of the attempted French revolution led by the Paris Commune also became visible in Buenos Aires. In 1875 a mob of anticlerical immigrants, incited by rhetoric borrowed from the Commune, set a Jesuit seminary ablaze, razing it to the ground. Later that same year the Argentine authorities discovered a group of conspirators plotting the overthrow of the government because 'it governs absolutely, imitating the monarchies it has replaced'. Reported links between the conspirators and the Commune led the French minister in Buenos Aires to condemn them as 'bloodthirsty fools'.[21]

Compared with the events in France in either 1830 or 1870–71 the 1848 revolution had much less direct and immediate influence in Buenos Aires. The 1848 movement provoked neither a new intellectual fashion nor a body of followers or imitators. With Rosas acting as the great barrier, the reactions remained confined to the liberals exiled in Chile and Montevideo led by Echeverría, Sarmiento and Alberdi. Responding to European events, first Echeverría, writing in Montevideo, and later Sarmiento, writing in Chile, issued ambiguous, unenthusiastic endorsements. In July 1848 Echeverría greeted the creation of the Second Republic in France with rhetorical acclaim, confessing that his analysis borrowed heavily from Pierre Leroux, a leading French publicist of the doctrines of the Comte de Saint-Simon. In these terms, following Leroux, the recent revolution in France became an affirmation of the perfectibility of society. It would destroy the restraints on men imposed by the ownership of property and capital and 'inaugurate throughout the world the era of the complete emancipation [of humanity] through the support of the foremost people of the world. To achieve that magnificent and inspiring hope of humanity, France raised itself to its feet in February and proclaimed the Republic.' Echeverría hoped that the revolution would ultimately affect Spanish America, although, as he carefully emphasised, only by influencing the intelligentsia as opposed to the masses.[22] He offered a positive view of the revolution, but his comments remained perfunctory and derivative, stopping at the early stages of the movement. While celebrating the outbreak and results of direct popular action in France, Echeverría appeared reluctant to endorse it in Latin America.

Writing in early 1849, Sarmiento urged his readers 'to love the French revolution because it proclaims justice between the peoples, equality among men and the law of reason'. Nevertheless, in another piece, he noted the ongoing struggle in France at that point between monarchist

21 Ducros to Paris, no. 20, 22 Nov. 1875. Correspondance Politique, vol. 51 (Foreign Ministry Archive, Paris).

22 Quoted in José Ingenieros, *La evolución de las ideas argentinas*, book IV: *La restauración* (Buenos Aires, 1937), pp. 32–7.

and republican forces, and cited the recent election of Louis Napoleon Bonaparte as president of France to illustrate the dangers of universal suffrage.[23] A few years later, in another positive comment on the revolutions, he declared that in 1848 he ceased to be an Unitario supporter of political centralisation. Having seen some of the abuses of centralisation in Europe, he became a committed supporter of a federal system.[24] Sarmiento viewed the revolution as a cathartic act that could become a source of physical and intellectual inspiration, but not at all as a model for emulation. Some occasional, if never unqualified, endorsements for the revolutions appeared in his writings or recorded remarks, but on balance he regarded them with deep hostility. In 1846, the Chilean government (specifically Manuel Montt, then the minister of education) commissioned Sarmiento to travel to western Europe to examine the current state of public education. He visited France, Italy, Switzerland, parts of Germany, Spain and Morocco, and spent a brief period in England before sailing to New York. On close encounter, Europe – that 'sad juxtaposition of grandeur and collapse, and of wisdom and brutality' – created mixed impressions. In Paris Sarmiento became enthralled by one of the great parliamentary debates between Guizot and Thiers before the fall of the Orléans monarchy. However, the ignorance of Guizot's chief advisers of affairs in the Rio de la Plata deeply affronted him. Sarmiento satirised an official he met by claiming he made absurd parallels between French and Argentine politics. He treated Rosas as a kind of Louis Philippe. He made a ludicrous parallel between Rosas's thugs and spies known as the *mazorca* and the Orléans party. He treated the gauchos, ridiculously, as an Argentine version of the French petty bourgeoisie. In France Sarmiento noted the corruption of the Orléans regime, which governed with a mere pretence at democratic participation and employed lavish patronage and sinecures to sustain itself.[25] In all Europe Sarmiento found Prussia alone worthy of any interest, chiefly because it used education as an instrument of state control and indoctrination. Nevertheless, the United States became the real object of his enthusiasm. In Massachusetts Sarmiento established the ties with Horace Mann that ultimately led to the proposals for popular education in Argentina with which his name and posthumous reputation became closely associated. Following his return to Chile, Sarmiento retrieved the letters he had sent to his friends in South America and published them as his *Viajes*. In the preface, written after the revolutions

23 Sarmiento, quoted in Tulio Halperín Donghi, *Proyecto y construcción de una nación (Argentina 1846–1880)* (Caracas, 1980), p. 176.

24 Quoted in Benjamín Vicuña Mackenna, *La Argentina en el año 1855* (Buenos Aires, 1936), p. 51.

25 Sarmiento, *Viajes*, pp. 86–116 (Letter to Antonino Aberastain).

of 1848, he reported how he had returned from Europe with an 'alarming story of what he had seen'. He had a sense of a 'coming and imminent catastrophe' and a recognition that the 'current order of things' could not continue.[26] Sarmiento took from Europe an awareness of deepening social tensions and the lesson that the Latin American elite should make every effort to prevent similar conditions developing in the Americas. He viewed the avoidance of communism as one of the chief objectives of the system of state education he was planning. In newspaper articles written in the mid-1850s he argued that many of Argentina's problems derived from adopting unsuitable foreign models. 'We should copy nothing from France', he urged in 1856, 'other than its fashions and its art.'[27]

Among the members of Argentina's liberal intelligentsia, a secondary figure, Félix Frías, became the strongest adversary of the 1848 revolutions. Frías passionately opposed Rosas and took a prominent part in the revolt against him in 1839–1840 when he served as the secretary to General Juan Lavalle, the commander of the Unitario rebel forces. Zealous Catholicism distinguished Frías from the other members of the group. His opposition to both the 1848 revolutions and to 'socialism' was rooted in Catholic ideas; he viewed Catholicism as a stronger instrument for achieving social and moral regeneration than liberalism. Between 1848 and 1853 Frías lived in Paris where he worked as the correspondent of a Chilean newspaper. He witnessed some of the most notorious incidents of the revolution, such as the assassination of the archbishop of Paris at the commencement of the June Days. Henceforth he became the inveterate foe of all the ideas and objectives of working class libertarian socialism. In letters to Alberdi in 1851 he denounced socialism as a 'plebeian philosophy of sensual arrogance ... the science of envy'. In communications to the deposed Guizot in Paris he attacked 'pure democracy' on the grounds it led to demagogy and tyranny.[28] Having lived during this critical period in France, Frías became one of the harshest critics of the radical movement in Chile led by Bilbao. In early 1852, soon after the defeat of the second rebellion in Chile, he denounced the Society for Equality as a group of 'young men [who] were repeating like parrots the same subversive slogans as in France'.[29] In a far-fetched comparison Frías likened Bilbao to Rosas. As the enemies of legitimately constituted government, he argued, Bilbao and Rosas alike were proponents of tyrannical authority. They were 'socialist' enemies of civil society because they threatened property rights.

26 Sarmiento, *Viajes*, p. 5.

27 Halperín Donghi, *Argentina 1846–1880*, p. 166, quoting *El Nacional*, 19 June 1856.

28 Jorge M. Mayer, *Alberdi y su tiempo* (Buenos Aires, 1963), p. 389.

29 Halperín Donghi, *Argentina 1846–1880*, p. 39. See also Félix Frías, *Carta sobre la situación actual de la República Argentina* (Buenos Aires, 1852).

Frías likened the defeat of the June Days of 1848 in Paris to the battle of Loncomilla in Chile in September 1851, which marked the defeat of the revolutionary movement. Had the rebels won, he claimed, Chile would have lapsed into disorder, class warfare and socialism. Anarchy and, ultimately, a tyranny like that of Rosas would have followed. 'People who sow anarchy will harvest bloody dictators,' he wrote. From Frías's Catholic, ultraconservative perspective, Rosas bore no resemblance to the European absolutists. Because he had confiscated the property of his enemies he was 'nothing less than socialism in power. What the barbarous theories [of socialism only] threatened to do in France, that enormous bandit [in Buenos Aires] carried out. "Take from the rich and give to the poor" is the favourite maxim of the European socialists. Rosas has been doing this for a long time.'[30]

For his part, Alberdi, who in this period lived in Valparaíso, hoped that the European revolutions would pressure Rosas to adopt a constitution. He described the movements in Europe as the start of a 'prodigious labour of regeneration [that] foretold the termination of the [Buenos Aires] dictatorship'. The 'arbitrary regimes of the Americas' like that of Rosas would be destroyed by the same 'great push of this century (*empuje del siglo*)' that was consuming the thrones of Europe. As events in western and central Europe unfolded, Alberdi oscillated between the idea that the European revolutions would push Rosas into political liberalisation and the hope he would offer concessions spontaneously. 'If General Rosas should imitate the absolutist sovereigns in Italy and Germany and grant a constitution and moderate liberty to Buenos Aires,' he wrote in the newspaper *El Comercio* in mid-1848, 'he will fulfil the destinies of his country. It cannot be asking too much to request a ruler who is a citizen [of a republic] to make the same concessions to liberty as men who rule as kings.'[31] Following the death of Echeverría in 1851, Alberdi wrote an obituary that became another attack on European socialism. Like nearly all the Argentina liberal intellectuals, he regarded the 'bourgeois' French revolution of 1830 as a great source of inspiration but rejected its more radical successor of 1848. He therefore described Echeverría in glowing terms in the obituary as the person who brought 'the excellent spirit and the ideas of every kind created by the French revolution of 1830' into Spanish South America. The *Dogma Socialista*, Echeverría's most influential work, he insisted, should be understood as 'a code and digest of principles' that had nothing to do with the term 'socialist' as used by 'French demagogues'. Echeverría had never cherished 'ambitions to alter

30 Halperín Donghi, *Argentina 1846–1880*, p. 39.

31 Mayer, *Alberdi*, p. 352.

the foundations of society as it exists'. Any attempt to link him with 'disturbers of the peace in Europe' represented a piece of pro-Rosas propaganda.[32]

In 1851, when Alberdi received the communications from Frías that attacked the radical movements in France and Chile, he agreed with him in rejecting 'democratic fanaticism and idolatry'. Alberdi held that the Spanish American republics had made the disastrous choice of democracy at the time they achieved independence. 'Born and raised to witness all the disasters [democracy] has provoked, I would never support it,' he declared. In his view, Britain and the United States, not France, represented the models of liberty most appropriate to Argentina.[33] In an essay titled 'The Argentine Republic in 1851' Alberdi emphasised that the country had to turn the clock back to the year 1810 at the start of the revolution for independence. A return to the past meant resuming the quest for a national congress and a properly constituted government. Every country in the Americas – even isolated and backward Paraguay – had a 'general government' and a constitution. In this statement France served only as a model to strengthen the case Alberdi wanted to make for a constitution in Argentina. 'Within two years of abolishing monarchy [France] has provided itself with a congress and a constitution despite all the obstacles there to republican government.'[34] In 1852, following the fall of Rosas, Alberdi published *Las bases*, the essay that strongly influenced the Argentine constitution of 1853. In this document, by supporting a strong executive and opposing universal suffrage, Alberdi once more tacitly repudiated the legacy of the 1848 revolutions.

Only Bartolomé Mitre, one of the younger Argentine liberals, expressed any enthusiasm for the democratic ideals of 1848. Mitre enjoyed long personal ties with Bilbao and Arcos, to whom he was closer in age than to Sarmiento and Alberdi. Working as a journalist in Chile, Mitre attacked the conservative government there on issues such as the failure to develop an education policy or to protect the freedom of religion and the press. In November 1850 the Chilean government closed down the newspaper Mitre worked for, and he suffered brief imprisonment following the rebellion of April 1851. In September that year he left the country to join Urquiza's army as it marched against Rosas in Buenos Aires. In this period some of his older contemporaries regarded Mitre as an Argentine Bilbao, another radical firebrand highly susceptible to French radical

32 Juan Bautista Alberdi, *Obras selectas. Nueva edición ordenada, revisada y precidida de una introducción por el Dr. Joaquín V. González* (Buenos Aires, 1920), vol. 4, pp. 478–80.

33 Mayer, *Alberdi*, pp. 396–7. See also Juan Bautista Alberdi, *Cartas inéditas a Juan María Gutiérrez y a Félix Frías* (Buenos Aires, 1953).

34 Alberdi, *Obras Selectas*, vol. 5, pp. 485–6.

influences. In Frías's comment, 'this boy's head is in France, and he's determined to sing to us the odes to liberty by Victor Hugo.'[35] Writing in the Buenos Aires newspaper *Los Debates* soon after the fall of Rosas, Mitre published the *Profession of Faith*, a document notable for its French borrowings. *Profession of Faith* began with an epigram by Lamartine: 'the great passion of our time is the passion for social perfectibility. The instrument of that passion is the press.' The manifesto proclaimed 'a new consciousness concerning liberty' and listed a determination to pursue many of the same objectives as the bourgeois (although not the working class) revolutionaries in France. The objectives included direct universal suffrage, freedom of the press, the right to hold meetings in public without restriction and public education 'as a means to moralise the masses and make them fit for the enjoyment of liberty'.[36] In the 1860s Mitre, the military and political architect of the Argentine national state, dominated by Buenos Aires, became the most powerful politician in Argentina. In 1862 he became president of the republic, and in 1865 was appointed commander-in-chief of the allied army in the War of the Triple Alliance waged against Paraguay. Accused of authoritarian and militaristic inclinations in his maturity, in his later years in opposition Mitre led a highly conservative faction of the Argentine oligarchy. Despite such associations, Mitre never abandoned the democratic ideas expressed in the *Profession of Faith*. While Sarmiento, Frías and Alberdi perceived the 1848 revolutions as a threat, Mitre helped to incorporate them into the political culture of Argentina and the Rio de la Plata.

Conclusion

The 1848 revolutions had a much more limited impact in the Rio de la Plata than in Pernambuco or Chile, chiefly because of the existence of the Rosas regime in Buenos Aires. Events in Europe influenced Argentina's liberal intellectuals, but mostly by pushing them into a more openly antidemocratic position. The revolution in France played an indirect part in the fall of Rosas in 1852, and provided Alberdi with an additional justification for the need to frame a constitution, the task accomplished in 1853. Guizot's vacillating policy towards Montevideo provided his enemies with some of the ammunition they used against him in February 1848. In the longer term, Argentines and Uruguayans assimilated the rhetoric of 1848 but never reproduced the events of that year. The European revolutions influenced political movements in Argentina, in

35 Mayer, *Alberdi*, p. 425.

36 Bartolomé Mitre, *Profesión de fe y otros escritos. Nota preliminar de Ricardo Levene* (Buenos Aires, 1956).

particular so-called *mitrismo*, the party led by Mitre, which adopted some of their more moderate ideas as enunciated in the *Profession of Faith*. At a later date the revolution of July 1890 in Buenos Aires, often known as *El Noventa*, appeared closest in style to the European revolutions of 1848. As with the French revolution, economic conditions strongly influenced *El Noventa*, which, again like the movement in France, occurred in protest at government corruption. As in the Paris June Days, the participants in the 1890 revolution in Buenos Aires fought out the struggle from behind street barricades. Leaders of *El Noventa* like Aristóbalo del Valle and Leandro N. Alem employed a democratic and romantic discourse reminiscent of 1848. Like the 1848 revolutions, *El Noventa* ended in a conservative restoration. Nevertheless, the similarities between 1848 in Paris and 1890 in Buenos Aires remained limited and largely superficial. Less a popular uprising, and not at all a workers' or a socialist movement, the 1890 revolution became a regional and local uprising led by the conservative classes of Buenos Aires. The 1890 revolutionaries were looking backwards, not forwards. For this reason they had very little of substance in common with the goals of the *quarante-huitards*.

6

Traces and Perceptions: A Chilean in Europe after the 1848 Revolutions

LEONOR GARCÍA MILLÉ

Foreign travellers are privileged witnesses of historical events. Indeed, by providing an outsider's view of local circumstances, the foreign gaze may uncover aspects unseen by the inhabitants of the place they are visiting. By representing an unfamiliar reality, and as representatives of their own country, travel writers can perform a doubly enriching service for their readers.

The mid-nineteenth century saw an increase in the number of Spanish American travellers visiting Europe. This resulted in the emergence of travel writing.[1] During this period travels were written by exiles and/or envoys sent by governments or newspapers. However, political unrest and economic stagnation ensured that Spanish American travellers were few and, consequently, travel accounts are scarce. It would not be until the 1880s, when export expansion promoted the formation of oligarchies, that the European tour would become institutionalised.[2] Travel books multiplied, written not only by politicians, but also by ordinary travellers, including women.[3]

Hence, the Europe of the 1840s was recorded in only a handful of travel accounts by the small number of Spanish American authors who

1 Although there are few studies of Latin American travel writing, the genre existed at least as early as the seventeenth century, see Lino Gómez Canedo, 'Dos viajeros mexicanos a Europa a fines del siglo XVII,' *Historia Mexicana*, 31 (1981), pp. 117–56. During the first decades of the nineteenth century, although travelogues are few, Spanish American views from abroad can be found in the letters or diaries written by members of diplomatic delegations in Europe or political exiles.

2 David Viñas, 'La mirada a Europa: del viaje colonial al viaje estético,' in David Viñas, *Literatura argentina y política. De los jacobinos porteños a la bohemia anarquista* (Buenos Aires, 1995), p. 168.

3 For studies about this period see George D. Schade, 'Los viajeros argentinos del 80,' in *Texto Crítico*, 10 (1984), and Frédéric Martinez, 'Representación de Europa y discurso nacionalista en los relatos de viajes colombianos, 1850–1900,' in Eduardo Posada-Carbó (ed.), *Wars, Parties and Nationalism: Essays on the Politics and Society of Nineteenth-Century Latin America* (London, 1995), pp. 55–70.

visited Europe at this time. Four travellers stand out: the Argentines Juan Bautista Alberdi and Domingo Faustino Sarmiento, who visited Europe in 1843 and between 1845 and 1846 (before the revolutions), along with the Mexican Manuel Payno and the Chilean Benjamín Vicuña Mackenna, who travelled in Europe in 1851 and between 1853 and 1855 (after the revolutions). Of these travellers, only Vicuña Mackenna analysed the revolutions of 1848 in any depth.

Juan Bautista Alberdi visited France, Switzerland and Italy in 1843, which he described as 'countries of selfishness, without any sensitivity'.[4] He was unable to perceive any sign of the impending crisis and his account comprised mainly descriptions of institutions, buildings and their interior decoration. Hence, when he visited the French Assembly he noted that he had been able to sit in the places of Louis Adolphe Thiers and Francois Arago,[5] but did not mention the monarchy of Louis Philippe, or say any more about the French people than that they were 'servile'.[6]

Sarmiento also visited Europe before the revolutions had taken place. But unlike Alberdi, he asserted in the prologue to the book that he had been able, if not to predict the revolutions, at least 'to forecast the crisis as a violent one ... (having been able) ... to judge the present state of affairs and institutions unsustainable'.[7] During his travels he had felt that he was walking over a minefield, with the rumblings of an imminent and inevitable crisis forever audible.[8] Sarmiento described Europe's social conditions with a critical eye, observing that European society was an 'unfortunate blend of grandeur and abjection'.[9] 'I come from Europe, where I had admired its monuments, I had gone down on my knees before its science and had been amazed by its artistic prodigies; but I had also seen millions of vile peasants, proletarians and artisans, degraded, unworthy of being counted among human beings.'[10] In Sarmiento's view political and religious rights were enjoyed only by a minority.[11] The European people were treated as minors, kept under state guardianship.[12]

Manuel Payno, on the other hand, arrived in Europe some years after the revolutions had been crushed. In his view, the 'people' were not the

4 Juan Bautista Alberdi, 'Impresiones de viaje,' in *Escritos póstumos* (Buenos Aires, 1901), vol. XV, p. 870.
5 Alberdi, 'Impresiones de viaje,' p. 867.
6 *Ibid.*, p. 928.
7 Domingo F. Sarmiento, *Viajes por Europa, Africa i América. 1845–1847* (Madrid, 1996), p. 5.
8 Sarmiento, *Viajes*, p. 5.
9 *Ibid.*, p. 86.
10 *Ibid.*, p. 334.
11 *Ibid.*, p. 333.
12 *Ibid.*, p. 317.

key agent for what had happened in France: 'In 1848 the revolution started in the press, it was followed in the cafes and in the boulevards, it continued in the Paris banquets and was concluded with the defection of the army'.[13] Contrary to Sarmiento, Payno did not see the Revolution as inevitable, and deemed it as 'one of the strangest and most unexpected' historical events.[14] He judged the monarchy of Louis Philippe as a peaceful and flourishing period, the monarch a man of talent, and the uprising incomprehensible.[15]

Only the Chilean Benjamín Vicuña Mackenna (1831–1886), who travelled throughout Europe in 1852 and 1853, and developed a deeper interest in the events of 1848 and their aftermath, devoted more pages to the subject. Vicuña Mackenna stands out for various reasons. First, he had followed the course of revolutionary movement with particular attention, even devotion. Moreover, as a liberal himself, he had participated in the abortive attempt in 1851 to overthrow the conservative government of Chile. Finally, his own journey to Europe was a self-inflicted exile resulting from his participation in Chile's Revolution of 1851.

What follows is an analysis of Vicuña Mackenna's representation of the revolutions of 1848 in Europe. The chapter begins with a brief overview of Chilean politics during the first decades of the nineteenth century, mentioning significant aspects of Vicuña's life. Then Vicuña's portrayal of Europe is explored through his account of the vestiges of the revolutions that he encountered on his travels. Finally, we will consider the images of France, the Austrian Empire and the Italian states drawn in the travel account.

Chile and Vicuña Mackenna

Benjamín Vicuña Mackenna was born on 25 August 1831 in Santiago, Chile, of a wealthy family. Chilean society at that time was aristocratic, agrarian, Catholic, authoritarian, paternalistic and peripheral.[16] Indeed, although Chile during these years was exceptional in the region for its stability, its political system was as authoritarian as anywhere in Latin America.

Since 1830 a conservative coalition had dominated the government. The so-called *pelucones* ('wigs' or conservatives) constituted a traditionalist

13 Manuel Payno, *Memorias e impresiones de un viaje a Inglaterra y Escocia* (Mexico City, 1997), p. 42.

14 *Ibid.*, p. 43.

15 *Ibid.*, pp. 43–4.

16 Alfredo Jocelyn-Holt, 'Liberalismo y modernidad. Ideología y simbolismo en el Chile decimonónico: un marco teórico,' in Ricardo Krebs and Cristián Gazmuri (eds.), *La revolución francesa y Chile* (Santiago, 1990), p. 327.

and authoritarian group that displayed great energy to reestablish order and social discipline after a turbulent post-independent period.[17] Accordingly, the constitution they established in 1833 strongly favoured the executive, allowing the president two consecutive five-year terms, meaning that he exerted uncontested power for ten years. The president was the centre of Chilean politics, 'a real monarch with republican title' as Donoso puts it.[18] Moreover, repression was routine and electoral intervention secured the conservative hold upon power.[19] In this presidential style of government, congress was oligarchical, its members subject to designation by the executive. *Martín Rivas*, Chile's first novel, depicts this feature of the political system in a dialogue; when Don Dámaso affirms that, depending on the people's will, he could be a deputy, he is corrected by Doña Francisca: in Chile, those elected belong to the government.[20]

Confronting the *pelucones* were the *pipiolos* ('youngsters'), young liberals who sought to reform society, and yearned for a real democratic republic that would lay the Spanish colonial and monarchical past to rest.[21] The struggle that would occupy these years was aimed at reducing the power of the president in order to achieve the independence of the congress.[22]

Having obtained a law degree at the tender age of eighteen, Vicuña Mackenna entered politics on the liberal side.[23] His coming of age coincided with a period that his contemporary Isidoro Errázurriz characterised as one of 'ferment of ideas and aspirations, feverish impatience and patriotic desires'.[24] Congress became a scene of conflict and political and literary debate occupied the educated classes. The early expansion of the educational system, and the introduction and diffusion of European – mainly French – books, encouraged the liberal revival of the 1840s.[25] Years later, Vicuña Mackenna recalled this period, affirming that Alphonse de

17 Sergio Grez Toso, 'El liberalismo popular: características y rol en la constitución del movimiento popular en el Chile decimonónico,' *Revista Chilena de Historia y Geografía* 163 (1997), p. 203.

18 Ricardo Donoso, *Las ideas políticas en Chile* (Santiago, 1967), pp. 85–6.

19 Simon Collier and William F. Sater, *A History of Chile, 1808–1994* (Cambridge, 1996), p. 56; J.M. Valenzuela, *Democratización vía reforma: La expansión del sufragio en Chile* (Buenos Aires, 1985).

20 Alberto Blest Gana, *Martín Rivas* (Havana, 1989), p. 33.

21 Cristián Gazmuri, *El '48' chileno: igualitarios, reformistas, radicales, masones y bomberos* (Santiago, 1992), p. 17.

22 Donoso, *Las ideas*, p. 86.

23 Ricardo Donoso, *Don Benjamín Vicuña Mackenna. Su vida, sus escritos y su tiempo* (Santiago, 1925), p. 25.

24 Isidoro Errázurriz, *Historia de la Administración Errázurriz* (Santiago, 1935), p. 242.

25 In 1835 José Victorino Lastarria created the Instituto Normal; the University of Chile was established in 1842 and new schools were also opened in this period, Ricardo Melgar, 'Francisco Bilbao y la rebelión de los igualitarios en Chile' in *Cuadernos Americanos*, 3:27 (1991), p. 55.

Lamartine's *Histoire de Girondins* brought a revolutionary impulse to all young *pipiolos*.[26] An additional catalyst was the presence in Santiago of Argentine Liberals, such as Vicente Fidel López, Domingo Faustino Sarmiento, and Juan M. Gutiérrez, driven into exile by Juan Manuel de Rosas, who contributed to the vigour of literary and political debate.[27] Political clubs appeared and, for the first time, Liberal debate addressed its appeal directly to ordinary Chileans, particularly artisans.[28]

In this atmosphere of expectation news of the revolutions in Europe in 1848 was followed with great interest by Liberals in Chile. Thirty years later Vicuña Mackenna recalled the reception in Chile to the news from Europe:

> We had seen it coming, we studied it, we understood it, we admired it: we would assimilate the lessons its leaders taught us, follow events the press, and identify with republican aspirations.[29]

Hence, Chilean Liberals not only admired the bravado of France's democrats, but also were able immediately to understand and to assimilate the lessons of their European mentors. Unlike the simple imitators of 1848 European revolutions described by Edwards, Vicuña Mackenna portrays an intellectual community that was active in its own right, well able to respond and relate to metropolitan developments.[30] Young Chileans saw themselves not only as followers of the revolution in Europe, but also as participants.

If, as Vicuña Mackenna affirms, the revolutions in Europe had been predicted by Chilean youth, this was because, as Cristián Gazmuri explains, young people were already accustomed to republican and democratic vocabulary and ideology.[31] French ideas were familiar to Chilean elites by the mid-nineteenth century. Moreover, the revolutions of 1848 were received by an already politicised and mobilised section of the population. Young *pipiolos* adapted European liberalism according to their own political interests and cultural codes.[32] They demanded 'a federalist, decentralised, and parliamentary democratic state' and sought a candidate of their own.[33] President Bulnes had been governing since 1841 and the proximity of

26 Benjamín Vicuña Mackenna, *Los girondinos chilenos* (Santiago, 1989), p. 29.

27 Iván Jaksic, 'Sarmiento and the Chilean Press, 1841–1851,' in Tulio Halperín Donghi, Iván Jaksic et al. (eds.), *Sarmiento* (London, 1994).

28 Luis Alberto Romero, 'La sociedad de la igualdad: liberales y artesanos en la vida política de Santiago de Chile,' in *Siglo XIX. Revista de Historia*, 2:3 (1987), p. 20; Daniel Riquelme, *La revolución del 20 de abril de 1851* (Santiago, 1966), p. 59.

29 Vicuña Mackenna, *Los girondinos chilenos*, p. 23.

30 Alberto Edwards Vives, *La fronda aristocrática en Chile* (Santiago, 1936), p. 64.

31 Gazmuri, *El '48' chileno*, p. 34.

32 Jocelyn-Holt, 'Liberalismo y modernidad', p. 325.

33 Maurice Zeitlin, *The Civil Wars in Chile (Or the Bourgeois Revolutions that Never Were)* (Princeton, 1984), p. 35.

elections motivated hopes.

Vicuña Mackenna participated in this political effervescence. He read French authors passionately, and, as a young *pipiolo*, became involved in liberal associational life. In 1849, he was elected secretary of 'Club de la Reforma' (the 'Reform Club'). Vicuña Mackenna was also among the founders of the 'Sociedad de la Igualdad' (the 'Society of Equality'). Formed in March 1850, this association enjoyed the participation of artisans and aspired to spread education to the working classes. His articles appeared in the Society's newspaper, *El Amigo del Pueblo (The Friend of the People)*.

This sudden and progressive radicalisation made the conservatives close ranks and support the candidacy of Manuel Montt, a repressive and authoritarian figure. On the opposing side, the 'Sociedad de la Igualdad' would finally become an instrument for the opposition to the Conservative candidate. Such was the instability provoked by meetings and marches, that the government dissolved the Society and imprisoned or exiled some of its leaders. Vicuña Mackenna was not among them and continued his political activity despite the state of siege imposed on Santiago; in February 1851 he, along with other liberals, supported the candidacy of General José María de la Cruz major of the southern province of Concepción. On 20 April 1851 the Valdivia battalion pronounced in Santiago. Although the Sociedad de la Igualdad had anticipated popular support, the general response was of indifference.[34] During the subsequent repression Vicuña Mackenna was arrested and sentenced to death. He was later pardoned and in July he escaped from prison to continue conspiring against the government. The confrontation was far from being settled.

Upon the Conservative Montt assuming the presidency in September 1851 a civil war broke out, mainly in the southern provinces. Having participated in the organisation of the uprising, Vicuña Mackenna was also involved in the ensuing military campaign. But this time government forces crushed the movement definitively, forcing Vicuña Mackenna into hiding on his family hacienda of Tabolango between January and November 1852. When peace was restored the opposition disintegrated, occasioning the young Chilean's decision to leave his country and embark on a tour. As his fellow conspirator, Santiago Arcos, affirmed in a letter from prison to Francisco Bilbao in 1852, the government was angry and set upon revenge upon those who had conspired against it.[35] On 26

34 Edwards Vives, *La fronda aristocrática en Chile*, p. 73. and Grez Toso, 'El liberalismo popular,' p. 205.

35 Santiago Arcos, 'Carta a Francisco Bilbao' in Alejandro Witker, *Chile: sociedad y política. Del Acta de Independencia a nuestros días* (Mexico City, 1978), p. 79.

November 1852 Vicuña Mackenna left Chile on board a ship owned by his father. He would not return until 29 October 1855, having spent almost two years in Europe (8 August 1853 to 9 July 1855). Vicuña Mackenna visited the United States, Canada, Mexico, France, England, Scotland, Ireland, the Italian states (Ligura, Piedmont, Tuscany, the Papal states, Lombardy and Parma) Switzerland, Austria, Bohemia, the German states (Prussia, Bavaria and Hanover), the Netherlands, Brazil and Argentina.

During his tour he wrote a diary, upon which his travel book is mainly based. However Vicuña Mackenna created a new narrative, with help of his memory, as well as a variety of documentary sources.

Europe as the scene of revolutions

In *Páginas de mi diario*, Vicuña Mackenna records how on his journey he kept on finding vestiges of the revolutions of 1789 and 1848: the sites of uprisings and confrontations, political inscriptions on walls, castles and dungeons that had served as prisons, and people who had participated in the upheavals. Not content with recording and commemorating these sites and incidents, the Chilean traveller also brought scenes from the revolutions to life:

> I remembered the popular scenes of this place, so many times consecrated by the popular assemblies against their tyrants, so many other times stained by the popular frenzy with blood and the martyrdom of illustrious victims.[36]

This, then, was an image of Europe in which, whatever the aftermath of the revolutions, the presence of the uprisings could still be felt.

In the early 1850s France, the German states and the Austrian Empire showed evidence of the events that had taken place there in 1848, and earlier, in 1789, in the case of France. When analysing Vicuña Mackenna's response to these countries, his own background has to be taken into consideration. James Buzard argues that travellers carry with them a set of constructed expectations derived from books, newspapers, pictures and other media. On their journeys they are in search of a synthesis between the image prevailing in their minds and the actual scenes of the places they are visiting: '(t)he "original" becomes itself when the viewer perceives that it suits its representations.'[37] Thus, what seems to be a continuous discovery of traces of revolution by Vicuña Mackenna, should not be interpreted as the awareness of elements that are merely there, but, on the contrary, should be seen as a conscious search for such vestiges. That

36 Vicuña Mackenna, *Páginas de mi diario*, I, p. 343.

37 James Buzard, *The Beating Track. European Tourism, Literature and the Ways to Culture. 1800–1918* (Oxford, 1993), p. 196.

anecdotes or data about social movements are frequently mentioned in the young Chilean's travels has more to do with the exiled author than with the situation of Europe in the 1850s.

As has already been said, Vicuña Mackenna was strongly influenced by the republican, liberal and democratic ideas received from Europe. He had participated actively in the uprising against the Conservative government in 1851. And he had been forced to leave his country due to this involvement. Consequently, he was eager to find evidence in Europe of a movement he had so much revered and to which he considered himself a pupil.

Not a tourist but a political exile, his observations were permeated by this particular bias. Paris, for example, was marked in his mind by political and social unrest:

> What place in Paris does not bring to memory some of the social and political traditions – at times horrific, at times sublime – that have regenerated the world since 89?[38]

A view of Europe as scene of revolutions, the place in which social movements were enacted for the first time, the source and home of ideas of social emancipation, is what characterises the Chilean's travel account. In the nineteenth century a journey to Europe was considered by Americans as a movement from the remote periphery to the centre of the globe. On arriving in Europe the Chilean traveller was reaching the source of social movements. Vicuña Mackenna was able to explain the Chilean movement, its roots, as well as its ultimate fate, by reference to European legends, places and monument. In providing what Gazmuri calls 'the paradigm of Chilean oligarchic youth', France played a fundamental role in setting the scene.[39]

If the idea of revolution was strongly embedded in Vicuña Mackenna's conception of Europe, another element that needs to be stressed is his conception of revolutions themselves. Gertrude Yeager affirms that Vicuña Mackenna was distinguished by his 'hatred of despotism' and his permanent belief in '(t)he people's right to revolution in the defence of freedom'.[40] In *Páginas de mi diario* revolutions appear as positive historical processes, the source of historical transformation and progress. Although they may temporarily be crushed, in the end they were considered inevitable. This conception was strongly embedded in Chile's peculiarly Conservative post-Independence history and in Vicuña Mackenna's own political and cultural background.

38 Vicuña Mackenna, *Páginas de mi diario*, I, p. 343.
39 Gazmuri, *El '48' chileno*, p. 27.
40 Gertrude Matyoka Yeager, 'Barros Arana, Vicuña Mackenna, Amunátegui: the Historian as National Educator,' in *Journal of Interamerican Studies and World Affairs* 19, 2 (1977), pp. 186–7.

For Vicuña Mackenna the Old World monarchies would sooner or later be overthrown. For example, he enthusiastically predicted the dethronement of Louis Napoleon: 'here (in Paris) can be found the mine that will blow up his throne, blown up like many others.'[41] Chile was no different in this respect. Constructed upon a revolution, a new one was waiting to destroy the Conservative hold upon power:

> Since Independence, Chile has had two revolutions. The first in 1829 constructed the PAST. The second in 1851 was the expression of an agitated and painful present. Today, the REVOLUTION OF THE FUTURE still awaits us.[42]

In Chile, as in Europe, revolutions were destined to shape the political future.

Traces and Perceptions

By the time Vicuña Mackenna arrived in Europe the monarchies had already reestablished themselves after the year of Revolution, regional unrest had been brought under control, and social and political reforms had been withdrawn. However, especially for a self-appointed revolutionary eager to discover vestiges of 1848, it was still possible to find traces of the movements. But they were just traces, for, arriving five or six years after the events, the Chilean was not able directly to witness the upheavals. Rather, he was obliged to provide information about the historical moment he was facing, the period that followed social and political defeat.

Inscriptions on the walls of Paris testified to the struggle of ideas between different parties. One of them expressed nostalgia for Ledru-Rollin, the former member of the Provisional Government:

> Oh! Famous Ledru Rollin, (...), when will you come to stain our shirts with the blood of the aristocracy![43]

Others had been drawn during the Provisional Government and mocked its benefits:

> Liberty to die of hunger! Equality in misery! Fraternity of Cain! This is the currency of the ferocious republicans![44]

After transcribing these and other inscriptions discovered during his stay in Paris, the historian concluded:

41 Vicuña Mackenna, *Páginas de mi diario*, I, p. 344.
42 *Ibid.*, p. 386.
43 *Ibid.*, p. 354.
44 *Ibid.*, p. 354.

> All these passionate inscriptions, made with soot of ruins over the ruins themselves, had a sad and at the same time solemn meaning.[45]

This sentence was not written by a conservative afraid of disorder. Its disillusionment was a consequence of the discovery of the remains of a shattered but unaccomplished revolution. In addition, noticing the blatant persistence of confrontation was unavoidable. The image is quite revealing: France was built and shaped by conflicting ideas displayed upon its ruins; progress through destruction. Notwithstanding this perception, Vicuña Mackenna comments solemnly on the sadness of the inscriptions, showing the reverence with which Americans regarded European history.

Meeting people, or simply observing them, provided an opportunity for the traveller to find witnesses of the revolutionary events and victims of the repression that followed the uprisings. When travelling by steamship from Venice to Trieste Vicuña Mackenna observed how a Hungarian soldier was seized and thrown into chains by Austrian soldiers. Indignation at this injustice was heightened when people were not allowed to give the man money. For the Chilean traveller, the control established by the Habsburgs was evident: 'Unfortunate Italians, Hungarians, and Polish, they even have to adore their oppressors' horses!'[46] He cited many other examples of oppression exerted in regions that had tried to liberate themselves from Habsburg rule. After the revolts in 1848, the Habsburg Empire attempted with violence and repression to recover and reassert its territorial control.

On another occasion, Vicuña Mackenna met an Italian waiter in a restaurant in Draguignan, France. A student at Pavia, he had been forced to leave his place of origin after participating in the movement against the Habsburgs, seeking refuge in France. Vicuña Mackenna could empathise with the waiter's craving to return to his country. The Chilean, after all, could verify that persecution and exile were the birthmarks left by the 1848 revolutions.

Besides affecting the European cities the revolutions of 1848 had also disturbed rural areas. In the Apennines a shepherdess told him about 'big people' who had traversed the mountains some years before. For the Chilean it was not difficult to guess who these 'big people' might have been:

> Perhaps they were Italian fugitives that have fought for freedom and were escaping from the Swiss in Naples, from the French in Rome, from the Austrians in Florence.[47]

45 *Ibid.*, p. 354.
46 Vicuña Mackenna, *Páginas de mi diario*, II, p. 179.
47 *Ibid.*, p. 116.

This image of Italians hunted down in their own land was a further reminder that behind the movements of social liberation there were struggles for national liberation against the foreign usurper.

In Vicuña Mackenna's understanding of a social revolution, and of any historical event, great men were the leaders of the process of change. The great names and personalities of European history and literature were familiar to the traveller. After all, knowledge of the Old World came through its writers, prominent intellectuals and politicians. Hence his travel account is full of names – Louis Blanc, Louis-Eugène Cavaignac, Alphonse Lamartine, Adolphe Thiers, François Guizot and Henri Lacordaire – whose ideas had illuminated the people. By acknowledging their importance he demonstrated his own knowledge of the European political scene and identified himself with these great European political figures.

An example of this mixture of hagiography and self-validation can be found in Vicuña Mackenna's account of Silvio Pellico. Pellico was an Italian patriot who had been imprisoned in 1820, sentenced to death in 1822 and then amnestied (the same trial that the Chilean had suffered thirty years later).

> Silvio Pellico, Oh that friend of the captive! On so many occasions he presented himself to me wearing his aureole of martyrdom and immense pain, in which I felt I could find some of my own reflected.[48]

By attributing to himself the characteristics and sufferings of an Italian nationalist, the Chilean revolutionary was establishing a link between their struggles. He was imagining a community of martyred revolutionaries, and one not confined to Europe.

In the autumn of 1853 François Arago, who had been minister of war and the navy for the provisional government, died. Vicuña Mackenna described the sentiment shown by attendants to his burial in Paris. In a blend of liberty and despotism, mourners and soldiers were present in number: around twenty thousand people lined the streets to pay their respects to the dead politician, while approximately six thousand soldiers were present to prevent disorders. The Chilean's belief in the power and tenacity of revolutionary ideas persuaded him of the imminence of social unrest. Napoleon III should fear the respect that Arago was receiving at his burial: 'Perhaps it was the rain that day that saved an improvised throne from a violent blast.'[49]

Driven by his interest in exiled revolutionaries, the Chilean historian also attended a meeting in London in November 1853. Republican exiles had gathered to commemorate the anniversary of Poland's revolution of

48 *Ibid.*, p. 194.
49 Vicuña Mackenna, *Páginas de mi diario*, I, p. 338.

1831. 1,500 people attended the meeting, most of them English. Lajos Kossuth, Giuseppe Mazzini and Louis Blanc were the notorious absentees because of sickness, jealousies and/or quarrels. However, Russian, Hungarian, Polish, German, Austrian and Italian speakers were also present:

> Each oppressed nationality had an apostle there, each failed revolution could count a martyr among that group of exiles.[50]

Several inflammatory speeches were heard, among them one of Ledru-Rollin who showed, in the view of Vicuña Mackenna, and naive belief in the proximity of victory. The Chilean historian instantly identified himself with this family of mourning exiles: 'How many of us, exiles, were there, united by the sympathy of pain!'[51] Had this impressive meeting taken place in Paris, Vicuña Mackenna was sure that it would have engendered a revolution. But, being held in front of an English audience, it was no more than a simple political meeting, punctually brought to a close at midnight.[52] An end to despotism, the death of monarchy and liberation of the oppressed could be pronounced from the safety of London, but it in a way that was harmless to any throne.

The overall image from Vicuña Mackenna's account is one of disillusion: the opposition was scattered or dead, 'all the great names are being persecuted by proscription or oblivion', monarchies had reestablished their despotism.[53] However, still present was the undiminished necessity, and even inevitability, of the emergence of republics and the destruction of monarchies.

For a republican, the perception of Europe in the aftermath of the 1848 revolutions was strongly influenced by the figures of the monarchs who held power. In *Páginas de mi diario* it is possible to find contempt for the figure of the monarch, though not necessarily for the individual who wore the crown. Monarchs were considered embodiments of despotism. The harshest remarks were reserved for Emperor Napoleon III, described as 'austere, sinister and imperious', a singular despot whose tyranny was absolute.[54] Abhorrent to the Chilean traveller, the French emperor was also unappealing to his subjects. In a parade, the emperor inspired 'public indifference', and even 'contempt', while in his public appearances he was greeted 'without enthusiasm or any other token of the expansion of the soul with which the people salutes its heroes.'[55]

50 *Ibid.*, p. 389.
51 *Ibid.*, p. 389.
52 *Ibid.*, p. 390.
53 *Ibid.*, p. 352.
54 *Ibid.*, pp. 340, 344.
55 *Ibid.*, p. 340.

Emperor Francis Joseph came off only slightly better. His physiognomy was described as agreeable and benign. But his expression lacked intelligence and he displayed arrogance and, Vicuña Mackenna concluded, 'he has no will of his own'.[56] The former king of Bavaria was an old imbecile and the duke Leopold III of Florence was 'a sanataic'.[57] Hence, while republicans were considered as martyrs and commanded the admiration of the author, kings deserved only his disdain and scorn.

During these prosperous years following the defeat of the Revolutions of 1848, Europe was calm. The revolutions had failed and become mere themes for tour guides. Vicuña Mackenna records some anecdotes of those 'good old days' told by guides: the window through which the princess Windischgrätz had been shot; Lamartine's seat in the Assembly where, the guide added as a curiosity, he had left 42 francs on 24 February 1848; the place where Louis Blanc stood to deliver speeches to artisan delegates; the prison where Barbés had been held, and so on.[58] Anecdotes could be varied according to the traveller's political inclinations. A French guide in Liorna bluffed about having participated in 1848 revolutions and when Vicuña Mackenna, tired of the servility and idle gossips of European guides, pretended to be a Bonapartist his interlocutor changed his speech swiftly starting to describe the rebellious crowd with harsh adjectives.[59]

The image of France, the Austrian Empire and Italy

According to Jean Blancpain, mid-nineteenth-century Chilean intellectuals were characterised by a 'revolutionary and francophile mimeticism'.[60] Certainly Spanish American intellectuals admired French culture. However, the tendency to imitate must be qualified. They borrowed what they considered would match their national reality and interpreted the ideas received from Europe accordingly. Nevertheless, the encounter with places so long admired inevitably provoked passionate remarks. France, in Vicuña Mackenna's view, was the 'centre of life and intelligence', 'fatherland of world civilisation', as well as 'the lighthouse that illuminates, although sometimes obscures, the journey of the human race'.[61] Admiration for France was almost an unavoidable position for any Chilean intellectual at that time.

56 Vicuña Mackenna, *Páginas de mi diario,* II, pp. 186–7, 188.
57 *Ibid.*, pp. 75, 102.
58 Vicuña Mackenna, *Páginas de mi diario,* I, pp. 293, 297.
59 *Ibid.*, p. 110.
60 Jean Blancpain, 'Cultura francesa y francomanía en América Latina: el caso de Chile', in *Cuadernos de Historia* Vol. 7, (1987), p. 19.
61 Vicuña Mackenna, *Páginas de mi diario,* I, pp. 277, 281–2.

Vicuña Mackenna spent eight months in Paris.[62] Throughout *Páginas de mi diario* he demonstrates a considerable knowledge of the history, writers, intellectuals and politicians of France. Among the authors he mentioned were Alexandre Dumas (father and son), Victor Hugo, Alphonse Lamartine, Chateaubriand, Pierre Auguste Beaumarchais, George Sand, as well as Jean Racine, La Fontaine, Molière and Moratin.[63] In addition to his admiration for the intellectual and political elites, the Chilean traveller showed great respect for the French people whom he characterised as combative, resistant to oppression, defiant against authority, even sometimes too eager to rise: 'those French people have barricades in place of heads'.[64] In France, more than in any other place he visited, Vicuña Mackenna sensed the dormant, but still latent, revolutionary impulse. This was particularly perceptible in Lyon: 'the darkest spectre that thrashes in the temple of despotic France despot during her insomniac night.'[65] While rural areas were considered as vessels of a passive population, Paris and Lyon were the repositories of an incendiary people.

The Chilean's admiration for France was not wholly uncritical. He also noticed flaws. In Paris, Vicuña Mackenna found misery and a city inhabited by injustice. A cemetery of tears and hunger, a lugubrious city of rags and mud, the capital of France seemed the capital of inequality. Poor neighbourhoods were seen as 'the Paris of barricades, insurrection and social mysteries'.[66] The Chilean blended revolutionary memories with Eugène Sue's description of the city. In the city's flagrant contrasts, the outrageous contradiction between opulence and misery, Vicuña Mackenna found justification for the violence and social upheaval of 1848, when 'during the horrendous June days, the French army fired two million cartridges at the people, and the people fired two million at the army'.[67]

Amidst death and initial reforms, the revolution had been crushed. Louis Napoleon was the anti-hero who bore the guilt for its sorrowful conclusion. Napoleon obtained the presidency, Vicuña Mackenna believed, thanks to the support of the army and the rural vote, whose ignorant population was fascinated by this character.[68] But Napoleon had also resorted to violence and repression: 'his hands have been soaked in blood.'[69]

62 Four in the summer of 1853 and four in the summer of 1854.

63 From Britain he mentioned Byron, Scott, Thackeray, Milton and Adam Smith. As for German authors he indicated Goethe and Schiller.

64 Vicuña Mackenna, *Páginas de mi diario*, II, p. 49.

65 Vicuña Mackenna, *Páginas de mi diario*, I, p. 455.

66 *Ibid.*, p. 285.

67 *Ibid.*, pp. 285–6.

68 *Ibid.*, p. 344.

69 *Ibid.*, p. 350.

Louis Napoleon was a modern Phillip II, whose 'holy tribunals – a modern Inquisition – had sent thousands of victims to Guyana to die of fever and plague'.[70]

A monarchy based on such terrible events could only engender an abhorrent government. Vicuña Mackenna believed the situation of France to be desperate: its public administration had lost any dignity, its most illustrious professors had abandoned their posts, the press was either plainly servile or suffered censorship, even the theatre was censored.[71] The word 'Imperial' seemed to be inscribed with gold letters on every public monument and building, haunting the republican traveller. Amidst all this imperial vanity, Vicuña Mackenna wondered: 'Who is it, France or Napoleon III, who merits the name 'Chiquito'? For if she were not so great, how could he possibly exist?'[72]

The Austrian Empire was different. Unlike France, where a tyrannical despot controlled a glorious but subdued population, Vicuña Mackenna, with characteristic anti-Habsburg flourish, deemed the whole race 'barbarian'.[73] As he approached Austria, he contrasted the Latin and Meridian races with those of the North:

> this boundary separates civilisation from barbarism, a great and fertile history from the despicable and selfish present, art and culture from the brute development of the elements of power, freedom from oppression and independence from usurpation, and finally, Italy from the Austrian Empire![74]

Even villagers he passed when travelling by train were judged by the same harsh light. Austrian subjects were not members of an oppressed class, but representatives of a brutal race.[75] Vicuña Mackenna conceded that the 'northern races' were the personification of modernisation and the achievement of materialistic goals. But he denied them any capacity for moral or abstract understanding.[76]

Vicuña Mackenna's image of the Habsburg Empire was of persecution and subjection. He witnessed many examples of state coercion on his journey: the Bohemian nobility uprooted from their land, forty thousand students of the University of Prague reduced to three thousand, songs prohibited in Lombardy, Austrian troops occupying entire populations, soldiers of different nationalities of the Empire scattered and kept away

70 *Ibid.*, p. 351.
71 *Ibid.*, p. 341.
72 *Ibid.*, p. 348.
73 Vicuña Mackenna, *Páginas de mi diario*, II, p. 180.
74 *Ibid.*, p. 179.
75 *Ibid.*, p. 180.
76 Vicuña Mackenna, *Páginas de mi diario*, I, p. 214.

from their places of origin.[77] Summarising the Austrian Empire: 'the army is everything. All the nation is a regiment.'[78]

A militaristic state welded together by arms, it was also a system that was forever falling apart, because it had constructed 'from a process of slow agglomeration of spoils and thefts'.[79] Understanding the country to have been built on military power alone, Vicuña Mackenna was unable to recognise any outstanding Austrian intellectual or prominent politician. Upon visiting Francis II square, the Chilean traveller mocked the caryatids representing Samson, Theseus and Hercules, suggesting that instead they should depict Josip Jelacic, Alfred Windischgrätz and Julius Haynau, the great repressors of 1848.[80]

Italy occupied a special place in Vicuña Mackenna's travel account. The Habsburg hold over Bohemia and Hungary inspired anecdotes and observations, but the Italian states provoked a stronger reaction in him. Passing through Prague he was more a traveller enjoying a city than a political commentator, while in Italy the author identified himself with the Latin cause.

Sorrow for the oppression of the Italian states dominates his account. Italy was everywhere marked by external invasion, its greatness based more on the glories of its history than on its present. 'Battlefield of all European wars, victim of all despotism', the peninsula had been looted and oppressed since the arrival of Alaric, king of the Visigoths, at the end of the fourth century.[81] He highlighted the courage of its people, prophesying not only their liberation but also their unification.[82] Vestiges of these confrontations were easy to find, and the Chilean stressed the violence and destruction inflicted by Austrian troops in 1849 during the reconquest. The outcome of this upheaval had been devastating. He mentioned how the students of the University of Pavia had been exterminated.[83] He also observed damage inflicted on buildings and monuments: in Piacenza Raphael's *Sistine Madonna* had been transferred to the Museum of Dresden, and the convent containing Da Vinci's *The Last Supper* had become a garrison for troops.[84] The whole city of Mantua 'today is only an immense troop barracks, sad and decrepit'.[85] Even when faced by the rich and progressive city of Milan, Vicuña Mackenna could

77 Vicuña Mackenna, *Páginas de mi diario*, II, pp. 185, 196, 9.
78 *Ibid.*, p. 195.
79 *Ibid.*, p. 184.
80 *Ibid.*, p. 190.
81 *Ibid.*, p. 80.
82 *Ibid.*, p. 180.
83 *Ibid.*, p. 160.
84 *Ibid.*, pp. 141, 152.
85 *Ibid.*, p. 167.

not simply admire it. He concluded that in its opulence and ostentation the city was searching for consolation or revenge for its imprisonment.[86] Upon leaving Italy, Vicuña Mackenna appealed for its emancipation and unification.[87]

Conclusion

A landmark in European history, the 1848 revolutions also played an important role in other parts of the world, particularly Latin America, where they served as a reference point. For conservatives they presented a warning of the dangers of liberalism and popular participation. Many Liberals, by contrast, saw them as a model to emulate. They observed the heroes, struggles and events of 1848, absorbing them into their own ideological habitats. This was not a passive exercise in admiration and assimilation, but rather a process of selecting and interpreting of the events of 1848 in accord with their own needs, ideas and experiences.

Benjamín Vicuña Mackenna was a distant follower and admirer of the European revolutions. He participated in a movement that emulated the French uprisings. He considered himself both a pupil of and a companion to the sufferings of the European heroes. His journey through Europe was guided by these pre-conceptions of the continent and of the events taking place there. His eyes were seeking what he had already learnt to admire. In this sense the image of Europe in *Páginas de mi diario* should not be considered a mere travel account, but rather the product of a self-appointed revolutionary about a place that he considered to be the fount of all revolutions.

86 *Ibid.*, p. 150.
87 *Ibid.*, p. 180.

7

Las revoluciones europeas de 1848 y su influencia en la historia política de Chile

CRISTIÁN GAZMURI

A mediados del siglo XIX se dieron en Chile lo que pueden considerarse ecos importantes de las revoluciones del '48', aunque un tanto desfasados con respecto a lo que fue ese episodio en Europa. En lo fundamental tales hechos fueron consecuencia de razones sociales y políticas internas del país, pero los motivos centrales del '48' europeo estuvieron también claramente presentes.[1]

Cuando se recibió en Santiago la noticia de la caída de Luis Felipe de Orleans y la instauración de la Segunda República francesa, se produjo una explosión de júbilo. En carta fechada en mayo de ese año, Leoncio Levraud, Cónsul General de Francia en Chile, informaba al Quai D'Orsay del enorme entusiasmo reinante: 'Esta tarde – escribía Levraud – en el teatro, la compañía italiana y los espectadores cantaron el Himno Nacional y La Marsellesa.' Levraud recibió incluso la visita del venerable Andrés Bello, quien difícilmente podría ser considerado revolucionario, el que acudió personalmente a felicitarlo.[2] El republicano Chile (que tomaba en serio su condición de tal) se felicitaba por la instauración de la forma republicana en la admirada Francia; los periódicos abundaban en elogios.

Hubo varias situaciones que se pueden incluir en este '48' chileno. De partida el nacimiento en el país de organizaciones que representaban a la cultura laica, liberal, filantrópica, utópica y anti-conservadora típica del '48' europeo. Es así que en 1850 nacieron en Chile la Masonería, los cuerpos de bomberos voluntarios (que hasta hoy son los únicos bomberos que existen en Chile) organizados por ciudades, barrios, colonias de inmigrantes de un mismo origen etc., 'forma de sociabilidad' típica de la Europa del '48', aunque en el caso concreto de la primera 'compañía de bomberos' fundada en el país el ejemplo imitado estaba más bien en los

1 Cristián Gazmuri, *El '48' chileno. Igualitarios, reformistas radicales, masones y bomberos* (Santiago, 1992).

2 Jorge Edwards, 'El decenio de Bulnes a través de los Archivos del Quai D' Orsay,' en *Boletín de la Academia Chilena de la Historia*, no. 74, (1966), p. 20.

Estados Unidos. Sin embargo, entre estas manifestaciones, las más importantes – nuevamente como en el caso de Europa – más que en la sociedad civil, estuvieron en el mundo de la política. La principal fue la formación de la llamada 'Sociedad de la Igualdad' (un grupo político, semi-revolucionario, bastante grande, el que puede considerarse el primer partido político moderno de Chile), así como su posterior rebelión represión y aplastamiento por el Gobierno conservador y autoritario.

La Sociedad de la Igualdad ha sido bastante estudiada, pero, a mi juicio no se ha dado debido énfasis a su cercano parentesco con las que fueron las sociedades políticas republicanas de la Europa, y en particular de la Francia de 1848. En la formación de la Sociedad de la Igualdad ciertamente estaba presente la problemática política chilena del momento, ligada a sucesión del Presidente Manuel Bulnes, un autoritario moderado y la oposición liberal a la candidatura presidencial de Manuel Montt, su sucesor designado y un autoritario radical. También influyó el ambiente de efervescencia social conectado con la 'Fiebre del Oro' en California, y, algo más interesante, la existencia en Santiago de un vasto sector artesanal, el que se constituiría en el grupo más numeroso entre el sustento político de la Sociedad de la Igualdad.

Prestemos atención a este último punto. El 'Amigo del Pueblo', diario que fue de la Sociedad de la Igualdad, habla de la existencia de 10.000 artesanos en el Santiago de entonces. Teniendo en cuenta que la población de la 'ciudad' de Santiago en la época bordeaba las 90.000 personas con algunas pequeñas variaciones estacionales, 10.000 aparece como un importante segmento. ¿Corresponde a la realidad lo afirmado por el diario? Veamos nuestros datos. Siguiendo la proporción que nos entrega el censo de 1854, de estas 90.000 personas, unas 51.500 habrían sido adultas. ¿Cuántos eran artesanos? Sabemos que en 1854 existían 31.498 artesanos en la 'Provincia de Santiago', para una población adulta de 142.204, vale decir, un 22.1 por ciento. En base a la misma proporción, tenemos que para esa fecha la cantidad de artesanos de la ciudad, sobre 51.500 adultos, debe haber sido de 11.330 y cuatro años antes, en 1850, año en que nace la Sociedad de la Igualdad, unos 10.800, aproximadamente. Es así que lo afirmado por 'El Amigo del Pueblo' parece ser cierto.[3]

Pero la Sociedad de Igualdad nació directamente como consecuencia de dos hechos externos a la situación político-social del Chile de mediados del siglo XIX. El primero fueron las noticias que llegaron al país de las revoluciones del '48' europeo, las que aparecieron publicadas en los periódicos a partir de mayo de 1848; y, el segundo, la conducta política de algunos jóvenes oligarcas chilenos que las vivieron personalmente (o al

3 Gazmuri, *El '48' chileno*, pp. 46 y sigs.

menos su ambiente previo) y regresaron a Chile por esos mismos meses o poco después. Ellos fueron los que movieron a la masa artesana, hasta entonces casi absolutamente pasiva políticamente.

Es efectivo que la admiración por lo que ocurría en Francia no duró mucho en el conservador Chile de mediados del siglo XIX. Meses después de recibida la noticia, cuando se supo de la revolución proletaria de junio en París, un nuevo discurso contrarrevolucionario se manifestó ahora con virulencia. Sin embargo, el entusiasmo por las revoluciones del '48' se mantuvo entre la juventud liberal ('pipiola') y entre el artesanado más informado y consciente. Prueba de esto fueron las características de la que sería la Sociedad de la Igualdad, particularmente durante su primer período.

Por otra parte, como se dijo, entre los jóvenes chilenos que, habiendo vivido el ambiente de la revolución francesa de 1848, y que, henchidos de romanticismo, llegaron a Chile por ese entonces, destacaban dos: Santiago Arcos y Francisco Bilbao. Arcos, nacido en Santiago de Chile en 1822, había vivido en París desde su infancia, donde recibió una esmerada educación. Había viajado por Europa y casi seguramente militado en una sociedad republicana y revolucionaria durante los últimos años de la Monarquía de Julio.[4] Llegó hasta Chile en febrero de 1848 después de haber viajado por Estados Unidos en compañía de Domingo Faustino Sarmiento.[5] Una vez radicado en el país, al comienzo se limitó a hacer vida social, sin ocultar, sin embargo, sus ideas políticas revolucionarias. Después de septiembre de 1848, rechazado por la buena sociedad justamente por esas ideas, optó por dedicarse activamente a la vida política e ingresó al llamado 'Club de la Reforma'. Este era una sociedad política informal compuesta por oligarcas liberales opuestos al Gobierno conservador ('Pelucón'). Allí Arcos intentaría desarrollar sus ideas revolucionario-republicanas y, en lo fundamental, liberales. Sin embargo, a poco de fundado, las limitaciones del Club de la Reforma como instrumento político se le hicieron evidentes. Captó claramente sus falencias, sin duda contrastándolo con los clubes revolucionarios franceses que bien conocía. Entonces pronunció una arenga que muestra cuan bien conocía lo que era un 'club republicano:

> La palabra inglesa 'club', tiene un significado de esfera o círculo. Un 'club' político es la concentración de muchas voluntades para formar un sólo espíritu, y determinar un propósito de bien publico. Su acción se extiende a otras armónicas (asociaciones correlativas), y se comunica con ellas por lazos de unión que mantienen continua correspondencia. La discordia es la peor de las enfermedades que pueden aquejar a un 'club'. La discordia lo hace

4 Sobre la juventud de Arcos, Cristián Gazmuri, 'Introducción'; Santiago Arcos, *Carta a Francisco Bilbao y otros escritos* (Santiago, Chile, 1990).

5 D.F. Sarmiento, *Viajes por Europa, África y América* (Santiago, Chile, 1849–1851), 2 vols.

> estéril, y entonces está próximo a disolverse como todo cuerpo orgánico que en la naturaleza pierde el equilibrio de su vida. Un club político, es síntesis de una idea generalizada. La corporación necesita concentrarse más aún, para crear en su seno propio un espíritu que represente, dirija y resuelva, con el nombre de directorio. En Chile no existen los clubes políticos. En Francia los miembros de un club someten su voluntad a un directorio, y este obra según su criterio.[6]

Las palabras de Arcos no ocultan el origen de sus ideas; incluso los términos que utilizó nos dicen bien claro las raíces del modelo que propone.[7]

Sin embargo, desilusionado del 'Club de la Reforma', Arcos también pudo darse cuenta que entre la juventud liberal, afrancesada, intelectual y admiradora de la herencia de la Revolución Francesa, existía un ambiente diferente.[8] Arcos distinguía entre estos jóvenes a Eusebio Lillo, Manuel Recabarren, Manuel Guerrero, Benjamín Vicuña Mackenna y al músico José Zapiola, los que, además de conservar el ardoroso entusiasmo de la juventud por las ideas liberales, había sufrido persecuciones a causa de ellas.

Si se trataba de modernizar la sociedad chilena, para lograr este fin era preciso contar con el instrumento político adecuado, ya utilizado en Europa. En otras palabras, era necesario realizar una mutación en las formas de sociabilidad política. En reemplazo de agrupaciones informales, semi formales o puramente instrumentales, como el 'Club de la Reforma', había que pasar a constituir organismos permanentes sujetos a normas y programas y con planes de acción precisos. Al parecer, Arcos concibió la formación de la Sociedad de la Igualdad los últimos meses del año 1849.

¿Por qué decidió Santiago Arcos fundar la Sociedad de la Igualdad? Ciertamente que su carácter rebelde influyó, como también su espíritu aventurero marcado por el romanticismo. Pero más allá de los rasgos de su personalidad hubo probablemente otros motivos menos subjetivos. De partida, el que ya hicimos presente: decidido a dedicarse a la política se vio en la necesidad de contar con un instrumento eficaz cuyo modelo conocía bien: una sociedad (o 'club') republicana. Pero creemos que hubo también otro, aún más de fondo: al llegar a Chile, y esto se deja ver vagamente en su artículo 'Cuentos de tierra adentro', Arcos se ha de haber sentido muy impresionado por la miseria, ignorancia y marginalidad, en

6 Antonio Iñiguez V., *Historia del período revolucionario en Chile, 1848–1851* (Santiago, 1905), p. 495.

7 'Todos saben que esa palabra (círculo) constituye el equivalente francés usual del "club" inglés,' Maurice Agulhon, *Le Cercle dans la France bourgeoise, 1810–1848* (Paris, 1977), p. 17.

8 Benjamín Vicuña Mackenna, *Historia de la jornada del 20 de abril de 1851* (Santiago, 1878), and *Los girondinos chilenos* (Santiago, 1902).

un sentido amplio, de la gran masa de la población chilena.[9] Tal como escribió en la *Carta a Francisco Bilbao*, de 1852, se dio cuenta que ser pobre en el Chile de entonces constituía más una condición vital que una mera situación económica. Finalmente, existe la posibilidad que todo hubiese sido conversado y más o menos planificado junto con Bilbao después de la llegada de éste a París en 1845. La rápida integración de Francisco Bilbao al directorio de la Sociedad de la Igualdad, a los pocos días de volver a Chile, en febrero de 1850, ayuda a esta hipótesis.

En realidad, más que un colaborador de Arcos, Bilbao se convirtió en su amigo y su igual en la dirección de la Sociedad de la Igualdad; lo que también se comprende por el hecho que Bilbao, quien se había iniciado en la vida pública ya en 1842 como secretario de la Sociedad Literaria fundada ese año, era una figura muy conocida en cuanto líder progresista y rebelde y dueño de una exuberancia verbal, tanto escrita como oral, notables. El que hubiese regresado a Chile con un contrato como empleado público, parece no haber entorpecido la decisión de Bilbao de transformarse en agitador contrario al Gobierno, algo inconcebible en el Chile de entonces. Sería expulsado del empleo pocos meses después.

Por cierto que no fueron sólo Arcos y Bilbao las únicas figuras catalizadoras del episodio de la Sociedad de la Igualdad. Vicuña Mackenna se ha referido a los llamados 'Girondinos chilenos', ejemplo del tipo de agitadores del ambiente 'cuarentaiochesco' que hicieron de Brissot, Roland y sus compañeros sus modelos, adoptando incluso sus nombres.[10] Además, tras la Sociedad de la Igualdad estuvo también latente la tradición política anti-autoritaria que venía desde la caída de Bernardo O'Higgins e incluso más atrás, desde la época de la Reconquista.

La primera reunión formal de la Sociedad de la Igualdad se celebró la última semana de marzo de 1850. Asistieron a ella seis personas: Arcos, Bilbao, Lillo, Zapiola y los artesanos ('obreros' en palabras de Zapiola) Ambrosio Larrecheda, sombrerero y Cecilio Cerda, sastre. El propio Zapiola y Lillo eran elementos de la incipiente clase media de entonces.

Dos días más tarde se realizó la segunda reunión a la que asistieron tres nuevos miembros. En esta segunda sesión se acordó que Arcos y Zapiola presentaran en la siguiente un proyecto de estatuto y un reglamento para el trabajo político por secciones. De lo anterior deducimos que Arcos (y Bilbao posiblemente) ya habían convencido a los demás acerca de la estructura a dar a la Sociedad. A esa tercera sesión acudieron otros tres nuevos 'igualitarios', dos artesanos y un ex-oficial de ejército, Luciano Piña. A

9 Santiago Arcos, 'Cuentos de tierra adentro,' en *Revista de Santiago* (Santiago, Chile, 1849).

10 Benjamín Vicuña Mackenna, *Los girondinos chilenos.*

proposición de este último se bautizó el grupo como 'Sociedad de la Igualdad'.[11]

La adopción de ese nombre no era una muestra de originalidad, la palabra 'igualdad' era la más importante del vocabulario político heredado de la Revolución Francesa y durante el '48' parisiense volvió a adquirir carácter simbólico. Bilbao, por su parte, logró hacer aprobar, tras larga discusión, la siguiente fórmula de admisión (o juramento): '¿Reconocéis la soberanía de la razón como autoridad de autoridades; la soberanía del pueblo como base de toda política y el amor y la fraternidad como vida moral?'; una mezcla entre el ideario político de Las Luces y el del catolicismo social tomado de Lamennais.[12]

Más allá de esa declaración de principios, el ideario que animaba a la Sociedad de la Igualdad era vago y poco coherente. En verdad, constituía una mezcla de los lugares comunes de la oposición liberal o 'pipiola' más radical, con elementos ideológicos republicanos y populistas tomados del imaginario del '48' europeo y de algunos autores liberales, católico-sociales y socialistas utópicos anteriores.[13] Por otra parte, sostiene José Zapiola, que en un principio la Sociedad no tuvo aspiraciones políticas contingentes, ni siquiera simpatías hacia bando político alguno. Pero esta afirmación aparece desmentida, desde el primer número, por el diario que comenzó a publicar la Sociedad de la Igualdad: 'El Amigo del Pueblo', cuyo principal redactor fue Eusebio Lillo pero en el que también colaboraron Arcos, Manuel y Francisco Bilbao y José Victorino Lastarria (al menos) y que proclamó desde el inicio: 'queremos que don Manuel Montt, fatal a las libertades públicas, fatal a la educación, fatal a la República, se anule para siempre.' La oposición al Gobierno autoritario y a los pelucones (Conservadores en el Gobierno) era pues clara, posiblemente porque los 'pipiolos' financiaban a 'El Amigo del Pueblo'.[14]

Pero a pesar de su debilidad doctrinaria y sus vínculos con la oligarquía opositora, la Sociedad de la Igualdad nacía con características nuevas, que la diferenciaban de las organizaciones previas en las que se agruparon grupos de artesanos u obreros y que fueron 'instrumentales' para una determinada campaña política y nada más. Esto fue así no sólo porque incorporó sectores artesanales en número muy elevado y desde sus inicios, sino, especialmente, por sus características novedosas en cuanto forma de sociabilidad política. Estaba estructurada por secciones de 24 individuos cada una, formando una red territorial. Cada sección estaba numerada y correspondía a un barrio de Santiago. Tenía además fórmula de iniciación

11 José Zapiola, *La Sociedad de la Igualdad y sus enemigos* (Santiago, 1902) p. 9.
12 *Ibid.*, p. 10.
13 Gazmuri, *El '48' chileno*, pp. 76–9.
14 'El Amigo del Pueblo', No. 1, 1 de abril de 1850.

y un estatuto, así como un reglamento de sesiones común para todos los núcleos. El estatuto estipulaba que en cualquier sección podía presentarse la 'moción de una reforma administrativa o social'; ésta sería comunicada a los demás grupos y si reunía mayoría de votos individuales sobre el total de los miembros de la Sociedad era aprobada.[15]

Como podemos apreciar muy poco había en común entre la estructura de la Sociedad de la Igualdad, forma de sociabilidad política formal, y las antiguas tertulias políticas, ocasionales e informales, en las que se había reunido hasta entonces el sector masculino de la oligarquía cuando se trataba de hacer política. Tampoco lo había, con las organizaciones políticas artesanales 'instrumentales' anteriores. En cambio, resulta notable la similitud entre la Sociedad de la Igualdad y los clubes republicanos y revolucionarios franceses que Arcos y Bilbao conocieron.

Por otra parte, la Sociedad de la Igualdad no se trataba de una sociedad secreta. A diferencia de los grupos carbonarios o las 'jóvenes' Italia, Alemania, Irlanda, España, etc., en boga en Europa por influjo de Mazzini, no ligaba a sus socios con un juramento existencial irrenunciable. No se conoce que haya propiciado o cometido acto violento alguno (al menos la de Santiago) antes del motín del 20 de abril de 1851, exasperada entonces por la persecución del Gobierno. Zapiola relata que 'recibíamos a todo el que quería incorporarse'. El propio 'Amigo del Pueblo' publicó un anuncio de la apertura de la Sociedad de la Igualdad. Para ingresar en ésta bastaba ser presentado por uno de sus miembros e inscribir su firma en el 'gran libro de registro'.[16]

En síntesis, la Sociedad de la Igualdad no sólo constituía una nueva forma de sociabilidad política para Chile, con características de partido político moderno, el primero en existir en Chile; significaba aún otra cosa: el ingreso a ese mundo político, también ahora de manera clara, de un 'sector social' no perteneciente a la oligarquía, quebrando así el monopolio que aquella detentaba hasta ese momento sobre la política.

En las semanas siguientes a su formación la 'Sociedad' creció tanto, que al poco tiempo hubo de aprobarse un estatuto complementario destinado a coordinar la discusión, creándose un sistema de reuniones generales cada 15 días, para lo cual hubo de arrendarse un amplio local. A comienzos de abril de 1850 los asistentes a las reuniones de la Sociedad ya llegaban a un centenar o dos.

Después de mediados de ese mes, la afluencia de simpatizantes aumentó aún más cuando el 'Club de la Reforma' decidió autodisolverse, incorporándose muchos de sus miembros – especialmente los más jóvenes – a la Sociedad de la Igualdad. Lo más granado de la oligarquía liberal se

15 Gazmuri, *El '48' chileno*, pp. 74–5.
16 Zapiola, *La Sociedad de la Igualdad*, p. 17.

mezclaba así con el mundo artesanal. Pero al hacerlo, como se verá, desvirtuaría su fisonomía original.[17] La Sociedad de la Igualdad llegaría a transformarse en un órgano de lucha contingente contra el Gobierno. El propio Santiago Arcos, en la *Carta a Francisco Bilbao,* se referiría, dos años después, 'al partido al que pertenecíamos entonces' refiriéndose obviamente al nexo que se contrajo (o fortaleció partir de entonces) con el grupo 'pipiolo' opositor al Gobierno.[18]

Pero, antes de referirnos a ese cambio en su orientación, queremos señalar que hubo todavía otro aspecto en el que la Sociedad de la Igualdad trajo una novedad en el mundo político chileno. De acuerdo con Iñiguez Vicuña, 'Junto con las sesiones de la Sociedad de la Igualdad comenzaron las clases, las conferencias y la discusión pública de los proyectos de mejora de la clase obrera, fin primordial que perseguían noblemente los fundadores de la institución.'[19] En verdad, casi desde su fundación, una de las actividades principales de la Sociedad de la Igualdad fue la dictación de cursos que sobre diversas materias se impartían gratuitamente a los artesanos. En un comienzo se ofrecieron cinco: 'lectura, escritura, primeras operaciones de aritmética, elementos de gramática castellana y geografía.' Después se enseñó también al menos un oficio, sastrería. En fin, se dictó un curso de 'economía política'.[20] Los cursos – como observamos – eran una mezcla de adoctrinamiento, difusión cultural, educación humanista e incluso técnica

Lucha contra la Iglesia y el gobierno

Ahora bien, no es de extrañar que la formación y el crecimiento rápido de la Sociedad de la Igualdad provocara en el gobierno, sectores autoritarios y conservadores en general, una fuerte preocupación. El Presidente Bulnes solicitó la renuncia al ministro del interior, Manuel Camilo Vial (quien quedó profundamente resentido) y pidió la formación de un nuevo ministerio a Antonio Varas, un autoritario, amigo íntimo y el más decidido partidario de Manuel Montt. Esto significaba la declaración de guerra a la Sociedad de la Igualdad. De inmediato, la prensa adicta y, en parte, subvencionada por el Gobierno, desató su artillería contra la asociación, acusándola de revolucionaria, de ser un peligro para el orden y la paz del país, de subvertir el orden público, etc.[21] Por cierto que estos ataques fueron debidamente respondidos por 'El Amigo del Pueblo'.

17 Santiago Arcos, *Carta a Francisco Bilbao*, p. 62.
18 *Ibid.*, p. 25.
19 Vicuña Mackenna, *Historia de la jornada*, p. 83.
20 Zapiola, *La sociedad de la igualdad*, p. 28.
21 Cfr., por ejemplo, 'La Tribuna', mayo–junio de 1850.

Además no impidieron que la Sociedad de la Igualdad siguiera creciendo, lo que naturalmente acrecentó la tensión.

El primer incidente político grave en que se vio envuelta la Sociedad de la Igualdad no se dio, sin embargo, con el Gobierno, sino con la Iglesia Católica chilena. Esta ruptura era consecuente con la línea impuesta por el catolicismo europeo y por la propia Roma, la que desde una aceptación inicial de las revoluciones de 1848 había pasado a su condena más absoluta. 'El Amigo del Pueblo' en su número 23, del 26 de abril de 1850, publicó un capítulo de la obra de Lamennais, *Palabras de un creyente*. La publicación, iniciativa de Francisco Bilbao, provocó un furibundo ataque de la 'Revista Católica', al que replicó, en peor tono, el diario igualitario con una sátira (presumiblemente escrita por José Victorino Lastarria) en la que se simulaba una condena eclesiástica contra la 'Revista Católica' firmada por 'Nos el Príncipe Pio Castroporci, Arzobispo de Padua, por la gracia de Dios y la Santa Sede'.[22] El sarcasmo produjo indignación.

Sin embargo, entrar en conflicto con la Iglesia Católica y todo el mundo católico del muy católico Chile de entonces constituía evidentemente una torpeza política que causó graves problemas internos dentro de la propia Sociedad de la Igualdad. Tanto así que se optó por acabar con 'El amigo del Pueblo', diario semi-doctrinario y reemplazarlo por 'La Barra', un periódico preocupado fundamentalmente de la contingencia política. Con todo, la pugna con la Iglesia no tendría, en definitiva, mayor trascendencia. Eran Montt y Varas, en la conducción política del Gobierno, los que estaban preparando el aplastamiento de la Sociedad de la Igualdad.

Hacia junio de 1850 la Sociedad de la Igualdad había alcanzado su máxima expresión en cuanto asociación republicana abierta al mundo artesanal según el molde que le diera Arcos, quien, en palabras de Vicuña Mackenna, fue 'el dictador absoluto de la Sociedad de la Igualdad durante los meses de marzo y abril'.[23] Ya funcionaban varias secciones, se mantenían reuniones generales periódicas, cursos, un diario y se contaba con unos doscientos miembros entre artesanos y jóvenes oligarcas liberales. Contaba además con un financiamiento adecuado a juzgar por los gastos de arriendo de sede y publicación del diario, los que se sufragaban sin problemas.

El resto de la oposición al gobierno y a la candidatura presidencial de Manuel Montt (los 'pipiolos' en general y la fracción pelucona 'vialista') estaba, en cambio, en la mayor desorganización y, como anotaba Lastarria, 'carecía de fuerza'. Aparecía entonces la Sociedad de la Igualdad como la única organización capaz de aglutinar a los enemigos del Gobierno y su candidato. Siendo estas las circunstancias, el nombramiento en el ministerio

22 'El Amigo del Pueblo', No. 33, 8 de mayo de 1850.

23 Vicuña Mackenna, *Historia de la jornada*, p. 93.

del interior de Antonio Varas, enardeció los ánimos de los desorganizados opositores provocando el comienzo del ingreso masivo de oligarcas opositores a la Sociedad. Desde entonces la Sociedad de la Igualdad se transformó en una gran asamblea conspirativa e insurreccional, dirigida por los caudillos de la oligarquía liberal e incluso 'vialistas', los que la llevaron por el que era también el camino tradicional para hacerse con el poder: la promoción de una sublevación armada con apoyo militar.

Paradojalmente la nueva orientación que veían tomar a la Sociedad de la Igualdad no podía menos que agradar al Gobierno y los 'pelucones'. El régimen autoritario del Chile de entonces, ciertamente podía sentirse desconcertado y relativamente inerme para impedir el ingreso masivo a la arena política del artesanado, estructurado en una asociación republicana y con objetivos de reestructuración de la sociedad chilena por medios pacíficos, a mediano o largo plazo, como eran los declarados; aún sabiendo que la asociación la financiaban sectores oligárquicos. Pero a una bulliciosa agrupación rebelde y conspirativa, acaudillada por figuras pipiolas y que no tardaría en comenzar sus aprestos bélicos sabía de sobra como tratarla. Diego Portales había dado la fórmula; bastaba la mano dura, todo lo dura que fuese necesario.[24]

La Sociedad de la Igualdad le hizo el juego al Gobierno. Volvamos a preocuparnos de esta asociación. Desde junio de 1850, se vio inmersa de lleno en una contienda cada vez más abierta con el régimen. Entregada a ese activismo político, su radicalización fue aumentando inevitablemente. Reclutando por centenares a nuevos adherentes, entre los meses de agosto y noviembre de 1850 se realizaron varias 'reuniones generales', seguidas de marchas por las calles céntricas de Santiago. Actos hostilizados de manera creciente por sucesivos bandos del intendente de la provincia. Hubo reuniones generales el 26 de agosto, el 30 de septiembre y el 14 de octubre. A esta última asistieron 1500 personas (de un total de 3400 que se inscribieron en la Sociedad de la Igualdad, de las cuales, 2000 posiblemente artesanos) y concluyó con un paseo en fila que hicieron los socios por la Alameda.[25] Iba a la cabeza Francisco Bilbao con su traje favorito de verano y llevaba en sus manos, con cierta unción de apóstol a manera de 'custodia', un pequeño árbol de la libertad hecho de mostacilla.[26]

Pero el 20 de octubre Manuel Montt era proclamado oficialmente candidato a la Presidencia de la República, con el apoyo del Presidente Bulnes; el 6 de septiembre *La Barra* editorializaba: 'Marchamos hacia la revolución', y el 21 de octubre se desataba en la siguiente arenga:

24 Gazmuri, *El '48' chileno*, p. 88.
25 Domingo F. Sarmiento, *¿A quien temen, a Montt?* (folleto), Santiago, 1850.
26 Vicuña Mackenna, *Historia de la jornada*, p. 206.

> Proclamar a Montt para candidato a la presidencia, es autorizar la revolución. Vale más reducir a cenizas el país, que permitir el triunfo de Montt.[27]

La pugna continuó subiendo de tono hasta que el 25 de octubre se publicaba un bando de la intendencia que prohibía los paseos masivos por las calles y ordenaba que las sesiones de la Sociedad de la Igualdad fuesen públicas y se permitiese el ingreso de cualquiera. Esto casi equivalía a ordenar su disolución.

Los igualitarios reaccionaron llamando a una nueva reunión general para el 28 de octubre. Sería la última. El día 26 de octubre se hizo público el himno de la Sociedad de la Igualdad, titulado, sin demasiada imaginación, 'La Igualitaria', un correlato simbólico de la 'La Marsellesa'. La canción se popularizó rápidamente, siendo cantada en coro por las calles los días siguientes. El 28 de octubre la ciudad presentaba, según Vicuña Mackenna: 'la serenidad, el ocio y la alegría de un día de fiesta.' El recinto de sesiones de la Sociedad (uno nuevo, con mayor capacidad para contener público, conocido como 'El Parral de Gómez') comenzó a llenarse de igualitarios desde la mañana. Hubo tres oradores: Luciano Piña, el artesano José María López y Francisco Bilbao. Éste comenzó su discurso batiendo en la mano un ramillete de flores que unas jóvenes admiradoras le habían proporcionado. Sus primeras palabras fueron las siguientes: 'El ruido del tambor, la publicación de órdenes represivas, el apresto de la tropa armada, parece anunciar al poder los peligros del combate. En presencia del aparato de guerra, la Sociedad de la Igualdad se presenta armada de flores'. Entonces fue el delirio: aplausos, lágrimas, entusiasmo indescriptible. Finalmente se tomó la resolución de rechazar la candidatura de Montt, lo que en verdad no significaba novedad alguna.[28]

Disolución y represión de la Sociedad de le Igualdad

El decreto de disolución de la Sociedad de la Igualdad, con el pretexto de una insurrección armada de una filial de ésta en la pequeña ciudad de San Felipe, fue dictado por el Intendente de la capital, Francisco Ángel Ramírez el 9 de noviembre de 1850. Además, el 'estado de sitio' fue declarado. ¿Que sucedió entre los igualitarios cuando ocurrió lo que se veía venir y casi se deseaba? ... Ante la actitud del gobierno, la agresiva y vociferante sociedad revolucionaria que hemos mostrado, pareció disolverse como sal en el agua. De hecho sobreviviría activo sólo un pequeño núcleo.

Un gobierno chileno de la época de los decenios tenía argumentos legales y de fuerza sobradamente eficaces para que una asociación compuesta por civiles no pudiese resistírsele. De los medios concretos de

27 *La Barra*, 29 de octubre de 1850.
28 Gazmuri, *El '48' chileno*, p. 100.

control usados por el gobierno, el más eficaz – antes de recurrir al uso de la fuerza militar – era el control político que se mantenía sobre los habitantes haciendo uso de su conscripción obligatoria en la Guardia Nacional (Cívicos).[29] Con éste se controló a la masa artesana. En cuanto a los dirigentes de la asociación: algunos (entre ellos Bilbao) se escondieron, otros (entre ellos Arcos) fueron exiliados al extranjero; aún otros fueron relegados o encarcelados. Este último caso fue el de todos los de origen artesanal.

El estado de sitio fue levantado a los 40 días, pero la Sociedad de la Igualdad había recibido un golpe irrecuperable. Bilbao publicó – desde la clandestinidad – varios manifiestos, algunos de los cuales aparecieron en un boletín manuscrito titulado – siempre sin mucha imaginación – *El Igualitario*, el que circuló de mano en mano, y fueron después reproducidos en *La Barra*, que había reaparecido una vez levantado el estado de sitio. Esta existencia de ultratumba, recibió su golpe definitivo con el fracaso (por poco) del sangriento motín de 20 de abril de 1851, casi el único episodio violento importante del '48' chileno (el otro se daría en Valparaíso el 28 de octubre de 1851).[30] Sin embargo, dejaría una herencia en la que podemos distinguir al menos tres aspectos.

En primer lugar el recuerdo de la Sociedad de la Igualdad se incorporaría a la cultura chilena en forma de una leyenda con particular fuerza entre grupos de la clase media que se iría consolidando en la segunda mitad del siglo XIX. De hecho el Partido Radical, que la aglutinó mayoritariamente y que llegaría gobernar, reconocía un hilo de filiación con respecto a la Sociedad de la Igualdad.[31] En segundo término, inauguró una forma de sociabilidad política en Chile que después recogerían otras asociaciones y partidos políticos. No es casualidad que ese mismo año de 1850, nacieran en Chile la Masonería, organización por cierto sin objetivos políticos directos, pero que comulgaba con los mismos valores racionalistas, laicos y anti-conservadores de la Sociedad de la Igualdad. La Masonería también observó (y mantiene) un patrón de sociabilidad similar al de la Sociedad. Lo mismo puede decirse del 'Cuerpo de Bomberos', vasta agrupación de voluntarios que llegó a tener cobertura nacional la que se mantiene hasta hoy, siendo la única organización que combate los incendios y otros accidentes de tipo urbano en todo el país. Los bomberos llegaron a constituir una 'hermandad' y el pertenecer a ella otorgaba (y otorga aún) un sello de identidad y una cultura ligada a la

29 *Ibid.*, pp. 103–4.

30 Véase Vicuña Mackenna, *Historia de la jornada*; Daniel Riquelme (ed.), *Andrés Bello* (Santiago, 1966); Daniel Riquelme, *La revolución del 20 de abril de 1851*; Gazmuri, *El '48' chileno*, pp. 111–12.

31 René León Echaiz, *Evolución histórica de los partidos políticos chilenos* (Santiago, 1949), p. 46.

filantropía laica. Su patrón de sociabilidad era y es el mismo de la Sociedad de la Igualdad y la Masonería.

Similares consideraciones pueden hacerse en relación a otras formas de sociabilidad políticas y no políticas nacidas en las décadas siguientes. Ya se mencionó al Partido Radical. Pero también hay que insertar en la misma línea de filiación al segundo 'Club de la Reforma', creado poco antes de la década de 1870, otra organización con cobertura nacional y que logró en buena medida lo que no había conseguido, en su momento, la Sociedad de la Igualdad: la reforma de la institucionalidad chilena.[32] En fin, en tercer término, el episodio de la Sociedad de la Igualdad sirvió para consolidar una generación liberal que fue la que transformó el Chile autoritario de la primera mitad del siglo XIX en el país liberal de fines de la centuria. Es efectivo que hacia 1850 ya existía liberalismo en el país, pero después de 1850 se dio lo que ha sido llamado, una 'religión liberal' que fue la causa principal de la transición desde el autoritarismo portaliano a la República parlamentaria.[33]

Una Generación Liberal

Preocupémonos de este último punto. ¿Quiénes fueron y quiénes llegarían a ser en la segunda mitad del siglo XIX chileno (o eventualmente en el extranjero como en los casos de Arcos, Bilbao, Mitre y Sarmiento) los jóvenes oligarcas que participaron en lo que hemos llamado el '48' chileno y cuáles fueron las ideas y valores que impusieron?

En relación a la primera parte de la pregunta. Es preciso mencionar, de partida, a Santiago Arcos, Francisco Bilbao y los 'Girondinos chilenos'; a José Victorino Lastarria, quien, al parecer también perteneció, aunque discretamente, a la Sociedad de la Igualdad, y que, en todo caso, simpatizó con ella; a Manuel Recabarren, Juan Bello, Rafael Vial, Domingo Santa María, Marcial González, Miguel Luis y Víctor Amunátegui, Pedro Ugarte, Manuel Bilbao, Francisco Marín, José Ignacio Víctor Eyzaguirre, Francisco de Paula Taforó, Bartolomé Mitre y otros 'Girondinos chilenos'; y a José Santos Lira, Pedro Francisco Lira, Justo Arteaga, Álvaro Covarrubias, Salvador Sanfuentes, Cristóbal Valdés y José Antonio Alemparte.[34]

32 Patricio Estellé, 'El Club de la Reforma de 1868–1871,' *Historia*, Nº 9, (Santiago, 1970).

33 Alberto Edwards, *La fronda aristocrática* (Santiago, 1945), pp. 148–9.

34 Esta lista de nombres de 'Girondinos chilenos' está tomada de Vicuña Mackenna, *Los girondinos chilenos*. Las mismas reservas que se pueden hacer a Lastarria en cuanto igualitario, caben en el caso de los hermanos Amunátegui y otros. Pero está claro que hacia 1850 todos estaban contra Montt y el Gobierno y muy posiblemente, si no militaban abiertamente, eran simpatizantes con la Sociedad de la Igualdad, Julio Cesar Jobet, 'José Victorino Lastarria y la democracia en Chile,' *Atenea*, Nº 359, May 1955, passim; Joaquín Rodríguez Bravo, *José V. Lastarria* (Santiago, 1892), p. 263.

Hemos visto que también estuvieron ligados a la Sociedad de la Igualdad o las agitaciones y rebeliones de 1850–51: José Zapiola,[35] Federico Errázuriz,[36] Fernando Urízar,[37] Eusebio Lillo,[38] Benjamín Vicuña Mackenna,[39] Manuel Guerrero,[40] Francisco Prado,[41] Pedro Félix Vicuña,[42] Vicente Sanfuentes,[43] Manuel Beauchef,[44] Pedro Nolasco Luco,[45] José Santiago Luco,[46] Luis Vargas,[47] Vicente Larraín Aguirre,[48] Bruno Larraín,[49] Luis Ovalle,[50] Rafael Garfias,[51] Paulino del Barrio,[52] Joaquín Lazo,[53] Félix y Juan Mackenna,[54] José Miguel Carrera Fontecilla,[55] Santiago Pérez Larraín,[56] Ramón Tagle Echeverría,[57] José del Carmen Stuardo,[58] Vicente Aldunate.[59] Muchos de estos hombres serían importantes figuras políticas en el Chile de la segunda mitad del siglo XIX.

Una breve síntesis de las carreras públicas de estas personas después de 1850 y hasta 1868 (en los casos más connotados, como los que llegaron a ser presidente de la república y algunos otros, incluimos cargos y funciones que desempeñaron después de dicho año) puede verse en la Tabla No.1.

35 J. Zapiola, *La Sociedad de la Igualdad y sus enemigos*, p. 9 y siguientes.

36 Expulsado junto con Arcos y Lastarria al Perú después del 7 de noviembre de 1850 ('La Barra', No. 131).

37 Inmiscuido en el 'Complot de los Cartuchos,' Vicuña Mackenna, *Historia de la Jornada*, passim.

38 Director de 'El Amigo del Pueblo' (J. Zapiola, *La Sociedad de la Igualdad y sus enemigos*, p. 17); 'La Barra', N° 131, etc.

39 Como lo reconoce en varias de sus obras citadas.

40 Zapiola, *La Sociedad de la Igualdad y sus enemigos*, p. 16.

41 Vicuña Mackenna, *Historia de la Jornada*, passim.

42 *Ibíd.*, p. 200.

43 *Ibíd.*, passim.

44 Zapiola, *La Sociedad de la Igualdad y sus enemigos*, passim.

45 *Ibíd.*

46 P. P. Figueroa, *Historia de Francisco Bilbao*, p. 207.

47 *Ibíd.*

48 Vicuña Mackenna, *Historia de la jornada*, p. 219.

49 *Ibíd.*, p. 177 (nota) y p. 234.

50 *Ibíd.*

51 Zapiola, *La Sociedad de la Igualdad y sus enemigos*, p. 40.

52 Virgilio Figueroa, *Diccionario histórico, biográfico y bibliográfico de Chile* (Santiago, FECHA) Vol. 2, p. 135.

53 Vicuña Mackenna, *Historia de la jornada*, p. 234.

54 *Ibíd.*, passim.

55 Ibíd., passim.

56 *Ibíd.*, p. 386.

57 *Ibíd.*

58 *La Barra*, No. 105.

59 Benjamín Vicuña Mackenna, *Diario de don Benjamín Vicuña Mackenna, desde el 28 de octubre de 1850 al 15 de abril de 1851* (Santiago).

Tabla 1: Carreras públicas de la Generación Liberal, 1850–1868

Nombre	*Carrera publica*
Alemparte, José Antonio	—
Aldunate, Vicente	—
Amunátegui, Miguel Luis	Historiador, diputado, Presidente de la Cámara de Diputados, ministro de estado, senador (liberal).
Amunátegui, Gregorio Víctor	Historiador, diputado, ministro de la Corte Suprema (liberal).
Arcos, Santiago	Escritor político; activista en Chile y Argentina, candidato a Cortes en España por el Partido Republicano Federal (liberal, al menos durante su estadía en Chile).
Arteaga, Justo	General, autor de un proyecto de Código Militar, Comandante en Jefe del Ejército en 1879 (liberal).
Bello, Juan	Diputado, secretario de legación en Francia, traductor al español del *Tratado técnico y práctico de economía política,* de Gustave Courcelle-Seneuil (liberal).
Beauchef, Manuel	Diputado, senador (liberal).
Bilbao, Francisco	Activista y líder revolucionario en 1844,1850 y 1851; exiliado de Chile, continuó con su activismo político en Perú y Argentina; fue además prolífico escritor político y social; se radicó en Argentina pero su influencia en Chile siguió siendo grande (liberal).
Bilbao, Manuel	Literato, historiador, periodista, se radicó en Argentina (liberal).
Carrera Fontecilla, José Miguel	Igualitario, dirigente del alzamiento de 1851 en La Serena.
Covarrubias, Álvaro	Diputado, ministro de estado, consejero de estado, ministro de la Corte Suprema, senador, embajador (liberal).
Del Barrio, Paulino	Ingeniero, fundador de la Escuela de Minas de Copiapó.
Errázuriz, Federico	Historiador, diputado, intendente de Santiago, ministro de estado, Presidente de la República (liberal).
Eyzaguirre, José I. Víctor	Sacerdote, historiador, escritor apologético y hombre público, una de las figuras más respetadas de la Iglesia chilena.

Garfias, Rafael	—
González, Marcial	Periodista, historiador, diputado, senador, Presidente del Senado (liberal).
Guerrero, Manuel	Agitador, fue vicepresidente de la 'Convención de los Pueblos' en 1875 (liberal).
Larraín Aguirre, Vicente	—
Larraín, Bruno	Diputado, intendente (liberal).
Lastarria, José Victorino	Diputado, ministro de estado, embajador, senador, ministro de la Corte Suprema (liberal).
Lazo, Joaquín	Diputado, senador (liberal).
Lillo, Eusebio	Periodista, alcalde de Santiago, intendente de Curicó, embajador, ministro de estado, senador (liberal).
Lira, José Santos	Diputado, senador, ministro de la Corte Suprema (liberal).
Lira, Pedro Francisco	Fiscal de la Corte Suprema.
Luco, Pedro Nolasco	—
Luco, José Santiago	—
Mackenna, Félix	—
Mackenna, Juan	Activo participante en las guerras civiles de 1851 y 1859. Murió en el exilio en 1860 (liberal).
Marín, Francisco	Diputado, senador (liberal).
Mitre, Bartolomé	Argentino; periodista y publicista en Chile; después de su retorno a su patria, fue historiador y connotado hombre público, Presidente de la República Argentina (liberal).
Ovalle, Luis	Diputado
Pérez L., Santiago	Senador (liberal).
Prado, Francisco	Minero e industrial, diputado (pipiolo, liberal).
Recabarren, Manuel	Diputado, ministro de estado (liberal-radical).
Sanfuentes, Salvador	Decano de la Facultad de Humanidades de la U. de Chile, ministro de estado, ministro de la Corte Suprema (liberal).
Sanfuentes, Vicente	Diputado, senador (liberal).
Santa María, Domingo	Diputado, ministro de estado, fiscal de la Corte Suprema, embajador (ministro) en Perú, senador, Presidente del Senado, Presidente de la República (liberal).
Stuardo, José del Carmen	Diputado (pipiolo, liberal).
Taforó, Francisco de Paula	Escritor sagrado, gran orador y figura muy

	destacada dentro del clero de Chile y Perú; senador y consejero de estado.
Tagle E., Ramón	Diputado (liberal).
Ugarte, Pedro	Juez (liberal).
Urízar, Fernando	Eterno conspirador anti pelucón (después de haber pertenecido a ese partido). Desterrado varias veces, diputado (liberal).
Vargas, Luis	—
Vial, Rafael	Periodista, fundador de varios periódicos en Chile y Perú.
Vicuña Mackenna, Benjamín	Historiador, periodista, escritor polígrafo, diputado, senador, agente diplomático, intendente de Santiago, candidato a la Presidencia de la República (liberal).
Vicuña, Pedro Félix	Padre del anterior. Conspirador pipiolo, tenía 45 años en 1850. Después de ese año fue periodista, prolífico escritor, diputado y senador (liberal).
Zapiola, José	Director del Conservatorio Nacional de Música, regidor por Santiago, memorialista (fue liberal, pero terminó conservador y católico).

¿Fueron lo que se podría llamar 'una generación'? El concepto de 'generación' ha sido bastante discutido como categoría histórica con sólidas raíces teóricas. En general es aceptado. Ortega y Gasset cree que las manifestaciones de relevancia histórica que realiza un hombre (y una generación) se dan durante dos etapas de su vida: las que llama 'de gestación o creación y polémica' que ubica entre los 30 y 45 años y la de 'predominio y mando' que ubica entre los 45 y 60.[60] En esta división podemos estar en desacuerdo con las edades fijadas y considerar la exactitud con que señala sus límites como superficial y sin base. Incluso señalar que, de serla, ésta sería una regla que se daría fundamentalmente en sociedades estables y que, aún así, admite muchas excepciones. Pero la hipótesis resulta insinuante y enriquecedor para comprender períodos históricos concretos.

En el caso chileno, que cumple con el requisito de la estabilidad, nos parece claro que el grupo de hombres que durante su juventud pretendieron revolucionar la institucionalidad y (en el discurso al menos) también a la sociedad chilena; una vez transformados en grupo dirigente

60 José Ortega y Gasset, *En torno a Galileo* (Madrid, 1982), pp. 34–67.

(vale decir cuando pasaron a la etapa 'de predominio y mando') llegaron a alterarla de modo muy importante, pero sólo en lo político-institucional. De este modo, el cambio se dio solamente en la forma de una nueva estructuración de la hegemonía oligárquica (de la República Autoritaria se pasó a la República Parlamentaria, pero igualmente oligárquica), dejando intocada y excluida, al resto de la sociedad chilena.

Efectivamente, parece indudable que muchos (casi todos) de los personajes que hemos visto participando en los episodios y revueltas mencionados, o, al menos, del ambiente que los rodeó; una vez maduros, si bien llevaron adelante los ideales juveniles en lo político, adquirieron una gran moderación en lo social. Combinación en definitiva compatible con su condición oligárquica, ya asumida plenamente y con la ideología liberal despojada de los fermentos de revolución social que la caracterizaban el '48'.

Este proceso fue más claro entre aquellos cuya rebeldía de la coyuntura de 1848–51 estuvo más bien ligada a la lucha pipiolo-pelucona y al antiautoritarismo, un fenómeno sólo político, que al espíritu 'Quarante-Huitard' que fue toda una cultura. Fue el caso de la mayoría de los hombres públicos de primera magnitud que figuran en la lista transcrita más arriba, como Federico Errázuriz Zañartu y Domingo Santa María. Incluso, si tomamos casos más extremos, como Eusebio Lillo, director del 'El Amigo del Pueblo', y Benjamín Vicuña Mackenna, verdadero energúmeno revolucionario en su primera juventud, ambos llegaron a adquirir el 'buen sentido' que dan el compromiso con el medio, una cierta fortuna en el caso de Vicuña y una respetable panza, en caso de ambos. 'Maduraron' como dirían los hombres 'cuerdos'. Vicuña Mackenna, en sus libros escritos 15 ó 20 años después del episodio que hemos relatado en el capítulo anterior, no deja de ironizar y señalar el romanticismo, ingenuo y absurdo que lo habría caracterizado. Es el caso de sus obras *Los Girondinos chilenos* e *Historia de la jornada del 20 de abril de 1851*; ambas una suerte de mea culpa que – además – muestran del afán lúdico del tremebundo historiador. Pero, dicho sea de paso, lo anterior no impidió al propio Vicuña Mackenna, conservar muchos rasgos de su atolondrada juventud revolucionaria durante su carrera política posterior. Por ejemplo: cuando lanzó su 'Campaña de los Pueblos' en 1875, hizo amplio uso del método de los 'banquetes' que remontaba su genealogía en cuanto forma de sociabilidad política informal al París de 1847 y 1848, así como al Estados Unidos que conoció en sus periplos de la década de 1850 en calidad de exiliado.

Pero los más decididos de los 'Quarante-Huitards' chilenos de 1850–51, que no actuaban simplemente dentro del contexto de la lucha pipiolo-pelucona o, en otras palabras, los menos comprometidos con el medio: Arcos y Bilbao, pero también Guerrero y Prado, no llegaron a ser figuras públicas importantes, en Chile al menos, y no sabemos cuál habría sido su actitud de haber adquirido esa condición. En el caso de los dos primeros, que dejaron el país casi inmediatamente después de haber concluido el episodio del '48', su idea de la necesidad de un cambio no sólo político sino también social, que afectara las estructuras, al parecer, no cambió.

Vicuña Mackenna acusó a Arcos, después que se encontrara con él en Nápoles en 1871, de haberse convertido en 'casi pelucón,[61] proyectando a nuestro juicio su propia evoluciény, tal vez, enojado con Santiago Arcos – al cual estimaba por otra parte – por haber vapuleado éste a los pipiolos – con los cuales Vicuña seguía identificándose fantasmalmente – en la *Carta a Francisco Bilbao.*[62] Pero la verdad es que Arcos había sido candidato a las Cortes en España representando a la izquierda (el Partido Republicano Federal) sólo dos años antes y difícilmente podía considerarse conservador.

Francisco Bilbao, a pesar de haber apoyado a la 'Confederación' y al caudillo Urquiza, que representaba lo tradicional, antiliberal y antimoderno, en las guerras civiles argentinas de fines de la década de 1850 (posiblemente como consecuencia del romanticismo americanista que lo caracterizaba por esa época), en su literatura política escrita después de 1850 y, en verdad, hasta su muerte, conservó su afán de revolucionario social; contradicción nada de extraña en Bilbao. Guerrero continuó siendo un agitador revolucionario toda su vida. Sólo Zapiola, hombre de compleja sicología (quien tampoco de transformó en hombre público, pero sí en organista en la Catedral de Santiago) terminó siendo conservador.[63]

Pero, el proceso a destacar es que, a diferencia de la actitud de los recién nombrados, la mayoría de los jóvenes oligarcas pipiolos igualitarios de 1850 perdieron sus afanes de redención social a medida que fueron adquiriendo respetabilidad y 'asentaron la cabeza' (como diría un Francisco Antonio Encina en serio o un Antonio Machado con sarcasmo), pero no los de liberalización política.[64]

Ellos transformaron la institucionalidad política autoritaria de la República Pelucona en la institucionalidad liberal que caracterizó a Chile

61 Vicuña Mackenna, *Historia de la jornada del 20 de abril*, pp. 46–7.

62 Arcos había sido, sólo dos años antes candidato a las Cortes españolas en representación del Partido Republicano Federal, vale decir la extrema izquierda. En esa ocasión escribió un folleto titulado, *A los electores de diputados para los próximas Cortas Constituyentes* (Madrid, 1869). En éste, defiende el federalismo, el liberalismo, los derechos de los más pobres, aún cuando se muestra abiertamente anti socialista; algo que, por lo demás, ya había dejado en claro en Chile en 1852 en *La contribución y la recaudación.*

63 Ventura Blanco, 'Introducción' a la primera edición de José Zapiola, *Recuerdos de treinta años*, reproducido en la edición que citamos aquí (Introducción), pp. XXVII a XXXVI.

64 Antonio Machado, 'Llanto y coplas a la muerte de don Guido,' Antonio Machado, *Poesías escogidas* (Madrid, 1969), p. 133.

después de 1870, fruto de las reformas constitucionales de la época de Errázuriz Zañartu y diversos documentos legales aprobados durante las administraciones siguientes, en especial las leyes laicas de la época de Santa María.[65] Incluso los pelucones (que luego se convertirían en 'conservadores' y 'monttvaristas'); en parte por conveniencia política, pero también porque fueron ganados por el signo de los tiempos, igualmente entraron a comulgar con la 'religión liberal' y favorecieron el proceso de transición desde el autoritarismo portaliano a la República parlamentaria.[66] Resumiendo: el programa político de la que había sido la Sociedad de la Igualdad y que caracterizó a la coyuntura del '48' chileno, por vago que fuese, se materializó, en buena medida, durante el siglo XIX, lo que no fue, el caso del programa social, el que hubo de esperar al siglo XX.

Aunque ya Marc Bloch prevenía sobre el peligro de dejarse llevar por el mito (o ídolo) de los orígenes en la explicación de una situación histórica, parece legítimo afirmar que el grupo de personas a que nos hemos estado refiriendo y que desempeñó un rol fundamental en la liberalización política y, en general, en la gestación del Chile moderno, había quedado marcada por las ideas y, más aún, por el 'pathos' rebelde y romántico de su vivencia juvenil liberal.[67] La preponderancia de la literatura política liberal – llegada desde Europa, y en particular desde Gran Bretaña – que se dio durante las décadas siguientes, reafirmaron esta opción, que representaba el signo de los tiempos en el ámbito de la cultura occidental, de la cual Chile se sentía parte.

Las nuevas formas de sociabilidad del Chile liberal: el Partido Radical

Pero si toda la generación de oligarcas jóvenes que participaron en las conmociones del '48' había quedado marcada por éstas, esta impronta fue especialmente notoria entre los que a partir de 1857, aproximadamente, constituyeron un grupo liberal, extremo en su rebeldía. Éste, andando el tiempo, formaría el Partido Radical, principal forma de sociabilidad política que haría de la difusión e institucionalización de la cultura del '48' su razón de ser. El año de 1858 este grupo creó un periódico bautizado 'La Asamblea Constituyente' y se organizó (todavía dentro del Partido Liberal o pipiolo) como grupo de presión opuesto a la formación de la 'Fusión Liberal-Conservadora' que se estructurara después de la crisis del peluconismo, consecuencia del escándalo que produjo la llamada

65 Julio Heisse, *Historia de Chile, El período parlamentario, 1861–1925* (Santiago, FECHA) Vol 1, passim.

66 Arturo y Samuel Valenzuela, 'Orígenes de la democracia, reflexiones teóricas sobre el caso chileno,' *Estudios Públicos*, No. 12, (Santiago, 1984).

67 Marc Bloch, *Introducción a la Historia* (México, 1965), p. 27.

'Cuestión del Sacristán'. Ésta dividió a los Pelucones entre 'Conservadores' incondicionales de la Iglesia Católica y el grupo 'Monttvarista' (por Manuel Montt y su ministro Antonio Varas) o 'Nacional', que siguió apegados a esos dos hombres públicos y que tuvo un carácter también conservador, pero laico. Ese mismo año también se fundaría, como forma de sociabilidad política, el 'Club de la Unión', el cual – después – derivaría a tener una función social puramente mundana.[68]

Como se sabe, a raíz del episodio de 'sacristán' el elemento pelucón o conservador católico militante, que ahora había experimentado el autoritarismo de Montt en carne propia, se acercó a los liberales, los que no le perdonaban a ese mandatario las persecuciones y exilios de 1850 y 1851.[69] Pero, a los liberales 'extremistas y rojos' como se les llamó, fuertemente doctrinarios en su laicismo, les resultó inaceptable un pacto con el sector conservador y clerical que se había escindido del partido de Gobierno. De allí su oposición a la 'Fusión'.

Los historiadores del Partido Radical están de acuerdo que este grupo de liberales anticlericales, que serían después el núcleo de la nueva agrupación política, no sólo habían pertenecido, sino que eran los herederos más directos de la 'juventud liberal de la época de Bulnes'.[70] Eran nuestros 'Quarante-Huitards' revolucionarios y afrancesados y que guardaban cierta fidelidad a sus ideas de entonces. Tanto así que para las elecciones de 1858 se formó, dentro de este sector, una 'Sociedad Política Obrera', alrededor de la cual se alinearon los elementos de la que fuera la Sociedad de la Igualdad.[71] Vicuña Mackenna fue candidato a diputado de esta asociación por la circunscripción de La Ligua. En cambio, los liberales dispuestos a fusionarse con los conservadores clericales, ahora distanciados del Gobierno de Montt, descendían, no de los igualitarios sino, en su mayoría, del tronco conservador vialista, escindido del peluconismo en 1849.

Entre los liberales laicos intransigentes y futuros radicales, estaban: Ángel Custodio Gallo, Francisco Marín, Justo Arteaga, Luis Rodríguez Velasco, Santiago Cobo Alemparte, Manuel Antonio y Guillermo Matta.

68 Ángel C. Espejo, *El Partido Radical, sus obras y sus hombres* (Santiago, FECHA). Antes ya había creado *La libertad*,' clausurado por el Gobierno de Montt y *El País*. Sobre el 'Club de la Unión', María José Larraín, *El Club de la Unión* (tesis de licenciatura, Universidad Católica, Santiago, 1995).

69 René León Echaíz, *Evolución histórica de los partidos políticos chilenos* (Santiago, 1949), pp. 58–59; Angel C. Espejo, *El Partido Radical*, pp. 95–129; Yerko Koscina, *El radicalismo como partido político; su génesis y su doctrina* (Santiago, 1956), pp. 44–5. Otras fuentes no se refieren a esta convención fundadora; la que, en todo caso, habría sido informal.

70 León Echaíz, *Evolución histórica de los partidos políticos chilenos*, p. 46.

71 Ricardo Donoso, *Vicuña Mackenna* (Buenos Aires, 1977), p. 85.

El grupo era dirigido por Manuel Antonio Matta, quien puede ser considerado la tercera figura clave entre los jóvenes que retornaron a Chile desde Europa en vísperas del año 1850. A pesar de su pasividad política durante los años 1850–51, Matta había asimilado las ideas y el espíritu del '48' europeo y, a diferencia de Arcos o Bilbao, supo integrar alrededor de su persona, después de su elección como diputado en 1855, un grupo permanente que hizo suyo y difundió ese legado. Eran liberales y el nombre de 'radicales' se les dio originalmente en la acepción adjetiva de la palabra, vale decir, para designar el sector más extremo e intransigente del liberalismo (pipiolos todavía) en particular en relación a sus posiciones duramente anticlericales, abiertas a una cierta sensibilidad social y a la modernidad en general.

Disuelta por el gobierno de Montt el intento de 'asamblea constituyente' de 1858 (de allí el nombre del diario), el grupo liberal 'radical' se manifestó de nuevo al año siguiente con motivo de la guerra civil que estallara.[72] Matta participó activamente en el conflicto de 1859, por lo cual fue condenado a muerte, debiendo abandonar el país en compañía de Vicuña Mackenna, Ángel Custodio Gallo y Guillermo Matta, radicándose en Inglaterra. Otro connotado futuro 'radical', Pedro León Gallo, de más activa participación en la guerra civil de 1859, también debió partir al exilio. Durante tres años vivió asimismo en Inglaterra, desde donde volvería en 1862.[73]

Lo que está claro es que de entre los ex 'Quarante-Huitards' chilenos, hacia 1857–58, era Matta y no Bilbao, como se suele afirmar, quien aportó la consistencia doctrinaria al grupo que fundaría el Partido Radical. Pero, si bien existente – como tendencia – desde 1857, el grupo liberal 'radical' no tuvo una estructura propia y una identidad diferenciada sino desde 1862. La mencionada guerra civil de 1859 fue determinante para que los liberales 'radicales', unidos por la derrota y el exilio, se cohesionaran y tomaran una voluntad de lucha que se transformó en una cruzada vital en el caso de la mayoría de ellos.

¿Cuáles eran las bases doctrinarias del radicalismo naciente? Originalmente, al menos, las mismas que hemos mencionado como propias del '48'; después irían incorporando nuevos elementos, notoriamente el positivismo. Desarrollemos el punto. Como hemos afirmado más atrás, el ideario y las formas de sociabilidad nacidas en Chile hacia la mitad del siglo XIX tenían su origen en las tendencias 'asociativas' (o 'societarias') comunes en el mundo político europeo de la primera mitad del siglo XIX, inspiradas por el socialismo utópico (lo que aparece, veladamente, en

72 'Lo Afirman,' Francisco Barría Soto, *El Partido Radical, su historia y sus obras* (Santiago, 1957); Yerko Koscina, *El radicalismo como partido político.*

73 Francisco A. Encina, *Historia de Chile,* Vol. XV, pp. 387–9.

algunos escritos de los dirigentes igualitarios; más en los de Bilbao que en los del liberal Arcos) y, más concretamente, en las sociedades republicanas francesas de 1848. Pero, después de 1855, aproximadamente, harían suya también la sociología positivista de Comte y sus seguidores (lo que aparece patente en los escritos de los líderes radicales de 10 años después; así como en muchos liberales, en particular Lastarria). En el caso de Manuel Antonio Matta hubo también, al parecer, una fuerte influencia del 'liberalismo evolucionado', de Stuart Mill.[74]

La tendencia positivista aportó la idea de privilegiar a la sociedad civil, en calidad de cuerpo intermedio entre el individuo y el estado, lo que naturalmente implicaba un debilitamiento de éste. Aspecto teórico que se adaptaba admirablemente a la contingencia chilena de los años que estamos estudiando (la lucha contra el autoritarismo encarnado en el régimen pelucón y el 'estado portaliano'). Por otra parte, si el del radicalismo se trataba de un ideario parecido (en la mayoría de sus puntos principales) al que hemos visto en el caso de la Sociedad de la Igualdad, era mucho más coherente, acentuando algunos rasgos que no aparecían claros en aquella 'Sociedad' de tan breve y agitada vida, en particular un laicismo racionalista y anticlerical militante y un anti centralismo acentuado.

En 1862, Manuel Antonio Matta definía así los principios doctrinarios que inspiraban al radicalismo chileno en su primera etapa:

> La reforma de la Constitución que reste los poderes omnipotentes del ejecutivo que origina abusos incalificables. La libertad electoral (que) debe generar el poder mediante el sufragio universal que impida las exigencias de una casta privilegiada cuyos derechos nacen por la cantidad de riqueza.
>
> La enseñanza laica, independiente de toda tuición confesional, lo que no significa, en ningún momento ataque a la religión, sino a la intransigencia religiosa. La conciencia (que) no debe presionarse para ganar adeptos por (¿para?) la idea religiosa, que merece el respeto de los ciudadanos
>
> La autonomía de las provincias por (¿para?) su descentralización administrativa que convierte a Santiago en Chile. El derecho edilicio que ponga vallas al autoritarismo de la metrópoli dirigida desde la Moneda.[75]

Pese a sus orígenes santiaguinos, el primer grupo organizado que podría calificarse propiamente de 'radical' se constituyó en la ciudad de Copiapó, región de origen de Manuel Antonio Matta, donde tenía fortuna, parientes y amigos, por donde había sido elegido diputado en 1855 y que había ya presenciado dos sublevaciones contra el Gobierno de Montt: durante la guerra civil de 1851, y la otra, más importante, en 1859.

74 Heisse, *Historia de Chile*, Vol. 2, p. 322.

75 Estas ideas están tomadas de artículos de Matta aparecidos en *La Voz de Chile* el año 1862.

En 1862, al retorno de Matta de su exilio en Inglaterra, ya mencionado, y probablemente bajo su inspiración directa, Ángel Custodio y Pedro León Gallo, con Fernando Chatel, Román Fritis, Pedro Pablo Zapata, Felipe Santiago Matta, Ramón de Fraga, Domingo Sanderson, José Ramón Zavala, Alejandro Walker, Pedro Nolasco Vivanco y otros, entre los cuales cabe destacar a Federico Varela, formaron en esa ciudad un grupo de análisis político y difusión de ideas.[76] Este grupo organizó, en noviembre de 1862, la llamada 'Fraternidad de Atacama' la que pretendía reunir miembros de un informal 'Partido Liberal Reformista', en el hecho el ala 'radical' del Partido Liberal atacameño, opuesto a la 'Fusión Liberal-Conservadora' de 1857, ahora gobernante.[77] A fines del año 1863, este grupo se transformó, propiamente, en un centro de activismo político con miras a las elecciones parlamentarias de 1864, creando una 'asamblea electoral' que, en el hecho, sería la primera 'asamblea radical' de Chile.

El hecho de la existencia en Santiago de un órgano periodístico de los liberales 'radicales' o 'reformistas' o 'rojos', como se les motejaba, el diario *La Voz de Chile*, que vio la luz pública en marzo de 1862 y se publicó hasta 1864, nos indica que también en la capital había renacido un grupo de las mismas ideas, aunque quizá más inorgánico que el copiapino. En el comité editorial del periódico figuraban: Manuel Antonio Matta, Antonio A. Arce, Roberto Souper, Ángel Custodio Gallo, Isidoro Errázuriz y Benicio Álamos. Resulta interesante observar que en este comité se daban cita futuros liberales de 'avanzada' como Isidoro Errázuriz, con radicales como Matta, Gallo y Álamos. En el diario también escribía Manuel Recabarren, uno de nuestros conocidos igualitarios y, antes, Girondino chileno y Alberto Blest Gana que allí publicó, como folletín, ni más ni menos que *Martín Rivas* y *El ideal de un calavera*.[78] Escribió en el diario también un tal Víctor Arcos, ¿pariente de Santiago Arcos?, ¿un seudónimo?[79] La Voz de Chile, en sus primeros números, junto a la crítica mordaz a los conservadores, publicó artículos políticos de tendencia liberal, destacando todo lo que se refería a la necesidad de 'organización' y 'asociación'.[80] La idea era promover la fundación de una nueva 'sociedad' política.

76 Espejo, *El Partido Radical*, passim.

77 *La Voz de Chile*, 24 de noviembre de 1862; citada por Pablo Toro en, 'El Partido Radical, nueva forma de sociabilidad política en el Chile del siglo XIX,' documento inédito.

78 Virgilio Figueroa, *Diccionario histórico, biográfico y bibliográfico de Chile*, passim.; Raúl Silva Castro, *Alberto Blest Gana* (Santiago, 1955), pp. 48–50. Alberto Blest Gana vivió el '48' en Francia siendo cadete de la Escuela Militar Preparatoria de Versalles; el episodio lo plasmó en una corta novela, *Los desposados*.

79 Raúl Silva Castro, *Prensa y periodismo*, p. 229.

80 Por ejemplo: 'Espíritu de asociación,' en *La Voz de Chile*, No. 11, 24 de marzo de 1862.

¿De qué sociedad se trataba? De la que pasaría a denominarse 'Unión Liberal'. En ésta se dieron cita los liberales radicales o rojos.[81] El 11 de abril siguiente, Juan Nepomuceno Espejo escribía sobre las intenciones de la nueva sociedad política, destacando la necesidad de crear asociaciones y partidos estables y unidos más allá de la contingencia.[82] La reunión constitutiva de la Unión Liberal se llevó a efecto en casa de Ramón de la Fuente el día siguiente a la convocatoria. En la elección de directiva que se realizó entonces, Manuel Antonio Matta obtuvo la primera mayoría con 98 sufragios. Otros asistentes que obtuvieron votos fueron: Isidoro Errázuriz, Pedro Félix Vicuña, Melchor de Santiago y Concha, Bruno Larraín, Álvaro Covarrubias, Fernando Urízar Garfias, Juan Bautista Reyes, Nicolás Figueroa, Federico Errázuriz, Aniceto Vergara Albano, Guillermo Matta, José Victorino Lastarria y Ramón de la Fuente. No todas estas personas se convertirían en radicales después y por eso la de Copiapó debe considerarse la primera asamblea radical de Chile y no esta santiaguina 'Unión Liberal'. Algunos de los miembros de esta última (como Isidoro y Federico Errázuriz) continuarían siendo liberales y no ingresarían a la 'asamblea radical' de Santiago cuando ésta se formó en 1864, pero cuya emancipación definitiva de la Unión Liberal se produciría en 1865 con motivo del debate constitucional de ese año. Desde entonces se puede considerar al sector liberal 'radical' de Santiago como un grupo definitivamente diferenciado del liberalismo, aunque todavía (y hasta 1888) informal.[83] Como podemos apreciar, de entre los miembros de la Unión Liberal, los dos Errázuriz, Federico e Isidoro, Pedro Félix Vicuña, Bruno Larraín, Lastarria, Urízar Garfias y Álvaro Covarrubias están en la lista de Igualitarios, Girondinos y 'Quarante-Huitards', chilenos que figura más atrás. Una relación de filiación entre los hombres de 1850–51 y el liberalismo extremo, radical o rojo, de la década de 1860 parece clara.

Otros liberales rojos, de esa primera época, en Santiago, Copiapó y Valparaíso, fueron, según Encina: el también ex igualitario, Eusebio Lillo, Juan Nepomuceno Espejo, Juan de Dios Arlegui, José Francisco Vergara, José Alfonso, Ricardo Claro Cruz y Juan A. Palazuelos.[84] Lista a la que habría que agregar a Gerónimo Costa y Francisco Donoso quienes figuran entre los organizadores de un banquete en honor a Pedro León Gallo, en noviembre de 1863.[85] En ese año 1863, al menos, cinco figuras liberales 'radicales' o partícipes de la 'Unión Liberal' ostentaban cargos de

81 Isidoro Errázuriz, 'La Unión Liberal, sus antecedentes y su importancia,' *La Voz de Chile*, 29 de marzo de 1862.
82 *La Voz de Chile*, No. 27, 11 de abril de 1862.
83 Sergio Guilisasti Tagle, *Partidos políticos chilenos* (Santiago, 1964), p. 134.
84 Encina, *Historia de Chile*, vol. 15, p. 383.
85 *La Voz de Chile*, 10 de noviembre de 1864.

diputados: Manuel Antonio Matta, Tomás Gallo, Juan Nepomuceno Espejo, Ricardo Claro Cruz y Manuel Recabarren.

Tal como las personas – liberales ex igualitarios en su mayoría – cuyas carreras públicas reprodujimos en la Tabla No.1, estos 'proto radicales', fueron adquiriendo un gran peso político en Chile a partir del Gobierno de José Joaquín Pérez. Igual que lo hicimos con aquellos de la primera lista, sigamos los hitos fundamentales de la carrera pública, posterior a 1863, de estas personas. En la Tabla No. 2 que sigue no repetimos las carreras públicas de los personajes que figuran en la anterior.

Tabla 2: Algunas Carreras Públicas despues de 1863

Nombre	*Carrera publica*
Álamos, Benicio	Ministro en Perú, diputado (radical).
Alfonso, José	Juez, ministro de la Corte de Apelaciones, ministro de estado (radical).
Arce, Antonio	—
Arlegui, Juan de Dios	Juez, diputado, Superintendente del Cuerpo de Bomberos de Chile, primer Serenísimo Gran Maestro de la Masonería chilena (1862) (radical).
Claro Cruz, Ricardo	Diputado, senador (radical).
Cobo, Santiago	—
Concha, Melchor de Santiago	Diputado, senador, ministro de estado (liberal).
Costa, Gerónimo	—
Chatel, Fernando	—
De la Fuente, Ramón	—
Donoso, Francisco	Diputado, senador suplente (radical).
Errázuriz, Isidoro	Diputado, senador, ministro de estado (liberal).
Espejo, Juan Nepomuceno	Diputado (radical).
Figueroa, Nicolás	Diputado, intendente.
Fritis, Román	Escritor, periodista (radical).
Fraga, Ramón	—
Gallo, Pedro León	Diputado, senador (radical).
Gallo, Ángel Custodio	Diputado (radical).
Gallo, Guillermo	—
Gallo, Tomás	Diputado (radical).
Matta, Manuel Antonio	Diputado, senador, embajador, ministro de estado (radical).
Matta, Guillermo	Diputado, senador, intendente, embajador (radical).

Matta, Felipe Santiago	Diputado (radical).
Matte, Augusto	Diputado, senador, ministro de estado (liberal).
Palazuelos, Juan A.	Diputado, fundador de diario 'La Ley' (radical).
Reyes, Juan Bautista	—
Rodríguez V., Luis	Senador, ministro de estado (radical).
Sanderson, Domingo	Regidor (radical).
Souper, Roberto	—
Varela, Federico	Diputado, senador (radical).
Vergara Albano, Aniceto	Diputado, embajador, ministro de estado, ministro de la Corte Suprema (liberal).
Vergara, José Francisco	Diputado, senador, ministro de estado, candidato a la Presidencia de la República, Superintendente del Cuerpo de Bomberos, Serenísimo Gran Maestro de la Masonería (radical).
Walker, Alejandro	—
Zabala, José R.	—
Zapata, Pedro Pablo	—

Resulta evidente que la mayoría de los personajes santiaguinos, de Valparaíso y del norte, que aparecen en la Tabla No. 2, al igual que los actores del '48' chileno ya incluidos en la Tabla No. 1, ocuparon, en su mayoría, altos cargos públicos en el Chile de la segunda mitad del siglo XIX, en particular los capitalinos y porteños, así como algunas de las figuras más destacadas de la región de Atacama. Es así que el Partido Radical, que tanta importancia tuvo en la historia de Chile posterior y que existe hasta el día de hoy, debe pues también insertarse, en herencia del '48' chileno.

La herencia del '48' chileno en el mundo popular

¿Pero, fue sólo entre unos pocos oligarcas y la clase media en formación que el '48' chileno dejó una herencia ideológico-política y social? Nuestra opinión que su legado ideológico-político entre los sectores populares urbanos, incluso entre los artesanos, no parece haber sido importante. Es probable que la Sociedad de la Igualdad haya sobrevivido en la leyenda y tradición oral populares; pero en los años y décadas posteriores al episodio, no se tiene evidencia de una herencia orgánica y significativa, que se manifestara en la actitud política o en la social de esos sectores. Esta rápida caída en el olvido del episodio del '48' entre los sectores populares de Santiago y de Chile puede haberse debido a que el artesanado santiaguino de 1850 era un segmento social destinado a desaparecer dentro de un Chile que comenzaba a integrarse a la modernidad; a que su nivel de conciencia político-social era precario y no fue capaz de trasmitirlo al proletariado que nacería poco después. Existió la leyenda – tempranamente aparecida – de que la Sociedad de la Igualdad había sido un engaño.

La diferencia con Europa, donde la memoria histórica y el ideario del '48' popular se perpetuaron es clara. Naturalmente esto tuvo una relación directa con el momento histórico y con la trascendencia y cariz de los episodios allá y aquí. El '48' francés (y europeo) fue una conmoción mayor que tocó la esencia del devenir histórico del país galo, que vivía una Revolución Industrial. En tanto el '48' chileno fue un episodio, que aunque no tan intrascendente como lo han pintado los historiadores conservadores y de grandes consecuencias, indirectas, en el futuro mediano, no puso en peligro al sistema en el corto plazo, ni acabó con el 'peso de la noche', que vivió su tardía apoteosis política durante el Gobierno de Montt. En Francia y en Europa, en cambio, el '48' significó un episodio histórico clave que provocó el quiebre definitivo e inmediato del mundo surgido del Congreso de Viena y de la Santa Alianza. Y aunque fracasó en acabar con las monarquías y el autoritarismo, al menos en los países de Europa Occidental, fue el entierro del 'Antiguo Régimen'.

En Chile la mencionada rebelión del 20 de abril de 1851 tuvo más de motín militar en la tradición pipiola que de sublevación popular. Pero encontramos nuevamente una cierta presencia de los sectores populares del '48' chileno en algunos episodios de la guerra civil que estallará en septiembre de ese mismo año; la que – por otra parte – obedeció en lo fundamental a causas ajenas al espíritu igualitario del año 1850.[86] Nos referimos, principalmente al – también mencionado – episodio alzamiento artesanal del 28 de octubre de 1851 en Valparaíso, último motín verdaderamente popular de la coyuntura que estamos estudiando.

Así, sin perjuicio de que los motivos ideológicos centrales y la simbología del '48' continuaran apareciendo fugazmente por muchos años en los motines y revueltas contra Montt y aún después; la posterior intervención en política de los artesanos que pertenecieron a la Sociedad de la Igualdad se redujo a la militancia radical de Larrecheda y Samaniego y a la intervención de un ¿artesano? ex-igualitario llamado Juan Silva quien fue elegido vice-presidente de la Asamblea Popular Democrática en apoyo de Vicuña Mackenna en la Campaña de los Pueblos de 1875, junto al entonces radical y también ex igualitario, pero nada popular, Manuel Guerrero.[87]

86 Benjamín Vicuña Mackenna, *Historia de los diez años de la administración de don Manuel Montt* (Santiago, 1862).

87 Lorena Ríos y Eugenio Ortega F., *La Campaña de los Pueblos de Benjamín Vicuña Mackenna*, trabajo inédito.

Con todo, en 1875, con motivo de la campaña presidencial de Vicuña Mackenna, Artemón Frías, delegado por Chañaral a la 'Convención de los Pueblos' afirmaba en público: '¡Gloria eterna señores a la memoria de nuestro malogrado compatriota Francisco Bilbao y la del gran socialista Lamennais, su digno maestro!'[88] La primera Convención de 'Partido Demócrata', formado mayoritariamente por artesanos,[89] se realizó el 14 de julio de 1889, al cumplirse 'el primer centenario de la Revolución Francesa';[90] nuevamente el hilo de filiación se manifestaba. Y en 1898 se fundó en 'Partido obrero Francisco Bilbao', que, entre otras cosas, proponía la reforma integral de la propiedad inmobiliaria y la reforma agraria (arts. 32, 40 y 41 de su programa). Después con la llegada de las ideas socialistas y anarquistas a las organizaciones políticas populares la herencia del '48' chileno parece perderse entre estas.

¿Pero si los hombres de condición artesanal que participaron en el '48' chileno no tuvieron gran figuración pública después, ni sus ideas prendieron seriamente en los medios populares chilenos, que ocurrió con su participación en las organizaciones sociales y laborales que se crearon en los años siguientes? En 1853 existió en Santiago una 'Sociedad Tipográfica' en la que, al parecer, militaron ex igualitarios.[91] La organizó el artesano peruano Victorino Laynes y se trataba de un grupo apolítico, lo que no impidió que fuese prohibida por el Gobierno de Montt y Laynes fuese relegado a Talca. En 1855 se crearía otra 'Sociedad Tipográfica' en Valparaíso y en el año 1858 surgieron la Sociedad de Artesanos de Valparaíso y la Unión de Artesanos de Santiago.[92] En 1862, Fermín Vivaceta, quien se consideraba discípulo de Francisco Bilbao, con la ayuda de Demetrio Lastarria, creó la 'Sociedad Unión de Artesanos de Santiago' y el mismo año nacía otra asociación similar en La Serena. Probablemente en estas organizaciones militaron ex igualitarios; pero, en todo caso, las fundadas por Vivaceta perseguían objetivos mutualistas y diferentes a los de la Sociedad de la Igualdad, aun cuando el lenguaje simbólico de la Revolución Francesa todavía se usaba en sus manifiestos, uno de los cuales decía que pretendía promover 'un sistema de asociación capaz de producir libertad, igualdad y fraternidad'.[93]

Una de las primeras obras de la Sociedad Unión de Artesanos de Santiago, fue crear una escuela nocturna para artesanos. ¿Reminiscencia

88 Benjamín Vicuña Mackenna, *La Convención de los Pueblos* (Santiago, 1876), p. 75.
89 De hecho el único partido político (propiamente tal) de artesanos que existió en Chile.
90 Julio Cesar Jobet, *Temas históricos chilenos* (Santiago, 1973), p. 201.
91 Hernán Ramírez, *Historia del movimiento obrero en Chile* (Concepción 1986), p. 166.
92 *Ibid.*
93 Fermín Vivazeta, *Unión y fraternidad de los trabajadores sostenida por las asociaciones cooperativas*, citado por Hernán Ramírez, *Historia del movimiento obrero en Chile*, pp. 168–9.

de la Sociedad de la Igualdad? Puede ser, pero es preciso considerar que la idea de fundar escuelas nocturnas para obreros estaba en el pensamiento mutualista y cooperativista europeo y, en particular, en Owen a quien Vivaceta admiraba y esa tradición poco tenía que ver con el '48'. También debe tenerse presente que el mutualismo que venía, fundamentalmente, de las enseñanzas de Proudhon, a quien jamás se le mencionó en 1850, y que fue uno de los teóricos que Arcos atacó más virulentamente en *La contribución y la recaudación*. De todas estas organizaciones mencionadas, sólo la formada por Vivaceta estaba destinada a durar y ejercer influencia en el mundo del trabajo manual santiaguino.

Pero que un cierto legado del '48' pervivía, fantasmalmente, es indudable. En 1872 se fundó en Valparaíso otra 'Sociedad de la Igualdad'.[94] Ignoramos que características e importancia tuvo, pero la misma escasez de noticias nos lleva a presumir que esta última fue poca. En Copiapó hubo aun otra asociación del mismo nombre por los mismos años, pero integrada por juventud burguesa del liceo. Existieron durante el siglo XIX chileno otros intentos de implementar iniciativas sociales ligadas de una u otra forma a la coyuntura del '48' europeo y francés, aunque no con la forma de sociabilidad representada por la Sociedad de la Igualdad. En 1863, el ingeniero, matemático y abogado Ramón Picarte, que había vivido en Francia entre 1859 y 1861, intentó fundar Sociedades de Sastres y de Zapateros, las que fracasaron. El año siguiente planteó otra iniciativa: la creación de una 'Sociedad de Trabajo para Todos' que se proponía ser a la vez una cooperativa de producción y de consumo, sociedad de socorros mutuos y caja de ahorros. Tampoco tuvo éxito. Pero el infatigable Picarte, en 1866, intentó una iniciativa aún más audaz: la fundación, cerca de Chillán, de un 'falansterio' a imitación del 'de Fourier' en Francia.[95] Al parecer el nuevo proyecto tampoco prosperó, pues no tenemos noticia de su materialización. Hasta donde llegan nuestros conocimientos no hubo relación entre Picarte y los ex-igualitarios . En todo caso, la iniciativa del falansterio se trató de la única de verdadero contenido socialista-utópico que se dio en Chile.

Pero si la herencia del '48' chileno entre los sectores populares, en la realidad laboral y social, también fue débil, perduró – como decíamos atrás – con más fuerza en el ámbito de la cultura. La leyenda en torno a la figura de Bilbao, transformado en símbolo y prócer, perduró tanto entre individuos de la naciente clase media, como entre sectores obreros. El año 1866, Genaro Abasolo, un discípulo y admirador escribió un libro titulado

94 Ramírez, *Historia del movimiento obrero en Chile*, p. 162.

95 Pedro Pablo Figueroa, *Diccionario Biográfico de Chile* (Santiago, 1897), p. 462. Como se sabe, Fourier nunca fundó un falansterio, sus discípulos intentaron la creación de varios, sin éxito.

La religión de un americano, libro, desde el título, claramente influido por los escritos de Bilbao y pródigo en citas de Quinet, Michelet y Proudhon (el Proudhon post '48' que entonces estaba de gran boga en la izquierda francesa y se había reconciliado con algunas instituciones fundamentales de una sociedad cristiana tradicional, sobre todo la familia, y que por lo tanto podía conciliarse con escritores católico-republicanos como Quinet).[96]

En fin, calles principales de ciudades principales de Chile fueron bautizadas con el nombre de Francisco Bilbao, que llevan hasta el día de hoy y su retrato ha adornado todas las galerías de próceres republicanos progresistas que han existido y existen. Que contraste con Arcos cuyo nombre sólo recuerdan dos pequeñas calles de barrios periféricos de Santiago y de quien no se guarda retrato alguno. El resto de los dirigentes de la sociedad de la Igualdad, incluidos los artesanos, al parecer fue olvidado hasta que, en el siglo XX, algunos historiadores los han rescatado. Parte de la historiografía socialista chilena (Julio César Jobet y otros) ha mostrado a los dirigentes de los motines de 1850 como los fundadores del movimiento político y laboral obrero en Chile. Por nuestra parte, aunque reconocemos en la obra de Jobet un aporte al conocimiento de la época, por lo recién escrito, no podemos estar de acuerdo con lo sustancial de su tesis. Es efectivo, como se hizo presente, que el episodio la Sociedad de la Igualdad representó la primera actuación masiva del mundo del trabajo manual urbano en la arena política chilena; pero, como también vimos, todo el episodio se dio en el marco de lo que todavía era un escenario controlado por la oligarquía, fue muy corto. Lo limitado del legado dejado por toda la aventura en el mundo popular chileno, pensamos que confirma este aserto. La herencia, que quedó y que fue efectivamente muy importante en la historia de Chile posterior, fue recibida, como lo hemos visto, por sectores mesócratas, y, en menor medida, oligárquicos, en especial de provincias, tanto en materia ideológica como de un patrón o forma de sociabilidad política.

Conclusión

Hemos visto que el '48' chileno, La Sociedad de la Igualdad, los motines de los años 1850 y 1851, aun sin incluir a la guerra civil que se dio ese último año; pero, más aún, la 'cultura' en que estuvieron insertos estas acciones, tuvieron dimensiones y alcances sociales importantes, dependiendo del sector social que las hizo pervivir, y que dejaron un legado considerablemente más trascendente que el que la historiografía, especialmente la conservadora, ha mostrado. Legado del que quedan muestras importantes aún en el presente.

96 Genaro Abasolo, *La religión de un americano* (Santiago, 1866).

Esto equivale a afirmar:

1) Que esos episodios fueron más importantes *en su momento* que lo que nos han mostrado los autores recién aludidos, pero, paradojalmente, no algunos de liberales del siglo XIX, que los vivieron y también hicieron su historia. Además de Vicuña Mackenna, Barros Arana e incluso literatos como Blest Gana o Daniel Riquelme, les concedieron mucha importancia.

2) Que dejaron un legado ideológico en la forma de un fortalecimiento del pensamiento o, mejor dicho, una visión del mundo racionalista, liberal y progresivamente laicizante. Desde entonces, la idea de modernizar Chile adquirió dimensiones mucho más vastas que el mero desarrollo económico y educacional como fue concebida en los decenios de la República Autoritaria (pelucona).

3) Que esta herencia se acrisoló – más que entre los sectores populares – fundamentalmente entre grupos de clase media y de la alta burguesía 'de origen no hispano' que se estaba consolidando y enriqueciendo entonces. Entre estos hombres nacieron y se consolidaron nuevas formas de sociabilidad que tal como había sucedido en Europa, eran el correlato natural de esa cultura o visión de mundo que hemos mencionado en el punto anterior.

No parece coincidencia que tres de estas nuevas formas de sociabilidad, la Sociedad de la Igualdad, la Masonería y el Cuerpo de Bomberos Voluntarios nacieron el año de 1850. Eso indica su vínculo directo o indirecto, pero indudable, con el espíritu del '48', que llegó Chile desfasado, pero ya aquí, ayudó a debilitar, hasta poner en jaque, a la República autoritaria, que estaba experimentando (y siempre había experimentado) tensiones. Su quiebre se haría definitivo después de 1870.

4) Que, en términos generales, los hombres de la oligarquía tradicional y la nueva burguesía, que en su juventud participaron el llamado '48' chileno, llegaron, muchos de ellos, a ocupar los más altos cargos públicos de la institucionalidad chilena; constituyéndose en una verdadera 'generación' que transformó al Chile pelucón en el liberal de la segunda mitad del siglo XIX.

5) Que las nuevas formas de sociabilidad que los agruparon; jerarquizadas y estructuradas en forma de una red de núcleos que progresivamente fue cubriendo el territorio nacional, cobraron extraordinaria importancia entre el elemento burgués masculino chileno de la época y décadas posteriores, cumpliendo una función de pedagogía político social modernizadora hasta el punto de influir decisivamente en el desenvolvimiento histórico del país.

6) Que, de este modo, el proceso recién descrito constituye, indirectamente, uno de los pilares históricos del siglo XX chileno en sus características políticas, sociales y culturales.

8

The Influence of the European 1848 Revolutions in Peru*

NATALIA SOBREVILLA PEREA

Although in Peru there was no 'Cuarentaiocho', the ideas of 1848 fuelled an already vigorous debate between liberals and conservatives and were important in giving ideological support to the 1854 revolution that abolished both slavery and the Indian tribute.[1] As in the other Latin American cases presented in this collection, the press, artisans and intellectuals played an important part in the diffusion of the new ideas imported from abroad. This chapter explores the impact of European ideas on ideological debate in mid-nineteenth century Peru, and how ideas were transmitted through the press, both in Lima and the provinces. Specifically, the chapter will analyse the 'democratisation' of politics – the participation of artisans and the appearance of the first organised political party – in the presidential campaign of 1850, and assess how the *quarante huitard* spirit influenced both the 1854 revolution liberal constitution of 1856.

Peru in the nineteenth century is mostly known for its economic history. The wealth that originated from guano, the bird dropping fertiliser, and how it was used and abused by the governing caudillos and elite, has attracted the attention of specialists. Until the 1990s, the politics and ideological debates of the period, and the important social changes of nineteenth-century Peru, had escaped modern historiography. This has changed with a growing body of work looking at the national question, tribute, Indians and regional studies.[2] Compared to the more conspicuous

* This chapter owes much to the comments of my colleagues in Lima and London, especially the editor, Guy Thomson, and the series editor, Eduardo Posada-Carbó.

1 In the 1920s, Jorge Guillermo Leguía wrote a seminal work on liberalism, and published an essay, 'Las ideas de 1848 en el Peru,' in *Estudios Históricos* (Santiago, 1939), pp. 113–44.

2 Recent regional studies include Sarah Chambers, *From Subjects to Citizens, Honor, Gender, and Politics in Arequipa Peru, 1780–1854* (Philadelphia, 1999), and Charles Walker, *Smoldering Ashes, Cuzco and the Creation of Republican Peru, 1780–1840* (Durham, NC, 1999).

impact of the European Revolutions of 1848 in north-eastern Brazil, Chile and New Granada, events in Peru do not seem as tightly linked. Yet, when these are examined more closely, it is evident that the ideas and new forms of political association accompanying the 'springtime of the people', and the sheer feeling that the world was changing, had a marked impact in Peru. These currents benefited Peru's Liberals, who gained important political victories between 1846 and 1856. The encouragement Liberals derived from events in Europe also made Peru's Conservatives more certain of the threat they were fighting against.

Peruvian independence from Spain was a protracted affair. The first rebellions in 1812 in the south, sparked by Argentine influence, were defeated by a strong viceroy who possessed the largest Spanish garrison of the continent. Peru became the centre of Spanish resistance until 1821 when General José de San Martín declared independence. The Royalists moved the viceregal government to highland Cuzco and fighting continued. Lima was twice retaken and final victory was only attained with the capitulation of the Spanish to Bolívar's forces after the Battle of Ayacucho in 1824.

The post-independence period was one of instability. Bolívar failed in his attempt to establish the Federation of the Andes under his lifelong presidency and Peru began its campaign to achieve what it considered its historic boundaries, which for many included Guayaquil and Bolivia. Peru fought wars over both territories. Civil strife then engulfed the country in anarchy. Six constitutions were promulgated between Independence and 1836, but none managed to provide the country with a durable institutional framework.[3] Cuzco leader, Agustín Gamarra, emerged from this fighting as the most powerful leader in Peru. His rivalry with Andrés de Santa Cruz, the strongest man in Bolivia, ensured another two decades of war. Both men shared the vision of uniting Peru and Bolivia into a single state, but whereas Gamarra thought Bolivia should be annexed to Peru, Santa Cruz believed in a confederation of equal states. Between 1837 and 1839 the Bolivian leader was able to put his vision into practise and a joint state was established. However, this provoked the opposition of Chile, Argentina and the Peruvian emigrés led by Gamarra.

After the defeat of Santa Cruz, and of the liberal forces that had supported him in Peru, Gamarra took power for a second period, backed by the 1839 conservative Constitution of Huancayo. However, the south

3 Heraclio Bonilla, 'Peru and Bolivia from Independence to the War of the Pacific,' in Leslie Bethell, *Cambridge History of Latin America* (Cambridge, 1985), vol. III, p. 248. Also significant is the Bolivian popular mobilisation known as 'the republic of artisans', during the presidency of Manuel I. Belzú (1848–1855), about which little yet has been written.

of the country remained restless, becoming a centre for Liberal conspiracy. Gamarra's chief aim in his second term was to annex Bolivia so as to ensure Santa Cruz would never return to power. In this endeavour he met his death in the battle of Ingavi, outside La Paz, in 1841. The Peruvian state then disintegrated as rival regional caudillos competed for power.[4] With the invasion of Bolivian troops the period known as the 'Anarchy' began. This lasted for more than three years, after which Ramón Castilla, hero of both the campaign against the Spaniards and the Peru-Bolivia Confederation, defeated the forces of Manuel Ignacio de Vivanco, the self appointed Director of the country.

Returning to the 1839 Huancayo Charter, but without alienating the Liberals, Castilla emerged to revalidate Gamarra's legacy. Aided by the revenue generated by the export of guano to Great Britain, Castilla was able to restore Peru's credit-worthiness and consolidate the country, after more than three decades of uncertainty and revolt.

The Ideological Debate

Caudillos have often been seen as the only important forces operating in post-independence hispanic America. However, as Paul Gootenberg reminds us, they did not operate in a vacuum: 'high-ranking figures influenced and even determined government policy from the time of independence'.[5] Described as *hombres de bien*[6] or *hombres de traje negro*,[7] these men dominated the political debate as well as the middle and upper echelons of the government, which were split between liberals and conservatives. The death of Gamarra brought the rise of a Conservative who was to dominate Peruvian politics for the next quarter of a century; Bartolomé Herrera. Born in Lima in 1805, orphaned at the age of five, Herrera was raised by his uncle, a priest who provided him with the best education available. By the age of twenty he was a doctor in both law and theology and soon after became a priest.[8] He lived in relative obscurity in his parish of Lurín until 1842, when Francisco Vidal, the caudillo who briefly held power before Vivanco, met him en route to Lima and became

4 Paul Gootenberg, 'North-South: Trade Policy, Regionalism and Caudillismo in Post-Independence Peru,' *Journal of Latin American Studies*, vol. 23, (1991), p. 303.

5 Peter Blanchard, 'The "Transitional Man" in Nineteenth-Century Latin America: The Case of Domingo Elías of Peru,' *Bulletin of Latin American Research*, vol. 15, (1996), p. 161.

6 Michael Costeloe, *The Central Republic in Mexico, 1835–1846: Hombres de Bien in the Age of Santa Ana* (Cambridge, 1993).

7 Jorge Basadre 'Los hombres de traje negro,' *Letras*, (Lima, 1929), vol. I, pp. 29–59.

8 Fredrick Pike, 'Heresy, Real and Alleged in Peru: An Aspect of Conservative–Liberal Struggle, 1830–1875,' *Hispanic American Historical Review*, vol. 47, (1967), pp. 54–5.

interested in his ideas.[9] Herrera was invited to deliver the sermon at Gamarra's funeral and used this opportunity to call for order.[10] He considered the country's political instability was caused by 'the loss of the habit of obedience among citizens', asserting that political authority derived from God and therefore should be obeyed.[11] The sermon brought Herrera to the attention of Conservatives and he was appointed Rector of the Colegio de San Carlos, the most important state-funded school. While the political situation worsened during the 'Anarchy', Herrera reorganised the college by including his favourite French authors – Cousin, Constant and Guizot – in the curriculum.[12] His aim was to train a new generation that would 'dry out the tears in Peru.'[13]

Ever since the defeat of the monarchism of San Martín in the 1820s Liberals had dominated political debate, if not government. They had written several constitutions. By appointing weak executives that could be led by congress, Liberals had tried, but failed, to restrict the power of the caudillos. One of the most important exponents of liberalism in the country was Francisco de Paula González Vigil. Born in Tacna in 1792, trained in the ideas of the Enlightenment at the seminary of Arequipa, this priest was elected to congress in 1827. In 1832, González Vigil rose against Gamarra's authoritarianism with what became a famous phrase: 'I must accuse, therefore I accuse.'[14] During the 1840s, when most other liberal priests had renounced their once heretical views of the state's dominance over the Church, Vigil dedicated himself to writing his 'Defence of the authority of governments and bishops against the pretensions of the Roman Curia'. The publication of the first volume 1848 earned Vigil excommunication. Vulnerable after surviving the Roman Republic, Pope Pius IX is reputed to have lamented that 'Even in the land of Saint Rose, I am persecuted.'[15]

While the Liberal–Conservative debate dwelled mostly on the issue of relations between Church and state, a new group emerged to take on *caudillismo* led by Domingo Elías, a rich and successful merchant and

9 Jorge Guillermo Leguía, 'Don Bartolomé Herrera, su labor en el Convictorio de San Carlos,' *Estudios Históricos* (Santiago, 1939), pp. 63–100.

10 Jorge Basadre, 'Los hombres de traje negro', p. 46.

11 Pike, 'Heresy, Real and Alleged', p. 55.

12 Ricardo Cubas Ramacciotti, 'La propuesta nacional y educativa de Bartolomé Herrera: la reforma del Convictorio de San Carlos 1842,' unpubl. BA thesis, PUCP, Lima 1998, pp. 55, 56.

13 Hugo Garavito Amézaga, *El Perú liberal: partidos e ideas políticas de la Ilustración a la República Aristocrática* (Lima, 1989), p. 170. Carmen McEvoy 'Formando la Nación, usos y abusos del paradigma republicano,' in Carmen McEvoy (ed.), *Forjando la Nación* (Lima, 1999), p. 208.

14 Pike, 'Heresy, Real and Alleged', pp. 58–9.

15 Jorge Guillermo Leguía, 'El Apostolado de Vigil,' in *Estudios Históricos*, p. 43.

landowner. In 1844, in the midst of the 'Anarchy', Vivanco the 'Director', had left Elías in charge of the government of Lima while he travelled to Arequipa to suppress Castilla's uprising. Blanchard observes that Elías was chosen precisely because he was not a civilian without the military backing to challenge Vivanco.[16] In spite of this, while the two caudillos prepared to fight in the South, Elías pronounced against both, as exponents of authoritarian military rule. The *Semana Magna* (as this uprising in Lima was called) favoured peace and civilian government. Inspired by the French idea of an armed citizenry, a National Guard organised along occupational lines and barricades was established, reminiscent of the 1830 Paris uprising. Yet the language of fraternity was exclusive to 'the "decent" people preventing its extension to plebeian sectors.'[17] Students at San Carlos organised a personal guard for Elías and the city prepared its defence against the forces of José Rufino Echenique, who threatened to retake it for Vivanco. Echenique, the military commander in the region, realising that the outcome of the civil war would depend on the battle between the two main caudillos, decided not to intervene. Elías and Echenique accepted Castilla's victory as an opportunity for peace.[18]

Domingo Elías, who after these events became known as 'the man of the people', had established the School of Nuestra Señora de Guadalupe in 1841, for the education of his children and for the diffusion of liberal ideas.[19] He appointed Sebastián Lorente, Spanish Liberal and *doceañista*, to direct it. Among the subjects taught were political economy, natural and constitutional law, classical and modern history, calculus, physics, Latin, French, English, arithmetic and book-keeping.[20]

During the initial years of Castilla's government, Bartolomé Herrera kept a low profile. But on 28 July 1846 Herrera asserted in a sermon commemorating the twenty-fifth anniversary of Independence that all the political troubles of the Republic had been God's punishment for the 'impious and anti-social errors that were spread through the influence of

16 Blanchard, 'The "Transitional Man",' p. 168.

17 Victor Peralta, 'El Mito del Ciudadano Armado, La "Semana Magna" y las elecciones de 1844 en Lima,' in Hilda Sabato (ed.), *Ciudadanía política y formación de las naciones. Perspectivas históricas de América Latina* (Mexico City, 1999), pp. 231–52.

18 Elías tried to impose conditions to Castilla and to be recognised as the political power in the north. *Informe sobre las causales del fracaso de las negociaciones entabladas entre el Gral. Ramón Castilla y los miembros de la Junta de Gobierno de su presidencia en Arequipa*, Agosto 21 de 1844, D10616 Manuscript collection in the Biblioteca Nacional (Peru). Failing at this Castilla, Elías's chances in the 1844 elections disappeared, Peralta, 'El Mito', p. 247.

19 '[Para] evitar que sus hijos mendiguen en paises extraños una mediana educación', a letter to *El Comercio* written upon the opening of the school on 9 Feb. 1841.

20 *El Comercio*, 8 Feb. 1848, article commenting on the final exams presented in the College of Guadalupe in Dec. 1847.

the French Revolution'.[21] He claimed that 'the ruin of nations, as of individuals, is of their own making.' To prevent punishment, nations should respect God's will that legally constituted government be obeyed.[22] Herrera also denied the existence of sovereignty of the people; sovereignty was a quality possessed only by God. Vigil considered this sermon more in tune with the court of Isabel II than a commemoration the anniversary of a free and democratic republic.[23]

The sermon caused uproar in Liberal circles, prompting high court magistrate, Benito Laso, a well-known Liberal who had supported Bolívar, to launch a polemic in the press. He argued that, once sovereignty was taken away from the people, an absolutist government, as in Asia or in Europe of the Dark Ages, would be established.[24] Herrera replied by inviting Laso to prove that 'the people can be sovereign in the same sense that kings have been called sovereign'.[25] Laso then defined sovereignty, citizenship and liberty. Although respecting his opponent for the high level of the debate, Herrera admitted that further argument would be fruitless, as he came from another generation. Laso would simply quote Rousseau's *Social Contract*, and he would do the same with the new *Philosophy of Law* by Ahrens.[26]

But this was not the end of the debate. A series of anonymous articles appeared in the press during the following three months accusing Herrera of subversion and of defending absolutism. The main complaint was that Herrera's ideas were endorsed by the government who allowed them to be taught in San Carlos, the most important state school. Polemicists argued that the debate on popular sovereignty could have been abandoned if it were not the principle upon which the Nation itself was founded, and that Herrera should explain his position.[27] Finally, by the end of October 1846, the Rector of San Carlos declared that 'el pueblo', defined as individuals of all age and condition, did not have the right to make laws since they were based on eternal principles which only those accustomed to intellectual and scientific work were able to appreciate. 'The right to make laws belongs to the most intelligent, to the aristocracy of knowledge, created by nature', Herrera triumphantly asserted.[28]

21 Pike, 'Heresy, Real and Alleged,' p. 55.

22 Bartolomé Herrera, *Escritos y discursos* (Lima, 1929), vol. I, p. 71.

23 Leguía, 'Don Bartolomé Herrera,' p. 72.

24 Benito Laso, article in *El Correo Peruano*, 29 de Julio 1846, published in Herrera, *Escritos y Discursos*, p. 104.

25 Herrera, *Escritos y discursos*, p. 106.

26 Herrera, *Escritos y discursos*, p. 111; Garavito Amézaga, *El Peru Liberal*, p. 173.

27 'Un Patriota,' *El Comercio*, 24 Aug. 1846, in Herrera, *Escritos y discursos*, p. 119.

28 Herrera, *Escritos y discursos*, p. 131. For an analysis of his idea of citizenship see McEvoy, *Forjando la nación*, pp. 215–18.

Sovereignty of the people, as against intelligence, continued to be debated by the self appointed 'Patriots', an anonymous group opposed to Herrera and the School of San Carlos well into January 1847. What became clear and public knowledge in these six months was how the school's curriculum had dramatically changed from the days of the Liberal reform of Toribio Rodríguez de Mendoza (1770–1817). Herrera stressed the importance of science, specially mathematics, physics and philosophy, and the study of law. French and English were taught alongside Latin and Herrera himself taught philosophy following the rationalist ideas of Cousin.[29] His writings demonstrate the influence of François Guizot's theory of the sovereignty of intelligence that sought a balance between democracy and privilege. This had been adopted by the Orleanist restoration after the July 1830 revolution. In Peru Herrera used Guizot's theory to sustain the traditional order and to maintain elite domination of government.[30]

In 1849, a year after the events in Europe, Herrera was elected deputy for Lima and presided over the legislative chamber that was to discuss changes to the constitution.[31] The debate began in 1847 when an alliance between Domingo Elías and Ramón Castilla had added electoral reform to a proposal to reform the economy. Provincial electoral colleges would remain responsible for verifying congressional elections, but suffrage would be extended to include all taxpayers.[32] This issue featured prominently in the 1849 congressional debate, especially a proposal to extend the vote to illiterate Indians and mestizos until 1860. The Rector of San Carlos used this opportunity to promote the idea of the 'sovereignty of intelligence', continuing to support the ideas of French conservatives, even after their defeat in the 1848 revolution. Once again he argued that those who could not exercise a right properly should not possess that right. He considered that in a community of around one hundred, where only ten could read, the votes of the ninety illiterates should be appropriated by these ten. For Herrera, the only way to be fair to the Indian and the mestizo was by providing them with education.[33] Pedro Gálvez, a young graduate of San

29 Leguía, 'Don Bartolomé Herrera,' pp. 73–4. Leguía revised all the documents of San Carlos and notes all the changes Herrera made to the curiculum in his detailed footnotes

30 Francisco García Calderón, 'La evolucion de las ideas y los hechos,' in *El Perú Contemporáneo* (Lima, 1980).

31 Garavito, *El Perú liberal*, p. 177.

32 Vincent Peloso, 'Liberals, Electoral Reform, and the Popular Vote in Mid-Nineteenth-Century Peru,' Barbara Tenenbaum and Vincent Peloso (eds.), *Politics and Power, State Formation in Nineteenth-Century Latin America* (Athens, GA, 1996), p. 194.

33 Jorge Basadre, *Elecciones y centralismo en el Perú, apuntes para un esquema histórico* (Lima, 1980), p. 39.

Carlos, gave Herrera the greatest homage a student can give a former teacher, by opposing his views and defending the right of all to vote.[34] Following French liberals, Gálvez argued that a right could not be linked to the capacity to exercise it, pointing out the absurdity of fearing that ten would dominate the votes of ninety and not to fear when only these ten could vote. Gálvez, who ended his speech with a demand for the abolition of slavery, obtained 96 votes, defeating Herrera who only obtained nineteen.[35] Winning the vote extending suffrage was a great Liberal victory.

Peruvian *hombres de traje negro* kept abreast of the latest intellectual debates in Europe. The 1830 French revolution with its conservative thought influenced Herrera's adoption of Guizot. Moreover the enemies of *caudillismo* were inspired by the myth of an armed citizenry, the building of barricades, and a National Guard composed of citizens.

The Influx of Ideas

Intellectual debates in Europe were followed very closely in Peru where, as seen above, they were often mirrored. Not only were the main schools in Lima teaching the most fashionable European ideas, but a wide range of recent European books and news was available. Before 1848 *El Comercio* carried articles on the main political events and even reproduced speeches by important leaders such as Lamartine.[36] This newspaper also carried advertisements for the main bookstores in Lima that every other week published lists of the recently arrived books. French authors such as Guizot, Dumas, Hugo and Lamartine were easily accessible both in translation and in their original language. Spanish and Italian conservative and religious books were also quite popular.[37]

A rich description of the culture of the *tertulia* has been left by Ricardo Palma in *La bohemia de mi tiempo*.[38] Palma formed part of a generation of Romantic poets, all born after independence, who tried to create a new style of literature appropriate for the Republic. They were inspired by the classes in literature and history at the School of Nuestra Señora de Guadalupe given by its director, Sebastián Lorente, whom 'the new generation followed and listened to as if an apostle'.[39] The 'Bohemians' flourished between 1848 and 1860, the period when the Liberal movement achieved its greatest advances in Peru. They would meet after five at the

34 Basadre, 'Los Hombres,' p. 42.

35 Basadre, *Elecciones*, p. 40.

36 His speeches against customs in Marseilles, and on the liberty of Italy of 1847, were published in *El Comercio*, on the 12 and 13 of Feb. 1848.

37 *El Comercio*, 13 Jan. 1848, 8 March 1848, 17 March 1848.

38 Ricardo Palma, *La bohemia de mi tiempo* (Lima, 1948).

39 Palma, *La bohemia*, p. 18.

bookshop of the Gallego Pérez, to exchange books, talk politics and read aloud from the main newspapers.

News of the uprising in Sicily, carried by *El Comercio* on 8 April 1848, or a letter from Mazzini to the Pope, translated entirely by George Sand and reprinted from a London newspaper, would have been eagerly commented upon in Lima's cafés. A month later, on 8 May, news of the events of February 1848 in Paris reached Lima. International news dominated *El Comercio* for the rest of the week. The reaction of Peru's liberals appeared on the following day in a letter signed by the 'true patriots', welcoming the events in Paris and warning Lima to be vigilant and to hold their government accountable: 'Patriots of Peru and of everywhere, Glory to republican France! And if any *stupid despot* should humiliate you, imitate the sublime example of the great civilising nation of the world.'[40]

After the events in Paris the share of international news increased. Between the eighth and tenth day of each month an eagerly awaited package arrived via Panama. On the first day a summary of the main events would be published, interlaced with speeches by the most important participants. Letters from the main European gazettes, from Peruvians in Europe, as well as the debates of the Assembly in Paris, would then be combined with articles from other parts of America. The news coverage extended even to detailed debate of the new French and Prussian Constitutions (both published in their entirety). Events in France, Italy and Prussia received most coverage while events in Austria, Russia, England and Spain were also followed closely. Once all the interesting news had been published, and before the next package had arrived, editorials would analyse the European situation, summarise the year's events and print the work of the most important contemporary historians. The interest on the European events diminished slightly during the presidential campaign in late 1849. Yet Lima's newspapers never ceased covering the political situation in Europe.[41]

News of 1848 was not confined to Lima. Liberal newspapers in the provinces also followed events in Europe closely. Cuzco's vigorous press witnessed the foundation of two new liberal papers in this period, *El Demócrata Americano, periódico político, literario y mercantil* in 1846 and *Los Intereses del País* in 1848.[42] The editors of *El Demócrata Americano* considered it their duty to 'co-operate in the diffusion of the enlighten-

40 *El Comercio*, 9 May 1848.

41 *El Comercio*, between 1848 and 1850.

42 Claudia Rosas Lauro, 'Los ecos del "48" en Cuzco,' *Yachaywasi Revista de la Universidad Nacional Federico Villareal* 'El regreso de la historia política,' (Cuzco) No. 7, (March 2000), pp. 51–7.

ment' and to educate the people by providing them with foreign news. They considered events in Europe in 1848 to be so close to their reality that the news they received seemed to be written for their own country and province.[43] *El Demócrata* contrasted Herrera's conservative ideas with those emanating from Europe, and concerning itself in particular with issues relating to artisans.[44] In July 1848 several articles in favour of workers' organisations were published, including a 'Catechism of the Artisan', written by Schemit, to inform 'compañeros' of their rights to freedom of association.[45]

Los Intereses del País was created as a direct reaction to the events in Europe. It carried as its slogan a quote from E. de Girardin: 'When a nation has come to know its rights, it can only be governed by these lessons, because there is no other way to prevent successive revolutions and oppressive governments.'[46] In the first number the editors explained that their newspaper was to be dedicated to 'spread some of the sparks of the enlightenment among the people to prepare the nation for necessary changes.' They also considered that by learning from the example of Europe they would 'save the country many tears'.[47] *Los Intereses* was openly protectionist, in deference to its artisan readers, and also advocated the rights of the Indians and equality of all.[48] It included an eclectic mix of European and local news as well as lengthy editorials. These newspapers demonstrate how the ideas of 1848 had spread throughout the country and had a real impact in areas far from the coast.

The events of 1848 also had an impact on Europeans living in Peru. The French consulate in Lima maintained an updated record of its countrymen, who were expected to register upon arrival as well as to inscribe the rest of their families.[49] Once news of the abolition of slavery in France had reached Peru, consular authorities could check up on their compatriots, as French living abroad were forbidden from owning, buying or selling slaves, or risk losing their citizenship.[50] The Italian community in Lima became involved in the events of 1848 too. A newspaper called *La Italia Libre*, managed from the sweet shop of Mr Ghirardelli, was published in the capital, while letters from leading members of the Italian

43 *Demócrata Americano*, no. 158, 4 March 1848.

44 In 1847 the *Demócrata Americano* intervened in the debates on the press, on the sovereignty of the people and intelligence, *Demócrata Americano*, no. 158, 4 March 1848.

45 *Demócrata Américano*, no. 177, 21 July 1848.

46 *Los Intereses del País*, no. 1, 4 July 1848.

47 *Ibid.*

48 *Los Intereses del País*, no. 1, 2 Aug. 1848.

49 *El Comercio*, 10 July 1848 and selected numbers between 1848 and 1850.

50 The news reached Peru on 10 July 1848, *El Comercio*.

community, exhorting their compatriots up and down the Pacific coast to support the Roman Republic, were printed in *El Comercio*.[51] A section of the *Giovane Italia* had been founded in Lima by the Republican leaders led by Doctor Manuel Solari, an exiled cousin of Giuseppe Mazzini.[52] Recent immigrants also had a role in transmitting the radical social philosophies in vogue in Europe during the 1840s among Lima's artisans.[53]

Artisan Participation in Politics

A measure of the influence of European events in Peru was the increased importance of artisans in politics. Just as in New Granada, artisans became crucial in the presidential campaign of mid-century as the constitutional reforms of 1847 and 1849 allowed them greater political participation. The guilds had changed radically since independence: masters no longer exercised the same power over their apprentices and workers, whose possibilities of bargaining had increased with changes in the structure of society. By 1848 18 per cent of artisans were foreigners, together taking 40 per cent of manufacturing profits (indicated by tax levels). Despite the success of immigrant craftsmen, local artisans never campaigned for their exclusion, as they had with foreign merchants. Foreign artisans were welcome because locals felt they could learn their techniques, as well benefit from the prestige of having foreigners working in their establishments as Lima consumers were ever more eager to embrace European tastes. A consequence of foreign intrusion into Lima's craft life was that European ideas would be shared in workshops where reading of newspapers and the discussion of news became important activities.

Paul Gootenberg has described the advent of free trade to Peru and the strength of protectionism in the early years of the Republic. He has observed that the final offensive against free trade occurred between 1848 and 1852, after which the Liberal, guano-enriched elite triumphed in implanting an open economy. The campaign to obtain the passage of the 'Artisan Law', late in 1849, shows how mobilised artisans could become in favour of protectionism. During congressional debates, artisans crowded the galleries 'to remind deputies that "they knew very well to whom they owed these benefits".'[54] José María García, a cigar maker, addressed Congress in October 1849 reading a long and impassioned plea by Lima's

51 *El Comercio*, 6 August 1848.

52 This group organised collections to support the fighting in Italy. Giovanni Bonfiglio, *Los italianos en la sociedad peruana* (Lima, 1994), pp. 114–20.

53 Paul Gootenberg, 'The Social Origins of Protectionism and Free Trade in Nineteenth-Century Lima,' *Journal of Latin American Studies*, Vol. 14, (1982), p. 342.

54 Gootenberg, 'The Social Origins,' p. 349.

guild in favour of protectionism.[55] A law giving unprecedented powers to the guilds was finally passed unanimously on 21 of December 1849. All imports of competing goods were liable to a 90 per cent duty based on the guilds' price evaluations. Artisans were delighted, as they felt that their voices had finally been heard. Miguel Guzmán, described by Gootenberg as a 'radical leader', published a pamphlet in verse, entitled 'Triumph of the artisans, Free Peru in its progress', celebrating the victory of 'law and reason' against the 'foreign usurper' who had kept Peruvians in poverty.[56]

Yet this was a Pyrrhic victory for Lima's artisans. 'Sensing the tide against them in 1850 and the betrayal of their old political-allies, Lima artisans,' asserts Paul Gootenberg, 'launched a series of bitter attacks against liberals, the Congress, and the guano elites ("aristocrats" all). This was Peru's delayed and miniature "1848". In the early months of 1850 Lima's popular Jacobins stridently demanded even more protectionism and an independent political mobilisation to get it.'[57] This description of a 'mini 1848' conjures up the idea of a mass protest movement, not found in the accounts of the time. In 1850 Lima's artisans were still elated with the passing of the import tax law in their favour. At the start of the year, news and action were directed almost entirely at the presidential campaign. Artisans participated widely in the election, particularly in a press debate defending the new protectionist law against Liberal opposition. This centred mainly around the 'students of political economy' who published articles supporting free trade in *El Comercio*, and the *Progresistas*, a new political group composed of businessmen, who had started a campaign in favour of pure liberalism in their weekly, *El Progreso*. The protectionist law was revoked only in 1852 by the newly elected administration.

Paul Gootenberg sees artisan mobilisation as an important part of the contest for the presidency:

> Artisans organised numerous meetings for the candidates and propaganda spread through the ranks. The most vocal came out as partisans of Vivanco, a *limeño* with nationalistic pretensions, against Echenique whom they vilified for his allegedly hostile acts towards artisans. However, all contenders sought artisan votes, pledging to safeguard 'national industry'.[58]

Both Vivanco and Echenique, then, had artisans in the ranks of their supporters. Initially around October 1849, artisans seem to have joined Vivanco's side, publishing articles accusing Echenique not only of being

55 *Ibid.*, p. 348.

56 *Ibid.*, p. 350, and Miguel Guzmán, *Triunfo de los artesanos, Perú libre; en su progreso. Viva el nombre de García y las leyes del Congreso* in 'Colección de Volantes, 1849,' Biblioteca Nacional, Lima.

57 Paul Gootenberg, *Between Silver and Guano*, p. 89.

58 Gootenberg, 'The Social Origins', p. 350.

Bolivian but also of trying to bully artisans into supporting him.[59] The *echeniquistas* responded on 12 December 1849, accusing the opposition of trying to buy the artisan vote. This article was considered subversive and the anonymous author, 'An artisan, friend of the one last night' claimed that he had to feign sickness to prevent being prosecuted. In a second article, published 28 of December, the 'amigo' reminded the *vivanquistas* that artisans would never vote for them because they could never forget how their leader had neglected them during the 'Directorate', when he had ordered all uniforms to be produced abroad.[60]

Although both articles were anonymous, they are characteristic of the style of Miguel Guzmán, the 'radical leader' and ardent *echeniquista* who, in 1850, published countless articles to convince his fellow artisans that he was their best candidate.[61] In his article 'Seduction of Artisans', Guzman defended himself against the *directoriales* whom he accused of publishing an article to offend artisans, their laborious and honest work, and to make them believe that Echenique despised them. The author then asserted that the meetings of Echenique's opponents, the *vivanquistas*, could not 'even reach ten men, to do so they need to include eight jobless drunkards'.[62]

The influence of the events in France in 1848 is clear in Guzmán's article of 16 February 1850:

> Artisans! If the cultivated France, only by willing it, has just reconquered its primitive rights, overthrowing the throne and crown that for so many years had become a tyranny and a despotism that reigned as the only master and owner of this fortunate nation, in the same way, and with the same feelings of liberty, we shall teach this handful of men that have lost the path of justice, considered this nation their property and we their slaves, and, dominated us with their brutal will.[63]

Parisian influence is evident not only in the rhetoric used during these elections, but also in the adoption in Lima of the banquet as a form of political mobilisation. Detailed descriptions of one such event, held in honour of Echenique, were recorded by his opponents. According to the followers of Vivanco, those attending the meeting were armed with guns and daggers and their shouting in the streets was such that shopkeepers had to close their establishments. *Vivanquistas* also claimed that after the banquet, a group of drunkards attacked a *pulpería*, hurting and robbing

59 'Atentado Escandaloso and Señores Echeniquistas,' in *El Comercio*, 26 Oct. and 14 Nov. 1849.

60 'Un Maestro de Artesano,' *El Comercio*, 12 and 28 Dec. 1849.

61 *El Comercio*, 5 and 30 Jan., 16 Feb. 1850.

62 *El Comercio*, 7 Jan. 1850.

63 *El Comercio*, 16 Feb. 1850.

its owner.[64] The following day an article denying *vivanquista* accusations appeared, signed by the supposed ring leader, Manuel de Soto, who claimed that 'It is good that a man says what he wants, even if it is only founded on conjectures, but to openly lie without remorse is the worst.'[65] Historian, Jorge Basadre, describes another public demonstration in favour of Vivanco in which a crowd of around four thousand, wearing red buttons, met near the bullring to see huge kites painted with the emblems of liberty and the republic as well as a big balloon from which flowers and verses were thrown to the masses.[66]

In Arequipa, where the presidential campaign was as hotly contested as in Lima, artisans were also divided between the *echeniquistas* and *vivanquistas*. On more than one occasion the parades in favour of one or the other candidate ended in stone throwing at the houses of political opponents. One of the most visible leaders of these public confrontations was Diego Masías, a small landowner and local politician. He was accused of having organised the stone throwing against the house of Marshall Blas Cerdeña.[67] In the file of the proceedings we find a rich description of the meetings organised by the artisans, which usually comprised between eighty to a hundred people, and were mainly to talk and drink *chicha*. They got out of hand when some well-known member of the opposition would appear and not cheer the candidate of the group's choice.[68] Elite groups found these public displays very threatening and were opposed to what they considered was the manipulation of artisans.

El Club Progresista

On 28 July 1849, as a reaction to these massive demonstrations, a new player entered the political arena. The *Club Progresista* was the first attempt to organise a political party that believed in reason and organised discussion as the means to attain progress and democracy. Its president was Francisco Quirós, José Sevilla and Pedro Gálvez its secretaries. Together they edited *El Progreso*, a weekly published each Saturday, containing the political and administrative programme they wished to see implemented in Peru. From the first issue the inspiration of European events was evident: 'In France, after half a century of trials, confrontation and socials transformations, an administrative system more complete and analogous to the progress of modern civilisation, has been proposed.'[69] The Club, as

64 *El Comercio*, 15 Jan. 1850.

65 *El Comercio*, 16 Jan. 1850.

66 Jorge Basadre, *Historia de la República del Perú* (Lima, 1961), vol. II, p. 915.

67 Archivo Departamental de Arequipa, Prefectura 1848–49 leg. N°17.

68 Archivo Departamental de Arequipa, Prefectura 1848–49 leg. N°17.

69 *El Progreso*, 28 July 1849.

its members called themselves, presented itself as an impartial observer of the situation, whose only interest was the progress of the nation.

Resembling more a magazine than a newspaper, *El Progreso* contained lengthy articles on diverse matters, and analysis of the current national and international situations, advocating liberty, education and free trade. The Club criticised Herrera's opposition to allowing illiterate Indians the vote, and, as part of a campaign against unfair taxes, *El Progreso* published a series of articles attacking the colonial Indian head tax that was still in place. Indians, *El Progreso* asserted, were living under worse conditions than in the colonial period: 'When our forefathers oppressed the Indian, they did it openly; they did not give them rights on paper to then take them away in reality.'[70] This denunciation of the situation of the Indian struck a chord in other regions of the country, and these articles were reprinted in *La Alforja*, a local paper in Ayacucho.[71]

On 8 December 1849 the Club presented its political programme. It argued that for Peru to progress, the political state and resources of the country must be studied with 'impartiality and true patriotism'. The *Progresistas* considered that a change of government was the ideal moment for analysing the work of the outgoing administration, as a lesson for the next. They stressed their independence from the existing political parties and announced they would only chose between the candidates after their programmes for government had been presented, as, on the base on personal attacks, they had found no difference between the candidates.[72] In the next number they reasserted these principles and began what they called the 'trial of the parties'. Their critics accused them of being unable to participate in the elections as they had no candidate and therefore no head.

The Club criticised the campaigns both of Vivanco and Echenique for using every possible means to win, and, especially, for supporting the economically unsound 'Law of the Artisans'. They abhorred the way in which both parties abused the democratic system by using violence at the polls. The day after the ballots had been cast for the electoral colleges, the *Progresistas*, disillusioned by the way in which supporters of both candidates had acted, presented the idea of a third candidate.[73] They did not mention any person in particular, but of the possibility of there being someone else who could be a better president. They asked newspapers in

70 *El Progreso*, 13 Oct. 1849.

71 *La Alforja, periódico eventual de Ayacucho*, 15 and 19 Dec. 1849.

72 *El Progreso*, 8 Dec. 1849.

73 Although the franchise had been extended to nearly all adult males, elections still were indirect. Once the provincial electoral colleges were in place, they chose their representatives to Congress and their presidential candidate. Peralta, 'El Mito', p. 249.

the rest of the country to react to the idea.[74] A lengthy debate followed. While many papers from the provinces were open to this option, Echenique's newspaper, *El Rimac*, led the opposition. During the following six months the discussion grew ever more fierce. The main accusation against the Club was its refusal to announce a candidate, because it feared the true character of the person becoming known to the press.

The idea of a third candidate continued to be debated and it was not until two months before the electoral colleges were to meet that the Club presented its candidate: Domingo Elías, founder of the liberal Guadalupe school and leader of the *Semana Magna* uprising. A well-known liberal, reputedly one of the richest men in Peru, Peter Blanchard has described Elías as the 'Transitional Man' for mid-century Peru.[75] In 1845 he had been elected deputy for Ica and, later that year, councillor of tate. From this position, he questioned the government's economic management and, in 1849, called for an extraordinary Congress to assess the government's response to the problem of the devalued Bolivian currency that was entering the country.[76] In October 1850 there was a failed attempt to assassinate him. It was in this context that his candidacy was announced.[77]

The electoral colleges met in late December 1850 and, by the first week of January, it was clear that Echenique had won by a landslide with 2,590 votes. Elías fared much better than expected with 775 votes. Vivanco was the real loser as a result of the appearance of a third candidate, obtaining only 368 votes. Other candidates included San Román, a general from Puno with indigenous support, who obtained 268 votes, and Bermúdez, another late-comer who had become Ramón Castilla's candidate, obtained only 59 votes. Initially the president had favoured Echenique, but later decided to back Bermúdez, and was therefore accused of trying to disrupt the elections. Three other candidates obtained 36 votes between them. Of the 154 remaining votes, many were not counted for being spoiled with inscriptions for and against Elías, as an 'hombre del pueblo' or an 'hombre de frac'.[78] Castilla was not eager to leave the presidency. Although his period lasted only until April 1851, he awarded himself extension until July.

74 *El Progreso*, 18 Feb. 1850.

75 Blanchard uses this term to describe the way in which Elías managed to combine his political liberalism with other more conservative traits, Blanchard, 'The "Transitional Man",' pp. 168–70.

76 Juan Luis Orrego, 'Domingo Elías y el Club Progresista: los civiles y el poder hacia 1850,' *Histórica*, Lima, Vol. XIV (1990), pp. 337–8.

77 *El Progreso*, 9 Oct. 1850.

78 Basadre, *Historia de la República*, p. 920; *El Comercio*, Jan. and Feb. 1851; *La Alforja*, 11 Jan. 1851.

Echenique's Government

The transfer of power was not entirely peaceful as Arequipa rose up behind Vivanco. Echenique finally asserted his authority and peace was established by his moderately conservative government. Lima soon became a hub for exiled thinkers, both radical and conservative. The former came mainly from Chile after the failed uprising of 1851, and the latter from Colombia after the radical liberal movement took power there. Radical ideas were put forward by leaders such as Francisco Bilbao, Pedro Félix Vicuña, Victorino Lastarria and Federico Errázuriz from Chile. Conservatives included Julio and Sergio Arboleda, Manuel María Mallarino and Vicente Cárdenas from Colombia. After the liberal government had been established in Colombia, many conservatives came to Peru to strengthen the already powerful group led by Herrera, who by then was a minister of Echenique's government. Italian intellectuals also arrived in Lima after the defeat of the Roman Republic, among them Antonio Raimondi and Giusseppe Garibaldi. The former never participated in politics again but the latter was active from his arrival in 1851 until his final departure in 1853, mainly within the Italian community.[79] The presence of so many thinkers stimulated the debate in Peru even further.

The most influential thinker to come to Peru in this period was the radical Chilean leader Francisco Bilbao. Not only had Bilbao been in Europe in 1848 and 1849, but he had tried and failed to implement a radical revolution in Chile. Bilbao had spent part of his childhood in Lima when his father had been exiled by Diego Portales. After his return to Chile, he studied in the Instituto Nacional.[80] He was influenced by the ideas of Jean-Marie Lamennais, and in 1843 he translated *La Esclavitud Moderna*. In the following year, Bilbao published *La Sociabilidad Chilena* in which he argued that Chile had inherited the Middle Ages from Spain. Only with independence had ideas of the liberty of man and equality of citizenship arrived in Chile; ideas that he believed would become a universal religion. For his efforts, Bilbao was tried and found guilty of immorality and blasphemy but innocent of sedition. He left Chile thereafter to continue his studies in the *Collége de France* where he became close friends with his teachers, Jules Michelet and Edgar Quinet, as well as of Lamennais, the author he had admired since his youth.[81] He travelled

79 Garibaldi travelled in a Peruvian guano-loaded ship bound for China for most of 1852 but was politically active during his stay in Lima. Bonfiglio, *Los italianos*, pp. 120–4.

80 Alberto J. Varona, *Francisco Bilbao, revolucionario de América* (Buenos Aires, 1973), p. 42.

81 David Sobrevilla Alcazar, 'Francisco Bilbao y el Perú, El inicio del radicalismo en el Perú y su aporte a la abolición de la esclavitud,' *Repensando la tradición de Nuestra América, Estudios sobre la filosofía en América Latina* (Lima, 1999), pp. 123–4.

extensively across Europe and participated in the June days in Paris, defending barricades with Quinet. After the victory of the reaction, Bilbao remained in France until the end of 1849 when he returned to Chile.[82] There, with Santiago Arcos, he founded *La Sociedad de la Igualdad*, an association of artisans and intellectuals that was viewed with great suspicion by the government. After the abortive rebellion in Santiago in April 1851 against president Bulnes, when Bilbao had tried to build barricades, he was exiled to Peru.[83]

Once established in Lima Bilbao began to organise the *Sociedad Republicana* which he described as: 'a society of youths to abolish slavery and strengthen *rationalism*.'[84] He also published an article in *El Comercio* arguing that slavery was incompatible with Catholicism on a rational basis and that it should therefore be abolished. Pursued by the Echenique government, especially by Herrera, Bilbao spent the next three months in the sanctuary of the French legation. After a warning from the president that to speak against slavery would be to drag the country in disorder and chaos, Bilbao promised not to become involved in the politics of Peru and was allowed to stay. He dedicated his time to writing a life of Saint Rosa of Lima, in which he stressed the saint's concern with the Indian and the slave, rebuking Peruvian society for allowing these unjust systems to remain.[85] Separated from politics, Bilbao drew close to the youth that, under the influence of Spanish liberals Sebastian Lorente and José Joaquín Mora, were developing Peruvian romanticism. Bilbao contributed, along with members of this group – Ricardo Palma, Manuel Nicolás Corpancho, José Casimiro Ulloa and Clemente Althaus – to the *Revista Independiente* (1853–1854).[86]

After the slave uprising in Trujillo early in 1851, the issue of abolition became more pressing. Also, as a consequence of campaigning by French-influenced liberals, abolition became a more widely accepted issue. Although the revolt in Trujillo was localised and bloodless, the injustice – even the illegality – of the system became more apparent. The reasons given by the slaves in support of their bid for freedom were, first, San Martín's decree of 1821 that had freed all children born to slaves, and, secondly, the terrible conditions existing on the haciendas. Fernando Casós, a young liberal and romantic writer, in his partly autobiographical novel *Los amigos de Elena*, presents the best-known account of the uprising.

82 Sobrevilla Alcazar, 'Francisco Bilbao', p. 124.
83 *Ibid.*, p. 125.
84 A. Donoso, *El pensamiento vivo de Francisco Bilbao,* quoted in Sobrevilla Alcazar, 'Francisco Bilbao', p. 127.
85 Varona, *Francisco Bilbao*, p. 144.
86 Varona, *Francisco Bilbao*, pp. 145–6.

The narrator accepts the responsibility for the uprising in his preaching of liberty to a black sacristan of the convent of Santa Clara who then popularised the idea through his singing.[87] According to this account, Casós was the author of the slaves' demands for freedom, based upon their constitutional rights.[88] However, Peter Blanchard doubts Casós's participation and points instead to two mixed-race tailors, Gregorio Tejada y Olaya and Valentín Baca, who were approached by eight blacks in the market for help with composition of the petition.[89]

These tailors must have already acquired a reputation for abolitionist sentiment, for they were involved in an uprising with a high degree of organisation. Some 150 blacks from the surrounding valleys travelled to the city to demand their freedom, carrying the petition. The prefect fled, and as the slaves faced no resistance, they decided to take the local garrison, free the prisoners and declare themselves free men. When the blacks returned to Trujillo the next day, citizens awaited them in shock and fear in the city, convinced that they had come to loot and kill. But by now, a local militia had been organised. Shots were fired in the air in the main square, frightening the slaves who fled in panic. During the following days ninety-seven slaves were recaptured, and their liberty was rescinded. The ringleaders were put on trial. The mulatto tailor, Gregorio Olaya declared that he was just a follower of Elías whose struggle was liberty for all. This was a very generous interpretation of the *Progresista* doctrine, which although promoting freedom never directly called for the freedom of slaves. Indeed, Elías was the largest slave owner in the country. The events demonstrate, however, how Lima newspapers such as *El Progreso, El Comercio*, and local ones such as *La Alforja* in Ayacucho, the *Demócrata Americano* and *Los Intereses del País* in Cuzco, had provided a medium for the diffusion among Peru's artisans of the ideas of 1848, such as the abolition of slavery. Blanchard suspected that the mulatto tailors might have had political linkages, as only Olaya and Baca were sentenced to death. Two years later, even they were amnestied.[90]

The issue of slavery remained in the public imagination with *El Comercio*'s publication of *Uncle Tom's Cabin* in 1852.[91] With the arrival of Chinese bonded workers, the need for slaves to work in plantations

87 Fernando Casós, *Los amigos de Elena o diez años antes* (Paris, 1874).

88 Hector Centurion Vallejo, *Esclavitud y manumisión de negros* (Trujillo, 1954), pp. 16–17.

89 Peter Blanchard's analysis of the Trujillo uprising is based upon research in Trujillo's archives, Peter Blanchard, *Slavery and Abolition in Early Republican Peru* (Delaware, 1992), pp. 114–19.

90 Blanchard, *Slavery*, pp. 114–19.

91 More on the dismantling of slavery as an institution see Cristine Hünefeldt *Paying the Price of Freedom, Family and Labor among Lima's Slaves 1800–1854* (Berkeley, 1994).

decreased.[92] Slavery had ceased to be an important part of coastal agriculture and it was only maintained in two departments, Lima and Trujillo. On the other hand, the civil code recognised a series of rights for slaves. All those born after 1821 were *libertos* who, after a certain age, were considered free and were to be paid a wage. All children born to *libertos* were immediately free.

The 1854 Revolution

Slavery was not the issue that generated most debate and criticism of the Echenique regime. More controversial was the consolidation of the internal debt. This process had started during Castilla's presidency and was the repayment of the old debt generated during the process of independence and the initial years of the republic. The measure had been conceived as a way to channel earnings from guano into the local economy, as well as to help build local capital that had been destroyed. Initially, the consolidation had been seen as a positive measure, but during the presidency of Echenique the number of recognised consolidation bonds increased exponentially and there was a feeling that corruption had taken over and that those surrounding the president were the only ones profiting. A second measure that angered the opposition was the conversion of the internal debt bonds to the external debt. Although a plausible economic explanation was later given by Echenique in his memoirs, his political opponents saw it merely as a way to ensure the payment of the debt no matter how the economy developed.[93]

Liberals, who had prepared a plan for government in 1850, but had been defeated in the elections, now believed that force was the only way to implement the ideas emanating from the 1848 European revolutions. On 12 August 1853, *El Comercio* published an open letter to the president by Domingo Elías, denouncing Echenique's government and especially the way in which the consolidation was being carried out. Elías warned him that guano was running out and that the country would be in severe crisis if the falsified bonds continued to be accepted as real. The next day the president assured readers that Elías's real motive for the attack was that he had not been allowed to present some bonds to the consolidation board and that he had even tried to bribe him. It must be noted that Echenique had taken from Elías the profitable guano-loading contract. Elías denied charges of bribery and denounced the office where the fake

92 Domingo Elias had held the monopoly of importation of chinese coolies to Trujillo and Lima since 1849.

93 José Rufino Echenique, *Memorias para la historia del Perú* (Lima, 1952), p. 205.

bonds were prepared.[94] Public opinion was incensed. Anger about the consolidation and conversion of the internal debt fuelled the general grievance at the devalued Bolivian currency continuing to enter the country. It was further fuelled by the generalised rejection of the government's support for the conservative expedition led by Juan José Flores that left Peru for Ecuador to fight the liberal regime. Echenique was considered a corrupt conservative leader lacking the courage declare war on Bolivia and stop the devalued currency entering the country.

On 16 August 1853, Elías was arrested, but freed on the guarantee offered by some important businessmen that he not intervene in politics. Seeking asylum in the French legation, Elías fled under the cover of darkness to Ecuador. From Guayaquíl, he organised an unsuccessful expedition to Tumbes in October of 1853. Once again, the '*hombre del pueblo*' escaped prison and landed in Ica, his home turf, from where he once again rebelled early in 1854. By now, Elías had contacted Castilla who, feeling ignored by the government, agreed to support the rebellion and travelled south. On the 7 January 1853, Elías was defeated at Saraja. Meanwhile in Arequipa, a group of artisans led by two well-known liberals, Diego Masías and Domingo Gamio, assuming that the entire north had risen, and unaware of Elías's defeat, rebelled. With the arrival of Castilla to lead the rebellion, and with no *echeniquista* leader daring to face the caudillo, all of southern Peru fell into his hands.[95]

In the central Andes a middle ranking leader, Fermín del Castillo, rose with the backing of liberals, José Gálvez and Sebastian Lorente, both teachers in the Guadalupe School, who had waited until the end of the school year to join the rebels.[96] In February 1854, Indian tribute was abolished in this region of the revolt. Five months later, Castilla and his secretary Pedro Gálvez decreed the abolition of tribute throughout the country. After five years of campaigning – in Congress, *El Progreso*, and from the Guadalupe School – this represented a great victory for the liberals. Recent historiography has shown, however, that the liberals did not understand how tribute had continued to bee seen by Indians as a guarantee to access village commons.[97] Initially, ending tribute helped the

94 *El Comercio*, 12, 13 and 16 Aug. 1853. According to Blanchard Elías reaction was the one of a typical caudillo, that when threatened, attacked. Blanchard, 'The "Transitional Man",' p. 170.

95 Juan Gualberto Valdivia, *Las revoluciones de Arequipa* (Arequipa, 1958), vol. II, p. 123.

96 José was Pedro Gávez's younger – and even more liberal – brother, who rose to prominence during this campaign.

97 Víctor Peralta, *En pos del tributo. Burocracia estatal, elite regional y comunidades indígenas en el Cusco rural (1826–1854)* (Cusco, 1991), pp. 130–5. Mark Thurner, *From Two Republics to One Divided. Contradictions of Postcolonial Nationmaking in Andean Peru* (Durham, NC, 1997), pp. 44–53. Florencia Mallon, *Peasant and Nation: The Making of Post-colonial Mexico and Peru* (Berkeley, 1995), pp. 180–1.

revolutionary forces as they gained the support of the Indian population who did not yet understand the repercussions of the abolition.[98] Echenique, however, still had a very loyal army that had vowed to defend the constitution and that could be paid promptly. He did face opposition in some areas due to the unpopularity of force conscription.[99] The government forces marched to the Andes in July where they met the rebels. The two armies stood face to face at the bridge of Izcuchaca, some shots were fired, but there was no battle. The armies remained camped the following two months, no one daring to make the first move. In October, Castilla resolved to march towards Lima but stopped half way. Unaware of this manoeuvre until too late, Echenique was left no option but to follow, losing many of his troops during exhausting marches and counter marches. Eventually he decided to cut his losses and return to Lima, leaving Castilla in charge of most of the country.[100]

In November 1854, once in the capital, Echenique took a desperate measure to try to gain some popular support. He passed a decree offering liberty to all the slaves that enlisted in the army for two years. His government had believed in a progressive dismantling of slavery and he himself declared in his memoirs that he believed slaves should be free, not because that state was prejudicial to them, but because it was inappropriate for human dignity.[101] Some slaves enrolled in the army but demanded guarantees for their liberty. As a counter measure, Castilla decided to completely abolish slavery, causing Echenique's newly gained support dissolve. Many have interpreted this event as a proof that Castilla was a born-again liberal. Others have seen it purely as a cunning measure to defeat Echenique. The 'liberator', as Castilla became know after abolition, ensured that the owners were not alienated by including in the decree assurances that the state would reimburse them for all the slaves they owned. Moreover, ex-slaves would not be allowed to leave their ex-masters immediately, so to prevent a crisis. How opportunistic Castilla was is demonstrated by the provision that slaves fighting with the enemy would not be liberated. Castilla's liberal secretaries, José and Pedro Gálvez and Manuel Toribio Ureta, who had been campaigning for the abolition of slavery for many years, must have had an influence upon Castilla's change of heart.[102]

98 Liberals considered that tribute should be changed to a poll tax paid by all citizens. This measure was unenforcable and in many regions local authorities continued to charge tribute.

99 Thurner, *From Two Republics*, p. 47.

100 Basadre, *Historia de la República*, pp. 1085–8.

101 Blanchard, *Slavery*, p. 193.

102 Carlos Aguirre, *Agentes de su propia libertad, los esclavos de Lima y la desintegración de la esclavitud 1821–1854* (Lima, 1993), p. 298.

Slave support was the key to Castilla's final victory over Echenique in the first days of 1855. Both armies had been camped between Lima and Miraflores for nearly six weeks. Finally, on 5 of January 1854, they both decided to attack. Echenique was unable to take advantageous of his better position because Castilla had the better intelligence, obtained from the blacks in the area.[103] While the battle was raging at La Palma to the south of the city, the bells in the church of San Pedro in Lima began to toll, rang by Francisco Bilbao who took over this church with some civilian groups that rose in support of Castilla.

The Chilean exile was instrumental in Echenique's downfall. Once Elías's letters were published in 1853, Bilbao was deported to Guayaquíl where he wrote *La Revolución de la honradez* attacking the president, under siege. In this pamphlet, published in the Castillista newspaper of Cuzco *El Triunfo del Pueblo*, Bilbao used all his skill to destroy an already discredited regime, while pinning all his hopes upon Castilla, whom he praised as a protector of freedom of the press and the best administrator in Peruvian history.[104] Bilbao returned to Peru in late 1854 and lived under cover. After Echenique promised liberty to those slaves who enrolled in the army, the Chilean exile published a furious public letter denouncing the policy as sign of the president's fear and desperation.[105]

On 15 January 1855 Bilbao published the *Noticia de la Victoria* in *El Comercio*, in which he described the rebellion and analysed the reasons for victory. A provisional government was formed with Castilla as president, Pedro Gálvez as minister of Justice, Manuel Toribio Ureta as Minister of Government and Foreign Affairs, and Domingo Elías, as Finance Minister. Liberals dominated the cabinet and elections for a National Convention that would draft a new constitution were called for. The elections were the first ever to be based upon direct and universal male suffrage for all except those who had fought with Echenique. Many conservatives considered this the worst of all worlds, as newly manumitted blacks were enfranchised, while those who had supported the previous regime, many of whom were important members of society, could not vote. A flood of gazettes, papers and pamphlets were issued by both sides. The official paper, *La Voz del Pueblo*, was edited by Sebastián Lorente, and, Bartolomé Herrera, now out of power, edited *El Católico*.

In February 1855 Bilbao published *El Gobierno de la Libertad*, his most important work on political and constitutional theory in which he proposed a series of advanced democratic ideas for the new charter that was to be drafted by the National Convention elected that same month.[106]

103 Blanchard, *Slavery*, p. 197.
104 *El Triunfo del Pueblo*, Cuzco, 24 May 1854.
105 Sobrevilla Alcazar, 'Francisco Bilbao', pp. 128, 129.
106 Sobrevilla Alcázar, 'Francisco Bilbao', pp. 129, 130.

These ideas were not adopted by the new assembly installed in July 1855.[107] During the discussions for the new constitution, Bilbao entered the debate on religious freedom, which became very incensed. Herrera led the campaign against him from his newspaper, publishing public petitions in defence of Catholicism against other religions, from all the provinces of Peru, mostly by women. Such was the opposition to Bilbao's anti-religious ideas from the most conservative sectors of society that the Chilean was jailed and public processions held against him. Herrera published an article accusing his liberal enemy of corrupting the 'simple souls' of Peruvians and of trying through this to destroy the country, but advocating release from prison and exile.[108] Bilbao's disciple Enrique Alvarado defended his mentor's ideas but found so little space for radical liberal debate in Peru that he finally left for Europe never to return.[109]

The new constitution designed by the liberals followed many of the proposals presented by the *progresistas.* It abolished the Council of State, replacing it with two vice-presidents. The presidential term was cut from six to four years. The system of regional government through prefects was maintained, but greater autonomy was granted to municipalities, with committees formed in each district to arrange local affairs and take charge of local funds.[110] The new constitution also prohibited the state collection of Church tithes, and abolished military and ecclesiastic *fueros.* Liberals failed, however, to separate Church and state. Though they did manage to give the legislature more power than the executive, it still had less control over the military.[111] The president also established a Junta de Examen Fiscal to review all the debts recognised by Echenique's government.[112]

The new constitution was a great victory of Peru's liberals. Finally Peruvians possessed a written charter that contained most of the ideals they had been advocating for a decade. However, their victory proved to be shortlived. It did not take long for Castilla to become weary of his liberal ministers, who only lasted in power until August 1855. The new constitution was never implemented. Castilla managed to stay in power by manipulating a conservative uprising in Arequipa in 1856, enabling him to discard the liberal constitution and to direct a new Congress led by Bartolomé Herrera to write a new one. The 1860 constitution was not as conservative as the 1839 Huancayo charter it replaced. And some of the

107 Basadre, *Historia de la República,* p. 1104.
108 *El Católico,* Lima, 23 May 1855.
109 Sobrevilla Alcázar, 'Francisco Bilbao', p. 130.
110 Clements Markham, *A History of Peru* (repr. Chicago, 1992), p. 349.
111 Frederick Pike, *The Modern History of Peru* (London, 1967), p. 106.
112 Valdivia, *Las revoluciones de Arequipa,* p. 152.

innovations introduced in the 1856 constitution were retained, in spite of Herrera's protests. This would be the enduring constitution in Peruvian History.

Conclusions

The impact of the European Revolutions of 1848 in Peru can be found in the way the news from Europe influenced intellectual and political debates and nourished currents of romanticism. The press was crucial as a channel for the diffusion of ideas both in Lima and the provinces, allowing issues to be more widely discussed. As a result Liberalism emerged to become a powerful political force in the decade between 1846 and 1856. The Guadalupe School played a very important part in the development of liberalism in Peru as it provided an opposing view to the evermore conservative College of San Carlos under Herrera. The teachers and director of the Guadalupe School participated in the main debates of the period and even in the civil war of 1854.

Artisans participated in politics in a more direct way, first by pressing for more protection for their trades through a law and later by supporting different presidential campaigns. The extension of voter qualifications in 1849 brought a democratisation of the country, evidenced in the 1850–51 elections. New forms of political mobilisation imported from Europe, such as the banquet and the political club, were also brought into use. The *progresistas,* a party embodying most of the principles of 1848, had a clear plan for government but lost the election. After democratic means for implement their plans had failed, liberals promoted Peru's first revolution that involved mass mobilisation.

The presence of Francisco Bilbao in Peru in the early 1850s was a crucial link to the events of the European 1848. The Chilean intellectual had not only participated in the barricade building in Paris but had brought European ideas and practices to Latin America, first to Chile where he created the Sociedad de la Igualdad, and then to Peru where he tried to set up the Sociedad Republicana to fight slavery. As an exiled thinker Bilbao had the opportunity to share his ideas with local intellectuals as he did by collaborating in the local romanticist publication. He also participated in the agitation that led to the 1854 liberal revolution and was instrumental in writing against the Echenique regime.

Slavery was a decaying institution in Peru by 1848. Yet the quickening of liberal debate inspired by the European revolutions redoubled the efforts towards abolition, ensuring that it would come sooner rather than dying the slow death to which it had been destined. The radical liberal ambience encouraged by 1848 eased the efforts of the slaves themselves to undermine the system, and facilitated the legal changes introduced in the

Civil Code of 1852. Although it can be argued that abolition was a result of the particular interests of caudillos competing for power in a civil war, the impact of ideas and example of the European revolutions of 1848 cannot be denied.

What did become clear with both the abolition of slavery and the Indian head tax was that elite and masses in Peru continued to be deeply divided. Even progressive liberals were unable to connect to a wider constituency. It was impossible for elite intellectuals to agree with artisans due to differences in political economy as it was impossible for both groups to connect with Indians because of the cultural, spatial and political gulf that separated them. The abolition of tribute is the prime example of that division. Liberals regarded it as the most important step towards the incorporation of Indians as citizens. For Indians the end of tribute signalled the loss of control over village commons, resulting in haciendas taking their land and appropriating their labour.

The triumph of the liberals was enshrined in the new constitution of 1855, a direct heir to the ideas of 1848. But, just when everything seemed prepared for a more democratic Peru, reaction gained the upper hand. The same caudillo who had led the liberals to power destroyed this option by choosing more moderate and conservative supporters, who, also influenced by the events in Europe, had decided that the country was not ready for such radical change.

9

New Granada and the European Revolutions of 1948*

EDUARDO POSADA-CARBÓ

On 7 March 1849, congressmen of New Granada (Colombia today) gathered in the Santo Domingo Church in Bogotá to select the new president of the republic. As none of the three major candidates had managed to attract an absolute majority of the electoral colleges, as required by the constitution, it was then up to Congress to settle the dispute. This was far from being a simple matter. The divisions among the electorate were also reflected in the composition of Congress. And congressmen were not left on their own to choose the president. Inside the church building the 84 members of Congress were surrounded by a large crowd – estimates vary between 1,500 and 4,000 people – most of them artisans, craftsmen and students largely in support of the *progresista* candidate (Liberal), General José Hilario López. Only after the fourth round of votes, and in the middle of allegations that some of them had been intimidated by the crowd, congressmen finally elected López as the President of New Granada. Following the news, the crowd went on to celebrate in the streets – 'music, fireworks and cheers were heard everywhere: the people of Bogotá seemed overjoyed by the victory of the *progresista* party.'[1] According to a contemporary witness of the events, 'a patriotic feeling had just been awakened ... from a long dream, after receiving encouraging energies from the immense European revolution'.[2]

There is little doubt that the 1849 presidential election developed in an atmosphere that echoed the spirit of the 1848 European revolutions. This was a major landmark in the history of Colombia. It unfolded a period of rapid economic, social and political reforms, including the final abolition of slavery, the introduction for the first time of direct elections

* I would like to thank Guy Thomson for his encouragement and observations. I am also grateful to Malcolm Deas and Gustavo Bell, who gave me access to valuable documents. Research for this chapter was also possible thanks to the kind assistance of Gilma Rodríguez at the Banco de la República in Bogotá.

1 J.M. Restrepo, *Historia de la Nueva Granada* (Bogotá, 1963), vol. II, p. 106.

2 S. Camacho Roldán, *Escritos varios* (Bogotá, 1895), p. 347.

and male universal suffrage, the adoption of absolute freedom of the press, and a series of drastic measures against the Catholic church. It also unfolded a period of popular mobilisation and radical politics that to some extent resembled the events in Europe: 'Nowhere else in Latin America', Malcolm Deas has observed, 'did the events of 1848 ... find such eager followers and imitators among the politicians, artisans, students and even soldiers of poor isolated New Granada'.[3] Similarly, Jaime Jaramillo Uribe has suggested that very few European movements have had as much of an impact on Colombia as the French revolution of 1848.[4] More recently, Peter Jones has singled out Colombia, together with Pernambuco, as two of the regions where the revolutions of 1848 spread beyond Europe.[5] Yet Germán Colmenares for one has raised some questions about the ways the European revolutions were read and reinterpreted by the politicians in New Granada to foster their own interests, underlining the difficulties in establishing the causality of events.[6]

What then was the real impact of the 1848 European revolutions in New Granada? How can we measure the influence of European events on the 1849 presidential elections, and on the period of political reform and social upheaval that followed? What sort of comparisons can we establish between events in Europe and those in New Granada? This chapter is an attempt to answer these and other related questions. In the first part of the essay, I examine some of the major developments in New Granada since it became an independent state in 1830, as a background to the mid-nineteenth-century reforms. In this section, I also try to identify some of the features that set the *neogranadino* experience somewhat apart from European developments, while also identifying those elements of the European revolution that caught the imagination of *neogranadinos*. In the second and third parts of the chapter, I turn to the 1848–49 presidential election, showing how this electoral campaign and its subsequent results encouraged the 'democratisation' of politics in New Granada. Here I will

3 M. Deas, 'Venezuela, Colombia and Ecuador,' in L. Bethell (ed.), *Spanish America after Independence, c.1820–1870* (Cambridge, 1989), p. 233. A similar experience was that of Chile, see C. Gazmuri, *El '48' chileno. Igualitarios, reformistas radicales, masones y bomberos* (Santiago, 1992), and his chapter in this volume. For a contemporary account, see B. Vicuña Mackenna, *Los girondinos chilenos* (Santiago, 1989). As the chapters of this volume make clear, the impact of 1848 in Latin America went beyond the usual examples of Colombia and Chile.

4 Jaime Jaramillo Uribe, 'La influencia de los románticos franceses y de la revolución de 1848 en el pensamiento político colombiano del siglo XIX,' in *La personalidad histórica de Colombia y otros ensayos* (Bogotá, 1997), p. 162.

5 P. Jones, *The 1848 revolutions* (London and New York, 1997, sixth repr.), p. 3.

6 See G. Colmenares, *Partidos políticos y clases sociales en Colombia* (Bogotá, 1997, first published in 1968). See also Jay Robert Crusin, 'The revolution of 1848 in Colombia,' PhD thesis, University of Arizona, 1978.

focus my attention on the 'varieties of revolutionary experience' in New Granada: the emergence for the first time of a mass electorate, its unprecedented mobilisation, the spread of associations, 'politics in the streets', the role of newspapers, and other 'contours of public life' – as described for Europe by Jonathan Sperber.[7] In the final section, I reflect on the difficulties of measuring the overall impact of the European revolutions in New Granada, in spite of their undeniable significance on the history of the republic.

New Granada first became independent from Spain in 1819, in an initial union with Venezuela and Ecuador – the so-called Gran Colombia – that came to an end in 1830.[8] As a newly independent nation-state, New Granada did not have to face any nationalist movement from within, although some of the provinces did press for a federal arrangement. There was no need for a Mazzini or a Kossuth. 'Nationality, the passionate creed of intellectuals' that invaded 'the politics of central and east-central Europe',9 was generally absent from the concerns of New Granada.

The country adopted the republican principle, and a presidential system under a representative government of sorts. Unlike parts of Eastern and Southern Europe, where by 1848 the existence of parliament was considered a novelty,[10] New Granada's experiences with congresses dated from the beginning of the independence struggle. From 1832 presidential and congressional elections took place every four years. Elections were indirect and held under a restrictive suffrage, although not restrictive enough to exclude all popular sectors. Literary restrictions were introduced but their implementation was postponed for two decades. Income restrictions were also introduced but in a vague fashion: only those considered 'economically dependent' were excluded from the franchise. Artisans, craftsmen and small farmers were therefore given the vote. As elections became contested, all competing factions tried to expand their electoral base. Artisans and other popular sectors, for example, were already heavily

7 I follow here ch. 4 of his book *The European Revolutions, 1848–1851* (Cambridge, 1994).

8 See D. Bushnell, *The Santander Regime in Gran Colombia* (Newark, DE, 1954). For a general history of Colombia, see Bushnell, *The Making of Modern Colombia. A Nation in Spite of Itself* (Berkeley and Los Angeles, 1993).

9 Lewis Namier, *1848. The Revolution of the Intellectuals* (Oxford, 1992), p. 33. Marco Palacios has suggested that the 1848 revolutions set out to the *neogranadinos* the challenge to imagine themselves (beyond the confines of the upper classes) as a modern nation. In this sense, as Efraín Sánchez has shown, the work of the *Comisión Corográfica* (1850–59) had 'nationalist' aims. But this was entirely different from the 'nationality' problem of the Central Europeans. See Marco Palacios, *Parábola del liberalismo* (Bogotá, 1999), pp. 87–8; and Efraín Sánchez, *Gobierno y geografía. Agustín Codazzi y la Comisión Corogáfica de la Nueva Granada* (Bogotá, 1998).

10 Sperber, *The European Revolutions*, p. 148.

involved in the presidential elections of 1836/7, and in the vice-presidential and congressional elections of 1838.[11] This year, a *Sociedad Democrática-Republicana de Artesanos i Labradores Progresistas* was established in Bogotá, to instruct 'the different classes of the state in the maintenance of their interests (and) in the knowledge of their public rights'. Alongside this relatively active public life, a political press flourished. The conservatively inclined regime of the 1840s introduced provisions against libel in the press, but they do not seem to have been as tough, as for example, the French press law of 1835, nor had the *neogranadino* state the power to enforce them.[12]

Thus there was no political absolutism to fight against in New Granada. By 1848, however, a succession of governments linked to the Conservatives (the expression was precisely coined this year) had been in power since 1837, when the candidate backed by the liberal administration of Francisco de Paula Santander, General José María Obando, had been defeated by the opposition candidate José Ignacio de Márquez. This is not the place to explain the complex process that led to the formation of political parties in Colombia. Suffice it here to say that by the 1850s what was clearly known as the Liberal party was formed around the figures, first, of Santander and, later, Obando, backed by a core group of young profoundly anti-clerical intellectuals, who were influenced by a mixture of liberal ideals.[13] In turn, the Conservatives – also clearly identified as a party by the 1850s –[14] grew out of the fate of the Márquez government. Santander and Obando had accepted electoral defeat in the presidential contest of 1837, but in 1839 Obando led a revolution against the Márquez administration – the *Guerra de los Supremos* – in which Obando rallied the Indians and the Blacks in Southern Colombia, while appealing to the

11 See Eduardo Posada-Carbó, 'Alternación y república: las elecciones en Venezuela y Nueva Granada, 1835–1837,' in H. Sabato (ed.), *Ciudadanía política y formación de las naciones* (Mexico, 1999), and D. Sowell, *The Early Colombian Labor Movement. Artisans and Politics in Bogotá, 1832–1919* (Philadelphia, 1992). By 1848, the suffrage in New Granada seems to have been less restrictive than in France, where 'small middling businessmen were excluded along the learned and professional classes and, of course, the workers and the peasants'; see Priscilla Roberts, *Revolutions of 1848. A Social History* (Princeton, 1980, first published in 1952), p. 15; see also Geoffrey Ellis, 'The Revolution of 1848–1849 in France,' in Evans and Pogge von Strandmann (eds.), *The Revolutions in Europe*, p. 29.

12 Press controls had also been strong in Germany since 1819. See Wolfram Siemann, *The German Revolution of 1848–1849* (Basingstoke and London, 1998), p. 110.

13 For an outline of the programme of the Liberal party published in 1848 by Ezequiel Rojas, see Gerardo Molina, *Las ideas liberales en Colombia, 1849–1914* (Bogotá, 1975), pp. 20–6.

14 The first Conservative platform was actually published in 1849. See 'Programa conservador de 1849,' in Directorio Nacional Conservador (ed.), *Los programas conservadores de 1849 a 1949* (Bogotá, 1952), pp. 47–8.

disaffected nationwide.[15] The government won the war, sent Obando into exile and set itself the task of reimposing order in the republic. A new constitution was adopted in 1843, strengthening the executive and conferring powers to the Catholic Church, while the Jesuits were called back into the country.

If there was no 'political absolutism' proper in New Granada, by the mid-nineteenth century Liberals nevertheless identified the Conservative regimes with the survival of a colonial legacy that needed to be destroyed: the unfinished job of the independence revolutions had to be completed. A rhetoric against the 'aristocrats' and the 'oligarchy' therefore flourished. Hence Liberals labelled the Conservative constitution of 1843 as 'monarchist' – a label often used by the *obandista* (Liberal) press to disqualify the Conservative regime.[16] Newspapers of Liberal leanings, such as *El Sentimiento Democrático*, challenged their opponents to 'speak the truth and acknowledge without scruples' what they were for: 'a king, absolutism, privileges'.[17] 'Why did the February revolution of 1848 find so much sympathy in the American republics?' asked Ramón Mercado, governor of the Buenaventura province during the López's administration. Mercado had no doubts: Independence from Spain had brought very few changes to the new republics. The legacy of three centuries of colonial domination was reduced to despotism, fanaticism and social and racial inequalities. These features of 'españolismo y coloniaje', in Mercado's view, remained dominant in the southern provinces by 1848 – there 'feudalism reigned'.[18] In 1852, the *obandistas* still warned their followers of the dangers of a possible return to colonial times: 'you would return to slavery, to pay tithes … and all sort of forced contributions with your labour, only to favour a faked aristocracy surrounded by wealth'.[19]

By 1848, New Granada's two million population was scattered throughout a vast territory, but a large portion was concentrated along the three

15 On the nature of this war, see Rebecca Earle, 'The War of the Supremes: Border Conflict, Religious Crusade or Simply Politics by Other Means'?, in Earle (ed.), *Rumours of Wars: Civil Conflict in Nineteenth-century Latin America* (London, 2000), pp. 119–34.

16 See *El Triunfo del 7 de marzo* (Ciénaga), 7 Feb. 1850.

17 *El Sentimiento Democrático* (Cali), 29 Nov. 1849. Similarly, *El Artesano* identified the Conservatives with those in favour of 'absolutism, dictatorships, noble distinctions, and constitutions that favour on the executive a sort of monarch with the title of president', *El Artesano*, 17 March 1850. Gerardo Molina has observed that in 1849 the Liberal party found its *raison d'etre* in the 'anti-colonial'; see *Las ideas liberales*, pp. 35–38.

18 See Ramón Mercado, *Memorias sobre los acontecimientos del sur de la Nueva Granada durante la administración del 7 de marzo de 1849* (Bogotá, 1853), pp. V, VI, XII.

19 *La Tribuna Popular*, no. 9, 1852, quoted in Francisco Gutiérrez Sanín, *Curso y discurso del movimiento plebeyo, 1849–1854* (Bogotá, 1995), p. 99.

branches of the Andes. This was by and large a rural country, although rural life was not entirely devoted to farming and cattle raising: trade, small manufacturing, mining, shop-keeping, were all part of the rural landscape.[20] Its poor and depressed economy depended on a decaying mining sector, until tobacco exports took-off after the abolition of the tobacco monopoly during the administration of General Tomás Cipriano Mosquera (1845–49).[21] There was no landed aristocracy proper, of the kind found in Europe. Vast estates – the Mexican hacienda or the Argentine estancia – had very few parallels in New Granada's mid-nineteenth century. Of course some of the wealthiest families owned land, but the major source of wealth was probably trade, in the major urban and commercial centres. Urban activities – commerce, the law, holding office, politics, and journalism – were also the major sources of political power and influence.[22] Urban centres, however, did not concentrate large numbers of people. Bogotá, the capital of New Granada, had no more than 40,000 inhabitants by 1848. Medellín hardly had 15,000. Cali had a similar population, while Popayán had 6,000 people. A large number of *neogranadinos* lived in towns and villages of between 1,000 and 2,000 people. The age of steam power was yet to arrive in New Granada; there was no large-scale manufacturing.[23] But there was an active artisan sector – shoemakers, tailors, masons, carpenters and the like – who resided in the major cities, but who could also be found in smaller towns and villages throughout the country.

20 For a description of post-independence New Granada, see Deas, 'Venezuela, Colombia and Ecuador'. For a contemporary account, see Isaac Holton, *New Granada: Twenty Months in the Andes* (New York, 1857). For contemporary analysis on New Granada's economy, see W. Will's collection of essays, in Malcolm Deas, *Vida y opiniones de Mr William Wills* (Bogotá, 1996), vol 2.

21 See L. Helguera, 'The first Mosquera administration in New Granada, 1845–49,' PhD thesis, University of North Carolina, 1958.

22 On these and related points, see Frank Safford, 'Social Aspects of Politics in Nineteenth-century Spanish America: New Granada, 1825–1850,' *Journal of Social History* (1972), and his expanded Spanish version, published in Safford, *Aspectos sociales del siglo XIX en Colombia* (Medellín, 1977). See also M. Deas, 'El caciquismo en Colombia,' *Revista de Occidente* (Oct., 1973).

23 This element of 'dimension' should always be borne in mind when comparing the developments in New Granada with those in Europe. George Rudé has rightly warned us that by 1848 in France three-quarters of its population still worked the land, and that there were only 5,000 steam engines – 'the age of the great industrial employer, like that of the factory worker was yet to come'; but there were already about one million people living in Paris. It is also true, as Ellis reminds us, that Paris's population accounted only for 3% of the French total; but its 35.5 million inhabitants contrasts with the figure of 2 million *neogranadinos* living in a larger and much less integrated territory. See Rudé's chapter on the 1848 revolutions in his book *The Crowd in History* (London, 1995), p. 164, and Ellis, 'The revolution of 1848–1849 in France,' p. 28.

In this sparsely populated and poor country, political alignments rarely followed class divisions. Indeed, the most important source of partisan conflict during the nineteenth-century was probably the Church.[24] This should not be surprising. The more historians look into political conflict in the nineteenth-century – be it in Europe or in Latin America – the more they appreciate how important religion, and social attitudes towards the Church were in shaping political life, an observation also applied regarding the 1848 European revolutions.[25] Indeed, issues around religion were prominent in splitting the artisan movement. Ambrosio López, one of the founders of the Sociedad de Artesanos in Bogotá, complained about the speeches against the Pope in their meetings, while considering that such anti-religious manifestations betrayed the origins of their association.[26]

However, there were certain social conflicts which impinged upon partisan politics during the mid-nineteenth century. One of these revolved around the issue of the survival of slavery. Although a decaying institution after independence, slavery was still significant in certain regions of New Granada, particularly in the south, where slaveholders were even resorting to the Bible in support of the institution.[27] By 1848 slavery was already in decay – the number of remaining slaves in the whole country did not exceed 27,000; a large proportion of them living in the southern provinces.[28] And the issue carried weight among significant sectors of the population in some regions. As suggested above, the Liberal opposition used the 'threat' of the return of slavery to rally their followers – a call guaranteed to find an audience above all among the free black population.

A second cleavage that came close to becoming a class conflict involved artisans. Artisans strongly resented the reduction of tariffs made by the

24 For an overview, see Fernán González, *Poderes enfrentados. Iglesia y estado en Colombia* (Bogotá, 1997).

25 See comments by Sperber, *The European Revolutions*, p. 52. See also Austen Ivereigh (ed.), *The Politics of Religion in an Age of Revival* (London, 2000). According to de Tocqueville, the elections of the 'ecclesiastics' to the Constitutent Assembly in 1848 was in part due to the 'very widespread and quite unexpected return of a great part of the nation to a concern with religious matters'; see his *Recollections. The French Revolution of 1848* (New Brunswick and London, 1997), p. 103. On Catholic political activism in Germany during 1848–49, see Siemann, *The German Revolution*, pp. 101–4.

26 Ambrosio López, *El desengaño* (Bogotá, 1985, first published in 1851), pp. 17, 26–7. See also Venancio Ortiz, *Historia de la revolución del 17 de abril de 1854* (Bogotá, 1972, first published in 1855), pp. 26–7.

27 *Esclavitud está apoyada en los libros sagrados*, leaflet, Cali, 12 March 1847.

28 See J. Leon Helguera, 'Antecedentes sociales de la revolución de 1851 en el sur de Colombia (1848–1849), *Anuario Colombiano de Historia Social y de la Cultura* (Bogotá: Universidad Nacional), vol 5, 1970, p. 56.

Mosquera administration in 1847.[29] They were nevertheless split during the 1848/9 presidential election. Once José Hilario López entered the presidency, the Liberals were openly divided into *Gólgotas*, who favoured low tariffs and opposed the power of the army, and *Draconianos*, allies of the artisans' cause, who closed ranks in defence of their interests during the movement that later led to the short-lived military revolt of General Melo in 1854. However, in 1851 Ambrosio López still lamented: 'Today we (the artisans) are divided, very divided, to the point of being broken into pieces'.[30]

A third social conflict worthy of notice was related to land problems in the South, especially in the Cauca region. The 'cuestión ejido', as the dispute about the enclosure of communal lands around Cali was refereed to by contemporaries, fuelled serious social unrest.[31] A significant number of peasant families, backed by local authorities, mounted a protest campaign against the *hacendados* who had fenced the land in February 1848, restricting therefore access to pasture and to public pathways. 'Long live the people, death to the white man', was the cry of the protesters on 20 and 21 May that year, when violence took over Cali and its rural surroundings. A fragile public order prevailed in the province during the period 1848–1851. It was thus in the Cauca region, besides Bogotá, where the events of 1848 probably took the most radical turn.

New Granada's contemporary historian José Manuel Restrepo recalled how news of the February revolution in Paris was only fully appreciated in distant Bogotá three months later, on 11 May 1848.[32] Fear of political upheaval was already running high, as *neogranadinos* learnt of earlier events Caracas, where disenchanted followers of the defeated liberal candidate in the Venezuelan presidential election stormed Congress on 24 January 1848, killing four deputies.[33] The news from Europe, therefore,

29 R. Gilmore, *El federalismo en Colombia, 1810–1858* (Bogotá, 1995), vol 1, p. 168. See also Sowell, *The Early Colombian Labor Movement.*

30 Some divisions, however, remained. For a debate between two leaders of the artisan movement, see López, *El desengaño.*

31 For different contemporary versions of the events, see *Reseña histórica de los principales acontecimientos políticos de la ciudad de Cali, desde el año 1843 hasta el de 1855 inclusive* (Bogotá, 1856), and Mercado, *Memorias sobre los acontecimientos del Sur.* See also Helguera, 'Antecedentes sociales de la revolución de 1851,' and Gutiérrez Sanín, *Curso y discurso del movimiento plebeyo.*

32 Restrepo, *Historia de la Nueva Granada*, p. 80.

33 José Gil Fortoul, *Historia constitucional de Venezuela* (Berlin, 1909), vol 2, ch. XIII ('El 24 de enero), pp. 230–55. The events in Caracas were constantly refered to by contemporary observers and the press. See, for example, *El Sufragante* (Cartagena), 24 May 1849; and *Ojeada sobre los primeros catorce meses de la administración del 7 de marzo, dedicada a los hombres imparciales i justos* (Bogotá, 1850), p. 3. See also Gabriel Francisco Porras, *Alrededor del 7 de marzo de 1849* (Cartagena, 1930). The *caraqueñada,*

added to an atmosphere of social and political tension which became more acute as the presidential election approached. 'The February revolution', wrote the Chilean Benjamín Vicuña Mackenna, 'took us by surprise (during the agitations of)... an electoral period'.[34] As with Chile, news of the European revolutions fell in the middle of an electoral campaign in New Granada. A brief examination of the 1848–49 presidential election and its aftermath could therefore illustrate to what extent the politics of New Granada were receptive to the revolutionary events in Europe.

The press was at the centre of this campaign. As in previous presidential elections during the early republic, newspapers, leaflets and pamphlets played a crucial role in the 1848–49 presidential elections. New periodical publications were set up in support of a particular candidate or to oppose the government. In Bogotá alone, *El Aviso*, *La América* and *El Neogranadino* appeared in 1848 to back the opposition Liberal candidate, while *La Epoca* and *El Progreso* were established in support of the Mosquera administration. In Cali, as a contemporary observer noted, 'several citizens devoted themselves to writing, and from all corners of the republic we weekly received newspapers, leaflets and letters' with news of the candidates.[35]

Salvador Camacho Roldán would later observe that the opinions of the candidates on various issues – abolition of slavery and of the tobacco monopoly, in particular – were not clearly known, although he admitted that given their antecedents and personal contacts, it was not difficult to identify where they stood politically.[36] Moreover, the electoral literature that flourished during 1848–49 – in newspapers, leaflets and pamphlets – made their position fairly clear regarding a wide array of issues.

How much distance the various candidates took from the existing Mosquera administration served as a good indicator of their respective standings. On 17 March 1848, a petition signed by more than one hundred people in Popayán launched Rufino Cuervo for the presidency.[37] But the candidacy of Cuervo, a Conservative, was repeatedly disqualified for being too close to Mosquera: Cuervo faced 'the inconvenience of having

as contemporaries often referred to the events in Caracas, was kept alive in the public memory. In 1853, the 'democráticas' threatened Congress with a *caraqueñada* if their demands were not attended to. See Ortiz, *Historia de la revolución*, p. 36.

34 Vicuña Mackenna, *Los girondinos chilenos*, p. 33.

35 *Reseña histórica de los principales acontecimientos políticos de la ciudad de Cali*, p. 14.

36 S. Camacho Roldán, *Memorias* (Bogotá, n.d.), vol 1, p. 28.

37 *Presidencia de la república. Los ciudadanos que suscribimos proponemos para Presidente de la república en el próximo período al dr Rufino Cuervo*, Popayán, 17 March 1848, photocopy of a contemporary leaflet in the private collecion of Gustavo Bell (GB), Barranquilla.

been originally nominated by the president'.[38] A second Conservative candidate, José Joaquín Gori, took trouble to distance himself from the president: 'artisans ought to be warned', a leaflet read, 'that Dr Gori is not the candidate of General Mosquera. His policies will be different from those of (Mosquera)'.[39] These were vague terms. Nevertheless, it was well known that Gori was a favourite candidate with the Church. The policies of the Liberal opposition candidate were more clearly expressed. The Liberal programme published in *El Neogranadino* seems to have been López's platform. Earlier in 1848, López promised his followers that he would allow the popular Liberal leader Obando to return from exile, expel the Jesuits from New Granada, and fire Conservatives from office.[40] He also assured artisans that he would protect them against foreign goods.

Artisans were nevertheless split, as already noted. In Bogotá, a *Sociedad de Artesanos* was established in October 1847 (an apparent heir to the earlier society – established in 1838 – which had vanished following the civil war of 1839–42). On 4 May 1848, the society – which by April that year claimed a membership of 300 – met to discuss its involvement in the presidential election.[41] The president of the society favoured Gori, but the majority agreed to support López.[42] Indeed, a significant sector of the artisan community in Bogotá seems to have originally voted for the Conservative Gori. Artisans were warned that López was constitutionally impeded to deliver his promise of banning foreign goods. They were also warned of López's anti-clericalism and were urged to read the pro-López press carefully to avoid later disappointments.[43] However, as the election polarised between López and Cuervo after the results of the electoral colleges were published, artisans, together with other popular sectors, seem to have rallied behind López.

Mid-nineteenth-century elections followed a slow process, conditioned by a relaxed calendar and the natural difficulties of communications. The primary electors voted during the last eight days of June 1848, to select members of the electoral colleges who, in turn, met during the first eight days of August to elect the president.[44] By October that year, the results

38 *A los electores*, Bogotá, 10 July 1848; *Carta de un elector a otro*, Bogotá, 26 June 1848, photocopies of contemporary leaflets in the private collection of GB. See also Camacho, *Escritos varios*, p. 363; Posada Gutiérrez, *Memorias histórico-políticas* (Medellín, 1971), vol 3, p. 355.

39 *A los artesanos de Bogotá* (Bogotá, n.d., but certainly 1848), photocopy in GB's private collection.

40 Restrepo, *Historia de la Nueva Granada*, p. 76.

41 See Sowell, *The Early Colombian Labor Movement*, pp. 41–4.

42 *Ibid.*, p. 43.

43 *A los artesanos de Bogotá*.

44 Restrepo, *Historia de la Nueva Granada*, p. 84.

from the electoral colleges were finally published: López, 725 votes; Gori, 384; Cuervo, 304.[45] As none of the candidates received an absolute majority of votes in the electoral colleges, the election was left to Congress, which met on 6 and 7 March 1849.

Modern historians have yet to reconstruct in detail the events that finally led to López's election by Congress, the development of what was – even by contemporary standards – an extremely long process, full of uncertainties. This proved to be a highly contested dispute, 'generating a heat hitherto unknown'.[46] A contemporary account of politics in the southern town of Cali gives evidence of much electioneering. Opinion there seems to have divided into two camps, around López and Gori respectively. Electoral competition forced both parties to widen their appeal. Electoral agents visited 'even … the far distant suburbs to seduce and commit their partisans':

> … And what a surprise! Men who had never before dared to greet or even looked at the poor plebeians … could now be seen visiting their miserable huts: melted by love, they warmly shook their hands, they asked them about their women and praised their little children for being happy and chubby, making more promises to them than to a bride …[47]

In addition to promises and social niceties, these electoral tours were occasions to reinforce the images of the respective candidates. If López became president, his followers claimed, 'the chains with which the oligarchy has oppressed the people will be broken'. Gori, in turn, was portrayed as 'the father of religion', a civilian that would respect 'public liberties'.[48] As the polls opened in late June, political activities were centred around mobilising voters in an atmosphere of communal festivity. The streets were taken over by both parties and their parades, accompanied by bands of music.[49] Once the polls had closed, public attention focused on the count.

Partisan feelings further intensified once the results of the electoral colleges were known in October. New newspapers, like *El Neogranadino*, were launched to increase public pressure on Congress. By February 1849, the *Sociedad de Artesanos* in Bogotá was holding meetings 'almost daily … to prepare an election strategy'. According to Sowell, 'the agreed-upon

45 *Ibid.*, p. 89. Overall results of the June elections are unavailable. The only available figure are those of the electoral colleges. To my knowledge no historian has ever attempted to estimate the size of the primary electorate for this period. See David Bushnell, 'Elecciones presidenciales colombianas, 1825–1856,' in Miguel Urrutia and Mario Arrubla, *Compendio de estadísticas históricas de Colombia* (Bogotá, 1970), pp. 258–66.

46 Camacho Roldán, *Escritos varios*, p. 347.

47 *Reseña histórica*, p. 14.

48 *Ibid.*, pp. 15–16.

49 *Ibid.* pp. 18–19.

approach 'was to frighten the weak (members of Congress)', and therefore press them to vote for López.[50]

The events of 7 March 1849 – when Congress met at the Santo Domingo Church to reach a final decision – were the subject of conflicting views and interpretations, almost immediately after the voting took place.[51] According to Restrepo, by early March artisans in Bogotá, more specifically the members of the Sociedad Democrática – referred to as the 'democráticos' – were joined by people coming from the northern suburbs of the capital city, who belonged to the marginal sectors of society: 'chosen among the most daring bullies with the most sinister faces that could be found in the whole city'. On 7 March, as described at the beginning of this chapter, thousands of people surrounded congressmen, while they voted. Restrepo echoed Conservative complaints of threats against their lives and physical harassments from the crowd inside the church. Daggers, in this version, were very much in evidence: some Congressmen, as a result, were forced to vote for López.[52] Those closer to López, such as Salvador Camacho Roldán or the editors of *El Neogranadino*, favoured a different story. Conservatives feared that 'the people of Bogotá would stage a twenty-fourth of January' (in references to the events in Caracas); they saw 'daggers and assassins' everywhere. It was it all in their imagination. Camacho Roldán, who witnessed the gathering, claimed that he never saw 'not even the pommel of a knife', that none of the congressmen were threatened. For Camacho, as for *El Neogranadino*, the events of 7 March were above all expressions of patriotism.[53]

Whichever version was correct, they all agree that an enthusiastic crowd surrounded congressmen while they were voting throughout the day. They also agree on the description of popular joy when Congress finally elected López. About 4,000 people – 10 per cent of Bogotá's population – celebrated in the streets. Even Mosquera left the comforts of

50 Sowell, *The Early Colombian Labor Movement*, p. 45.

51 For pro-Liberal contemporary accounts of the events, see *El Neogranadino*, 10 March 1849, and articles by Salvador Camacho Roldán in *El Siglo*, 22 and 29 April, 1849, reprinted in his *Escritos varios* (Bogotá, 1895), pp. 340–366. José Eusebio Caro, founder of the Conservative party, published his version of 7 March. See also Restrepo, *Historia de la Nueva Granada*, and Angel and Rufino Cuervo, *Vida de Rufino Cuervo y su época*, in Rufino José Cuervo, *Obras* (Bogotá, 1987), vol. IV. For a later conservative interpretation by a contemporary, see Posada Gutiérrez, *Memorias histórico políticas*, pp. 354–75. For different interpretations by twentieth-century historians, see Porras, *Alrededor del 7 de marzo*, and Camilo Gutiérrez Jaramillo, *José Hilario López. Un hombre de su siglo* (n.p., 1997), pp. 243–57.

52 Restrepo, *Historia de la Nueva Granada*. Angel and Rufino Cuervo also claimed that 'gangs of callous swines from neighbouring villages arrived every day to support the "democráticos"'; *Vida de don Rufino Cuervo y su época*, p. 417.

53 Camacho Roldán, *Escritos varios*, 344–50, and *El Neogranadino*, 10 March 1849.

the presidential palace to join the crowd, which he harangued with the populist language of the day: 'I have erred for being an aristocrat; aristocracy is for me such a dirty thing, as the mud on my feet.'[54]

The election of José Hilario López on 7 March 1849 did not close a chapter of social and political upheaval in New Granada. Quite the contrary: it opened it. For *El Neogranadino*, 'the sun of the seventh of March enlightened a new era for New Granada, an era of hope and happiness, of progress and social improvement'. His election was received as part of a wider movement, where the principles of 'liberty, fraternity and equality' have been accepted as 'dogmas': 'France has proclaimed them, and presented them to the astonished eyes of Europe ... The whole world shakes ... to free itself from its chains'.[55]

The programme of reforms implemented by the López administration was wide-ranging. A republican tone permeated all official communications. On 10 April 1849, a law stated that instead of the title 'His Excellency', the expression 'citizen' ought to be used when referring to any official, including, of course, 'citizen president López'.[56] The reforms went beyond these formalities. Within the next two years, the state monopoly over tobacco production and trade was finally abolished. The size of the army was reduced from 3,300 to 1,500 (with a maximum of three generals). University degrees were abolished. The Jesuits were expelled from the country – a move for which responsibility lay, according to a French correspondent in the *Revue de deux Mondes*, with Sue's *El Judío Errante*.[57] Church privileges were curtailed while city councils were given the right of *patronato*. The central state lost power over fiscal matters, now devolved to the provinces. Industrial schools to train artisans, in an attempt to emulate the national workshops in France, were set up, although the idea was never fully implemented. Absolute freedom of the press was established. And slavery was finally abolished. Most of these laws were incorporated in the new constitution of 1853, which also opened the doors for a federal system and adopted direct elections under male universal suffrage.[58] According to Restrepo these reforms were the work of several enlightened men of New Granada who, influenced by the 1848 French revolution, 'conceived and took on the task of changing everything, even the very bases of society'.[59]

54 Camacho Roldán, *Escritos varios*, p. 353.
55 *El Neogranadino*, 10 March 1849.
56 According to Angel and Rufino Cuervo, this measure was taken 'because in France all the ancient titles of nobility were abolished,' *Vida de Rufino Cuervo*, p. 465.
57 Quoted in Jaramillo Uribe, 'La influencia de los románticos franceses y de la revolución de 1848,' p. 167.
58 See Gilmore, *El federalismo en Colombia*, vol 1, pp. 163–5.
59 Restrepo, *Historia de la Nueva Granada*, p. 80.

There were other significant political measures as well: Obando, the popular figure in exile, was allowed to return. On 25 February 1850, Obando made a triumphal entry to Bogotá. Some 1,500 'citizens' greeted him in the neighbouring village of Facatativá the previous evening. Between 7,000 and 15,000 people celebrated his return in the streets of Bogotá the following morning. Obando was then launched as the next 'popular' and 'democratic' presidential candidate, for the following elections of 1853.[60]

This reformist zeal did not proceed smoothly. Nor did it go unchallenged. A Conservative armed rebellion broke out in 1851, although it was soon suppressed.[61] More significantly, the Liberals were deeply divided around the issue of tariffs and the role of the army in the republic. The Liberal youth – the so-called Gólgotas, later to be renamed Radicals – favoured an extreme version of individual liberalism, including *laissez-faire* economic policies, and wanted to curtail whatever power the army retained. Initially they gained the upper hand in López's government, but in 1852 they resigned from their cabinet positions. Liberals from the old guard – known as Draconians for their sympathies with capital punishment – had closed links with the army since independence, and favoured protectionism. Their divisions were temporarily set aside during the election of 1853, when Obando was voted president almost uncontested in the electoral colleges – an unprecedented event in the electoral politics of New Granada since 1836.[62] However, Liberal divisions soon resurfaced. A group of Draconians, largely backed by artisans, supported the short-lived military coup by General Melo, who took power in Bogotá in 1854.[63] Gólgotas then joined forces with the Conservatives to restore civilian rule that year. A further Liberal backlash occurred in 1856, when the first presidential election under male universal suffrage took place – as had happened in France, the Conservatives, with the support of an active clergy, managed to win over the majority of the electorate. Moreover, the measures in favour of decentralisation meant that the state lost control over the reform process and, according to Gilmore, reinforced the power of local and regional oligarchies.[64]

60 Descriptions of these celebrations were widely echoed by the provincial press. See for example, *El Artesano* (Cartagena), 17 March 1850; and *El Triunfo del 7 de Marzo* (Ciénaga), 7 April 1850.

61 See Alonso Valencia Llano, 'La guerra de 1851 en el Cauca,' in Museo Nacional de Colombia (ed.), *Las guerras civiles desde 1830 y su proyección en el siglo XX* (Bogotá, 1998), pp. 37–58.

62 Out of the 2,008 members of the electoral colleges, 1,548 voted for Obando. The runner-up, Tomás Herrera, received 329 votes. Conservative Mariano Ospina came third with 36 votes. See Registraduría, *Historia electoral colombiana*, p. 115.

63 See the classic account by Ortiz, *Historia de la revolución*.

64 Gilmore, *El federalismo en Colombia*, vol 1, p. 181.

These backlashes, however, should not detract from the significance of the social and political upheaval that prevailed in New Granada throughout the 1850s and beyond. The impact of the Liberal reforms was longstanding. Slavery was not to return. During the following decades, freedom of the press generally prevailed, a fact that often impressed foreign visitors such as the Argentine Miguel Cané.[65] Civilian grip over power was further reinforced after the Melo rebellion was quelled. The army was almost dismantled: its size being reduced to 400 soldiers in 1856.[66] These numbers were slightly increased during the following years, but by the mid-1870s the British minister still thought that 'the army can scarcely be said to exist'.[67] The experience with male universal suffrage motivated a larger degree of partisan competition. The two emerging parties felt therefore compelled to strengthen their links with all social sectors, while the frequency of elections encouraged even higher levels of politicisation in an extraordinarily politicised community.[68] In the short-term, Conservatives could do little to stop the reformist zeal that was reinforced by a new Liberal constitution in 1863. They did prevail in two of the nine states that now formed the loose federal union renamed in the 1863 Constitution 'the United States of Colombia'. But only after 1886 would the country experience a nationwide conservative reaction, whose

65 Miguel Cané, *En viaje, 1881–1882* (Buenos Aires, n.d.), pp. 145–6. 'The press is quite free', reported the British Minister in 1874. 'General Report by Mr Bunch on the United States of Colombia for the year 1873–74,' *Parliamentary Papers, Consular Report* (London, 1874), LXXIV, p. 358.

66 Anthony P. Maingot, 'Social Structure, Social Status, and Civil-Military Conflict in Urban Colombia, 1810–1858,' in Stephen Thernstrom and Richard Senett (eds.), *Nineteenth-Century Cities: Essays in the New Urban History* (New Haven, 1969), pp. 328–43.

67 'General Report by Mr Bunch,' p. 360. The size of the army was then approximately 1000.

68 The literature has tended to undervalue the significance of the early experience with male universal suffrage by noting that the vote was again restricted in 1863 and even further in 1886. However, four of the nine federal states of the union kept male universal suffrage until 1886, while in two of the other states the new restrictions were relatively mild. The centralist system of 1886 introduced restriction to the suffrage for national elections, but accepted the principle of male universal suffrage for municipal and departmental elections. For the workings of the electoral system under both the 1863 and the 1886 constitutiones, see my essays, 'Elections and Civil Wars in Nineteenth-century Colombia: the 1875 Presidential Campaign,' *Journal of Latin American Studies* (Oct. 1994), 26:3, pp. 621–50; and 'Limits of Power: Elections under the Conservative Hegemony, 1886–1930,' *Hispanic American Historical Review* (May, 1997), 77, 2, pp. 245–80. For an overview of Colombian electoral reforms, see Eduardo Posada-Carbó, 'Fraudes al sufragio: introducción a la historia de las reformas electorales en Colombia, 1830–1930,' in Carlos Malamud (ed.), *Reformas electorales en España y América Latina, 1830–1930* (Mexico City, 2001).

roots could also be traced back to 1848.[69] The revolutionary atmosphere of the 1850s, strongly felt throughout the country, therefore left an enduring legacy in national politics. I shall return to this legacy, whose full appreciation requires a further look at the 'varieties of revolutionary experience' that sprung up after 1848, which bore striking similarities to those taking place in Europe and to which this chapter now turns.

The principle of 'freedom of association' was put into practice with a fervent zeal, even in the distant provinces of New Granada. As mentioned, a 'Sociedad de Artesanos' was established in 1847 – its original nature being that of a political club in support of the Liberal cause. But the 'Sociedades Democráticas de Artesanos' really flourished after López's election, now encouraged by the government itself.[70] These societies were despised by the likes of Restrepo as 'disastrous … real clubs of the French type, imitating the Jacobins'.[71] Others had only praise. 'The spirit of association has been developed, Sociedades de Artesanos are set up everywhere' – thus greeted *El Artesano* the opening of a new chapter of the Democráticas in Santa Marta.[72] The society established 16 new chapters in 1849, 21 in 1850, 66 in 1851, 9 in 1852; by 1853 some 141 Sociedades Democráticas had been opened throughout New Granada. In Bogotá alone, where in each of the major neighbourhoods a chapter was established, it has been estimated that the society could count on 4,000 members.[73] This is a substantial figure in a city of 40,000 inhabitants, relatively higher than the member-

69 The Conservative reaction was partly supported by dissident Liberals, known as *Independientes*, led by Rafael Núñez. For a recent interpretation of this period, see Marco Palacios, *Entre la legitimidad y la violencia, Colombia, 1875–1994* (Bogotá, 1995), chs. 1–2. I have examined Núñez's political thought against the bakground of Liberal reformism in 'Rafael Núñez, el Caribe colombiano y el orden nacional,' *Aguaita. Revista del Observatorio del Caribe Colombiano* (Cartagena, 1999), 2, pp. 8–22. The leader of the Conservative reaction was Miguel Antonio Caro; see his *Escritos políticos*, edited by Carlos Valderrama Andrade (Bogotá, 1990–93), 4 vols. On Caro, see Malcolm Deas, 'Miguel Antonio Caro and Friends,' *History Workshop* (1992), reprinted in his *Del poder y la gramática. Y otros ensayos sobre historia, política y literatura colombianas* (Bogotá, 1993).

70 See Jaime Jaramillo Uribe, 'Las sociedades democráticas de artesanos y la coyuntura política y social colombiana de 1848,' *Anuario Colombiano de Historia Social y de la Cultura* (1976), vol 8, pp. 5–18; and Sowell, *The Early Colombian Labor Movement*, ch. three.

71 Restrepo, *Historia de la Nueva Granada*, p. 76. Another contemporary publication also referred to the Democráticas as gangs sponsored by the government, a club of 'perverts', see *Ojeada sobre los primeros catorce meses*, pp. 15–19.

72 *El Artesano*, 6 April 1850.

73 Gilmore, *El federalismo en Colombia*, vol 1, p. 168; and Sowell, *The Early Colombian Labor Movement*, p. 47. Sowell quotes the figure of 2,500 members for Bogotá by 1850, and 10,000 for the whole of the country also by 1850.

ship of political clubs in Paris in 1848: approximately 70,000 in a city of 1 million people.[74]

Since its origins the meetings of the Sociedad Democrática were public and attracted 'people from all classes'.[75] As the Sociedades strengthened their links with the López administration, members of the cabinet, and even the President, attended their sessions in Bogotá. According to *El Sentimiento Democrático*, more than 800 people attended the Democrática's meetings in Cali, where one could see 'the rich, the poor, those with literary titles and those without them joined together, and where the feelings of humanity and fraternity flourish among all its members'.[76] If initially they had been established to instruct the popular classes about their rights as citizens, and later appeared as an appendix of the government, the Democráticas became embroiled in political and social conflicts which often acquired class and even racial connotations, although the nature of the Sociedades changed from town to town.[77] In Cali, for example, a popular oratory flourished, in speeches that 'had no other aim than to endlessly attack the dirty oligarchy', where it was said that 'it was necessary to stop the whites and rub their dirty cloaks on their nostrils'. Only those who 'wore *ruana* (*ponchos*) and no shoes' could genuinely claim to constitute 'the sovereign people'.[78]

The Democráticas were not the only societies to be established. The Jesuits, who had been active in setting up lay organisations in 1838, founded the Sociedad Congregación, with the apparent aim of instructing their members on the Christian doctrines of the Church.[79] They attracted 'humble artisans', and mostly sympathisers of the Conservatives. But the Conservatives set up their own societies. In Bogotá, the Sociedad Popular was established in opposition to the activities of the Sociedad Democrática. Their leaders were prominent members of the Conservative party, though they also attracted representatives of all classes. In Cali too the Conservatives set up an Amigos del Pueblo society, which claimed to count on 1,300 members. 'What do you make of this aristocracy?', thus Manuel María Mallarino replied to the accusations that his society was an exclusive club of the oligarchy.[80] The Populares referred to the Liberals as

74 Sperber, *The European Revolutions*, p. 158.

75 Bernardino Torres Torrente, *Sombras i misterios. O los embozados* (Bogotá, 1859), p. 74; and Camacho Roldán, *Escritos varios*, p. 343.

76 *El Sentimiento Democrático*, 6 Dec. 1849.

77 On the different nature of the Democráticas, see suggestions by Gutiérrez Sanín, *Curso y discurso del movimiento plebeyo*, pp. 168–75.

78 *Reseña histórica*, p. 28.

79 Torres Torrente, *Sombras i misterios*, p. 73.

80 See M.M. Mallarino, *Carta dirijida al Sr Dr Ramón Mercado* (Cali, 1854), p. 20; and *Ojeada sobre los primeros catorce meses*, p. 26. As the Amigos del Pueblo claimed to

'reds', claimed that their cause was 'the cause of God', and firmly opposed the election of López.[81] When the Jesuits were expelled, some 200 members of the Populares guarded their exit from Bogotá.[82] Similarly in Cali, a sociedad 'De amigos del pueblo' (friends of the people) was established, initially meeting on Sundays in the house of Sra. Joaquina Ortiz, and attended by 'the aristocrats, several clerics ... and *camanduleros* (roughs)'. But they soon widened their appeal to the poor, through 'offering them cash and loans at good terms'.[83] Violent clashes between the members of the Democráticas and Populares were frequent in both Bogotá and Cali.

Other political clubs also flourished. On 25 September 1850 the Escuela Republicana was established by the Liberal youth of Bogotá, mostly students from the Universidad Nacional and Colegio San Bartolomé. According to one of its founders, Aníbal Galindo, the Escuela was set up to 'propagate the liberals ideas of the programme of the 1848 French revolution'.[84] Their meetings were also attended by 'some of the most elegant and distinguished ladies of the capital'.[85] The composition of the Escuela Republicana, their activities and programmes, soon reflected the deep political and social divisions within the Liberal party. Members of the Republicana closed ranks behind López against the 1851 Conservative uprising. But they openly clashed with members of the Democráticas, and joined the Conservatives against the coup led by General Melo in 1854.

Yet the initial opposition to the Escuela Republicana came from the Conservatives. On 28 October 1850, leading Conservatives founded the Sociedad Filotémica, notably in antagonism to the Republicana, established a month earlier. The new society printed its own newspaper, where they published its programme, which included the 'emancipation of women, abolition of cast differences and the supremacy of the "bayonetas de la inteligencia".'[86] The Filotémica was also established to join efforts to fight cholera. In addition to the Filotémica, another Conservative association established in Bogotá was the Sociedad Niño Dios, formed by women, apparently for religious purposes but also with open political aims. Women

---

favour the same principles than the Sociedad Democrática, supporters of the latter attempted to unveil the real partisan (Conservative) agenda of the former; see 'Sociedad de Amigos del Pueblo,' in *El Sentimiento Democrático* (Cali), 20 Dec. 1849.

81 Torres Torrente, *Sombras i misterios*, p. 75.

82 Sowell, *The Early Colombian Labor Movement*, p. 65.

83 *Reseña histórica*, p. 29.

84 A. Galindo, *Recuerdos históricos (1840 a 1895)* (Bogotá, 1900), p. 53. See also José María Samper, *Los partidos políticos en Colombia* (1873) (Bogotá, 1985), pp. 40–2.

85 *Ibid.*

86 Torres Torrente, *Sombras i misterios*, pp. 78–9.

of this society paraded in the streets against Liberals, whom they referred to as 'reds, thieves, heretics and godless'.[87]

Indeed the streets were often taken over by politics. The election of López in 1849 or the reception given to Obando the following year, as described above, were themselves no doubt expressions of popular joy, and mass political demonstrations. The opposition did not stay still. The Jesuits, through the Sociedad Congregación, organised religious parades with clear political connotations. But the streets also became the stage of open and violent confrontations. The divisions between Gólgotas and Draconians led in Bogotá to clashes between 'cachacos' and 'guaches'.[88] Florentino González, a former secretary of finance responsible for lowering tariffs, was recognised in the streets of Bogotá on the evening of 8 June 1853 by a group of artisans, who 'beat him with sticks, leaving him in a very poor state'. Earlier, in May, members of the Sociedad Democrática surrounded Congress to demand higher tariffs. After the session ended, they assaulted some congressmen: 'and immediately a skirmish among two sides followed, distinguished by their costumes, those in *ruana* and those in jackets, or in other terms, *guaches* and *cachacos*; this subsided leaving behind an unhappy artisan stabbed to death.'[89]

Violent confrontations were more widespread, and left behind more casualties, in the southern region of the Cauca Valley, where social tensions seemed to have been escalating throughout the 1840s. Violence there was both urban and rural. Attacks against private property were frequent. Fences around the estates were destroyed, their houses and sugar plantations burnt, their owners and their families physically assaulted.[90] Indeed personal assaults against Conservatives intensified after a leaflet entitled *El Zurriago*, recommended Conservative partisans to use the whip (*zurriago*) against the 'reds'. As it turned out, almost in revenge, quite the opposite happened:

> ... several gangs, armed with *zurriagos*, ... patrolled the city during the nights... and they cruelly whipped any Conservative whom they caught. The *zurriagueros* were a mob of freed slaves from the haciendas roaming the

87 Similarly in Cali, 'varias mujeres conservadoras formaron una sociedad *sui generis*° con el objeto único de ayudar a los hombres en la política ... i pedir a Dios el total esterminio de los liberales, a los que no admitian en sus bailes i tertulias', in *Reseña histórica*, p. 33.

88 'Cachaco' was a pejorative term to refer to elegant members of the upper classes; 'guache' was used in reference to undesirable members of the lower classes.

89 Angel y Rufino Cuervo, *Vida de Rufino Cuervo*, pp. 522–3. On 18 June 1853, a 'cachaco', Antonio Paris, was killed by a group of 'guaches'. See *ibid.*, p. 523.

90 *Reseña histórica*, pp. 9–12, and 35–7; Gilmore, *El federalismo en Colombia*, p. 172; Cuervo, *Vida de Rufino Cuervo y noticias de su época*, pp. 482–3, and Gutiérrez, *Curso y discurso del movimiento plebeyo*, pp. 211–22.

> cities ... They were in gangs of 40 to 50 men, all of them covered in black *ruanas*: they moved in guerrilla fashion ... and as soon as they saw their victims, they fall on them like bloodthirsty vultures, and they whipped them to the bitter end.[91]

The Sociedades Democráticas and the national government tried to distance themselves from these 'excesses against property'. But it was acknowledged that some local authorities in the Cauca Valley were themselves behind those confrontations. In Buenaventura, Governor Mercado's newspaper, *El Pensamiento Popular*, published extracts from Proudhon and Blanc, while he supported the attacks against landowners and the privileged few.[92] Governor Gómez openly justified the developments in Cauca: 'the people who have reached liberty leaving behind oppression, frolic and enjoy themselves, getting sometimes angry against those who believed to have the power to humiliate them'.[93] Questioned in Congress, a member of the cabinet minimised the problem, by replying that these were mere 'retozos democráticos' (democratic frolickings).

'One of the most important results of recent scholarship on the revolution of 1848', Jonathan Sperber has observed, is the 'portrayal of the revolution as a pioneering venture in mass political mobilization'.[94] This was certainly the experience in New Granada, although, more than an abrupt break with the past, it is possible to identify here a continuing trend since independence. Nevertheless politics became more participatory, involving larger number of people. As political clubs and associations flourished, members of the popular sectors became more acquainted with new ideas and took the floor to give speeches to enthusiastic audiences. The electorate expanded significantly, following in particular the adoption of male universal suffrage in 1853. In the presidential election of 1856, more than 210,000 people went to the polls – some 40 per cent of those entitled to vote.[95] This was one of the largest South American electorates at the time – in Chile, by contrast, some 30,000 voted during this period.[96] Moreover, *neogranadinos* experienced a very intense electoral calendar: there was hardly a year without an electoral campaign in progress. As

91 *Reseña histórica*, pp. 36–7.

92 Gilmore, *El federalismo en Colombia*, p. 172.

93 *La Gaceta*, 26 April 1851, quoted in *Vida de Rufino Cuervo*, p. 484–5.

94 Sperber, *The European Revolutions*, p. 165.

95 See David Bushnell, 'Voter participation in the Colombian election of 1856,' *Hispanic American Historical Review* (51: 1971). With the available information, it is impossible to estimate the rate of growth of the electorate following the adoption of male universal suffrage. But I suspect that the abrupt jump in France – from 250,000 to 9,000.000 voters during the 1848 elections for the Constitutent Assembly had no parallels in New Granada; see J.P. Mayer, 'Introduction' in Tocqueville, *Recollections*, p. XXXV.

96 See Samuel Valenzuela, *Democratización vía reforma* (Buenos Aires, 1985).

elections were generally competitive, this forced parties to widen their appeal and expand their social bases. Artisans, close to the Liberals, acknowledged with regret that Conservatives were canvassing their quarters: 'only now they are so kind to lower themselves to the *canalla*... only now they call the poor 'brothers' and join them in meetings, and they nurture them and call the people 'sovereign', because only now they need them'.[97]

Political mobilisation was not restricted to the vote. Nor it was limited to men. Women, as observed above, paraded in the streets. In their houses, the better-off hosted political meetings. Women signed political petitions, and attended meeting at political clubs.[98] There were women with ribbons cheering López during his election on 7 March 1849, although women seem to have been more prominent rallying behind the cause of religion.

'Let us *all* speak, let us *all* discuss, let us *all* debate, for we *all* are citizens with equal rights and equal obligations,' thus *El Artesano* stated its position, when it first appeared in Cartagena in February 1850. As already noted, the publication of newspapers and leaflets flourished during the 1848/9 electoral campaign. This trend continued after López's election. *El Artesano* was one of several newspapers established to support López's programme. López's victory was celebrated in the very name given to a newspaper set up in Ciénaga, *El Triunfo del 7 de Marzo*, in late 1849. *El Cienaguero Libre* and *El Pueblo* were also founded in this province as Liberal newspapers. The latter aimed at being the voice of the recently established Sociedad Democrática in Santa Marta, a practice followed elsewhere: in Cali, the respective society published *El Sentimiento Democrático*. Conservatives did not stay still. And this 'explosion' of the press, much in evidence in the provinces, was more intense in the capital city of Bogotá. The trade in books also flourished during this period.[99]

According to Gilmore, the number of newspapers, leaflets and pamphlets in New Granada was never as large as those published during the decade after 1848.[100] Newspapers were of course the centre of political debate. As in France, their headquarters were 'arenas of discussion', and of political organisation.[101] The press, in Gilmore's words, 'faithfully reflected the effervescence of its time".[102] The press was of course the

97 *El Artesano*, 24 May 1850.

98 *Vida de Rufino Cuervo*, p. 437.

99 For suggestions of this, see Jaramillo Uribe, 'La influencia de los románticos franceses y de la revolución de 1848,' p. 164.

100 Gilmore, *El federalismo en Colombia*, p. 139.

101 See comments on the role of the French press in Agulhon, *The Republican Experiment: 1848–52* (Cambridge, 1983), pp. 16–18, Roberts, *Revolutions of 1848*, pp. 40, 55. On the press in Germany, Siemann, *The German Revolution*, chapter 7.

102 *Ibid.*, p. 139. For comparisons with Europe, see Sperber, *The European Revolutions*, pp. 151–3.

main vehicle through which the major ideals of 1848 were spread. *El Neogranadino* carried transcripts of debates in the French National Assembly, and reprinted chapters of Proudhon's latest books.[103] Even in the provinces, newspapers such as *El Porvenir*, in Cartagena, and *El Censor*, in Medellín, started to publish Lamartin's *Les Girondins* at the end of 1848. During the following three decades, according to Jaramillo Uribe, there was hardly a newspaper, in Bogotá or in the other major cities in the provinces, that had not published in the *folletón* section either an essay, an article or a fragment of a book by Lamartine, Victor Hugo, Eugene Sué or Louis Blanc.[104] After quoting Ledru-Rollin's words in the French National Assembly, *El Neogranadino* argued that the republic should not have any laws regulating the press.[105] But while the Liberal press praised the virtues of the European revolutions, Conservative newspapers attacked the impact of those events in New Granada.

If 1848 had shaken Europe, reflected the Conservatives Angel and Rufino José Cuervo, the consequences of that year's events in New Granada 'were more deplorable, and the scandals greater'.[106] A French publication in 1851 agreed: 'what European demagoguery classifies as its most extreme is daily put into practice by *Granadino* demagoguery, using the same names, the same terms, adopting the same formulas and looking for the same results of destruction and anarchy'.[107] Yet for the Liberal *El Neogranadino*, the European developments were the cause of celebration: 'the sacred principles of *liberty, equality and fraternity* prevail everywhere, today they have become political and religious dogmas among all enlightened peoples'.[108] Contemporary Liberals such as Anibal Galindo, José María Samper or Salvador Camacho Roldán agreed that their political education had been much influenced by the French revolution of 1848. These developments in New Granada, however, were just a parody of the French events, according to José Manuel Restrepo – though a parody with 'disastrous' results.[109]

Modern historians have acknowledged the revolutionary upheaval

103 See Gilmore, *El federalismo en Colombia*, pp. 156–7, and *El Neogranadino*, 10 March 1849.

104 Jaramillo Uribe, 'La influencia de los románticos franceses y de la revolución de 1848,' pp. 165–9. The *folletón*, or *folletín*, section was devoted to the translation of foreign literature – usually French, and seems to have been a common practice for newspapers elsewhere in Latin America. See, for example, the *folletín* section in *El Mercurio*, where they serialised Alejandro Dumas's and Chataubriand's books, *El Mercurio* (Santiago), 29 March 1849, and 5 Dec. 1850.

105 *El Neogranadino*, 18 Nov. 1848.

106 *Vida de Rufino Cuervo y su época*, p. 463.

107 Quoted in Gilmore, *El federalismo en Colombia*, p. 151.

108 *El Neogranadino*, 10 March 1849.

109 Restrepo, *Historia de la Nueva Granada*, p. 80.

that New Granada experienced by mid-nineteenth-century, but the extent to which this was influenced by the European revolutions is open to debate. Jay Robert Crusin has argued that what happened in New Granada 'was an independent movement brought on by local problems and conditions, only slightly influenced by foreign ideas'.[110] Measuring the impact of the 1848 revolutions beyond Europe is certainly no easy task. How foreign ideas were read, reinterpreted, and reshaped in New Granada merits further attention. There is strong evidence, however, to suggest that the events in New Granada were neither a 'parody' of the French revolution, nor an 'independent movement ... only slightly influenced by foreign ideas'. As this chapter has shown, the country underwent a period of radical reform that gained momentum after the election of López in 1849. It is true that this was not an abrupt break with the past, as some of the reforms were rooted in the earlier developments of independence. Long unresolved problems resurfaced in 1848. Political tensions were also exacerbated by violent events in neighbouring Venezuela. And the reform programme of the Mosquera administration (1844–49) opened the way for further conflicts. Yet it is hard to account for the hectic course of events without taking into serious consideration the impact that the European revolutions had in New Granada.

Perhaps it would be more precise to refer to the impact of the 'French' rather than the 'European revolutions'. 'My own perception of the 1848 revolution in France', Geoffrey Ellis has recently observed, '... stresses ... its essential *Frenchness*.'[111] Indeed some of the features of the European revolutions that were not part of the French picture – nationalism and internationalism – were also absent in New Granada. The possibility of the return of any dynasty from the ancien regime was certainly here a 'dead issue', even before 1848. And if Herzen despised French Liberals for their lack of radical socialism, his feelings about the Liberals Gólgotas, whose programme prevailed in New Granada, would have been similar.[112] The press did not fail to register the wider European revolutionary movement, and the 'European revolutions' entered the vocabulary of those who constantly referred to the events of 1848.[113] However, it was above all France – French authors, French ideas and French revolutionary episodes – what was in the minds of *neogranadinos* when they looked at the European developments.

110 Crusin, 'The revolution of 1848 in Colombia,' p. iv. See Clara Lida's chapter in this volume.

111 G. Ellis, 'The Revolution of 1848–1849 in France,' p. 47.

112 *Ibid.*, pp. 48–50.

113 See, for example, *El triunfo del 7 de marzo*, 7 Feb. 1850; *Ojeada sobre los primeros catorce meses de la administración*, p. 9, and Mercado, *Memorias sobre los acontecimientos del sur*, p. V.

As the Cuervos recalled, 'the course of events in France was followed among us with the liveliest interest'. French writers – Sue, Lamartine and Hugo – were the favourite authors among the youth, Liberals and Conservatives alike.[114] According to Governor Mercado, 'the genius of the (French) revolution, of the men who were at its forefront, and of the peoples who made it happen, seemed to have been transplanted to New Granada'.[115] Speeches at the political clubs – which followed, after all, the French example – gave plenty of evidence of rhetoric where the French revolution figured prominently: 'Did you hear the cry of the latest French upheaval?' – asked a speaker in the Sociedad Republicana in 1850 – 'I believe you did' – he himself answered – 'it echoed in our horizons and our American condors flew under the shadow of the socialist eagles'.[116] Another speaker added that he favoured a *sui generis* socialism for New Granada.

However, as Gilmore makes clear, *neogranadino* intellectuals were highly eclectic. Furthermore, the impact of European socialist ideas, except in some Bogotá circles and in the Cauca Valley, was not strong. *El Alacrán*, a newspaper that often took radical positions, mocked the Liberal youth for the way they toyed with the word 'communist' – 'echo of the great word launched in Europe'.[117] And *El Neogranadino* explicitly distanced itself from 'communism as propagated in Europe by that proletarian majority oppressed by all sorts of aristocracies'.[118] There was, though, a Proudhonian, anarchist vein running through Liberal activism in mid-nineteenth-century New Granada.[119] But, above all, the ideals of the French revolution served to increase the momentum behind a set of reforms that aimed at granting political freedom, securing individual rights, giving autonomy to the provinces, and protecting freedom of industry and trade.[120] These reforms left an enduring legacy to the republic: in the civilian outlook of its institutions, in its competitive, often violent, partisan struggles, and in the historical weakness of its central government.

114 See Jaime Jaramillo Uribe, 'Tres etapas de la historia intelectual colombiana,' p. 124, and *El pensamiento colombiano en el siglo XIX* (Bogotá, 1982). See also the account by the Cuervos, *Vida de Rufino Cuervo*. The French geographer Elisée Reclus, who visited New Granada in 1855, observed that, for the youth in Santa Marta, France was 'the most glorious representative of the Latin races and the paramount of progress,' Reclus, *Viaje a la Sierra Nevada de Santa Marta* (Bogotá, 1947), p. 55.

115 Mercado, *Memorias sobre los acontecimientos del sur*, p. XXIX.

116 Torres Torrente, *Sombras i misterios*, p. 78.

117 *El Alacrán*, 28 Jan. 1849.

118 *El Neogranadino*, 3 March 1849.

119 On the influences of Proudhon, see Gilmore, *El federalismo en Colombia*.

120 See Gilmore, *El federalismo en Colombia*.

www.ingramcontent.com/pod-product-compliance
Lightning Source LLC
LaVergne TN
LVHW090024310826
846742LV00010B/23
9781900039437